Explorer Brittany

Lindsay Hunt

AA Publishing

Front cover (a): *shingle beach*
(b): *Belle-Ile, Morbihan*
(c): *women in traditional costume, Pont-l'Abbé*
Spine: *statue at Kermaria chapel, Pink Granite Coast*
Back cover: *polders, Mont Døl, Emerald Coast*
Page 2: *a traditional Breton lace* coiffe
Page 3: *the granite shoreline at Pointe du Grouin, Cancale*
Page 4: *fishing boats moored at Douarnenez, Cornouaille*
Page 5 (top): *half-timbered houses, Rennes*
Page 5 (bottom, left): *a detail from the calvary at Guéhenno*
Page 5 (bottom, right): *Stone Age Alignement de la Lande de Cojoux, near St-Just*
Page 6 (top): *a sunset over the sea at St-Briac-sur-Mer*
Page 7 (bottom): *the beach at Paramé, near St-Malo*
Page 8: *craggy rocks at Pointe du Raz, Cap Sizun, Finistère*
Page 9: *St-Malo – the Fort National at sunset*
Page 29: *the moated ruins of Hunaudaie castle*
Page 265: *Le Grand Hotel, Dinard*

Written by Lindsay Hunt
Revision verified by Elisabeth Morris
Original photography by Rick Strange and Steve Day
Edited, designed, produced and distributed by AA Publishing

Reprinted 1999, 2000, 2001
Revised second edition 1999
First published 1995

A CIP catalogue record for this book is available from the British Library.

ISBN 0 7495 2043 4

Published by AA Publishing (a trading name of Automobile Association Developments Limited, whose registered office is Norfolk House, Priestley Road, Basingstoke, Hampshire RG24 9NY. Registered number 1878835).

Colour separation by Fotographics Ltd
Printed and bound in Italy by Printer Trento srl

How to use this book

ORGANISATION

Brittany Is, Brittany Was
Discusses aspects of life and culture in contemporary Brittany and explores significant periods in its history.

A – Z
An alphabetical listing of places to visit.The book is divided into eight geographical areas, with places of interest listed alphabetically within each section. Suggested walks, drives and Focus On articles, which provide an insight into aspects of life in Brittany are included in each section.

Travel Facts
Contains the strictly practical information that is vital for a successful trip.

Hotels & Restaurants
A listing of the best places to stay and the best places to eat. Entries are arranged by region and graded budget, moderate or expensive.

ABOUT THE RATINGS
Most places described in this book have been given a separate rating. These are as follows:

▶▶▶ **Do not miss**

▶▶ **Highly recommended**

▶ **Worth seeing**

MAP REFERENCES
To make the location of a particular place easier to find, every main entry in this book is given a map reference, such as 176B3. The first number (176) indicates the page on which the map can be found, the letter (B) and the second number (3) pinpoint the square in which the main entry is located. The maps on the inside front cover and inside back cover are referred to as IFC and IBC respectively.

Contents

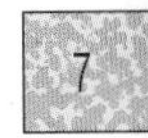

After a year living and working in Spain, Lindsay Hunt got hooked on travel. Since then, she has been a regular contributor to *Holiday Which?* magazine and has written a number of hotel and destination guides. She is familiar with many parts of France, from Flanders fields to the Savoy Alps, and has paced the length and breadth of Rivieran strands, clambered up innumerable Parisian hotel staircases and travelled round Burgundy's vineyards on a bicycle.

My Brittany

For decades, Brittany eluded me. Somehow, my visits to France always by-passed this ragged, north-western peninsula. In dim corners of my mind's eye, images of standing stones lingered, shrouded in Celtic legends and Atlantic mists. Gradually, this unexplored piece of the Gallic jigsaw grew more and more tantalizing, and when the opportunity came, I jumped at the chance to visit. So the truth is out: I am an enthusiastic but comparative newcomer to Brittany's charms – its lonely, seaweed-strewn Atlantic beaches; Concarneau's morning fish market; Carnac's orderly lines of ancient standing stones.

The way to discover Brittany is to drive round its dog-toothed coast, where the best of the region's attractions lie. Besides enticing ports like St-Malo and Vannes, you'll discover a hugely varied coastline of weirdly shaped granite boulders, wave-dashed promontories and placid lagoons. Stray inland via estuarine tentacles to discover the irresistible medieval towns of Dinan and Quimper, the remarkable religious art in the ornate parish closes of Finistère and the mighty Breton border castles.

Francophiles should be warned. In some ways, Brittany doesn't feel like France at all – something that many of its inhabitants regard with pride. In medieval times this was a separate duchy, and even after several centuries of integration, Bretons chafe under the reins of Parisian government. You still hear the Breton language spoken in the western regions of Finistère, and Breton hymns sung at the annual festivals and *pardons*, age-old local celebrations that still play a central role in Breton culture. Consider Brittany, then, not just as an isolated corner of France, but as a new-found land, and enjoy it as much as I did.

Lindsay Hunt

Brittany Is

The rocks of Brittany are among the oldest on earth. The Armorican Massif emerged from a sea that covered France over 500 million years ago. It formed two giant crystalline backbones that were taller than the Alps. Now time has filed them down to mere molehills less than 400m high.

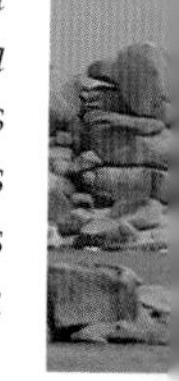

A HEART OF STONE Few regions are as geologically uniform as Brittany. Schist covers two-thirds of the land mass, the source of those ubiquitous grey-slate roofs. There are sparkling outcrops of quartz and feldspar, cliffs of blood-red porphyry, lodes of silver, lead and tin, sediments of kaolin and river-silt. Never far beneath the surface, though, is Brittany's true heart of solid granite, the primitive, elemental force that the artist Paul Gauguin admired. Granite influences Brittany's landscapes, its buildings – perhaps the rugged stoicism of its people. But Breton granite takes protean forms – wave-sculpted boulders, mysterious standing stones like marching soldiers, timeworn calvaries blotched with lichen, lace-fretted church spires...

Granite locks on a stretch of the Nantes–Brest Canal

THE BRETON LANDSCAPE Erosion over millennia has reduced Brittany's grand mountains to low stumps. The contours of the granite hills are gently rounded, like pudding basins. The sharper, toothier crests of upland regions such as the Monts d'Arrée and the Montagnes Noires are outcrops of schist or slate. Inland, much of the countryside was once covered in forest, which the ancient Celts called the *argoat* ('land of the woods'). Today, the woodlands have been depleted by man for fuel or ship timber, or to make way for usable agricultural land, and have dwindled to small patches.

Moorland or brushwood predominate in uncultivated areas but most of the region is an undulating plateau of fields divided by countless rivers, hedges, pollarded trees and stone walls. Granite boulders dumped by meltwater in glacial valleys form chaotic rockeries of moss and ferns.

Where the Breton interior lacks visual drama, the jagged coastline compensates amply. Its shore presents a spectacularly varied scene of cliffs, estuaries, beaches, marshes and dunes. Most striking of all are the granite rocks of the north coast, glowing fiery at sunset and worn by the elements into weirdly organic shapes that seem almost alive.

BUILDING IN GRANITE By far the commonest building material in Brittany is granite. The earliest shelters of all were probably the huge rounded boulders that lie tumbled in river gorges, some as big as houses, where remnants of very early prehistoric settlements have been discovered. When tools developed sufficiently to work the hard stone, granite was used through the ages in

Elven, one of Brittany's many granite castles

many types of structure, from the dolmens of the megalith-builders, through the fortresses of the Middle Ages, to today's whitewashed holiday homes. The stone appears in street cobbles and paving slabs, in the earth-covered banks around fields and, perhaps most memorably, in the churchyards, where gravestones, ossuaries and elaborately carved calvaries all consist of local rock. Breton churches are nearly always granite, too. The few cathedrals built of alien stone make a dramatic impact in Brittany – the jaundiced limestone of St-Pol-de-Léon or the pale tufa of Nantes startle amid the monochrome grey.

A MULTI-FACETED STONE Granite can seem gloomy and dark, lending itself only to squat, crouching buildings and coarse-grained sculpture. But when cut and dressed it takes on a new sparkle. The pink granite of the north coast is the colour of expensive bathrooms and exclusive boutiques. Kersanton stone, used in so many of the region's churches, is the stuff of intricate rood screens, altarpieces and tombs. Malleable when worked, it hardens over time, preserving the mason's chiselled outlines. However, most granite is notoriously stubborn, and ambitious projects such as large churches often took several centuries to complete. Many craftsmen abandoned the laborious task of vaulting in stone and turned instead to wood panelling, often vividly carved or decorated with frescoes.

The parish close at Guimiliau

On a map, Brittany's jagged profile looks something like a savage animal snarling at the Atlantic, but in reality it is the sea that snarls, battering its rocks with storms and gales. 'The sea is English by nature...she breaks our ships,' wrote the 19th-century historian Michelet in his Tableau de la France.

A CHANGING SHORE Aeons ago Brittany was one of the few parts of what is now France to lie above the waves, but prehistoric megaliths and fossilised tree trunks discovered below the waterline indicate that sea levels subsequently fell, then rose again. The drowned valleys (*abers*), inland seas and tidal marshes that characterise parts of the coast were created after the last Ice Age. What were once parts of the mainland are now islands and offshore reefs. Twice daily the tides strike deep into Brittany's land mass through its many estuaries. On the Rance they do so with sufficient force to generate 600 million kW of electricity each year (see page 62).

A WAY OF LIFE Before the Romans arrived, the inhabitants of Brittany were already experienced seafarers. The Gaulish Veneti were intrepid traders, loading their sturdy, leather-sailed boats with cargoes of tin to sell in distant lands. Throughout the centuries that followed, Bretons earned a living from the sea in many different ways. Fishing became a vital source of food and income for thousands of families. Whale and cod from the northern seas, and tuna and sardines from the south, have all brought prosperity at various periods. Traditional fishing fleets still cast their nets, but increasingly the fishing industry relies more on farming the seas than on hunting them. Oysters, mussels and salmon can be raised more or less predictably now, in captivity. Important subsidiary industries such as fish-canning or processing also depend on the sea. Shore-based livelihoods practised for centuries can still be earned today, including evaporating sea water for salt and gathering seaweed.

In the days of sailing ships and merchant adventurers, Bretons hunted the high seas for more than fish. Many ventured great distances in search of new territory: Jacques Cartier, discoverer of Canada, was one of the most famous Breton explorers. Other seafarers became corsairs (see page 68), the state-registered pirates based in St-Malo who plagued English, Spanish and Dutch fleets. Even less honourable scavengers were the wreckers of Finistère, who lured shipping on to their deadly reefs with false lights.

The French fleets (merchant and naval) have always been manned by a large proportion of recruits from Brittany, and going to sea remains a strong tradition in many families. So too is shipbuilding, once a thriving industry in Nantes, Lorient and St-Nazaire. Breton forests supplied much of the

Inspecting the previous night's catch at Concarneau's criée *(fish auction)*

Cap Fréhel's lighthouse guards the Emerald Coast

timber for France's early sailing ships and its famous hempen sailcloth flew from most of Europe's rigging.

COASTAL RESCUE The west Breton coast is studded with lighthouses and warning beacons to head shipping off its treacherous rocks. Despite these precautionary measures, disasters still occur, even with all the assistance of modern navigation equipment. The most spectacular shipwreck in recent years was that of the oil tanker *Amoco Cadiz*, wrecked off Finistère in 1978. The disaster was notable not for the loss of human life but for the hideous effect it had on the environment. Oil slicks ravaged the beaches, threatening countless seabirds and Brittany's vital tourist industry.

❑ Brittany has several excellent museums dedicated to various aspects of the sea. Among the best are Brest's Océanopolis (see page 99), Douarnenez's Musée du Bateau (see pages 152–3), Concarneau's Musée de la Pêche (see page 149) and the Musée des Marais Salants in Batz-sur-Mer (see page 230). You can also visit some lighthouses and clamber up them for panoramic views. One of the most interesting in Brittany is Creac'h on the island of Ouessant, which has a lighthouse museum (see page 109). One of the museums in the citadel of Port-Louis commemorates Brittany's sophisticated coastal rescue service. ❑

Sea-rescue services play a vital role on the Breton coast

Brittany has become increasingly industrialised since World War II, but its economic base is obvious to even the most casual observer of its well-tended artichoke fields or pedigree dairy herds. Today over a million Bretons (about one-third) are actively engaged in farming, and over 60 per cent of the land is cultivated.

THE MANAGED COUNTRYSIDE The great natural forests that once covered the *argoat* (Breton interior) have steadily dwindled to coppices and stands of conifers over the centuries. Marshlands submerged by neap tides have been drained and reclaimed as pasture for *pré salé* lambs, whose meat has a distinctive salty flavour (see pages 16–17); unproductive heath has succumbed to the plough. Breton soils are acidic and not naturally very fertile; they need considerable coaxing to produce high yields. Seaweed and *maërl* (estuary mud) are used as fertilisers.

From high vantage points in the Monts d'Arrée or the Montagnes Noires you get a clear impression of the modern countryside. It is unquestionably man-made, a chequered landscape known as *bocage* – tamed by hedges, tree-lined dikes and banks of earth and stone. There is little true wilderness, nor in most places is it especially picturesque.

THE MARKET GARDEN Though land units have increased in size, the typical Breton farm is still relatively small, and usually family-run. There are no vast prairies or Texan-style ranches, yet Brittany manages to produce a huge proportion of France's total agricultural output. Ille-et-Vilaine is its top milk producer; Fougères hosts the biggest cattle market in Europe. The region as a whole raises about half of all the pigs and chickens in France and grows the lion's share of its market vegetables. Artichokes, cauliflowers, peas and beans are the main crops, but carrots, onions, salad vegetables and brassicas also figure high on the list. Many of Brittany's cabbages, grown extensively around Lorient, end up as German sauerkraut. Even the humble potato, once falsely accused of spreading cholera in Brittany, now occupies many hectares.

Testing the potato crop at Cancale, on Brittany's Emerald Coast

One of the most fertile areas of Brittany is the Ceinture d'orée (Golden Belt) which runs along the north coast, in particular around

The artichoke season near Roscoff

St-Pol-de-Léon. Fertilised for centuries with seaweed, the alluvial soils are exceptionally productive. A trip through the region close to harvest time reveals a purposeful hum of activity, as laden tractors and juggernauts roar along the roads transporting produce to the marketplaces, or the docks at Roscoff. The scale of the operation, and the perfection of these splendid crops, can hardly fail to impress.

About a third of the cultivated land is devoted to cereals and animal fodder. Apples are grown around Fouesnant and the Rance valley, mostly for cider or juice, while Plougastel is famed for its strawberries. The crops on which Brittany once grew rich – flax for linen and sailcloth, and buckwheat – no longer figure largely, and vines thrive only in the south-eastern corner, near Nantes.

POLITICAL CLOUT These days the vote of the small farmer is crucial to the survival of any French government, and the agricultural lobby influences many political decisions, both in Paris and more significantly in Brussels. Even industrial workers have a keen vested interest in the well-being of the farming community; about a third of the Breton factory workforce is involved in food processing of one sort or another.

As the world's second largest exporter of agricultural produce after the US, France pays careful heed to its farming interests (whose antagonism to European Union (EU) quotas and anger at surpluses periodically manifests itself in strikes and violent confrontation). Indeed the French government's support of the industry is sometimes at the expense of goodwill among its EU neighbours. While Brittany exports its cabbages and crustaceans, it has aggressively resisted low-priced foreign imports. This trend towards protectionism may have far-reaching effects. Will the new EU agricultural policy, aimed at regulating production, be successful?

The range and quality of foodstuffs produced in Brittany indicate the important role that good food plays in the daily life of the region. There is much to enjoy, particularly seafood and pancakes, a wide range of charcuterie, *and delicious cakes like* kouignamann *– more readily eaten than pronounced.*

The ubiquitous crêperie

COCKLES AND MUSSELS Breton seafood is predictably superb; Brittany is one of France's foremost fishing regions, and the range available in markets and restaurants is staggering. Visit a *criée* (fish auction), or commercial fish farm for some idea of this marine cornucopia. Those less keen may be unable to look another *moule* in the eye by the end of their trip to Brittany, dreading the prospect of yet another *assiette de fruits de mer*.

Enjoying oysters at Cancale

They are daunting sights, those platefuls of seaweed and crushed ice, piled so precariously with curious sea creatures that extracting any one of them threatens a deluge. Whatever else you find on your plate there are almost certain to be mussels and oysters, which are prime local products. Winkles, crayfish, clams, crabs and scallops may also put in an appearance.

If you prefer your fish hot, try a traditional Breton *cotriade*, or fish stew. Freshwater species of fish reach the kitchens too: *brochet au beurre blanc* is a classic dish of pike in the Nantais white butter sauce. Most Breton of all, though, is lobster, often prepared in a special sauce of tomato, shallots and cognac (*homard à l'armoricaine*). On many menus it appears as *homard à l'américaine*, a misspelling attributed to a mistake made by a Parisian restaurant.

MEAT PRODUCTS Perhaps steak Chateaubriand is the most widely known Breton meat dish. But Brittany is more famous for its dairy produce than its beef. More typical meat products include the *pré salé* (salt meadow)

lambs raised on the salt marshes of Ouessant and Mont-St-Michel, with a characteristic salty flavour. *Gigot à la bretonne* (roast leg of lamb with haricot beans) is a local speciality. Pork is also produced in great quantities and *charcuterie* takes many forms – especially sausages, black pudding and *andouille*, a sort of pork haggis. Hearty peasant soups and casseroles such as *kig-ha-farz* often contain ham or bacon. Some of France's most succulent chickens come from around Rennes, while the *challan* is a delicious duck from the Nantes region.

PANCAKES Once, pancakes were a staple of the Breton diet, replacing bread in poor homes. You will find *crêperies* everywhere in Brittany, and *crêpes* are a cheap, quick way of satisfying hunger pangs. The variety of fillings offered is legion, and imaginative to the point of eccentricity. Two names are used for them: *crêpe* and *galette*. Generally, *crêpes* are made with a batter of wheat flour and usually have sweet fillings, while the more traditional *galettes* are made with the heavier buckwheat flour and are most often savoury. The distinctions between the two are, however, blurred in different parts of Brittany. You can buy them either ready made in packets or tins, though they are much nicer warm and fresh.

Terrace dining in Rennes

Crêpes dentelles are paper-thin, lacy pancakes, a speciality of Quimper.

CAKES AND PUDDINGS Like many Breton dishes, desserts tend to be rich and heavy. One famous local dessert is *far breton*, a solid flan which usually contains prunes or raisins. Other specialities include *kouignamann*, a delicious cake of sugar, butter and almonds, and *galettes de Pont-Aven* (not to be confused with pancakes) are buttery biscuits like shortbread.

❑ A recipe for *far breton*:
125g wheat flour, 125g sugar, 4 eggs, 750ml milk, 250g prunes, 2 tbsp rum, 2 sachets vanilla sugar, pinch of salt.
Preheat oven (240°C/465°F/gas mark 8), sift the flour into a basin and add sugar, salt and vanilla sugar; make a well and add the eggs. Stir to a smooth paste. Heat the milk with the rum and prunes. Pour on to the paste and mix vigorously. Pour this batter into a buttered dish and bake at 240°C/465°F/gas mark 8 for 10 minutes, then at 200°C/392°F/ gas mark 6 for 30 minutes, until well browned. Serve warm. ❑

Like all Celtic regions, Brittany is a land of storytellers, full of legends and folklore. Intense piety and religious fervour often go hand in hand with a belief in fairies, elves, demons and witches that stretches back to pagan times.

THE ARTHURIAN MYTH When Celtic settlers arrived in the 6th century from Wales and Cornwall they brought with them shadowy tales of the saintly protector-king who fought the invading tribes of Saxons. The legends of Arthur became established in the mysterious forests of Brittany, where they still live on today. The forest of Paimpont (see pages 216–17) is identified as the Brocéliande of the ancient stories, where the Knights of the Round Table began their Quest for the Holy Grail, and where the great wizard Merlin was ensnared by Viviane, Lady of the Lake. Other legends of Brocéliande tell of the magic Fontaine de Barenton, whose water splashed on a nearby stone and summoned storms and a fierce knight in black armour, or of the Val sans Retour, where Morgan le Fay imprisoned faithless lovers. Today these colourful associations are by no means discouraged by the Breton tourist industry.

The love potion takes effect on Tristan and Isolde

TRISTAN AND ISOLDE The most famous version of the Tristan legend filters through Wagnerian opera. Tristan, prince of Lyonesse, was sent to Ireland by his uncle, King Mark of Cornouaille, to fetch Mark's betrothed princess, Isolde. On their return, Tristan and Isolde accidentally drank a magic love potion intended for Mark and Isolde on their wedding night, and the inevitable happened. The star-crossed lovers fled from Mark's wrath to a friendly kinsman, the Duke of Hoel, where (depending on which particular version you follow) they either lived happily ever after or died tragically of broken hearts...

THE LOST CITY OF YS This is one of Brittany's most enduring legends, a subject beloved by 19th-century Romantic painters. In the 6th century King Gradlon ruled Brittany from Ys, a beautiful island city in the bay of Douarnenez. This was protected from the sea by sluicegates, which only the king could unlock. The king's daughter, Dahut, fell in love with a handsome young man (the Devil in disguise), who persuaded her to steal the keys one night. The Devil unlocked the gates at high tide and

Merlin's spell haunts the Fontaine de Barenton

❑ Elves known as *korred* are the equivalent of the 'little people' of other Celtic traditions. They are hunchbacked dancers and magicians less than a metre high, with cats' claws for hands and goats' hooves for feet. Folklore declares they brought the standing stones to Brittany on their backs, and they help mortals by sharpening knives or lending oxen. Unfortunately, today's tourists have driven them all away! ❑

the city began to flood. Gradlon woke in the nick of time, raised the alarm, mounted his horse and fled across the causeway, with Dahut clinging behind. But the waves were swift, and the horse grew weary of the extra load. A heavenly voice commanded Gradlon to drop his wicked daughter in the sea and immediately the waves subsided, allowing the inhabitants to escape to the mainland. But Ys, like Atlantis, vanished for ever. Gradlon set up a new court in Quimper, while Dahut turned into a mermaid and lured many sailors to their doom.

ANKOU, DEATH'S COACHMAN

Ankou is the Breton incarnation of death, a skeletal figure with a scythe depicted on tombs, charnel-houses and calvaries throughout the region. He drives a creaking cart piled high with bodies and spares no one. One story tells of the blacksmith in Ploumilliau who spent all night sharpening Ankou's scythe in an effort to placate him, instead of attending midnight mass. Next day he discovered that he, too, was destined for Ankou's cart. On dark nights crossing lonely moors, many a Breton peasant has been horrified by the sound of rumbling wheels.

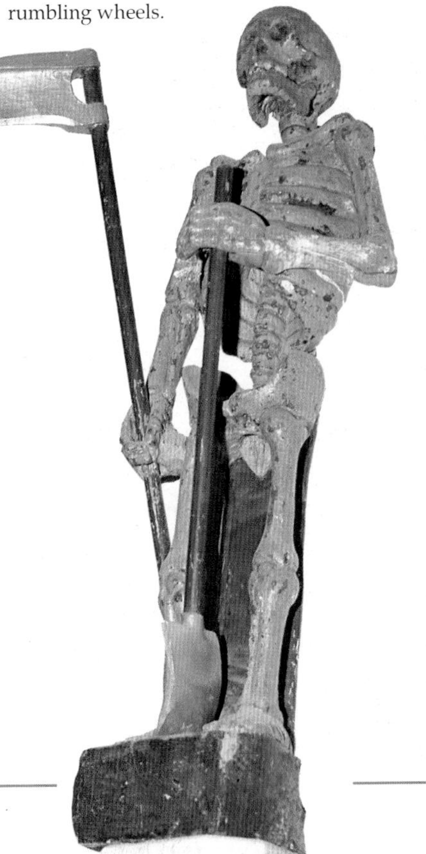

Ankou reaps the harvest of souls in Ploumilliau church

Few regions of France are as overtly pious as Brittany. Even in today's sceptical times mass is well attended in rural communities. Breton churches and enclos paroissiaux *(parish closes) are well cared for, and the shrines of the region's seven thousand, seven hundred, seven score and seven saints are revered.*

BRETON SAINTS Brittany's many saints appear sculpted in countless churches or wayside shrines, in local legends and in hundreds of place-names. Some are undoubtedly apocryphal, and a large proportion have never been formally recognised by the Church. Miraculous or super-natural events were associated with them, and many were attributed specific healing or protective powers against the ills of everyday life. The Seven Healing Saints celebrated at the Chapelle Notre-Dame-du-Haut near Moncontour (see page 213) are typical examples. Some saints looked after animals, such as St Golgan (sick horses), St Cornély and St Herbot (guardians of horned cattle). Others warded off lightning (Ste Barbe) or brought rain (St Vio).

Many Breton saints date back to the early wave of Celtic settlers fleeing Anglo-Saxon invaders in Britain during the 5th and 6th centuries. Evangelist monks then appeared in great numbers on Breton shores. The Seven Founding Saints set up the first seven dioceses of Brittany: Samson (Dol), Maclow (St-Malo), Brieuc (St-Brieuc), Tugdual (Tréguier), Paul the Aurelian (St-Pol), Corentin (Quimper) and Patern (Vannes).

ST ANNE The cult of St Anne began to be venerated in western Europe around the time of the crusades. Anne, mother of the Virgin Mary, was enthusiastically adopted as a patron and spiritual guardian of Brittany. She was (of course) a Breton, who somehow travelled to Judea to give birth to Mary, then came back to her native land, where Jesus and Peter visited her. Her name embraces aeons of Breton tradition; she is hazily identified with the all-powerful Celtic deity Ana, and also with the beloved Duchess Anne, an icon of Breton independence (see pages 36–7). Two famous *pardons* celebrate her, in Ste-Anne-la-Palud and in Ste-Anne-d'Auray (the largest and most revered shrine in Brittany).

St Yves, patron saint of lawyers, lies buried in Tréguier

ST PAUL THE AURELIAN St Paul travelled with St Samson to Brittany in the 6th century, and is one of the most famous of the Seven Founding Saints. His bishopric was St-Pol-de-Léon, where his relics are still kept in the cathedral. His final island refuge was Batz near Roscoff, where he captured a troublesome dragon

St Anne is revered in many parts of Brittany

with his stole and threw it into the sea. He died on Batz at the great age of 104.

ST YVES Yves Helori (1253–1303) was born at Minihy-Tréguier. The patron saint of lawyers, Yves combined religious duties with his work as a magistrate and advocate in Tréguier, and was famously incorruptible in an age when most lawyers took bribes. He was a champion of the poor, and is often depicted standing between a well-dressed client and a man in rags, an image which relates to the most famous story about him: a rich man sued a beggar for loitering by his kitchen door and 'stealing' his cooking smells. St Yves heard the evidence, declared the rich man had won his case, and awarded him appropriate damages – the sound of a coin rattling in a tin! Yves led an ascetic life and died at the age of 49. He is buried in Tréguier cathedral.

❑ A medieval joke relates how St Yves died and arrived at heaven's gates at the same time as a group of nuns. St Peter said to the nuns, 'You'll have to wait a while; we're crammed with nuns already.' Then he turned to St Yves, and asked who he was. 'A lawyer, sir', replied St Yves. 'Then come straight in,' said St Peter. 'You're the first one we've had.' ❑

Though Brittany is a fierce defender of Celtic traditions, comparatively few people still use Breton as their everyday language. Music, however, is thriving, and new interpretations of the old folk tunes produce a widespread awareness of Breton culture.

THE LIVING LANGUAGE Breton belongs to the so-called Brythonic group of Celtic languages, closely related to Welsh and Cornish in the UK. Some words have very similar counterparts in Welsh – *menez/ mynydd* (mountain), *yenez/ynys* (island) and so on – and some prefixes to place-names, such as *'pen'* or *'lan'*, are the same. The Breton hymn *'Bro Goz Ma Tadon'*, translates exactly into the Welsh national anthem, *Hen Wlad fy Nhadau* ('Land of My Fathers'), and is even sung to the same tune. Rumours that the Bretons and the Welsh can understand each other are, however, greatly exaggerated, though canny Breton onion-sellers taking the boat from Roscoff may have mugged up a few words of Welsh before reaching Wales, the better to sell their wares.

There are four distinct dialects in Brittany, spoken in Côtes-d'Armor, North Finistère, Cornouaille and the Morbihan. Like other Celtic languages, Breton has been subjected to great changes of attitude in the last couple of centuries. After Brittany officially became part of France, the Paris-based government attempted to suppress Breton language and culture, which it perceived (sometimes accurately) as a subversive influence. Since the inauguration of the Institut Culturel de Bretagne in 1981, which was set up to safeguard all aspects of Breton culture, the language has experienced something of a revival. It is now taught in schools and universities, heard on radio and television, and published in books and

*The Breton flag (*Gwen ha Du*, meaning 'White and Black'), designed in 1923 by the architect Morvan Marchal, is the only national flag that uses no colour*

Breton mingles with French on many signposts in Brittany

magazines. Despite this, many would say that the native language is in decline, and that efforts to revive it in the face of a continual onslaught from French-speaking mass media are artificial. About 600,000 people still speak Breton, mostly the elderly in Trégor and Finistère (Basse Bretagne), or separatists. Eastern Brittany (Haute Bretagne) has always allied itself more closely with French culture for obvious geographic reasons.

MUSIC AND DANCE Music is a strong social bond in Brittany. The Celts brought with them their bardic traditions of singing and storytelling. Long songs or poems (*lais*) were accompanied by musical instruments, often harps. Oral traditions went through a revival during the 18th century, and collections of folksongs began to be published.

Today's musicians continue this trend, encouraged by the spread of Celtic festivals and a renewed tourist interest in folk music. Music is now Brittany's most vigorous and versatile transmitter of Celtic culture, transcending the language barrier. You can see typical Breton instruments such as the *bombarde* (oboe), the *biniou* (bagpipes) or the *vielle* (hurdy-gurdy) in many museums, but try to hear them being played. All through the summer, concerts and festivals offer an opportunity to hear or even take part in Breton musical events (see page 28).

BRETON SEPARATISM Nationalist groups have existed in Brittany ever since the Act of Union lumped it with France in 1532. So far, luckily, terrorism has not played a great part in Breton politics (though the occasional statue has been blown up and, in 1977, the mirrors of Versailles were smashed by a Breton activist), but there are extreme voices, committed to more than putting a BZH (*Breizh* – Brittany) sticker on their cars. Some disaffected groups overtly ally themselves with terrorist organisations such as the IRA or the violent Basque separatists ETA.

Piping Celtic themes at a local festival

The Celtic temperament adores competitive activities, and trials of strength and team games have an enthusiastic following. For visitors, too, Brittany offers endless opportunities to enjoy active outdoor pursuits.

BRETON GAMES The local form of wrestling (known as *ar gouren* in Breton) can be seen at a number of summer festivals, such as the Fête de Locmaria at Belle-Isle-en-Terre. Breton wrestling is a bit like oriental judo: the wrestlers wear a voluminous garb of long shorts and loose shirts, and exchange three smacking ritual kisses before commencing battle. Other trials of strength are similar to those that can be seen at the Scottish Highland Games or in Spain's Basque country – tug-of-war, lifting a heavy stone, caber-tossing or discus-throwing. *Tire-baton* is a typical Breton sport, where the contestants attempt to lift each other with a pole. Brittany also has its own forms of those other popular Celtic team games, hockey and rugby. Breton sports are mostly conducted in a spirit of good humour and fun today, but in earlier times post-*pardon* games could degenerate into deadly inter-parish rivalries resulting in drunken brawls and broken heads.

TOURIST ACTIVITIES Brittany's changeable climate has always encouraged a fair degree of seaside activity rather than torpid sunbathing. Dinard's Victorian visitors used to amuse themselves by playing croquet on the sands. Today, however, the range of activities available to holidaymakers is much more extensive, with specialist sports such as hang-gliding, parascending, windsurfing and sand-yachting, as well as the more traditional resort pastimes of golf, riding, cycling and tennis.

Watersports All types naturally proliferate in the region's coastal areas, though Brittany's inland waterways and lakes also provide many opportunities to canoe, cruise, sail and fish. Windsurfing (*planche à voile*) is especially popular along the south coast, though experts head for the Plage de la Torche on the Penmarc'h peninsula. The Golfe du Morbihan offers excellent scuba-diving. Quiberon is one of Brittany's best sailing bases, and the clear waters of the Iles de Glénan are a marvellous place to practise sailing or diving.

Angling There are about 9,200km of shoreline or river bank in Brittany, offering sea, river or lake angling;

Checking the score at palet. *'Who won that round?'*

Brittany's inland waterways offer an endless source of relaxation

there is even underwater spear fishing off shore. Ask at the local tourist office about regulations on permits and the like. Alternatively, you can join in the simple pleasure enjoyed by countless Breton families of searching for shellfish in rockpools at low tide. All the equipment you will need (spades, rakes, nets or buckets) should be available locally.

Golf Brittany now has over 30 golf courses, many on the coast in lovely scenery. Dinard is the oldest and most fashionable centre, but golf is a more sociable, family-oriented game in France than in many other countries, and course etiquette is generally unstuffy, though fees can be quite high.

Cycling Each *département* has a local *Comité départemental de Cyclotourisme* which dispenses information and organises cycling events, and in most towns you can hire a bike from a cycle shop or the railway station for a day's outing.

Riding Brittany has many *centres équestres*, and organised riding holidays (by yourself or in a group with a guide) are easily arranged. Some of these treks include overnight accommodation. Like canal cruising, riding through Brittany adds a whole new dimension to the countryside. If motorised transport seems too pressurised you can opt for lower levels of horse-power in a *roulotte*, Brittany's version of a Romany caravan.

❑ In the evenings in quiet town squares you often see a sight familiar to visitors to all parts of France – all-male gatherings of local elders playing what looks like *boules* or *pétanque*. In Brittany, however, flat discs like quoits are thrown at the target instead of a ball. This Breton game is known as *palet*. ❑

The Celtic love of dressing up and making merry shows through in Brittany's festivals, which provide a continual backdrop of pageantry to any summer visit. Originally the festivals were religious events, but now they reflect many aspects of local culture.

PARDONS The *pardon* is one of the most distinctive aspects of Breton life, and virtually every parish holds one at some time during the year (some places have several). The word *pardon* implies forgiveness of sins, which was the purpose of the original medieval ritual. The inspiration for local *pardons* is still a fervent communal expression of spiritual contrition, followed up in a lighter vein by feasting and fun. Increasingly, *pardons* are used as occasions to cement Breton solidarity with some sort of festival or fair, and inevitably more than half an eye is cocked towards the tourist trade and an associated fresh influx of revenue. The *pardons* also present an opportunity to wear those elaborate costumes now stuck in the wardrobe for special occasions.

In some *pardons* darker echoes of the ancient Celtic gods can be heard. At Plougastel's midsummer festival, young children are passed over the flames of a bonfire, a tradition that harks back to rituals of human sacrifice. Some Christian *pardons* are held at the same times of year as older pagan festivals (harvests, or the summer and winter solstice, for example), and the forms of worship reflect the Celtic belief that gods or saints returned to earth at certain auspicious seasons.

FOLKLORE FESTIVALS After the solemn hymns and long religious services, *pardons* generally take on a much more cheerful tone. Locals in bright costumes parade embroidered banners and statues of their patron saint through the streets, while stallholders sell all kinds of crafts, souvenirs, *crêpes* and cider. Afterwards, there may be dancing and traditional music, or a sports competition featuring typical 'trials of strength' – perhaps Breton wrestling or a tug-of-war.

Many secular folk festivals have appeared in the past century. Largest of all is Quimper's Festival de Cornouaille, a massive gathering of Celtic artists, musicians and dancers. This is one of the best places to see regional costumes and enjoy Breton music. Rennes holds its Tombées de la Nuit in July, another huge celebration of all things Breton, with modern rock music thrown in. Lorient's Festival Interceltique is a further

Stepping out in style at one of Cornouaille's popular festivals

The male version of the coiffe

chance for Celtic cousins to join hands and dance a gavotte to the harp, the *bombarde* and the *biniou*. Dinan's medieval Fête des Remparts or Pont-Aven's Fête des Ajoncs d'Or (Gorse-flower Festival) have been immensely popular in recent years. Châteauneuf-du-Faou and Guingamp both hold annual festivals of traditional dancing.

Several festivals have charitable origins – Concarneau's Fête des Filets Bleus (Blue Nets Festival) began as a fundraising exercise for the distressed families of redundant sardine fishermen. Others celebrate local livelihoods: Fouesnant's Fête des Pommiers (Apple-tree Festival) honours its cider industry, and Paimpol remembers its Icelandic fishermen in a Fête des Terre-Neuvas et des Islandais. Blessings of the Sea ceremonies (for example, at Carantec or Douarnenez) propitiate the gods of the deep.

Many Breton communities now rely heavily on tourist revenue and promote colourful spectacles or *fest-noz* (night festivals) as a way of attracting summer visitors. Some of the more famous annual events are a great draw, and accommodation fills up fast. If you are planning to visit a particular town in high season, check its diary for crowd-pulling junkets, and book well ahead.

The calendar of events overleaf gives a selection of the larger festivals and *pardons*. Any tourist office can provide advice about events happening locally, though they may be vague about those taking place further afield. For further information, and an annual programme of events throughout Brittany, contact the Fédération des Comités de Fêtes Traditionnelles de Bretagne, Kerholen, 29540 Spézet (tel: 02 98 93 91 58).

Pont-l'Abbé is one of the best places to see traditional costumes

Calendar of events Most of Brittany's cultural events and festivals are geared to the short tourist season. Little happens between November and April.

Some of the following events are moveable feasts and vary from year to year, so it is best to check precise dates with the local tourist office.

May
Quintin Pardon
Tréguier Pardon de St Yves

June
Le Faouët Pardon de Ste Barbe
Rumengol Pardon de Notre-Dame
St-Jean-du-Doigt Pardon du Feu (Pardon of the Fire)

July
Binic Fête de la Morue
Dinan Festival International de la Harpe Celtique (harps)
Fouesnant Fête des Pommiers
Lamballe Festival Folklorique des Ajoncs d'Or
Locronan Petite (annual) or Grande Troménie (every sixth year, next one takes place in 2001)
Morlaix Les Mercredis de Morlaix
Nantes Carnival and arts festival
Paimpol Fête des Terre-Neuvas et des Islandais
Pont-l'Abbé Fête des Brodeuses (embroidery festival)
Quimper Festival de Cornouaille
Redon Fête de la Batellerie (canals festival), Festival de l'Abbaye
Rennes Les Tombées de la Nuit
Ste-Anne-d'Auray Grand Pardon
St-Malo Festival de Musique Sacrée

August
Carantec Blessing of the Sea
Carnac Grande Fête des Menhirs
Châteauneuf-du-Faou Festival International de Danses et Traditions Populaires
Concarneau Fête des Filets Bleus
Erquy Festival de la Mer
Fédrun Brière Festival
Fougères Festival du Livre Vivant (historical pageant)
Guingamp Festival de la Danse Bretonne
Lorient Festival Interceltique
Perros-Guirec Fête des Hortensias (hydrangeas)
Plomodiern Fête du Menez-Hom
Pont-Aven Fête des Fleurs d'Ajoncs (gorse flowers)
St-Briac-sur-Mer Fête des Mouettes (seagulls)
Ste-Anne-la-Palud Pardon
Cap Sizun Fête des Bruyères (heather)
Vannes Grandes Fêtes d'Arvor

September
Camaret Blessing of the Sea
Le Folgoët Grand Pardon
Josselin Pardon
Hennebont Pardon
Penhors Pardon
Tronoën Notre-Dame de Tronoën Pardon

Traditional Breton costumes are worn with pride on festival days

Brittany Was

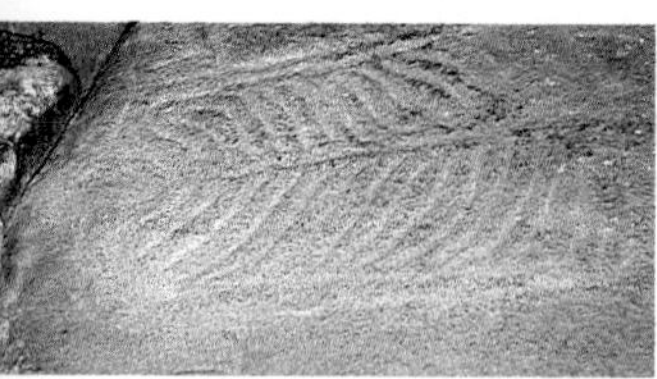

Very little is known about the enigmatic people who raised those standing stones in lines around Carnac over 6,000 years ago. After wrestling with all the theories it is tempting to assume that the alignments are an elaborate Stone Age joke, constructed simply to baffle posterity.

EARLIEST INHABITANTS Scarcely anything remains of any civilisation before the megalith-builders. The earliest signs of human settlement in Brittany date from the Old Stone Age (about 8000 BC, well before the megalithic period). Brittany seems to have been more sparsely populated at this stage than other more fertile regions of France, perhaps because there were so few caves to provide natural shelters (Brittany has virtually no lime-stone). What communities there were seem generally to have lived on or near the coast, subsisting on a monotonous diet of shellfish eked out with scraps of meat from captured game. A few signs of ritual graves and domestic hearths have been unearthed from the mesolithic or Middle Stone Age period (about 6000–3500 BC), mostly in Morbihan and Cornouaille.

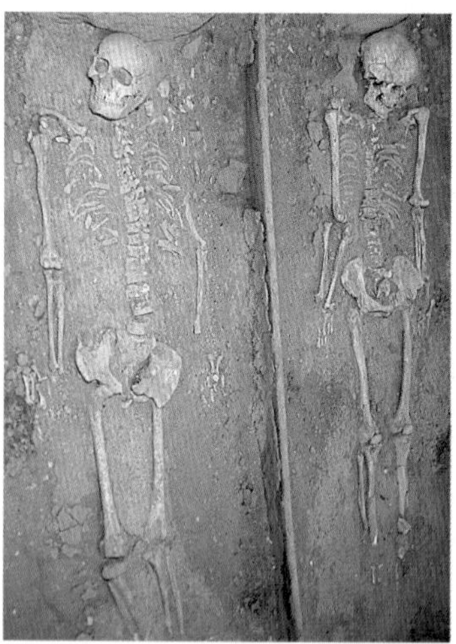

Reconstructed Iron Age necropolis at St-Guénolé's Musée de la Préhistoire

SETTLING DOWN As time went on, the hand-to-mouth existence of these early peoples became more ordered and settled. The climate grew colder, and the lack of natural caves may have encouraged them to create their own shelters by piling up stones and earth. Gradually, the possibilities of building more complex structures opened up. When the climate grew more favourable again, farming techniques were developed. Wild plants were cultivated and improved, including wheat, barley, lentils and a primitive kind of apple.

ARCHITECTS IN STONE Monuments similar to those found in Brittany can be found all over the world, dating from widely differing periods. Not all, even within Brittany, can clearly be related to each other, nor do they all have a common purpose. The earliest Breton megaliths can be identified with reasonable certainty as burial places. These are dolmens (literally 'table stones'), or passage graves. They usually consist of flattish slabs of rock assembled into a roofed chamber with an entrance at

❑ If you visit any of Brittany's museums you will almost certainly see dozens of metal axe heads. These smooth, greenish artefacts are so beautifully shaped that it is easy to suspect some modern factory is churning them out to boost the tourist trade. Weapons of smelted metal were once as precious as jewels. Nearly 400 Bronze Age hoards have been unearthed in recent times all over Brittany, containing about 20,000 axes made of 10 tonnes of bronze. ❑

Standing stones, Carnac

one side. Some are enclosed in mounds of earth and stone (cairns).

A second group of similar but more extended monuments are called gallery graves (*allées couvertes*). The third and most mysterious type of all are the menhirs, or standing stones, in some places solitary, elsewhere arranged in rows, or *alignements*. These are thought to date from between 4500 and 1800 BC, the neolithic (New Stone Age) period. By far the most impressive and numerous of these *alignements* stand near Carnac (see pages 184–5).

At some time during the Bronze Age (1800–600 BC), new settlers appeared who were known as the Bell-Beaker people because of their style of pottery. Brittany's most recent megalithic monuments date from this period, by which time both tools and skills had developed considerably. Ornate gold jewellery, shaped axe heads and decorated pottery reveal great artistry and craftsmanship, and indicate a knowledge of metalworking.

THEORIES Some historians believe the stone lines were masterminded by a caste of priest-kings in order to determine the correct dates for sowing and harvesting crops from the movements of the stars. Although it is known that the stones were used by later cultures for ritual purposes, no theory yet proposed about their original function is entirely convincing.

Alignement *at Cojoux*

The first wave of Celtic peoples arrived in Brittany during the Iron Age, calling their new home Armor – 'The Land by the Sea'. After the departure of the Romans, the Celts returned again in the 5th and 6th centuries AD, this time from Britain.

THE EARLY CELTS It seems likely that the new arrivals merged gradually with the previous inhabitants rather than conquering and supplanting them. The Bronze Age dragged on late in Brittany, and full 'Celticisation' of the population did not take place until around 500 BC. The Celts were skilled metalworkers and potters. They built hill forts surrounded by earthworks to protect themselves from interlopers, and barrows to bury their dead. Some were farmers and stock-breeders, while others were adventurous seafarers who traded Armor's mineral wealth as far as the Mediterranean.

The Celts were a warlike people, and their military exploits were often ill-advised. After they dared to attack Rome in 387 BC, it is scarcely surprising that the Romans resolved to quell them. The task was made easier by the Celts' lack of any sense of political nationhood. They were essentially a tribal people who allied themselves around strong, individual leaders but frequently fought among themselves. Thus divided, they fell. The Romans steadily picked them off all over Europe using a subtle mixture of diplomacy and military action.

By the time Julius Caesar launched his Gallic Wars in 58 BC, Brittany (or Armorica, as the Romans called this outpost of Gaul) was inhabited by five identifiable Celtic tribes. The powerful Veneti, who spearheaded the resistance movement against the Roman invasion, inhabited the Morbihan area. Their epic sea battle against Caesar's fleet marks the turning point of Roman supremacy in Gaul.

Granite blocks form the doorway in the wall of the Camp d'Artus, Finistère, a town established by the Armoricans in the 1st century BC

THE BATTLE OF THE VENETI By 56 BC one of the few remaining pockets of Gaul yet unconquered was Armor, a wild and infertile but potentially rich metal-producing region. Caesar attempted bloodless infiltration by taking Armorican hostages. Most tribes acquiesced, but the proud Veneti seized Roman envoys in reprisal. Caesar determined to teach them a lesson. The Veneti were a seafaring race who controlled the tin mines and the lucrative Atlantic trade. Their sturdy sailing ships were designed for rough seas and heavy cargoes, and numerically and structurally they far outstripped the slow, oar-propelled Roman galleys. However, a period of dead calm left the Veneti's sailing ships helpless, while the lighter Roman craft rowed towards their bows, hurled grapnels at the rigging and pulled down their sails. Thus immobilised, the Veneti were soon captured.

The battle took place somewhere off the Rhuys peninsula in the Golfe du Morbihan, and was allegedly watched by Caesar himself from a nearby hill. Caesar was not a magnanimous victor; the Veneti were ruthlessly massacred, mutilated or sold into slavery.

Gaius Julius Caesar (100–44 BC), Roman general and statesman

The 4th-century BC Celtic Kermaria Stone, found at Kermaria en Pont-l'Abbé, Finistère

ROMAN BRITTANY The Romans left no great reminders of their existence in Armorica. They improved the roads and replaced the camps of the old Celtic tribes with stoutly walled cities (Rennes, Vannes and Nantes) but their purpose in occupying Armorica was more to take from it than to add. There are no aqueducts or amphitheatres to admire in Brittany, and evidence of the Gallo-Roman period is mostly confined to museums. Rennes' Musée de Bretagne (see page 221) has a good Roman section; so too does Corseul's town hall museum, near Dinan (see page 50).

THE FALL OF THE EMPIRE Roman supremacy in Gaul and neighbouring Britain brought a peace that lasted until the 5th century AD, when the legions were hurriedly recalled to defend Rome from barbarian hordes. Thus unprotected, Great Britain was subjected to Viking raids and invasions by Angles and Saxons, who steadily drove the indigenous Celts westwards to Wales and Cornwall, whence they set sail for Armorica and their long-lost Celtic cousins. Many of their leaders became the saints of the new Celtic dawn. They renamed Armorica after their old homeland – Brittany (Little Britain).

The old gods were soon supplanted by Christianity after the arrival of the British Celts, who also brought their language (unadulterated by the Low Latin which later turned into French) and their Arthurian myths. Under continual threat of invasion, the disparate Celtic groups were gradually forged into a nation.

FRANKS AND NORSEMEN In AD 799 the petty kingdoms of Brittany were easily subjugated by the Franks and placed under a governor, Nominoë, a Breton noble and a protegé of Charlemagne. At Redon in 845, Nominoë expelled the Franks and made Brittany an independent state under his ducal authority. Nominoë's son and heir, Erispoë, took the title of King of Brittany.

Another heroic leader, Alain Barbe-Torte (Crookbeard), repelled the Norse invasions of the 10th century and became the last Breton king. He took measures to strengthen Brittany's defences against invasion, and built many fortresses. After Barbe-Torte's death, dissent among the nobles plunged Brittany into a long period of fighting and confusion.

THE WAR OF SUCCESSION When Duke Jean III (1312–41) died childless, the succession for the Duchy of Brittany was contested by his half-brother, Jean de Montfort, and his niece, Jeanne de Penthièvre, wife of Charles de Blois, the French king's nephew. The English under Edward III supported Jean de Montfort, while the French allied themselves with Charles de Blois and his wife. The confusing struggle lasted 24 years, complicated by the wider issues of the Hundred Years War. One of the most memorable incidents of the long campaign was the Battle of the Thirty in 1351, a chivalric fight between 30 knights from each side near Josselin (see panel on page 188). The French side won this epic tournament, but not the war: the Montforts eventually claimed victory when Charles de Blois was killed at the Battle of Auray in 1364. Jean IV (son of Jean de Montfort) succeeded to a much impoverished duchy.

BERTRAND DU GUESCLIN (1320–80) This great medieval warrior was born of minor nobility near Dinan, the eldest of ten children. He came of age – conveniently for a military man – just as the Hundred Years War began. Bertrand's interests were thoroughly active – hunting, hawking and fighting. He detested academic pursuits and remained illiterate all his life. Apparently he was so ugly and boorishly

Jean de Montfort, head of a new dynasty

aggressive that his parents disowned him when he was young. He became the leader of a lawless peasant gang, and thus honed his fighting skills. At a tournament to celebrate the marriage of Jeanne de Penthièvre and Charles de Blois in 1338, Bertrand appeared in disguise and acquitted himself so well in the lists that when his identity was revealed his father was instantly reconciled with him.

Du Guesclin seized the chance of military adventure during the War of Succession, when he backed Charles de Blois and tormented the English supporters of the Montforts. When he was captured after the Battle of Auray, the French ransomed him for a massive 100,000 crowns. After many more adventures in Spain and elsewhere, mostly fighting the English, Du Guesclin became Constable of France in 1370. He died of fever, still on active service, in the Massif Central. Du Guesclin wanted to be buried in his native Dinan, but the journey was long and the summer hot, and bit by bit the great warrior's decomposing corpse was interred *en route*: entrails at le Puy, flesh at Montferrand and his skeleton at St-Denis. Finally, his heart reached Dinan, where it lies in the church of St-Sauveur (see page 52).

Du Guesclin rides roughshod over Dinan's main square

Bertrand Du Guesclin, hero of the Hundred Years War

❑ Du Guesclin was immensely courageous, and knew all the 'rules' of medieval chivalry. But he didn't always play by them; he fought to win. He was a master of cunning guerrilla tactics, and developed the use of gunpowder and new methods of siege warfare. His soldiers were taught to fight on foot, hand to hand, using ambushes and subterfuge. ❑

After the exhausting struggles of medieval times, the Duchy of Brittany entered its most glorious phase under the House of Montfort (1364–1532). But the seeds of Brittany's downfall lay dormant in its greatness, which represented a threat to French supremacy.

THE MONTFORT RECOVERY Things soon picked up under the firm Montfort leadership and trading possibilities blossomed, bringing a new wave of prosperity to Brittany. Salt and textiles were the economy's mainstays – linen and sailcloth were particularly important commodities. Art and architecture also flourished, and many of Brittany's most memorable Gothic cathedrals and castles date from this period.

The Montfort dukes reinforced their independence from France with a mighty chain of fortresses along the Breton Marches. By the end of the 15th century the strength of the Breton duchy was beginning to alarm the French monarchy, and the newly wealthy province looked an increasingly attractive prize. Duke François II, sensing which way the wind blew, sought allies abroad, and entered into a coalition against the powerful Anne de Beaujeu, then Regent of France on behalf of the young Charles VIII. Anne invaded Brittany and François II was defeated at the Battle of St-Aubin-du-Cormier in 1488. He was forced to sign a treaty and died (of shame, it is said) just two weeks later.

ANNE DE BRETAGNE (1477–1514) François II was succeeded by his daughter, Anne, who became Brittany's best-loved heroine but its last duchess. Anne lived only to the age of 37, but her dynastic marriages and astute personality had a huge influence on Brittany's destiny. When she entered the political arena she was very young. One of the terms of the treaty her father had signed after his defeat was that the French king should choose Anne's future husband. Even at the tender age of 12 she had already been

Though not physically prepossessing, Charles VIII won Anne's heart

betrothed by proxy twice for political reasons – once to the English Prince of Wales (King Edward IV's successor), then to a Habsburg prince, heir to the Holy Roman Empire. Both these powerful alliances represented a threat to French interests. Although pledged to another, Charles VIII of France broke off his engagement and made a determined play for Anne. He captured Nantes, besieged Rennes, and then proposed. The spirited Anne was in no mood to be browbeaten into marriage, but the pleas of her starving people swayed her and she finally agreed to meet Charles. Amazingly, the two got on well, and Anne soon became not simply Duchess of Brittany but also Queen of France. Brittany remained independent, but inevitably the bonds with France grew tighter.

Anne is described as small and frail, with a limp. Though not especially pretty, she was charming and intelligent, and very determined.

Charles was neither physically nor mentally prepossessing, but they seem to have been genuinely fond of each other. No heir survived the marriage; they watched all four of their children die in infancy, which caused them both enormous grief.

After seven years, Charles died of an accidental blow to the head. A clause in the terms of their alliance stated that Anne should marry Charles's successor in the event of his death, and this she duly did. Louis XII hastily extracted an annulment from his first marriage and married Anne. Again, she made the best of her arranged match and lived on good terms with her kindly but ailing husband, who treated her with great affection. Anne devoted herself tirelessly to the administration of Brittany and attempted to ensure its future independence. She toured the province and endowed it with great wealth. Once again, her desire for a healthy male heir for the duchy was thwarted; of her four later children, only two daughters survived. When Anne died in 1514, exhausted by her fruitless confinements, the whole of Brittany mourned.

Anne in characteristically devout pose, surrounded by patron saints

Despite Anne de Bretagne's endeavours, Brittany was irrevocably absorbed into the French kingdom when her daughter, Claude, married François d'Angoulême, the future king of France. The rights and privileges that Anne had fought so hard to retain were subsequently ignored and dishonoured.

Top: Jacques Cartier meeting the native people of Canada

UNION WITH FRANCE The Treaty of Vannes in 1532 proclaimed the 'perpetual union of the Country and Duchy of Brittany with the Kingdom and Crown of France'. In theory, Brittany was still permitted to control taxes and maintain its own army. In practice, however, its destiny now lay in French hands. The title of Duke of Brittany became obsolete, and the province was ruled by an appointed governor. Brittany's interests were represented by the *états*, a legislative parliamentary assembly based first at Nantes, then later at Rennes. Meanwhile, the region's assets and resources were stripped and its autonomy eroded. Many Breton citizens developed a lasting sense of grievance against central government.

BRITTANY OF THE 16TH CENTURY The new era of union began auspiciously enough for Brittany: the Breton explorer Jacques Cartier discovered Canada for the French Crown just two years later, in 1534; St-Malo, Nantes and Lorient grew enormously rich from seaborne trade and privateering; and architecture flourished with a profusion of elegant castles and country mansions. Popular religious art also reached great heights – many parish closes were constructed during this period (see pages 136–7). Later in the 16th century, however, the Wars of Religion caused terrible hardship and disruption in some parts of France. Brittany was not seriously affected because very few of its population were Protestants, but the Breton *Ligue* (a band of fanatical Catholics) implicated Brittany in various political plots. One of these *Ligueurs* was the cruel bandit La Fontenelle, who ravaged the Penmarc'h peninsula (see panel on page 153). The Edict of

Jacques Cartier adds Canada to France's colonial possessions

Cardinal Richelieu had a marked influence on Brittany's destiny

Nantes put a temporary end to religious strife by granting Protestant Huguenots civil rights. It was signed by Henry IV in 1598 at Nantes castle, where he is alleged to have exclaimed in amazement at the Duchess Anne's mighty fortress: 'God's teeth, they are no small beer, these Dukes of Brittany!'

THE *ANCIEN RÉGIME* In 1610 the accession of Louis XIII (1610–43) ushered in a new era. He appointed as Governor of Brittany Cardinal Richelieu, who lost no time in making his mark on the province. Fortifications were dismantled at Richelieu's behest to discourage any insurrection. France's imperial ambitions dictated a massive upgrading of its naval defences, and the port of Brest underwent a startling transformation after 1636 when work began on the dockyards. Port-Louis on the south coast also became an important naval stronghold, though the first India Company founded by Richelieu failed. The Breton landscape began to change too. Huge quantities of timber were felled for the French fleet of sailing ships and the great forests of the *argoat* dwindled. Some trees reappeared, however – it was during this period that the cider apple was imported to Brittany from neighbouring Normandy, changing its drinking habits for ever. The vines that once struggled in Brittany's damp climate were confined to the region around Nantes and the Loire Valley (on the spurious grounds that the Bretons were habitual drunkards).

In 1643 Louis XIII died, a year after Richelieu, and was succeeded by the redoubtable Sun King, Louis XIV, then only four years old. After a period of regency under his Sicilian mentor, Mazarin, Louis XIV decided at the age of 23 that he preferred absolute power. He appointed his finance minister, Colbert, Governor of Brittany, and once again the province was exploited. So lavish were the king's tastes that new sources of revenue were constantly sought. Besides continuing Richelieu's plan of building up the French fleet, Colbert had to find finance for palaces, colonial adventures and foreign wars.

Brittany provided a convenient cashbox for Louis XIV's extravagance, but not a docile one. Smouldering resentment erupted into violent protest against unjust and draconian taxation. The scene was set for revolt on a wide scale.

THE BONNETS ROUGES One of Colbert's first attempts to balance the Sun King's budget resulted in the so-called 'Stamped Paper Revolt'. Colbert decreed in 1675 that to be legally valid all documents must be recorded on special stamped paper. There was, of course, a stiff duty on the stamps, and payments filled the royal coffers. Tobacco and pewter, other commodities dear to the Breton heart (smokers and drinkers all), were also heavily taxed, despite an 'amnesty' Brittany had obtained at a massive cost of 2 million *livres* absolving it from further increases in taxation. Riots broke out in Rennes, Nantes and St-Malo, and troops were dispatched to punish the truculent Bretons. The local aristocracy joined in on the king's side and helped to crush the rebels.

Louis XIV, the Sun King, reigned from 1643 to 1715

The situation deteriorated when Colbert threatened to impose further taxes, including the hated *gabelle*, or salt tax. Armed peasants calling themselves the Bonnets Rouges (Red Caps) rampaged through 40 parishes, ringing the church bells to call supporters to arms. They attacked local châteaux and drank the cellars dry, demanding an end to long lists of grievances. Under the leadership of Sébastien Le Balp, a lawyer, 30,000 insurgents sacked Carhaix, but the revolt collapsed abruptly after Le Balp was killed. Dreadful reprisals followed, and the remaining ringleaders were broken on the wheel or sent to the gallows. Madame de Sévigné, observing these events, wrote that the frightened peasants destined for the scaffold had spirit left only to plead for a drink and a quick death. French troops were then billeted in Brittany, where their appalling behaviour, including rape and pillage, went unchecked. Rebellion was quelled – temporarily.

THE FRENCH REVOLUTION When the Bastille fell in July 1789, Brittany rejoiced, hoping for an end to the injustice it had felt since being annexed by France. The optimism was short-lived, however. The Breton temperament, though fiercely independent, was not naturally radical, and was quickly appalled by the godless excesses of the French

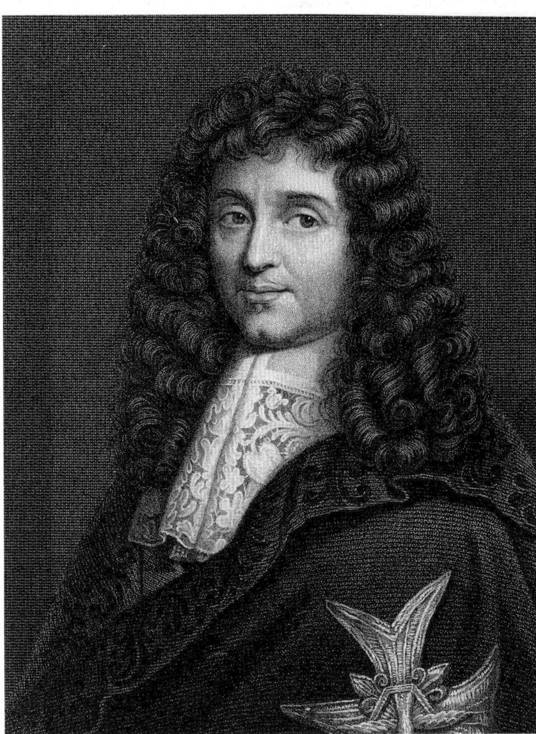

Jean-Baptiste Colbert, appointed superintendent of finances in 1661

Revolution. It also became clear that the Revolutionary ideals promised less, not more, autonomy for Brittany. The native language was discouraged in favour of French, and administration centred on Paris. Even the name of Brittany disappeared, submerged into five *départements*. Armies garrisoned in Brittany requisitioned rations from already depleted local stocks, and conscription was introduced.

One of the least successful ambassadors of the Revolutionary ideal was Jean-Baptiste Carrier, whose atrocities in Rennes and Nantes shocked even his Convention paymasters (see page 179). The scene was set for the emergence of a secret counter-Revolutionary movement called the Association Bretonne, founded by the Marquis de la Rouerie after the execution of Louis XVI in 1793. The rebels became known as the Chouans (see page 179) from their use of a screech-owl signal, and their rallying cry was '*Vive le roi, vive la bonne religion.*' ('Long live the King, long live the true religion.')

The novelist Jules Verne, born in Nantes in 1828

THE AFTERMATH

After some of the grim memories of the Revolution had been expunged in a brief decade of Napoleonic glory, Brittany settled down to lick its wounds. In the 19th century, canals and railways were built and the roads improved. A cultural revival took place, bringing a renewed interest in the music, folklore and language of Brittany. Pont-Aven became an artists' haven, and several local writers put Brittany on the map, notably Chateaubriand and Jules Verne. This new awareness of Breton identity took a political turn with the founding of the first separatist party, Strollad Broadel Breiz, in 1908. Economic unrest rumbled in some quarters, resulting in strikes and industrial riots among the fishing community in the early 20th century, when cod and sardine prices slumped. But before long, a much greater disaster engulfed the region.

By the end of World War I the Breton countryside had changed little compared with some parts of France, but its communities were devastated. World War II was less costly in terms of human lives, but the destruction it wrought changed the face of Brittany's coastal cities for ever.

THE GREAT WAR The huge memorial at Ste-Anne-d'Auray commemorates the dead of all modern wars, but the names of the dead of World War I make awesomely lengthy reading. Over 250,000 perished, the highest death toll per head of population of any region in the world. Brittany's maritime tradition meant that many of those killed were naval recruits.

The lost generation had a profound impact on both the region's psyche and its economy. The birth rate dropped dramatically, and emigration was rife between the wars. After the 1914–18 war many disillusioned survivors turned to separatist organisations to impart some meaning to their colossal sacrifice. Among the more militant of these groups were Gwenn ha Du (White and Black, taking its name from the Breton flag), a secret society responsible for a number of protest bombings, and Bezenn Perrot, which declared itself as a Breton army and whose aim was to eject the French from Brittany. The separatists attracted support by claiming that the valiant Breton war effort had been made on behalf of a government that had destroyed Brittany's autonomy and suppressed Breton culture.

WORLD WAR II After the pounding Brittany had received in the Great War, few expected its people would have the heart for another global conflict. Yet the Bretons provided one of the most spirited bastions of resistance against the German invasion. They accounted for a quarter of the Free French Forces summoned by General de Gaulle, and bravely endured a massive aerial onslaught.

At first, the fighting seemed a distant rumble beyond the eastern borders, but once Holland and

The moving war memorial at Ste-Anne-d'Auray

Belgium had fallen Brittany was all too close to the Maginot Line. By June 1940 the first German occupying troops arrived. Some expected the Bretons to welcome them as allies against their French oppressors; they were disappointed. By this time General de Gaulle had broadcast his stirring call to arms from England, and many Bretons were already on their way to join him – the Ile de Sein was deserted except for women, children and old men. An effective Resistance network was set up all over Brittany, to which many Allied servicemen owe their lives.

By 3 August 1944, when the Liberation of Brittany began under

An emotional welcome for American troops entering Rennes in 1944

the command of George Patton's US VIII Corps, 30,000 Bretons were in arms. Six weeks later several historic Breton ports – St-Malo, Brest, Lorient, St-Nazaire – lay in unrecognisable fragments.

Although the war damage has since been repaired, bitter memories linger in some places, expressed on grave-stones and memorials throughout Brittany. Many German visitors flock peaceably to Brittany today in Audis and BMWs, bringing welcome tourist revenue, but many older Bretons simply never speak of that period of their lives.

The submarine pens at St-Nazaire

❑ From Plage Bonaparte beach near Paimpol, a massive rescue operation codenamed Shelburne was mounted by the Resistance and the British Royal Navy during World War II. Allied aircrew shot down over German-occupied territory, or escaped prisoners-of-war, were smuggled across France to the north coast of Brittany to await a coded message relayed by BBC radio transmitters: '*Bonjour à tous dans la maison d'Alphonse*'. This was the signal to assemble beneath the cliffs on Plage Bonaparte, where a Dartmouth gunboat would slip quietly past enemy defences to collect them. Moonless nights were chosen for the escape missions, but even so they were extremely risky: 'To right and left of us were German listening posts...Ten miles away, there was a radar installation and a battery of medium guns...' Memorials near the beach and on the surrounding cliffs now com-memorate the brave participants in Operation Shelburne. ❑

Since World War II, Brittany has slowly recovered, its economy boosted considerably by the tourist industry, though many farmers and fishermen still feel they get a raw deal from Paris. While rural populations drift to the towns in search of work, weary city-dwellers gaze longingly towards the Breton countryside, dreaming of rustic bliss.

DOWN ON THE FARM During the 1960s agricultural prices slumped and, with no organised marketing strategy to protect them, farmers suffered badly. In time-honoured fashion they took the source of their grievances to Paris and dumped them in the streets – an episode that became known as the Artichoke War. One unexpected by-product of this farming tussle was the creation of Brittany Ferries (see page 113). Since the 1960s, agriculture has enjoyed a great renaissance in Brittany, bolstered by enormous windfalls of cash from the European Union (EU). Protests still recur, though, sometimes erupting in violent confrontation against imported produce.

POWER LINES Brittany has new industries, too, from space-age telecommunications and high-tech electronics to controversial nuclear power stations. The Bretons have complained vociferously (and sometimes successfully) about having nuclear power plants dumped in their quiet backwaters, comfortably distant from France's main population centres. Much more enthusiastically received was the innovative Rance estuary dam near St-Malo – the world's first tidal power station, inaugurated in 1967 (see page 62).

Nuclear and tidal power help generate Brittany's electricity

Pleumeur-Bodou, centre for French telecommunications

DIVERTING THE LOIRE In 1973 France underwent one of its periodic bureaucratic upheavals and redrew the map, leaving Brittany with just four *départements* instead of the former five. Loire-Atlantique in the south-east joined the neighbouring region of Pays de la Loire. Psychologically, many Bretons have never accepted this change, and regard it as just another idiotic imposition by Parisian pen-pushers. Most inhabitants of Loire-Atlantique still regard themselves as Bretons, at least as far as that great natural divide, the River Loire. Economically, however, the transition cannot be ignored. Nantes, Brittany's old capital and one of its most populous and prosperous cities, now heads another region, taking with it the lucrative Muscadet wine trade and a significant proportion of tourism. La Baule, formerly Brittany's most sophisticated seaside resort, and Brière Regional Nature Park, now pay dividends elsewhere.

FORGING AHEAD In 1962 Brittany basked briefly in a welcome glow of world attention when the giant radar antennae at Pleumeur-Bodou transmitted (and received) the first transatlantic satellite broadcast via *Telstar*. Today, Brittany is still the centre of the French telecommunications industry. Other large employers are Citroën, near Rennes, and Renault, which has a plant near Lorient. Massive amounts of money have been poured into Breton cities such as Brest, which were badly damaged during World War II. The Brest Charter, ratified in 1988, encouraged large-scale investment in new city facilities and in education. This has resulted in the creation of new roads and bridges and the development of the Technopôle Brest-Iroise, a vast complex including research centres, higher education establishments and businesses.

Road, rail and air links with the rest of France have also become a major priority. The regional airline, BritAir, and the advent of the high-speed train (TGV – *Train à Grande Vitesse*) have done much to make Brittany less isolated. New road bridges, particularly the one at St-Nazaire, provide a gateway to the south.

World recession, though, has hit the region badly. Unemployment is still high, and rural depopulation is a problem. Traditional industries such as shipbuilding and steel have dwindled to a fraction of their former importance. Fishing is also suffering from aggressive foreign competition and the cutbacks caused by EU attempts to conserve fish stocks. One other maritime harvest is being investigated with great interest, however – offshore oil. So far Brittany has experienced only the minus side of the drilling business, when laden tankers founder against its reefs and spoil its precious beaches. But the region looks enviously towards its Celtic relatives in Scotland, hoping that somewhere off Finistère lies similar buried treasure.

The Rance tidal dam – a power provider

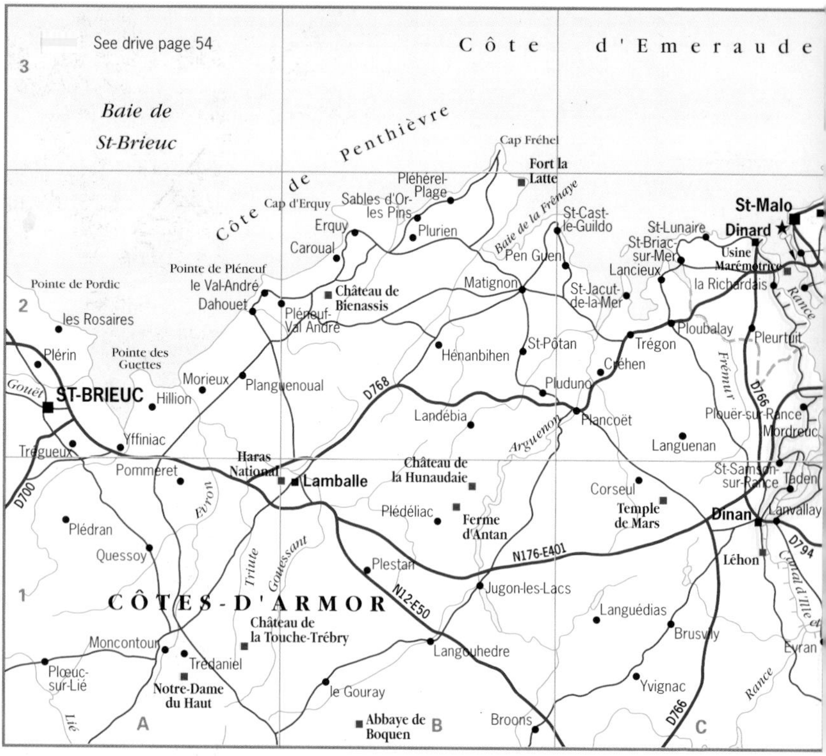

See drive page 54

Côte d'Emeraude
Baie de St-Brieuc
Côte de Penthièvre
Cap Fréhel
Fort la Latte
Cap d'Erquy
Pléhérel-Plage
Sables d'Or-les Pins
Plurien
Erquy
Caroual
Baie de la Frênaye
St-Cast-le-Guildo
Pen Guen
St-Malo
St-Lunaire
Dinard
St-Briac-sur-Mer
Lancieux
Usine Marémotrice
la Richardais
Rance
Pointe de Pordic
Pointe de Pléneuf
le Val-André
Dahouet
Château de Bienassis
Pléneuf-Val André
Matignon
St-Jacut-de-la-Mer
les Rosaires
Plérin
Pointe des Guettes
Hénanbihen
St-Pôtan
Trégon
Ploubalay
Pleurtuit
Frémur
Créhen
Gouët
ST-BRIEUC
Hillion
Morieux
Planguenoual
D768
Pluduno
Landébia
Plancoët
Arguenon
D766
Plouër-sur-Rance
Mordreuc
Yffiniac
Trégueux
Languenan
Pommeret
Haras National
Lamballe
Château de la Hunaudaie
St-Samson-sur-Rance
Taden
Corseul
Temple de Mars
D700
Evron
Plédéliac
Ferme d'Antan
Dinan
Lanvallay
Plédran
D794
Quessoy
Gouessant
Plestan
N176-E401
Léhon
Canal d'Ille et
Triute
Jugon-les-Lacs
CÔTES-D'ARMOR
N12-E50
Languédias
Château de la Touche-Trébry
Brusvily
Moncontour
Evran
Tredaniel
Langouhedre
Plœuc-sur-Lié
Notre-Dame du Haut
le Gouray
Yvignac
Lié
Abbaye de Boquen
Broons
D766

Mock-Gothic villas overlook the harbour at Dinard. Close proximity to the Gulf Stream ensures mild average temperatures and a profusion of palm trees

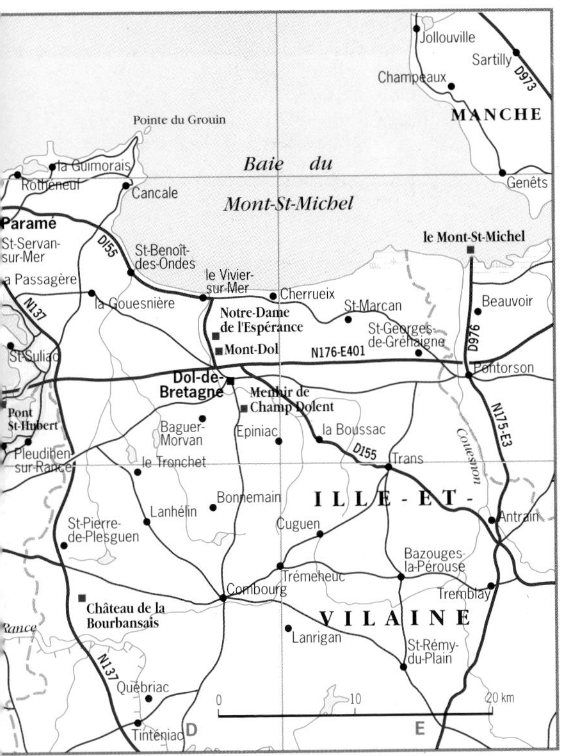

THE EMERALD COAST Grassy clifftops and lush fields, not water, give this northern stretch of coast its poetic name. Sometimes though, even the sea takes on a luminous greenish hue, more often jade or turquoise than emerald. Whatever its colours, the Emerald Coast is undeniably picturesque, its jagged edges lunging into the Channel in a series of rocky headlands, deeply cut by sandy bays and river estuaries, and peppered with islets. The best views are from the sea, so if you have a fine, calm day to spare take a boat excursion from one of the larger resorts. The main coastal road (D786) runs some way inland, and to see the best bits of scenery you must take detours. The roads around Cap Fréhel and Pointe du Grouin lead to the most spectacular viewpoints. Inland, the countryside is tamer – mostly pastureland, orchards and stands of maize.

DUTCH LANDSCAPES The Emerald Coast proper begins at the Pointe du Grouin just north of Cancale, and stretches west to the bay of St-Brieuc. The eastern section of Ille-et-Vilaine, bordering on Normandy, is completely different: a low-lying landscape of salt marshes, mud flats and great wide skies, reminiscent of the Netherlands. Once, the brackish pastures around the bay of Mont-St-Michel lay beneath the waves, but are now reclaimed polders. Ivy-hung poplars and willows line the watercourses, leading the eye towards straight horizons pierced by church towers and occasional windmills. The River Couesnon forms the boundary between Breton and

THE BRETON CLIMATE
If you have ever experienced Brittany in a westerly gale you will never forget it. Plage de la Torche or Pointe du Raz in a Force 10 is a sight to behold. In October 1987 hurricane gusts ripped up the ancient forest of Huelgoat in a few minutes. Yet the Breton climate is also surprisingly mild. Softened by the Gulf Stream, its winter temperatures are similar to those on the Côte d'Azur, while the sea temperatures are only a fraction lower than those of the Mediterranean. Even more startling, the annual rainfall in Dinard (698mm) is actually lower than in Nice (868mm).

Norman territory, and the historic vagaries of its now-canalised course have transferred one of France's most magnetic places of interest to Normandy, not Brittany. At least once in a lifetime, though, every visitor to France should make the pilgrimage to the sea-moated abbey of Mont-St-Michel, and St-Malo is the nearest entry port.

PLACES TO VISIT St-Malo itself is a major attraction. Now faithfully restored after wartime damage, it is one of France's largest ports, and it deserves at least half a day's exploration. Other highlights lie within easy reach: the gorgeous old town of Dinan at the head of the Rance estuary, and the scenic headlands of Grouin and Cap Fréhel, an easy drive – or better still, boat trip – away. Inland, the historic towns of Lamballe, Dol-de-Bretagne or Corseul are worth a passing glance, if not a pilgrimage. This easterly section of Brittany (Haute Bretagne) is less overtly regional than the far west. Breton is rarely spoken here, but you may occasionally hear a Breton hurdy-gurdy played by a folk group in St-Malo, and there are music festivals in Dinan and St-Briac-sur-Mer.

Apart from a few notable exceptions (Mont-St-Michel, Fort la Latte and the medieval part of Dinan), historic buildings are thin on the ground, and museums generally

A boat trip on the Rance estuary takes in the delightful old town of Dinan

unremarkable. But the area has several unusual sights. For curiosity value, visit the sculpted rocks at Rothéneuf, Cancale's oyster museum, the Rance tidal power station, and Lamballe's National Stud. Besides coastal boat trips, consider an excursion up the Rance valley to Dinan. If you're feeling wealthy, a spin round Mont-St-Michel in a light aircraft is an unforgettable experience.

Erquy combines seaside charm with a thriving scallop industry

SPLENDID SEAFOOD For *fruits de mer* addicts, the north-east Breton coast is superb. Cancale is the place to acquire a taste for oysters, available even in the months without an 'R'. Erquy is best for scallops, while mussels are produced in vast quantities at le Vivier-sur-Mer and St-Jacut-de-la-Mer, where they cluster prolifically like some strange maritime grape on thousands of dark wooden posts in the shallow seas. You can take a ride on the curious amphibious craft that trundles from le Vivier-sur-Mer to visit the mussel and oyster beds. Today's fishing fleets are smaller than before, and mostly venture only into local waters, but St-Malo has kept its deep-sea cod-fishing industry alive by introducing the latest in refrigeration technology to its trawlers.

SEASIDE ACTIVITIES The Emerald Coast has always been popular for its superb range of beaches. This part of Brittany is generally more sheltered from Atlantic gales than the western extremities of Finistère, but the mild climate is unpredictable and can be wet at any time of year. North Brittany is a place to bring bats and balls, buckets and spades, and watersports, riding and tennis are on offer everywhere. For an unusual spectator sport, head for Mont-St-Michel bay on a windy day, where sand-yachting is an exciting craze in Cherrueix or St-Benoît-des-Ondes. The best resorts for families are the more established places with safe beaches and plenty to do: Dinard, St-Cast-le-Guildo or le Val André. Erquy is a pleasant quieter choice, still with many of its original stone cottages; modern holiday homes have replaced these in many resorts. In July and August resort facilities are stretched to maximum capacity by a massive influx of French families, and every *gîte* is full.

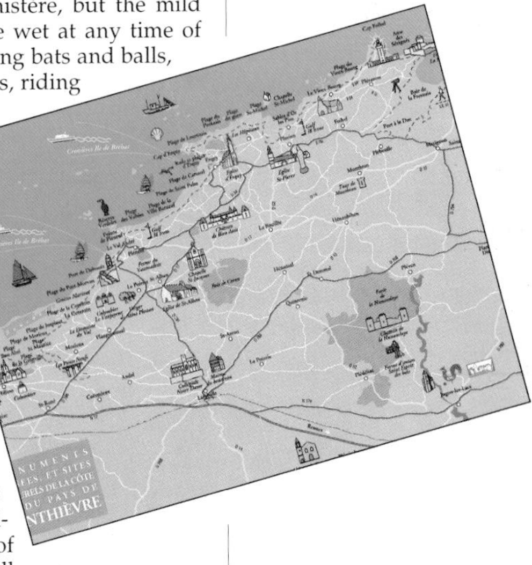

▶▶▶ REGION HIGHLIGHTS

THE OYSTER MUSEUM
At the Musée de l'Huître, in an oyster farm on the edge of Cancale, you can learn about the evolution of oyster-breeding techniques and the life and work of an oyster breeder. Visitors are shown the beds where the oysters are raised, the workshop where grading and packing take place, and can even enjoy a tasting. There is also a display of 1,500 seashells, and films on pearl fishing and other aspects of *ostréiculture*. *Guided tours* Jun–Sep, daily 11, 3 and 5 in French; 2 in English. *Admission charge*). Oysters can also be bought or ordered here.

La Cancalaise

LA CANCALAISE
This loving re-creation of one of Brittany's most beautiful sailing craft now takes tourists on cruises from Cancale. Once a year, in a colourful pageant called La Caravanne, the black-hulled *bisquines* used to set off from the port to drag nets along the seabed in search of wild oysters. Commercial oyster-farming has since made them obsolete. *La Cancalaise* is the last of the *bisquines*, a recently restored 45-tonner which takes up to 25 passengers at a time. Models of old *bisquines* are on display in the Musée des Arts et Traditions Populaires in Cancale's old St-Méen church (*Open* Jul and Aug, daily 10–6.30; Jun and Sep weekend afternoons. *Admission charge*).

►► Cancale *47D2*

After the muddy salt flats of Mont-St-Michel bay, Cancale provides the first real taste of Brittany's coastal drama, with grandstand views from its cliffs and headlands. Cancale is one of France's foremost producers of oysters, and they are sold cheaply and in prodigious quantities at seafood stalls or more pricily at a long string of colourful restaurants along the seafront. The muddy beaches are covered with shallow concrete beds or *parcs* where the oysters pass through their final stages of development.

Cancale is a split-level town, the main settlement separated from the picturesque port of La Houle by a long, steep, cobbled street. In the upper town the tall church belfry offers panoramic views. Other attractions include a couple of small museums: local history in the deconsecrated church of St-Méen, and a collection of accomplished wood-carvings by a local priest. More compelling is the **Musée de l'Huître (Oyster Museum)►►**, devoted entirely to Cancale's abiding passion (see panel).

► Corseul *46C1*

This small town north-west of Dinan is primarily interesting for its Gallo-Roman remains. Corseul was the capital of the Armorican tribe of the Coriosolites, mentioned in Caesar's *Commentaries on the Gallic War*. Excavations have revealed the former town of Fanum Martis, and the vestiges of a Roman villa near the modern town centre. Finds from the sites are displayed in a little **museum►** (*Open* Jul and Aug, daily 9–6, Sep–Jun closed Sat–Sun. *Admission charge*), housed in the town hall and in the Jardin des Antiques outside. Roman sandals, jewellery and figurines can be seen, including a tiny bronze of a boy on a lion's back. About 1.5km from the town on the Dinan road, in fields up a rough track, is the Temple of Mars (also known as the Temple of Haut-Bécherel), the half-shell of an octagonal tower dating from the reign of Augustus.

Oysters are cultivated in many places around Brittany's coast, and few restaurants fail to offer a plate or two. You may not find common or garden huîtres *on the menu; look out for* creuses *(large hollow oysters of the type known as Portuguese or Pacific),* Bélons *(flat oysters, the real natives of the Brittany coast) and* pieds de cheval *(the biggest and most costly).*

Pearls of great price The mystique of the oyster stretches back a long way: Romans gorged on them at their monstrous banquets; and wagonloads were transported daily to the court of Louis XIV at Versailles. But they were not only food for the rich; once oysters were plentiful enough on the Breton coast to form the staple diet for fishermen's families. By the 18th century they were much prized, gathered in vast quantities, and becoming scarce. Today, oysters are farmed like any other crop. Their high price is justified by the fact that they take four or five years to reach maturity.

How to eat them Oysters should always be eaten on the day of purchase. If you buy them from a stall, make sure the shells are tightly closed, or close when tapped, to show they are alive. Scrub well in cold running water, then insert a strong, pointed knife into the hinged end of the shell. Twist the blade to open the oyster and then lever along the upper shell. The oyster dies when its anchoring muscle is cut, but its nervous system may still retract slightly on contact with lemon juice. In a restaurant, the shells will usually be opened already.

The oysters should be creamy and fresh-smelling, sitting in a puddle of clear, salty fluid. You can either tip and swallow them directly from the shell or extract them with a fork. It may take a while to acquire the taste if you are not already an *aficionado*. Indeed, a good many folk go through life wondering what all the fuss is about!

OYSTER-FARMING
Earlier this century disease virtually wiped out the natural oyster stocks in the waters around Cancale, and now the young oysters (known as spat) are brought in from southern Brittany, where they are raised in the Bélon river and around Auray. The spat are placed in shallow rectangular beds, visible at low tide, where they develop in sacks of plastic mesh, undergoing a final purification process before being harvested. Farmers head out across the mud in tractors at the lowest tides every fortnight to tend the more distant beds.

AN 'R' IN THE MONTH
The belief that oysters are not fit to eat during the summer months stems from their breeding cycle, which lasts from May to August. After fertilisation, the female oyster takes on a milky appearance, and as the spat (larvae) develop it goes dark. The oysters look unusual at this stage, but are not harmful to eat; the varieties of oyster produced in Brittany are edible all year. That said, there is a greater risk of seafood poisoning in the summer, when ambient temperatures are higher.

Thousands of oysters go through their final stages of development on the beaches of Cancale

▶▶▶ Dinan 46C1

Wherever else you go in Brittany, try not to miss Dinan, one of the best-preserved towns in the region and an ideal sightseeing base for a day or two. Inevitably its attractions do not pass unnoticed and it can get very crowded in high season. The town stands high above the estuary of the Rance river, and is linked by regular boat trips to Dinard and St-Malo, though tidal conditions can make such excursions time-consuming (you can take a boat one way and come back either by rail or by bus).

The keep of 14th-century Dinan castle

Medieval Dinan grew rich initially on its riverine trade, and later on the proceeds of wool and cloth. The town is notable for its associations with the Breton warrior, Bertrand Du Guesclin (see pages 34–5), whose heart is buried in the church of St-Sauveur. Every September the Fête des Remparts celebrates the town's colourful past. Just outside the town, the abbey ruins of **Léhon** are worth a look (the next phase of restoration is due for completion in 1999).

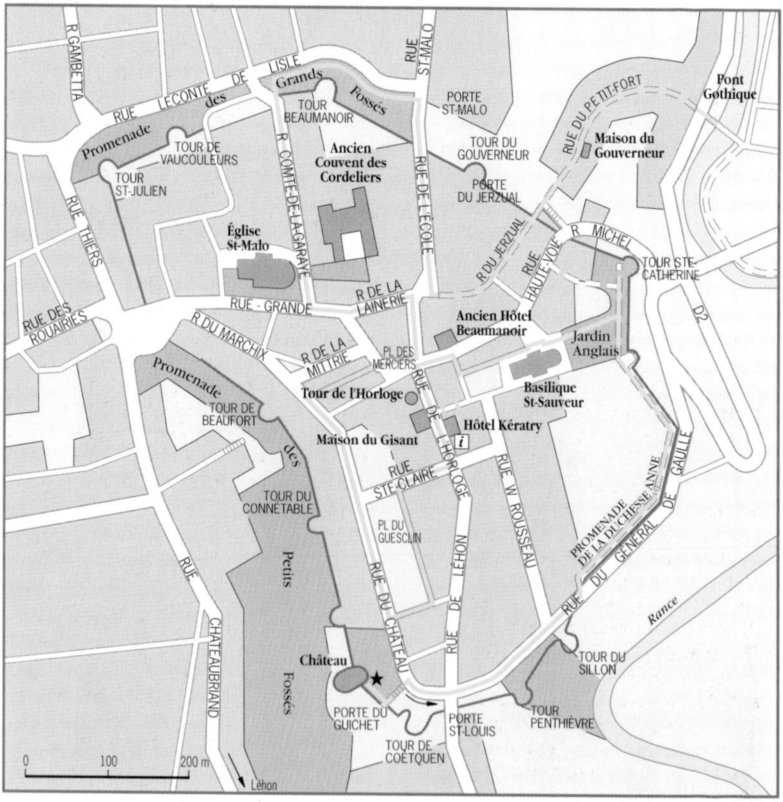

Above: arcaded buildings line the streets of Dinan's old town

Walk

The old town of Dinan

See map opposite.

Dinan has few obligatory tourist sights, but the cobbled old quarter is full of picturesque lopsided half-timbering. Ramparts encircle the old town, and are easy to follow via pleasant landscaped walkways. Allow about half a day.

Start from the **castle▶** guarding the southern side of the town, where a local history museum now occupies the machicolated keep. Follow the main rue du Château round the walls, picking up the **promenade de la Duchesse Anne▶** for splendid views over the Rance and viaduct. Beyond the orderly flowerbeds of the Jardin Anglais lies the church of **St-Sauveur▶**, bizarrely diverse in its architecture, combining Gothic and Romanesque styles. The present, slated steeple dates from the 18th century. Head back into town through the quaint old **Place des Merciers▶**. The **Tour de l'Horloge (clock tower)** on rue de l'Horloge has good views and deafens passers-by hourly with the memorial bell, a present from the Duchess Anne. Note the **Maison du Gisant** near by, where a headless stone statue lies. The pretty **Hôtel Kératry▶** houses Dinan's tourist office, which seems unable to offer a decent town map.

Turning down rue Ste-Claire, you reach a large, tree-lined square on which the horseback figure of the 14th-century military leader **Du Guesclin** surveys parked cars with some disapproval. This was the scene of his famous duel with Thomas of Canterbury, the English truce-breaker, at the siege of Dinan. The square, a fairground in the Middle Ages, now has a weekly market.

Weave back through **rue de la Cordonnerie** and up into the rue de la Lainerie, where the **Ancien Couvent des Cordeliers** (a Franciscan monastery, now used as a school) gives a fine view of the Gothic east end of the church of **St-Malo**. Follow the ramparts along the **promenade des Grands Fossés▶**, enter the town via the **Porte St-Malo** and walk down the rue de l'Ecole, then turn down the steep **rue du Jerzual** towards the **port**. Several charming old buildings, some converted into art studios, can be seen on the way down.

At the quayside, cafés and restaurants overlook a nautical scene, and there is a glorious view of the town from the other side of the bridge. A tourist train saves the walk back up, bumping over cobbles to reach the tourist office (summer only).

Above: a converted tidal mill

Drive

The Rance valley

See map on pages 46–7.

Dinard, Dinan and St-Malo form three compelling focal points on a narrow triangle of splendid estuary scenery. Allow the best part of a day for this 90km drive.

The Rance estuary is a classic example of one of Brittany's 'drowned valleys' (see page 111). The state of the tides makes an enormous difference to the estuary's appearance, and so varied are the Rance's tides that their forces have been harnessed for the world's first tidal power station. Typical scenery on this route consists of lake-like expanses of calm, glittering water flanked by fertile banks of woodland and apple orchards. Sheltered inlets provide mooring points for small craft. Boatyards, tidal mills, châteaux, churches and the elegant houses of wealthy corsairs can be glimpsed among the trees.

Starting from St-Malo, head south via St-Servan-sur-Mer, hugging minor roads close to the waterside rather than taking the main N137 where possible. Good vantage points include **la Passagère, St-Suliac▶** (a tidal mill and an ancient watch-tower) and **Pont St-Hubert** (a new suspension bridge across the river). At **Pleudihen-sur-Rance** the **Musée de la Pomme et du Cidre (Apple and Cider Museum)▶** offers visitors a glass of the potent local product.

Mordreuc supplements its fine river views with a ruined castle, while **Lanvallay▶** has tantalising views of the old town of Dinan. On the west side, detour to **Taden** where waterfowl, fish and campers congregate. The lock to the north (**Ecluse du Chatelier**) regulates the Dinan basin, another tranquil point for boat-watching. The menhir of **La Tremblay** can be tracked down near St-Samson-sur-Rance, leaning at a drunken angle. Tiny lanes potter northwards past the churches of **Plouër-sur-Rance** (carved tombs) and **la Richardais** (modern glass and frescoes). Ahead is the vast concrete barrage of the tidal power station (**Usine Marémotrice▶▶**), which can be visited from the Dinard side (see page 62).

Cider-making is a traditional industry around the Rance valley

▶▶ Dinard 46C2

'Pearl of the Emerald Coast', 'Nice of the North', trumpets the tourist literature about this sophisticated resort, modelled on the ritzy watering holes of the Riviera. It expanded massively from a simple fishing port in the mid-19th century after an American named Coppinger built a palatial villa on the cliffs. Wealthy British and American visitors followed his example, and soon the seafront was studded with mock-Gothic and Belle Epoque architecture. Many more holiday houses and apartments have appeared this century, along with ultra-modern resort facilities.

The attractions of Dinard's setting are instantly apparent: a natural amphitheatre of wooded heights overlooks three superb sandy beaches, with stunning views of St-Malo and the roadsteads of the Rance estuary. Dinard, washed by the tempering effects of the Gulf Stream, emulates the sunny south with its equable climate, and subtropical vegetation flourishes: mimosa, camellias, eucalyptus and palms. Some of the world's highest tides attract keen yachters, and smart races and regattas are an important aspect of the social calendar, along with tennis, bridge and afternoon tea.

Dinard today is still expensive, but less of a foreign playground. French families now throng the summer beaches, and volleyball and *boules* replace the croquet once played on the sands, along with children's clubs and *moules frîtes*. When the water is too chilly for sea-bathing, an Olympic-sized heated sea-water pool is the next best thing. At night the casino is the star attraction, but during the day Dinard concentrates on its beach life, ringing the changes with boat excursions along the Fréhel coast or up the Rance. St-Malo is an easy step across the barrage bridge or by shuttle ferry.

Two small museums offer wet-weather bolt-holes: the **Musée de la Mer** (*Open* May–Sep, daily except Sun morning. *Admission charge*) is devoted to the sea, with exhibitions of local sea creatures, stuffed birds and the polar explorations of Commander Charcot. The **Musée du Site Balneaire▶** is an unusual museum dedicated to the local history and development of the resort (see panel).

MUSÉE DU SITE BALNEAIRE

The ground floor of the museum houses the usual displays, but upstairs is a more idiosyncratic account of Dinard's development. Visitors included Debussy, Winston Churchill, the British King Edward VII and Vivien Leigh. There's a display of the cutlery and silver plate used in the grand hotels of the last century, a collection of foreign coins discarded near the casino, and a tableau of bathing costumes, becoming ever skimpier through the decades (*Open* summer, daily 10–6. *Closed* Sun. *Admission charge*).

The Plage de l'Ecluse, Dinard's main beach, makes for a delightful stroll

Emerald-topped cliffs at Cap Fréhel

►► Dol-de-Bretagne *47D2*

The 'Capital of the Marshes' now stands 8km inland, but centuries ago it was an island in the sea. In AD 709 a great tidal wave engulfed the low-lying land around the bay of Mont-St-Michel, leaving Dol stranded on its clifftop site above the waves. Eventually the waters retreated behind brackish salt marshes, which were gradually reclaimed from the sea. Today the countryside consists of maize fields and pastureland, chequered by dikes lined with poplar and willow, and pierced with church spires. The salty fields provide grazing for *pré salé* lambs.

Dol was founded by St Samson in AD 548, and was for many years an important ecclesiastical centre. Today it has no bishop, but its granite **cathedral►** still presides gloomily over the surrounding landscape. Behind the cathedral, several enjoyable streets contain quaint old houses sprouting unusual features at every turn: a granite shop bench outside one, pillars on another. Views from the public gardens, the Promenade des Douves, stretch over the marshes to Mont-Dol. The 16th-century treasury building beside the cathedral houses Dol's **history museum►** (*Open* Easter–Sep, daily 1.30–6.30; Jul–Aug 9.30am–7.30pm. *Admission charge*), a private collection of bewildering clutter, including prehistoric animal bones from Mont-Dol and statues of saints and madonnas.

Mont-Dol► is a strange, flat-topped granite mound 2km north of the town. Its modest 65m height takes on an awesome significance in this low-lying landscape, and views from the summit are extensive. From prehistoric times onwards it has attracted attention, and the site is dotted with holy wells and signs of earlier habitation. Pilgrims pay homage to the little chapel of Notre-Dame de l'Espérance, but most visitors today make more use of the small bar-restaurant near the disused windmill. You can walk or drive up the hill from the pretty huddled village of Mont-Dol, where the old **church** contains several ancient frescoes. **Les Trésors du Mariage Ancien►** (*Open* Jun–Oct, daily 10–6. *Admission charge*), daily displays traditional wedding treasures, including bridal dresses, trousseaux and a collection of Breton marriage 'globes' (symbolic ornaments protected in domed glass cases).

ST MICHAEL'S FOOT

One of many legends about Mont-Dol declares it to be the site of the apocalyptic struggle between Satan and the Archangel Michael. At the summit of the hill, various indeterminate marks in the rocks have been interpreted as the Devil's claw and St Michael's footprint, left as he leapt to Mont-St-Michel after his victory. You need plenty of imagination to reconstruct these.

View from Mont-Dol

An old mill at Dol

▶ Erquy 46B2

This agreeable fishing port, famed for its scallops, retains more of its original character than some of the Emerald Coast's resorts, and has a number of gorgeous beaches in exquisite settings. The town beach by the port is not the best; head for Caroual to the south-west or Cap d'Erquy to the north-west, where silver or grey-pink coves nestle among pine woods and bracken. At low tide you can reach the chapel-crowned islet of St-Michel. Inland, to the south of the main D786, lies the **Château de Bienassis**, a late-medieval edifice rebuilt in the 17th century and furnished in Louis XIV and Breton Renaissance styles (*Open* mid-Jun–mid-Sep, daily 10.30–12.30, 2–6.30. *Admission charge*).

▶▶▶ Fréhel, Cap 46B3

This renowned beauty spot is one of the Emerald Coast's most dramatic promontories, and shouldn't be missed. Gnarled grey cliffs of schist and sandstone streaked with red porphyry rise to a grand height of 70m above a sea of jade. The most impressive views of this section of coast are from the sea, and excursion boats ply regularly from St-Malo and Dinard during the summer.

Alternatively, you can drive to the cape along the tourist route and park by the square-towered lighthouse, which is open to visitors. Views extend to Bréhat, St-Malo and the Channel Islands on clear days. Seabirds crowd on the fissured Fauconnière rocks (now a nature reserve) to the west of the lighthouse, while human perches are provided at the Restaurant de la Fauconnière, with its spectacular cliff views (see the Hotels and Restaurants section, page 276). Walks around the cape are exceptionally beautiful, but don't expect to have the scenery all to yourself in the high season.

MENHIR DE CHAMP DOLENT

Just south-east of Dol-de-Bretagne, off the D795, is a standing stone about 9m high, stuck incongruously in a maize field. This menhir is alleged to have fallen from heaven to divide the armies of two warring brothers (Champ Dolent means 'Field of Sorrow'). It is said to be gradually sinking into the ground, a couple of centimetres every century, and when it vanishes completely the world will end. The stone is freely accessible from the road, and can even be admired from a picnic table, though it has no markings or particular features of interest.

South porch detail from Dol cathedral

A ruined tower at the Château de la Hunaudaie

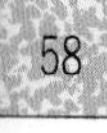

► Jugon-les-Lacs 46B1

The original houses clustered around the unusual saddle-backed 13th-century church in this little town are passably venerable (one of the oldest being the **Maison Sevoy** of 1634). Most of Jugon-les-Lacs' buildings are, however, much more recent, as the resort cashes in, tastefully enough, on its artificial lakeside setting. Grey-white holiday homes stretch towards the dammed twin rivers, and there are plenty of watersport facilities.

Several sights just outside the town add to its attractions as a base. The Cistercian **Abbaye de Boquen** lies in ruins about 15km south-west, and the **Ferme d'Antan** in St-Esprit-des-Bois has a typical Breton reconstruction of bygone rural life. The most striking excursion is to the **Château de la Hunaudaie►** (*Open* Jul–Aug, daily 11–6.30. *Closed* Sat morning. *Admission charge*), 9km northwards in deep forests. It dates from the 12th century, was enlarged over several centuries and battered into its present ruins during the Revolution. The monument is state-owned and its unpillaged parts are impressively preserved, including the Tour de la Glacière, Renaissance manor house and 15th-century keep. A local drama group enlivens the place regularly in high season, enacting humorous everyday stories of medieval folk.

THE NATIONAL STUD
The most interesting sight in Lamballe is the Haras National, France's second largest stud. In a palatial setting of dignified stable-blocks stretching round multiple courtyards, up to 400 horses were housed, notably the powerfully rounded Breton draught horses, English thoroughbreds, French trotters, saddle horses and Connemara ponies. The stud is open every afternoon, with guided tours of the stables (which now house 50 to 60 stallions and around 20 riding horses), carriage house, harness rooms and farriery in the summer. A riding school operates inside. Various equine events take place in Lamballe, including a Horse Festival in August.

►► Lamballe 46B1

A sizeable town these days, Lamballe has numerous industries related to its role as an agricultural centre – including animal foodstuffs and leather processing. It also hosts important cattle markets for the Penthièvre region. The most interesting part of Lamballe's old town is around the main square, Place du Martray, where several picturesque old houses can be seen. The best of these buildings is the half-timbered **Maison du Bourreau►** (Hangman's House), which contains an obliging tourist office and two good little **museums** (*Open* Jun–Sep, Mon–Sat. *Closed* Sun and hols. *Admission charge*). One recounts the town's local history in costumes, pottery and the like, while the other displays the lively charcoal drawings, watercolours and ceramics of the artist Mathurin Méheut, who was born in Lamballe in 1882.

Churches include **St-Jean**, containing a 17th-century altarpiece and organ; **St-Martin**, a priory with a strange little canopied porch; and the fortified collegiate church of **Notre-Dame►** at the top of the town, with its finely carved doorways and splendid rood screen.

► Lancieux 46C2

This small resort at the bridging point of the Frémur marks the easterly end of the Côtes-d'Armor coast and was originally a religious settlement founded by a British monk, St Sieuc. It is renowned for its excellent championship golf course (the second oldest in France) and a striking 18th-century bell tower, which is the last remnant of the town's original church. Like most of the resorts along this coast, Lancieux has lovely sandy beaches, the best of these being the Plage St-Sieu.

▶▶ La Latte, Fort 46B2

Open: May, daily 2.30–6.30; Jun–Sep, daily 10–6.30; Oct–Apr, Sat–Sun 2.30–5.30; guided tours. Admission charge

So photogenic is this coastal fortress that it was used as the set for the film *The Vikings* in 1957. It perches on a rocky promontory guarding the western entrance to the Baie de la Frênaye, just east of Cap Fréhel. Drawbridges cross two natural fissures in the rock, which form a sea moat at high tide. The crenellated castle dates back to the 14th century, but owes most of its present appearance to Louis XIV's ubiquitous military architect, Vauban (see page 176), who strengthened and remodelled it in the 17th century. During its varied history the castle has played host to medieval pirates, English spies during the French Revolution, White Russians, and the Old Pretender, James Stuart (son of England's James II, deposed by William of Orange).

Fort la Latte is now privately owned and still inhabited. One of its most interesting features is a kiln where cannonballs were heated to set fire to enemy wooden ships. There are panoramic views from the parapets and towers, and at the top of the gated track from the car park is a small menhir known as Gargantua's Finger.

▶▶▶ Mont-St-Michel 47E2

See pages 60–1.

Above: romantic Fort la Latte. Below: Cap Fréhel, home for thousands of seabirds, is a magnet to ornithologists

Rising mirage-like from swirling mud flats, this abbey-crowned granite island attracts more visitors than any other provincial sight in France. Technically it lies just beyond Brittany's boundaries in Normandy, but don't miss it if you are in the area.

THE MARVEL
'Climbing the steep narrow street, I entered the most wonderful Gothic building ever made for God on this earth, a building as vast as a town, full of low rooms under oppressive ceilings and lofty galleries supported by frail pillars. I entered that gigantic granite jewel, which is as delicate as a piece of lacework, thronged with towers and slender belfries which thrust into the blue sky of day and the black sky of night, their strange heads bristling with chimeras, devils, fantastic beasts and monstrous flowers, and which are linked together by carved arches of intricate design.'
– Guy de Maupassant.

TIPHAINE'S HOUSE
Behind the parish church near the foot of the Mount stands a quaint old house built by the Breton warrior Du Guesclin (see pages 34–5) for his scholarly wife, Tiphaine de Raguenel, in 1365. Du Guesclin, who commanded the garrison of the Mount during this period, left his wife studying astronomy and philosophy while he engaged in more active pursuits in the Spanish wars. Today the house is a small museum furnished in local style.

How long Mont-St-Michel will remain an island is uncertain: the bay is gradually silting up, particularly since the creation of the causeway connecting Mont-St-Michel with the mainland, which prevents tidal movements scouring away the sands. There are plans to replace the causeway with a bridge. The sight of the advancing tide is still remarkable, even if it is less swift than galloping horses (a common claim). High tides can still flood the car park, while at low tide over 10km of sand are exposed, and you can walk right round the Mount. Before the causeway was built, all pilgrims had to walk across the sands at low tide, many drowning on the way. A scene on the Bayeux Tapestry shows King Harold charitably rescuing some stranded Normans from quicksand.

Holy place The site has attracted attention as a holy place and a strategic vantage point for many centuries. Hermits arrived in about AD 500, and in AD 708 the Bishop of Avranches experienced a vision in which the Archangel Michael told him to build a church on the rock. The Normans took the project much further, fetching stone from the Chausey Islands, cutting it carefully into blocks and hoisting it up the perilous slopes. Later generations continued to build up and around the Mount until the 19th century. Sections collapsed several times, and had to be rebuilt. Today the structures seem as delicately poised as a house of cards, some cantilevered over thin air.

The base of the Mount is occupied by a village, and a good many touristy souvenir shops and fast-food outlets,

Fontaine St-Aubert
Chapelle St-Aubert
Bois de l'Abbaye
TOUR DU NORD
la Merveille
Cloître
Réfectoire
GRAND DEGRÉ
Abbaye
Entrée de l'Abbaye
Maison de la Truie-qui-file
TOUR BOUCLE
Église
TOUR GABRIEL
Logis Tiphaine
Église St-Pierre
Musée Historique et Grévin
TOUR CHOLET
Archéoscope
TOUR BASSE
GRANDE-RUE
Musée de la Mer
Porte du Roi
Porte de l'Avancée
Maison de l'Arcade
TOUR DE LA LIBERTÉ
0
50 m
TOUR DU ROI
TOUR DE L'ARCADE

The dramatic pyramid of Mont-St-Michel

which can be offputting. The commercialisation of the Mount is not a recent phenomenon; medieval pilgrims would have been plagued by beggars, touts, pickpockets and charlatans as they ascended. Once beyond the Grande-Rue the crowds immediately thin out and the atmosphere becomes noticeably more peaceful. Flights of steps seem to lead everywhere – and hence access is not easy for visitors with disabilities.

Admission to the island is free (though there are hefty parking charges); to visit the abbey you must join one of the excellent guided tours.

An architectural triumph The abbey church is a glorious blend of Romanesque and Gothic architecture. St Michael brandishes his golden sword from the highest pinnacle. The Gothic structures on the north side of the Mount, called la Merveille (the Marvel), house the domestic and guest quarters, and date from the 13th century. The buildings are regarded as some of the best examples of Gothic religious architecture in France. You pass through the Guests' Hall, the Knights' Hall and the Refectory (lit by mysterious invisible windows) to the cloisters balanced on the top floor, slim columns decorated with beasts and figures. Walks around the ramparts and gardens give marvellous views, and a better idea of this fantastically complex structure.

Left: visitors besiege the lower town in summer

ST-GEORGES-DE-GRÉHAIGNE

Before the building of sea walls and the canalisation of the wavering River Couesnon, this little village was virtually lapped by the sea, its hilltop site affording it some security from periodic inundations. A Benedictine church was built here in the 15th century, from which Mont-St-Michel is clearly visible. North-west of the village, off the road to le Vivier-sur-Mer, miniature models of regional monuments on a 1:50 scale are displayed, including one of Mont-St-Michel. The three-dimensional mini-version of this complex site gives an idea of how the various sections are piled on that vertiginous mound.

THE FLOUR AND THE GLORY

The monument showing a greyhound trampling a leopard in St-Cast-le-Guildo's rue de la Colonne commemorates a French victory over a British attack on St-Malo in 1758 (a reprisal for corsair plundering which constantly harassed British shipping). The Duke of Aiguillon, Governor of Brittany, directed operations from a windmill as British troops returned to their warships anchored in the bay of St-Cast. One of the Duke's political enemies, La Chalotais (Procurator of the Rennes Parliament), on hearing that the Duke had 'covered himself with glory', acidly remarked, 'Yes, and with flour as well, I suppose!'

Windmills were once a common sight along Brittany's north coast

►► Rance, Usine Marémotrice de la (Rance Tidal Power Scheme) *46C2*

Open: year-round, guided tours by appointment only, tel: 02 99 16 37 14. Admission free

A huge concrete barrage blocks the mouth of the Rance, creating a large reservoir upstream and used as a bridge by the St-Malo–Dinard road. There are parking places at both ends, from which you can walk across the dam on footpaths and watch the sinewy currents arc through the sluicegates to the generators housed in a vast tunnel within the barrage. The force is awesome.

The dam was opened in 1967, and spans 750m, curbing a reservoir of 22sq km. A lock enables boats to pass through. Around 600 million kW of electricity are generated by 24 generators each year, using both ebb and flow tides. It is slightly disappointing to learn that this massively imaginative and costly project generates only about 8 per cent of Brittany's total electricity needs, and although it sounds environmentally friendly its effects on local wildlife are significant: conservationists are concerned about the habitat loss of vast numbers of wading birds.

► Sables d'Or-les Pins *46B2*

For once, the tourist-brochure name does not deceive: the setting of golden sands and pines is truly breathtaking, though the resort itself (and even its glorious beach) is essentially artificial. The resort was constructed as a commercial enterprise during the late 19th century, which at one period lost an immense amount of money and was abruptly terminated. Luxury villas and hotels now stand in a curiously incomplete main street, supplemented by beach buggies, golf and watersports facilities. Swimming on some local beaches, including the beautiful Pléhérel-Plage to the north-east, can be dangerous because of the currents that swirl unpredictably around the sandbanks.

The ancient village of **Plurien** at the resort's southern end adds some historic weight, with a very early Knights Templar church and the remains of a Gallo-Roman villa.

► St-Briac-sur-Mer *46C2*

St-Briac stands on the Ille-et-Vilaine side of the Frémur estuary, whose panoramic cliff road (the Balcon d'Eméraude) and long bridge overlook amazing views. Not much happens here except the Fête des Mouettes in mid-August, when Breton bagpipes and folk-dancing take over the resort. However, migrant birds seem to like the town (barnacle geese and ducks drop in each year) and a wave of holidaymakers takes advantage of its south-facing sandy beaches with islet views. The harbour area still has a core of pretty old streets and alleyways.

► St-Brieuc *46A2*

Too large and city-like for comfort, its road systems complicated by deep river valleys, St-Brieuc is barely worth braving for casual sightseeing. However, it is a good shopping centre, and you can pick up picnic provisions in its new market. The cathedral of **St-Etienne►** is the town's most imposing building, a massive castle-like structure with fortified towers. The old streets around the cathedral are moderately picturesque.

►► St-Cast-le-Guildo *46C2*

The complex geography of this resort takes some fathoming. It consists of several separate districts: le Bourg is the administrative centre, with an aggressively modern church; l'Isle is the port; les Mielles is a resort area of hotels and shops; and la Garde is a wooded residential sector. Over half a dozen good beaches lie around the promontory, with attractive cliffs at Pointe de St-Cast and Pointe de la Garde. The fishing port specialises in scallops and clams, but self-catering developments and facilities for holiday activities show where this town's priorities lie. Several monuments stand on the cliffs around St-Cast: one is dedicated to Free French *evadés* (escaped prisoners) of World War II; another commemorates the Battle of St-Cast.

Le Guildo, to the south-east of the resort, has a ruined fortress, which was dismantled on Cardinal Richelieu's orders, and the strange **Pierres Sonnantes** (stones that make a metallic sound when they are banged together). Near by, the beach of Pen Guen is one of the most popular on the peninsula.

The fortress at St-Cast-le-Guildo guarded the Arguenon estuary; it was one of many in Brittany partly demolished at Richelieu's behest to discourage insurrection

HARNESSING THE MOON

The idea of using the tides to generate power is not new. Even in the 12th century monks were experimenting on a small scale, using the force of the ebb tides to turn mill wheels on the Rance. You can see one of these primitive tidal mills at St-Suliac, on the east bank. Today's massive barrage across the whole estuary would no doubt have astonished and fascinated those early monastic engineers.

Detail, St-Lunaire church

► St-Jacut-de-la-Mer *46C2*

This narrow peninsula rears cobra-like into the bay of St-Cast, changing shape phenomenally as the tides ebb and flow. At low tide you can walk to Ile des Ebihens (Ebihens Island), crowned by a tower; at high water it looks far out at sea (there is a good view of the island from the cliff at Pointe du Chevet).

Since the advent of tourism the resort has become much better known, but in earlier times the Jaguens were an isolated community who even had their own Breton dialect. The monks who first colonised the coast did their bit for regional harmony by building a causeway and joining St-Jacut, once a tidal island, to the mainland. The older part of the village has jettied gables and considerable character. Mackerel fishing takes place from the small port, and at low tide hundreds of *bouchots* (mussel posts) emerge from the waterline in the bay of Arguenon on the west side of the peninsula. Shrimping among the rockpools at low tide is popular with locals. St-Jacut has about a dozen beaches scattered around its long shoreline, though the sand here is interspersed with mud.

►► St-Lunaire *46C2*

This resort is now virtually an enclave of Dinard. Out of season it may seem dull, its smart holiday villas carefully shuttered, but in July and August, when it is colonised by a lively group of Parisian families, it is full of *joie de vivre*. The two main beaches are separated by a scenic promontory, the Pointe du Décollé. At the seaward end a natural rock arch called the Saut du Chat (Cat's Leap) spans a cave hollowed by the waves (Grotte des Sirènes), spectacular in rough weather. The 11th-century church in the old part of the village contains the tomb of St Lunaire, resting on an even more ancient sarcophagus. His statue, and those on other sculpted tombs in the church, are curiously flattened as though their subjects have been crushed by a steamroller.

JEANNE JUGAN (1792–1879)
Born into a fisherman's family in Cancale, Jeanne went into service in St-Servan after her father was lost at sea. Her mistress left her a legacy with which she set up a refuge for impoverished old people, feeding and clothing them by daily begging. Several saintly women joined her and formed The Little Sisters of the Poor, now scattered all over the world in some 300 communities.

ISLAND STROLLS
Several tiny islands lie just off St-Malo's shore, accessible from the town beaches at low tide. The Ile du Grand-Bé is the burial place of the writer François-Réné de Chateaubriand (1768–1848), just a plain granite slab surmounted by a cross facing the ocean. Fort-National, on another island, was built by Vauban in 1689. Guided tours include the dungeon and ramparts, from where there is a fine view of St-Malo.

Another of Brittany's multifarious calvaries; this touchingly naïve version can be seen at St-Lunaire

▶▶▶ St-Malo 46C2

The most attractive of any of the Channel ports, St-Malo has more visitors than anywhere else in Brittany, and though many do no more than race in and out of the ferry terminal it is well worth a day of anyone's time. If you can find accommodation (book ahead in summer) it makes an enjoyable and animated base, with good hotels and restaurants, plenty to see and do, boat trips galore, and sandy beaches near by.

The modern pleasure-boat marina at St-Malo

Spirit of independence The town is named after a Welsh monk, St Maclow, who settled in Aleth (now St-Servan) in the 6th century and founded a religious community. Local people retreated to what is now the walled citadel (then an island) to escape the Norsemen. Later, in more peaceful times, a causeway was built to connect the island to the mainland. The development of the harbour encouraged a strong seafaring tradition, and St-Malo built up a thriving trade with Spain and the Americas. During the 16th century it was an independent republic (one of the town's more truculent mottoes is *'Ni Français, ni Breton, Malouin suis'* – 'I am neither French nor Breton, but a citizen of St-Malo'), and few towns of its size have produced so many noteworthy inhabitants: explorers, writers, scientists and corsairs. The mansions of the corsairs sprang up all over town in their heyday (see page 68).

World War II St-Malo was occupied by the Germans and then heavily bombed by the Allies in August 1944, when much of the town was destroyed. After the war, it was painstakingly rebuilt in the old style. Some find St-Malo's granite architecture austere, or complain that it is 'fake'. A glance at Brest, Lorient or St-Nazaire (also badly damaged in the war but rebuilt in a brutal modern style) may put things in perspective.

THE DISCOVERY OF CANADA

Jacques Cartier, already in middle age, set sail across the Atlantic in 1534 in search of the fabled Northwest Passage. His first voyage took him to Newfoundland; two years later he sailed up the St Lawrence and, believing he had reached Asia, asked the native Indians where he was. They told him the name of their local village – Canada – and so the name of this vast new territory was established.

Rampart walkways

LES ROCHERS SCULPTÉS
A retired, partly paralysed priest, Abbé Fouré, spent over 25 years at the end of the 19th century creating a Disneylike wonderworld of over 300 monsters and grotesque figures, all carved out of rock. The effort involved in this labour of love is mind-boggling, though the results would perhaps interest a psychiatrist more than an art historian. Over time, the elements have blunted the outlines of the sculpted rocks, and at some point they will be completely eroded away. The windswept setting above a sapphire sea is remarkable.

Les Rochers Sculptés, at Rothéneuf, were carved in the 19th century

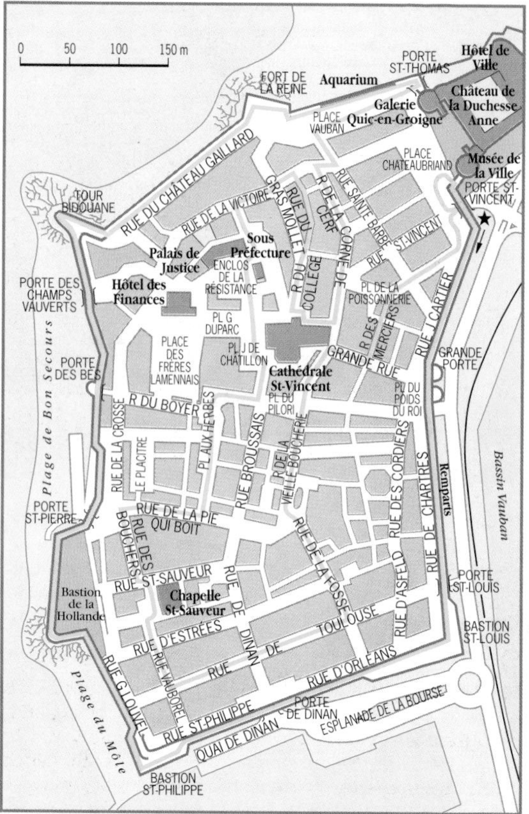

Points of interest St-Malo's main area of interest for visitors is *intra muros* ('within the walls'), in other words the restored old town behind the port area. The rest of the town is fairly nondescript, but the neighbouring communities of **St-Servan-sur-Mer**, **Rothéneuf** and **Paramé** are separate resorts. St-Servan's **Aleth Corniche▶▶** (a headland footpath) is a splendid walk at sunset, and the **Tour Solidor▶** contains an interesting museum recounting the voyages of Cape Horn sailors (*Open* Apr–Oct, daily 10–6. *Closed* Nov–Mar Mon and hols. *Admission charge*). Paramé has two fine beaches and a hydrotherapy centre. Both resorts have good hotels, quieter than those *intra muros*.

The resort of **Rothéneuf▶** lies to the east of the main town, its buildings petering out among cabbage fields. Further afield lies the grander and wilder countryside of the Pointe du Grouin. Rothéneuf was the birthplace of Jacques Cartier, discoverer of Canada. Cartier's home, restored as a museum, was the delightful 15th-century **Manoir de Limoëlou▶** on the outskirts of the village (follow signs for Manoir de Jacques Cartier). It is furnished in period style, with charts and mementoes of Cartier's voyages and an audio-visual show about his life (*Open* Jul–Aug, daily 10–11.30, 2.30–6; Jun–Sep, closed Sat-Sun; guided tours. *Admission charge*). The second of Rothéneuf's attractions is the **Rochers Sculptés▶**, a bizarre collection of cliffside rock carvings (see panel).

Walk

St-Malo *intra muros*

See map opposite.

The old walled citadel on its apron of sand (now firmly attached to the mainland) is a marvellous place for a stroll, best at high tide. Leave your car outside the ramparts and allow half a day, including museums.

Gates pierce the walls on all sides and the ramparts are freely accessible at several points, but the best place to start is **Porte St-Vincent▶**. From here you can make a complete circuit of the ramparts for a magnificent overview of St-Malo and its setting. Unlike the rest of the town, the walls are genuinely old, having survived even modern warfare virtually intact. Information panels point out features of interest, and statues of corsairs scan the horizon. On the seaward side you see the harbour, marina, town beaches, several fortified islands and a stretch of the Emerald Coast.

A restored tower of St-Malo's 15th-century castle

Above: view of the port

Inwards is a dignified townscape of 18th-century houses, tall chimneys and dormers.

Descend at Porte St-Thomas to visit the **aquarium▶** and **exotarium** (reptiles), then head for the cathedral of **St-Vincent▶** at the centre of the old town. Its main features are bright modern glass and the plain tomb of Jacques Cartier. Thread through the narrow old town streets past the Chapelle St-Sauveur (making a detour through the Porte du Dinan for views of the harbour and the rocky Aleth promontory), towards the castle, where the **Musée de la Ville▶▶** has good sections on St-Malo's seafaring past and famous people. A colourful waxworks museum is housed in the **Quic en Groigne tower▶**, popular with children.

The privateers of St-Malo harassed European shipping well into the last century – with full government approval. The most famous of them, Duguay-Trouin and Surcouf, are great local heroes.

CORSAIR RULES
Captured ships were taken back to France with their crew, whereupon their cargo or valuables would be sold and distributed. Ten per cent went to the king, two-thirds to the ship-owner or *armateur*, and the rest to the corsairs. How many ships were boarded illegally and simply scuttled at sea to avoid sharing the spoils is anyone's guess. St-Malo's town museum has a good section on the corsairs – including a sort of pirate's handbook, setting out the regulations.

PORCON DE LA BARDINAIS
Ironically in this town of privateers, the chosen career of Porcon de la Bardinais was to defend St-Malo's merchant ships from enemy corsairs, particularly the Barbary pirates, in the reign of Louis XIV. Captured in one skirmish and brought before the Dey of Algiers, la Bardinais struck a deal that he would try to negotiate a peace treaty with the king of France but would return to captivity if the proposal was rejected. It was, and Porcon honourably kept his promise to return to Algiers, whereupon he was strapped to a cannon muzzle and blown to bits.

Licensed to swashbuckle The corsairs were 'gentlemen pirates', sometimes of good family and high military or naval rank. The Crown awarded them 'letters of marque' signed by the king, which empowered them to seize merchant or warships of hostile countries – in practice, any that refused to stop and disclose their identity. The beautiful mansions in and around St-Malo give some idea of how profitable a business this was. Foreign governments were infuriated by their shipping losses, and the English, who sailed the high seas more than most, attempted several unsuccessful reprisal raids on Breton shores.

René Duguay-Trouin (1673–1736) Destined for the priesthood but led astray by a dissolute tutor, Duguay-Trouin went to sea early and showed great leadership qualities, becoming a commander at 24. During his short career at sea he captured over 300 vessels, including 85 English ships. At one point he was taken prisoner and held in Plymouth for a year, but made his escape in a longboat, disguised as a Swedish skipper. He was given a peerage at 32, and in 1711 he seized Rio de Janeiro from the Portuguese. This was his greatest adventure, but he returned in poor health and retired from seafaring soon afterwards.

Robert Surcouf (1773–1827) Surcouf came from a wealthy ship-owning family who hoped he would enter the Church. It quickly became apparent he had no such vocation, and he was sent to sea at 14. A commander at 20, Surcouf specialised in the rich pickings of the Indian Ocean. He undertook several daring raids on heavily armed British ships, capturing HMS *Triton* and an East Indiaman, the *Kent*, in 1800. He also retired early, at 36, to become an *armateur* (shipbuilder) in St-Malo, where he died, fantastically wealthy, at the age of 54.

Robert Surcouf spies booty from the ramparts of St-Malo

The tide retreats at le Val André

►► Le Val André 46A2

Founded in 1880 as a slightly less exclusive answer to smart Dinard, further east (see page 55), le Val André has a similar period feel. Large bow-fronted Victorian villas line the long, traffic-free promenade between two wooded headlands, interspersed with 1930s developments. The resort was built by the architect Charles Cotard, a colleague of Ferdinand de Lesseps, the French diplomat responsible for building the Suez Canal. The reason for the choice of site is immediately obvious: le Val André boasts one of the finest beaches in Brittany. At low tide a vast expanse of gleaming sand is exposed, freshly polished by the waves.

The older port of Dahouët, a popular sailing centre, lies to the south-west, offering boat trips to the Ile de Bréhat (see pages 76–7). Inland, the original village of Pléneuf-Val André adds shopping and a Tuesday market to the resort's seaside trappings of tennis courts, golf, a concert hall and casino. Coastal walks or drives to Pointe de Pléneuf or Pointe de la Guette offer panoramic views over the Baie de St-Brieuc and the seabird sanctuary of Ile du Verdelet.

MUSSEL-HUNTING

Out to sea, the tops of a myriad dark wooden poles are visible above the waterline. These are *bouchots*, which are used for mussel cultivation. Millions of seed mussels attach themselves in heavy clusters to ropes wound round the posts, where they grow until they are harvested between June and March each year. To see the mussel beds of le Vivier-sur-Mer at closer range, take a trip on the curious amphibious craft, Sirène de la Baie, which trundles over the muddy sand on wheels for a tour round the bay.

► Le Vivier-sur-Mer 47D2

Several centuries ago le Vivier was a significant trading port, the main sea outlet for the Pays de Dol region. Now all extensive seafaring has dwindled and le Vivier concentrates on shorebased enterprises. At low tide the waters of Mont-St-Michel bay retreat behind several kilometres of mud flats, leaving small boats stranded in the trickling channels.

Mytiliculture (mussel farming) is big business in le Vivier, which is responsible for about 25 per cent of France's total production (about 10,000 tonnes annually). The local *moules* are much prized for their flavour and succulence, a result of the rich plankton in the shallow seas around Mont-St-Michel. Tourism also plays a part in le Vivier's economy, and though the resort has no good beaches it does have leisure facilities and some fairly simple accommodation. Riding, cycling and sand-yachting are popular local pastimes.

Time ashore for one of Dahouët's fishermen

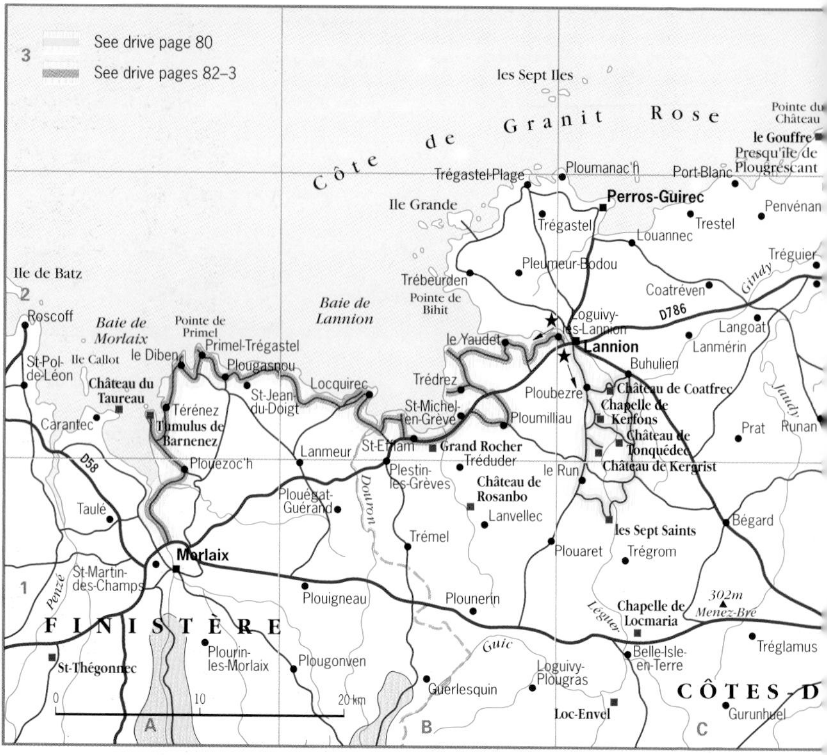

Looking out towards Costaérès castle and its rocky foundations, on a small island in Ploumanac'h bay

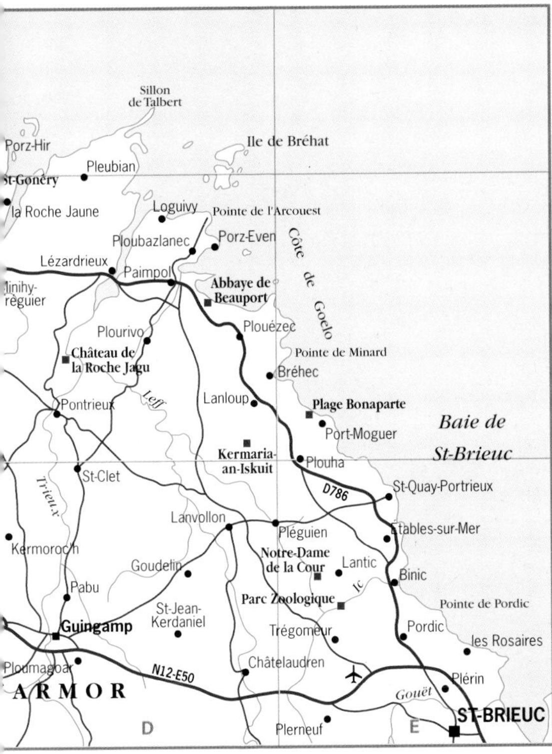

The Pink Granite Coast

THE PINK GRANITE COAST Brittany's northerly peninsulas face the sea in a welter of coastal drama. Their ragged promontories, deeply cut by river valleys, offer a great variety of brooding cliffs, expansive beaches, islands and coves. Most striking, however, is the richly coloured rock that gives the region its name, lying mainly between Paimpol and Trébeurden. These russet outcrops of granite are quite extraordinary, not merely in colour but also for the strange forms they assume. Not surprisingly, these often acquire fanciful names, such as the Turtles, the Pancakes and Napoleon's Hat. Ploumanac'h and Trégastel-Plage are the places that show this strange rock garden at its most spectacular, especially at sunset. When quarried and polished for building purposes the granite sparkles with diamond precision, and its attractive colour makes it popular for Parisian shopfronts and luxury bathrooms.

LONELY SHORES This chapter covers not only the Pink Granite Coast but also the adjoining stretches between St Brieuc and Paimpol, plus Lannion and Morlaix. Both are equally impressive in their way. The eastern section on St-Brieuc bay, with its sweeping grey cliffs and sheltered beaches, is sometimes called the Goëlo coast, after the local landowning family who built Beauport abbey. The Circuit des Falaises (see page 86) is worth exploring, not just for the brooding cliff scenery but for its historic associations as a Resistance headquarters in World War II: some of Brittany's most exciting escape stories are set on

►►► REGION HIGHLIGHTS

Tumulus de Barnenez *page 83*

Ile de Bréhat *page 76*

Ploumanac'h *page 86*

St-Jean-du-Doigt *page 83*

Trégastel *page 91*

Tréguier *page 92*

Right: the curious bent spire of St-Gonéry chapel on the Plougrescant peninsula crowns a 10th-century building that contains reliquaries, frescoes and lively wood-carvings

these lonely shores. The coast between Lannion and Morlaix straddles the Finistère border and is known as the Armorique Corniche. Only patchily pink, it makes a delightful drive for its pretty fishing ports and its glorious beaches (see pages 82–3).

The charms of the Pink Granite Coast make it one of Brittany's foremost holiday regions, and facilities are predictably extensive in the larger resorts of Perros-Guirec or St-Quay-Portrieux. Nowhere, however, feels overpoweringly urban, and as there are no major ferry ports along this coast, holiday traffic is more evenly distributed. Off the beaten track, especially if you are willing to walk, you can have whole beaches entirely to yourself.

UPPER AND LOWER BRITTANY
This chapter spans the divide between French-speaking Haute (Upper) and Breton-speaking Basse (Lower) Brittany. It may seem illogical to refer to west Brittany as 'Lower Brittany' and east Brittany as 'Upper Brittany' but this tradition stems back to Celtic times. Celts regarded the rising sun as the focal point of their world, and orientated their compass on it. So the east was the equivalent of our modern north and the west the south. Basse Bretagne has more colourful regional traditions and is divided into four districts based on ancient bishoprics: Trégor (Tréguier), Léon (St-Pol-de-Léon), Cornouaille (Quimper) and Vannetais (Vannes).

MARITIME TRADITIONS The inhabitants of the Pink Granite Coast have always gazed seawards for their livelihoods, trawling the rich cod-fishing waters of Iceland and Newfoundland and manning the French navy. Some were wreckers who lived on plunder, luring ships on to their deadly reefs with lanterns slung on cattle horns. Others pillaged neighbouring national merchant fleets as corsairs (see page 68). Even the region's historic inland towns, Tréguier and Lannion, stand on tidal estuaries and feel unmistakably briny.

The Breton character becomes more pronounced as the French border recedes, and from the Goëlo coast westwards, Celtic place-names appear more frequently, often with the prefixes *Tre, Pen, Ker, Plou* or *Lan*. Many of these settlements were originally founded by monks from Britain or Ireland fleeing the Norsemen in the Dark Ages. Annual events also indicate a sense of regional tradition, with the rituals of the festivals in Tréguier and Paimpol dating back centuries.

The restored 15th-century château of la Roche Jagu

The rocky shoreline at Trégastel is one of the most scenic stretches of the Pink Granite Coast

EXPLORING This northern extremity is surprisingly mild, and the sheltered Ile de Bréhat is a lush paradise of subtropical flowers and pink granite reefs. Even the worst sailor won't have time to feel seasick on this 15-minute hop. Equally enjoyable for bird-lovers is a spring jaunt around les Sept Iles off Perros-Guirec when the gannets and puffins are nesting. Take binoculars and a camera.

Even though most visitors favour the seaside, the hinterland is worth exploring too. Off the busy N12, two places repay a detour: the lively market centre of Guingamp with its mysterious Black Virgin, and the countryside around Belle-Isle-en-Terre where the land peaks at Menez-Bré.

Church architecture (Runan, Kermaria, Tréguier, Lannion, St-Jean-du-Doigt) and interesting châteaux (la Roche Jagu, Rosanbo, Tonquédec or Kergrist) are in plentiful supply. Prehistoric sights don't match the megaliths around Carnac, but if your tour is confined to northern Brittany, see the Barnenez tumulus near Morlaix and one or two of the dolmens around Trébeurden. The towns with the most character and best-preserved old quarters are Tréguier, Paimpol and Lannion, while the prettiest villages include Binic, Port-Blanc, Locquirec and le Diben. The best wet-weather venue by far is the futuristic Musée des Télécommunications at Pleumeur-Bodou. Spare half a day there, especially if you have children on board (see page 84).

DEATH'S GENTLEMEN GO BY...

In superstitious Trégor, near Pleumeur-Bodou, the Breton bogeyman, Ankou, was feared greatly by all the country people. Even in the early 20th century, local smugglers took advantage of people's strong beliefs to gain unhindered passage through the villages on dark nights. They loaded their contraband on to a cart with rag-wrapped wheels to reduce the noise. Then one of their number would dress up in a white sheet and brandish a scythe to frighten away any prying eyes.

The chapel of St-Hervé surveys a vast sweep of countryside from the summit of Menez-Bré

AN OLD-FASHIONED MILLIONAIRE

Marie Le Manac'h was a miller's daughter born in Belle-Isle-en-Terre. On a visit to Paris she had the good fortune to meet an extremely wealthy English aristocrat, who was so bowled over by her charms that he asked her to marry him. When she was left affluently widowed, Lady Mond returned to spend her remaining days in a château on the outskirts of Belle-Isle. She is buried with her husband in a fine marble monument in the ossuary of the Chapelle de Locmaria.

▶ Beauport, Abbaye de *71D2*

Open: mid-Jun–mid-Sep, daily 10–7, artistic events; late-Sep–early Jun 10–12, 2–5. Admission charge

Serious restoration work (scheduled for completion in 2009) is in progress on the abbey, which once held sway over 13 parishes. The abbey ruins lie just south-east of Paimpol, in a verdant setting overlooking the sea. Founded in 1202 by an order of la Lucerne monks called Premonstratensians, it was once a significant halt along a medieval pilgrim route to the shrine of St James at Santiago de Compostela in Spain. Its gates were left open as a sign of hospitality. In later centuries the abbey fell into decline, and was sold in 1790 after the last monks left.

Today, visitors are shown the evocative vestiges of the 13th–14th- century church, cloisters and a Gothic Norman chapter house. More intact sections are the Romanesque refectory, with a cellar below resting on great granite pillars, and the visitors' hostel, where a rare double-decker Breton box bed stands, big enough for a whole family. The local apple trees are pressed into service for cider, now processed in the 10th-century Duke's Room.

▶ Belle-Isle-en-Terre *70C1*

A brief detour off the N12 leads to this pleasant greystone town, swathed in woodland where two rivers meet. There isn't much to see in the town itself but it livens up greatly on the third Sunday in July when a *pardon* is held, followed by a more secular festival featuring Breton wrestling (see page 24).

Several places of interest lie close at hand. The chapel of **Locmaria▶** is just north of town, worth seeing for its 16th-century rood screen bearing polychrome statues of the Apostles. The marble tomb of Lady Mond conceals a tale of rags to riches (see panel). The church of **Loc-Envel▶**

(4km south) also has a beautiful rood screen and many carved and painted beams. A little further away (9km south-east) is **Gurunhuel**, where the church is in danger of collapsing and cannot be visited. The calvary outside, however, depicts an unusual scene of souls leaving the bodies of the two robbers crucified with Christ – one is received by an angel, the other by a demon.

The hill of **Menez-Bré▶** is another popular destination from Belle-Isle (9km north-east off the D116 Guingamp road). At 302m above sea level, this pudding-basin hill of gorse and grass is the highest point in northern Brittany. A brief yet steep ascent from the Trégorrois plateau rewards you with views of a valley-etched landscape, fringed by the distant sea and the foothills of the Monts d'Arrée. There's a viewing table, and the tiny chapel of St-Hervé provides a closer focal point (see panel).

▶ Binic *71E1*

This modest resort is by-passed by the main coastal road and overshadowed by the larger town of St-Quay-Portrieux to the north. Many visitors, therefore, miss the chance to discover this attractive low-key holiday base on the bay of St-Brieuc. Its grey stone and slate houses by the port once housed a sizeable deep-sea fishing community, whose intrepid seafarers used to leave their homes each April for six-month stints searching for cod in the waters of Newfoundland or Iceland. A little museum charts the history of Binic's fisherfolk. Now its fleet stays fairly close inshore, and the town supplements its tourist revenue with the sale of mud from the River Ic for fertiliser.

Penthièvre Pier is a good vantage point for Binic's beach. A scenic coastal footpath leads to the Pointe de Pordic and the splendid 3km beach of les Rosaires to the south. Inland, the **Jardin Zoologique du Bretagne** at Trégomeur, a 12ha wildlife park (*Open* Apr–Jun, Sep, daily 10–5.30; Jul–Aug, daily 11–6. *Admission charge*), and the pretty 15th-century chapel of Notre-Dame de la Cour at **Lantic** (stained glass and granite statuary) make a good day out.

ST HERVÉ

St Hervé is one of those mysterious Breton saints about whom many legends have grown. He cured mental disorders and irrational fears, and in local churches is often represented being led by a wolf. This was his guide, for St Hervé was born blind. When his mother was pregnant she prayed that her child would never witness the world's cruelty and dishonesty, and her prayers were answered all too well. Hervé's blindness, though, gave him the power to see into men's souls, and he was credited with great intuition. He became a celebrated poet, a monk and, some say, a horse-thief!

Flower-decked shopfronts at Belle-Isle-en-Terre

The Gothic shell of Beauport abbey's medieval church stands open to the elements

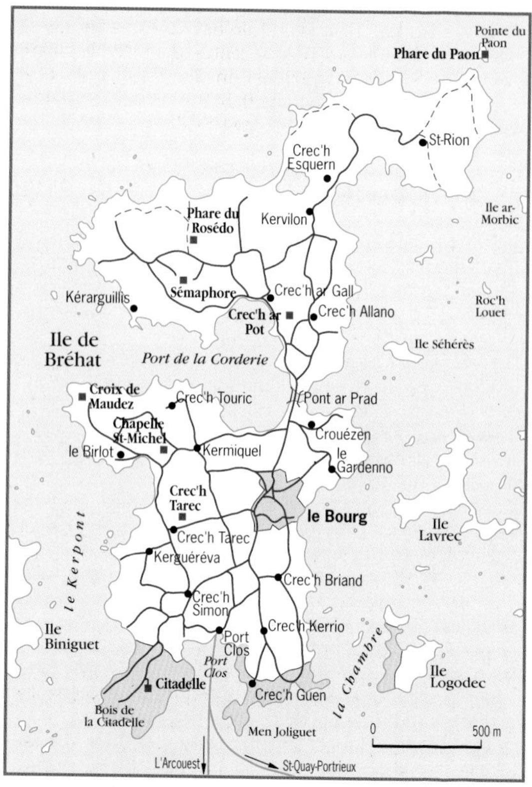

DUCKING THE STORMS
Bréhat's low-lying topography gives its residents and visitors an additional advantage. Atlantic rainclouds frequently pass right over the island, leaving it dry and sunny.

►►► Bréhat, Ile de *71D3*

Pointe de l'Arcouest, just north of Paimpol, is the closest point of access for this idyllic island. The Ile de Bréhat lies about 2km offshore, enticingly visible from the mainland as a low-lying wooded paradise encircled by a bracelet of pink granite reefs and islets. There is little to see or do on Bréhat, but the look of the place is hard to resist, and many eminent writers and painters have been enchanted by it. Now Bréhat's permanent population of about 400 is annually swollen to about 10 times that number in summer, when its three hotels are often fully booked. A pleasant alternative is its wooded campsite. All year round, Les Vedettes de Bréhat shuttle back and forth on 10-minute hops, hourly in summer. You can also reach the island (more lengthily) from Erquy, Binic and St-Quay-Portrieux.

Bréhat is effectively two islands balancing together and now firmly anchored by one of Vauban's useful bridges. No cars are allowed on the island, but a few tractors are used for local transport and bikes are available for hire. You can walk from one end of Bréhat to the other in under an hour, and waymarked paths lead all over the island.

NEW-FOUND LANDS
According to Bréhat legend, Columbus used the same route as the island's fishermen when he was on his way to the New World. A Breton sailor told him of the Bréhat route to the Newfoundland cod fisheries some eight or nine years before his first voyage in 1492. Could Bréhat sailors have been the first Europeans to reach America?

A turbulent past Despite Bréhat's apparent peacefulness, it has witnessed some grim episodes, notably at the hands of English raiders, who blew up its castle and massacred the local population at Crec'h ar Pot mill in 1409. Another mill, Crec'h Tarec, was an execution site during the 16th-century Wars of Religion.

Like most islanders, many of Bréhat's inhabitants chose a seafaring life. Its fishermen ventured great distances, and many became privateers in the 18th and 19th centuries. During World War II Bréhat remained under German occupation until 4 August 1944.

Island paradise Today ferries dock at Port Clos on the southern island, whereupon passengers disembark to explore an orderly subtropical jungle of hydrangeas, honeysuckle, mimosa, figs and geraniums, half-concealing elegant luxury villas in spacious gardens. Beaches of pink shingle stud the scalloped coastline, and some of the reefs are accessible at low tide. The northerly island is bleaker, with wilder beaches and a desolate coastline. Head here for quiet picnics; alternatively, try the pine-clad slopes of the Bois de la Citadelle at the southwest tip of the island.

Bréhat has only one main village, **le Bourg,** where houses are grouped around a square surrounded by plane-trees and overlooked by the pink-granite bell tower of the church. The island's tourist office is also situated here. Other sights include the chapel of St-Michel, where just 39 steps lead to a grandstand island view, and the Croix de Maudez, an 18th-century calvary commemorating a Celtic monk. La Corderie, surrounded by palatial Parisian holiday homes, is a magnificent rounded bay, Bréhat's main anchorage for pleasure craft. There is an interesting tidal well at Le Birlot (*Open* Jul–Aug). At the northern tip of the island is Paon lighthouse, which commands marvellous coastal views amid a profusion of wildflowers and seabirds. Inland, Rosédo lighthouse dates from 1862.

The ferry terminal at Pointe de l'Arcouest gives a dramatic view of the reefs of Bréhat

WOLF-SCARING
A few weeks after Guingamp's annual *pardon* in July the town lays on more festivities. The Festival de la Danse Bretonne in mid-August helps to keep local traditions thriving, with Breton music and dancing. A special shepherds' dance is performed, accompanied not by music but by stamping feet, allegedly to frighten wolves away.

Right: the Black Virgin at Guingamp
Below: wooden caryatids adorn some of the old houses in Lannion

▶ Guingamp *71D1*

This large, busy town lies on the main N12, some 30km inland. Its modern industrial outskirts do not entice, but if you are passing by, the dignified, well-kept old centre is well worth a visit. Once Guingamp was a Roman way-station, and it was heavily fortified during the Middle Ages when it grew wealthy on the cloth trade (some say Guingamp is a corruption of the word *guingan*, or 'gingham', allegedly first produced here). It has continued to prosper, and has expanded greatly with engineering works and food-processing factories. It is also an agricultural centre with a good market. If you have no objection to staying in towns, Guingamp makes a comfortable and strategic excursion base for some attractive parts of the *argoat* (inland Brittany), particularly the wooded Trieux valley and the lonely calvary villages to the south.

Little remains of Guingamp's fortifications except a couple of sections of ramparts and a ruined castle with weighty drum towers. Its main sight is the 14th-century church of **Notre-Dame-de-Bon-Secours▶** on the pedestrianised main street. One of its twin Gothic towers collapsed in the 16th century and was replaced by a Renaissance version. Inside and out, the basilica is full of interest, with a fine doorway at the west end, graceful pillars and buttresses in the chancel. However, the bit not to miss is the separate chapel on rue Notre-Dame, which houses Guingamp's revered **Black Virgin▶**, another of those dark images allegedly brought back from the crusades. A July *pardon* celebrates the Virgin, with bonfires lit in the Place du Centre, a seemly square of cafés and half-timbered houses. The square's most striking feature is a lovely Renaissance **fountain▶** of lead and stone, adorned with winged griffins and spouting nymphs.

Another building worth seeing is the **town hall▶** (*Open* Mon–Fri, 8.30–12.00, 1.30–5.30, Sat 8.30–12.30. *Admission free*) in the Renaissance hospice or Hôtel Dieu, formerly a monastery. Some parts are open to visitors, including the cloisters and 18th-century Italianate chapel, and Pont-Aven School paintings are on display.

▶ Lannion *70C2*

The second-largest town in the Côtes-d'Armor and the administrative centre of the Trégor region, Lannion stands at the head of the Léguer estuary. The hilly old port spreads both sides of the river, bordered by long quays and wooded towpaths which high tides often submerge. Fishing boats, some abandoned in the mud, line

The elaborately carved doorway of Notre-Dame-de-Bon-Secours, Guingamp

the waterfront, and the huge monastery of St Anne is a prominent landmark. In the old town, beautiful 15th- and 16th-century houses form a stately picture in the cobbled Place du Général Leclerc and along the streets near the sundialed church of St-Jean-du-Baly. Some of these houses are corbelled and turreted, while others are carved with caryatids, dragons and impish faces.

Lannion's most interesting building occupies a wide vantage point at the top of the town up a long flight of steep steps. The church of **Brélévenez▶** dates from the 12th century, when it was founded by the Knights Templar. Remodelled in the 15th century, it is alive with curious features: a stoup just inside the main entrance, used for measuring tithe wheat; a Romanesque crypt eerily half visible beneath the chancel, and an intricate apse festooned with carved capitals and pillars. If you can't manage the 142 steps to the church, it can be reached by a circuitous trek through backroads; the helpful tourist office by the waterfront can provide a map.

Lannion makes an excellent excursion base – though traffic congestion is a problem in summer – and is also an attractive shopping centre for lace, antiques and crafts. There is an especially lively atmosphere on Thursdays, when a market is held in the main square, and during the Shrovetide carnival, but at any time the town feels pleasantly animated. The pulse of the local region can be felt here, and many roads meet at Lannion.

CHATEAU DE ROSANBO

Not far south-west of Lannion stands this château, built on a former castle-topped rock over the River Rosanbo. The existing buildings date from various periods from the 14th to the 19th centuries, and the interior is richly furnished with tapestries, silverware and books (the library once belonged to Louis XIV's finance minister). Terraced grounds inspired by Le Nôtre, the famous French landscape gardener, surround the château (*Open* May and Jun, daily 2–5, Jul and Aug 11–6.30; guided tours. *Admission charge*).

Picturesque houses, slate-hung or timber-framed, stand on Lannion's main square

Drive

Inland from Lannion

See map on pages 70–1.

Though most people head for the spectacular coastline of Trégor, its wooded river valleys can be equally appealing, and the River Léguer is no exception. A few detours are essential on this 45km drive to see the points of interest. Allow half a day.

Heading south from Lannion along the D11, turn off past Ploubezre for the **Chapelle de Kerfons▶**, built during the 15th and 16th centuries. The chapel's outstanding feature is a rood screen with carved panels of the Apostles. Further south is the ruined **Château de Tonquédec▶**. It was demolished at the behest of Cardinal Richelieu to prevent insurrection, but a couple of towers and some of the curtain walls are still intact.

From yet another side-turning on the left side of the road is the **Château de Kergrist▶**, intact and still inhabited.

Above: the woodland setting of Tonquédec castle

The gardens are open all day and from them you can see the partly Gothic, partly neoclassical exterior of this fine manor house (*Open* afternoons). The gardens differ in style, passing from formal parterres to naturalistic landscaping and woodland.

Continuing south along the D11, turn left for **les Sept Saints▶**, south of le Run. This 18th-century chapel is built on top of a large dolmen, accessible from a door in the south transept. A curious legend is associated with the chapel, which is dedicated to the Seven Sleepers (or Saints) of Ephesus, a group of Christians who were walled up by the Emperor Decius in a cave in the 3rd century for refusing to renounce their faith. They awoke miraculously 200 years later, when they were released. The Seven Sleepers are mentioned in the Koran, and a pilgrimage to the chapel is organised each summer as a gesture of Christian–Muslim friendship.

Head back northwards up the D31. At Buhulien turn left for the ruins of the **Château de Coatfrec▶**, dating from the 16th century. The remains of a tower and parts of the domestic wings lurk beneath an ivy coat.

►► Paimpol 71D2

Sheltered in a deep cove at the north end of the bay of St-Brieuc, Paimpol is an attractive, bustling port packed with pleasure craft and chandlery. It doesn't have any good beaches but its pleasant, workaday atmosphere attracts plenty of visitors who prefer its more authentic charms to those of purpose-built holiday resorts. The town's two harbour basins are modern and practical rather than aglow with nautical character, but the surrounding buildings are harmoniously shuttered and dormered. The Repaire de Kerroc'h (now a hotel, see Hotels and Restaurants, page 269) was built by a former corsair.

There are more delightful old houses scattered throughout the cobbled town centre, especially around the Place du Martray, where a daily market displays the pick of fresh local produce, such as oysters, garlic, carrots and lettuces. Once Paimpol was an important deep-sea fishing port

whose menfolk set sail *en masse* for the rich cod-fishing waters off the coast of Iceland. In the heyday of the trade at the turn of the century, over a hundred vessels worked from the port. The last boats sailed in 1935, and since then Paimpol has turned to inshore fishing and the less arduous cultivation of oysters in the nearby Trieux estuary. If you wander through the old town, you may spy a beautiful old chemist's shopfront advertising 'directly imported' cod liver oil.

Paimpol's **Musée de la Mer (Maritime Museum)►** (*Open Jun–Sep, daily 10.30–1, 3–7. Admission charge*), on rue de la Benne, contains memories of dangerous voyages, with charts, models and navigational equipment. An old Breton schooner rescued from the scrapyard, *Le Mad Atao*, acts as a floating annexe to the museum in high season – a strange contrast to its fibreglass fairweather neighbours' clanking aluminium rigging. Not far from the quayside is another small museum of regional costume. A statue in the town commemorates the Breton songwriter Théodore Botrel, who was born in Paimpol (see panel, page 162).

Modern sculpture (above) and models of sailing ships (left) are some of the objects on display at Paimpol's Maritime Museum

81

PIERRE LOTI

The author Pierre Loti (1850–1923), who lived in Paimpol's Place du Martray, set one of his novels here, *Pêcheur d'Islande* (Fisherman of Iceland), a classic seafaring story made into a silent film in 1924. Loti (whose real name was Louis-Marie Julien Viaud) worked at sea himself for over 40 years, eventually becoming a captain.

EXCURSIONS FROM PAIMPOL

Take the scenic road to Pointe de l'Arcouest, where boats leave for the Ile de Bréhat (see pages 76–7). On the way, detour down a side-road to the hamlets of Perros-Hamon and Porz-Even. The little chapel of 1770 at Perros-Hamon lists the names of those lost at sea, and the Widow's Cross marks the spot where the women of Paimpol would stand gazing out to sea in the hope of seeing sails. South-east lie Pointe de Guilben, the Abbaye de Beauport (see page 74) and the Circuit des Falaises (see page 86).

Craft moored at Paimpol

Above: low tide in Locquirec bay

Drive

The Armorique Corniche

See map on pages 70–1.

This 70km drive straddles the coastal borderlands of Finistère and the Côtes-d'Armor, through a varied landscape of vast sandy beaches, rocky headlands and pretty fishing ports. The coast is jagged and there is no obvious main road, so just follow the lanes closest to the sea. Allow half a day.

If you have time, detour westwards from Lannion via the Léguer estuary, best at high tide. The coastal scenery is beautiful here, and several small churches are worth inspecting. The 15th-century church at **Loguivy-les-Lannion** has a wooden altarpiece depicting the Adoration, with shepherds in local costume playing Breton instruments. The chapel at **le Yaudet** contains a carved panel of the Virgin and the Trinity. Further south, **Trédrez** once had as its rector the redoubtable St Yves, patron saint of lawyers (see page 21). Notice the angels and strange beasts carved on the ends of the beams. Inland, **Ploumilliau**'s 17th-century church contains more carved and painted panels and an unnerving sculpture of Ankou, the grim reaper, ready with scythe and spade to gather in his human crop.

The Corniche proper starts at **St-Michel-en-Grève▶**, a small resort with a pretty seafront church. It is surprisingly low key considering that it stands on one of Brittany's star beaches, a magnificent 4km crescent of perfectly golden sand that stretches 2km out to sea at low tide. Sand-yachting and many other sports activities take advantage of the beach. Behind, a rocky knoll called the Grand Rocher is 80m high, and is worth the climb for panoramic views. Further along, **St-Efflam** has a chapel with a domed fountain dedicated to the local hermit saint who lived at nearby Plestin in AD 470, vanquishing dragons and doing good works.

Locquirec▶, a popular resort and fishing port, occupies a scenic headland where affluent villas take advantage of the views. The church was built by the Knights of St John and has a Renaissance bell tower. Westwards lies a series of glorious beaches, visible from the high viewing points beside the coastal road at Marc'h Sammet (good picnic spots on a clear day). **St-Jean-du-Doigt▶▶** has one of the most interesting parish closes in the area (see pages 136–7), with a triumphal arch and a beautiful Renaissance fountain. The parish gets its name from its celebrated relic, the first joint of John the Baptist's index finger, which was brought here in the 15th century. The sacred finger was dipped in water and the water was then used to anoint the eyes of those afflicted with an infection: the Duchesse Anne was cured of an eye complaint in this way and in gratitude she donated enough funds to complete the church in its present ambitious style. Ask for permission to see the sacred finger, and the church's other considerable treasures.

Westwards, **Plougasnou** and a series of pretty fishing ports (**le Diben, Térénez**) offer superb driving past deep sandy bays, shellfish farms and rocky headlands. One of the best vantage points is **Pointe de Primel▶**, accessible only on foot from the resort of Primel-Trégastel.

The last worthwhile sight before Morlaix lies well down the estuary, amid artichoke fields and swathes of gorse. The **Tumulus de Barnenez▶▶** is one of the best prehistoric sights in northern Brittany. A huge mound of terraced brown granite nearly 80m long and about 8m high conceals two separate mounds of different stone, one predating the other (4400 BC) by about 200 years. Eleven separate south-facing burial chambers overlook the estuary; most are blocked off for safety reasons but you can peep inside a couple. There are no carvings or interesting bits of tomb to see, and the few finds are on display at the visitor centre or in local museums. The site is carefully fenced off and it is fairly expensive to visit, but the guided tours are excellent (leaflets are available in English).

St-Jean-du-Doigt's churchyard fountain depicts the baptism of Christ

Yacht masts jostle for space in Perros-Guirec's popular marina

ST GUIREC
This Celtic monk arrived from Welsh shores in the 6th century and settled in a hermitage on the spectacular Pink Granite Coast. St Guirec's talents spanned a wide range: he was variously associated with the cure of retarded children, abscesses and fiery tempers. Despite his celibate status, he also acted as something of a marriage guidance counsellor, and would patiently listen to the hopes and fears of young women nearing their wedding day. Until the original wooden statue of St Guirec in the oratory at Plage St-Guirec was replaced with a more durable granite version, girls hoping to find a husband would stick a pin in his nose.

►► Perros-Guirec *70C2*

This is the largest resort on the Pink Granite Coast, and for a traditional family beach holiday there are few places to beat it. Well equipped, and spacious enough to disperse the summer crowds, it attracts older visitors as well. Two superb beaches lie to the north-west; southwards, a serpentine corniche road meanders past a gritty foreshore to the busy marina. On this side of town a small waxwork museum chronicles a century of turbulent local history from the Revolution onwards, while a casino, congress centre and thalassotherapy centre occupy the attractive seafront at Trestraou beach. A short footpath leads to the rocky tip of the promontory, Pointe du Château, from where a panoramic view of the coast can be seen. The semaphore signal station to the west provides another scenic vantage point.

Architecturally, the resort has no great features of interest or special Breton charm, but its unusual church of **St-Jacques►** is worth seeking out in the town centre. Huge trefoil motifs decorate the porch, surmounted by a spiky bell tower like a German helmet. Inside, carved capitals crown its Romanesque pillars, and there is a Gothic nave. One of the best walks from Perros-Guirec leads along the old watchpath to Ploumanac'h (see page 87). Three-hour boat trips to the bird sanctuary at les Sept Iles (see page 90) are another favourite excursion.

►► Pleumeur-Bodou *70B2*

The heathlands around this small village, north-west of Lannion, feature one unmistakable landmark – a giant white puffball structure surrounded by banks of satellite dishes. This futuristic sci-fi scene marks the site of France's telecommunications research organisation, the Centre National d'Etudes des Télécommunications (CNET), whose proudest moment came in 1962 when it received the first signals from the American satellite *Telstar*. Since 1991 it has been attracting visitors with the fascinating and brilliant displays of the **Musée des Télécommunications►►** (*Open* May–Sep, daily 10–6.

Detail from Notre-Dame-de-la-Clarté chapel, near Perros-Guirec

Admission charge). This lively exhibition with hands-on displays charts the progress of message-relaying from the earliest semaphore systems to state-of-the-art modern technology. Find out what happens when a trawler digs up a transatlantic telegraph cable, or how to use a radio-fax. The highlight of a visit is a Radôme (radar dome) show, when you enter the huge dome for a high-tech account (in French) of satellite communication.

Not far from the museum's exit is the **Planetarium▶**, which supplements its starlit presentations with more down-to-earth details about Brittany today, these being relayed across a 67m auditorium. Programme times are posted outside (or tel: 02 96 15 80 32).

Just opposite the Planetarium, a Gaulish village has been created along the lines of those made famous by France's beloved Asterix cartoons. Thatched huts stand beside a pond, and you may find a friendly pig snuffling about somewhere. Proceeds go to a charity for Third World education.

THE RADOME

The huge white globe at Pleumeur-Bodou measures over 200m in circumference and could shelter the Arc de Triomphe easily, yet its Dacron casing is only 2mm thick. To resist storms and high winds the air pressure inside is increased. The *Telstar* transmission was the first live television broadcast to be relayed across the Atlantic, from Andover in Maine just after midnight on 11 July 1962.

The Radôme and visitor centre at Pleumeur-Bodou

THE HOUSE IN THE ROCKS
A favoured spot for coach stops on the Plougrescant peninsula is Castel-Maur, where a tiny stone cottage buttressed between huge lumps of granite stands isolated by the sea. The Kerguezec family first built their remarkable house in the 1860s, and descendants still live there today. So picturesque is the setting that the house was used in a tourism campaign several years ago. It is now a postcard cliché of Breton charm, so popular that leaflets beg you to respect the owners' privacy.

►► Plougrescant, Presqu'île de *70C3*

This ragged peninsula makes a fine excursion from either Tréguier or Perros-Guirec and can easily be tackled in half a day. Minor roads close to the shoreline can be confusing to follow, but the *route touristique* called the Circuit de la Côte des Ajoncs is some help. As the name suggests (*ajoncs* means 'gorse'), gorse makes a bright splash on local heathland throughout the summer.

Starting from Perros-Guirec, the drive through Louannec (where St Yves was once rector) is fairly dull until after Trestel. **Port-Blanc►**, a delightful fishing village resort, is the first bright spot. Stone villas gaze out over a mass of craggy islets, some of which have been commandeered for celebrity holiday homes. The chapel of **Notre-Dame►** stands on a grassy hill, its roof sweeping almost to the ground and with a typical stepped wall belfry at one end. Inside, St Yves adjudicates between a rich man and a poor man.

Brittany's most northerly peninsula, tipped by the **Pointe du Château►►**, is a magnificent sight at sunset. Near by, signed paths lead to **le Gouffre►**, a chasm between rocks where the sea boils. Don't miss the pretty house at Porz-Hir (see panel). Round the headland, **St-Gonéry►** has a fascinating church with a stumpy spire of lead, bent completely out of true as though knocked by some giant bird. Ask for the key at the shop opposite.

The scenic coastline of the Plougrescant peninsula

Finally, detour to **la Roche Jaune** on the Jaudy estuary, which is famed for its oysters.

►► Plouha *71E1*

Plouha itself is of no great interest but from here it is possible to explore the dramatic slice of coastline south of Paimpol. Tourist authorities have devised a signposted route called the **Circuit des Falaises**. Highlights are the **Pointe de Minard►►** and the huddled port of **Bréhec.** For history buffs, though, the best destination lies just north of Plouha at **Plage Bonaparte►►**, which was the scene of a daring series of escapes during World War II (see page 43).

►► Ploumanac'h *70C2*

This smaller offshoot of Perros-Guirec is one of the most striking places in which to see the Pink Granite scenery. The resort is popular with young families, its pretty beach backed by a cluster of cheerful cafés, shops and restaurants. Fishing trips and excursions to the bird sanctuary at les Sept Iles leave from the bustling port to the south. The smaller island offshore was once the home of the author Henryk Sienkiewicz, who wrote *Quo Vadis?*

DANCING WITH DEATH
Inland from Plouha, the small gold-stone chapel of Kermaria-an-Iskuit (the House of Mary who Cures) makes a fascinating detour. Inside (ask locally who keeps the key if the chapel is locked), vivid frescoes illustrate the frailty of all mortal things in a *danse macabre*. In one section three noblemen out hunting encounter three dead men in a cemetery who assure them:
'Nous avons bien este en chance
Autrefoys, comme estes à present
Mais vous viendrez à nostre dance
Comme nous sommes maintenant.'
('We were like you once, but you will join our dance one day.')

Some say that St-Saens' *Danse Macabre* was inspired by these paintings. The rest of the chapel has many oddities and is thoroughly memorable.

Walk

Le Sentier des Douaniers

The 6km coastguard's watchpath by the seashore from Perros-Guirec leads past an astonishing wilderness of rose-tinted boulders weathered into curious shapes. The walk is much more attractive than the road route, which is mostly built up. Allow about 90 minutes each way.

From Perros-Guirec the path begins at Plage de Trestraou, hugging the shore beneath the cliffs. At first it is unspectacular, with views of les Sept Iles and claw-like headlands.

At Pors Rolland the rocks suddenly change gear, transmogrifying into weird forms strewn chaotically over the seafront like unclaimed suitcases. The most peculiar of all are in the Parc Municipal, an orderly conservation zone where each formation is given some fanciful name – for example, the Tortoise and the Armchair. The neat, polished number-posts of pink granite scattered around the park show the different qualities of this extraordinary stone when artificially cut instead of eroded naturally by wind and waves. One of the largest and most remarkable rock formations is called **Château du Diable▶** (Devil's Castle). A pink lighthouse stands guard over the headland.

You can follow the rocks right round to Plage St-Guirec, where an oratory and a statue mark the local patron saint. At the research unit housed in the Maison du Littoral on the edge of the park, there is a small display on local geology and natural history to attract passing visitors.

Above: granite formations at Ploumanac'h

Costaérès castle near Ploumanac'h

Walking is Brittany's most popular recreational activity, and with over 4,500km of waymarked routes there is no shortage of choice – along canal towpaths (chemins de halage)*, coastguard tracks* (sentiers des douaniers)*, forest trails or open countryside* (sentiers de pays)*.*

THE TRO BREIZ
The cathedrals of the Seven Founding Saints were the subject of a great medieval pilgrimage called the Tro Breiz, which had to be completed in under a month. Those who didn't do it in their lifetime had to undertake it after death – at the rate of a coffin's length every seven years – before they could rest in peace. The tradition ended during the 16th-century Wars of Religion, but today's tourist-pilgrims can still follow the ancient route.

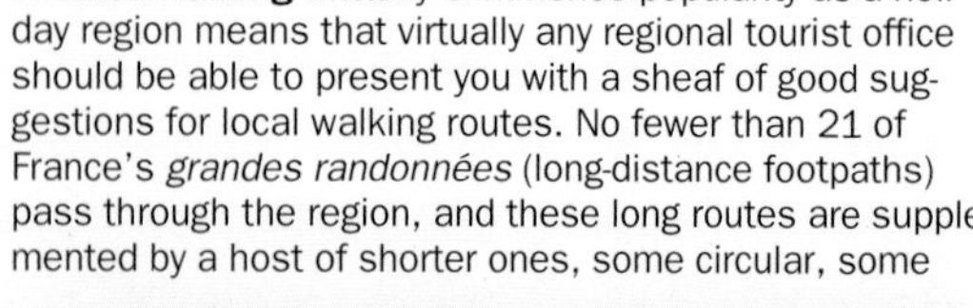

Themed walking Brittany's immense popularity as a holiday region means that virtually any regional tourist office should be able to present you with a sheaf of good suggestions for local walking routes. No fewer than 21 of France's *grandes randonnées* (long-distance footpaths) pass through the region, and these long routes are supplemented by a host of shorter ones, some circular, some linking particular themes. The Tour des Monts d'Arrée takes in some of the parish closes; the Tour des Chouans explores the sites associated with the Royalist counter-Revolutionaries; a Circuit Brocéliande tours the Arthurian landscapes of the Forest of Paimpont. You can even retrace the footsteps of medieval pilgrims on the Tro Breiz, an 800km trek around all the cathedrals and shrines of Brittany's seven founding saints (see panel). At one time all Bretons hoping for a place in heaven attempted this walk – a tall order in the days when signposts, campsites and rest huts were less readily available.

Feet (or wings) are the only way to reach the summit of Roc'h Trévézel

Undemanding terrain Compared with some regions of France, Brittany has little true wilderness and no significant mountains, so its scenery scarcely matches Alpine or Pyrenean heights. On the other hand, most of it is accessible to any walker of moderate fitness. All you need is sensible footwear (trainers are fine for lighter routes in the summer), a good map (the IGN 1:50,000 series is excellent for walking) and preferably a compass. Be prepared for changeable weather with light waterproofs, a warm sweater and a sun hat, and take along something to drink and some emergency rations. As in all areas that are intensively farmed, not all footpaths across agricultural land are readily accessible or clearly marked.

USEFUL ADDRESSES
For more on walking, contact the Maison Départmentale des Sports, Randonnée pédestre, 13B avenue Cucille, 35000 Rennes, or ABRI (Association Bretonne des Relais et Itinéraires), 9 rue Portes-Mordelaises, 35000 Rennes. Robertson McCarta produce several good walking books and maps on Brittany, including English-language versions of the French IGN Topo Guides (122 King's Cross Road, London WC1X 9DS).

If you are at all interested in birds, don't forget to pack your binoculars. Brittany's location on the western seaboard makes it the first landfall for a wide variety of migrant birds. Inland, the region's diverse habitats offer sanctuary to many unusual species.

Coastal reserves Two of the most important island reserves in Brittany are les Sept Iles off Perros-Guirec (see page 90), where gannets and puffins breed at the southerly limit of their range, and the Ile des Landes near Cancale. There is no public access to either of these sanctuaries, so you can see the birds only with fieldglasses from a boat. Koh Castell near Sauzon on Belle-Ile (see pages 180–1) is also a good place to watch seabirds, and Ile Grande, near Trégastel, has an ornithology centre where sick birds are treated. The reserve on Cap Sizun (see page 173) is open to visitors from March to September, and the Maison de la Baie d'Audierne on the Penmarc'h peninsula (see page 158), with a 600ha reserve of pools, marshland and sand dunes, has good information for bird-watchers at the visitor centre.

The best times to visit reserves are spring and summer, when nesting birds can be seen, although autumn can be an exciting time for migrating species. In winter the Golfe du Morbihan (see pages 192–3) is home to the largest concentration of seabirds and wildfowl on the French Atlantic coast.

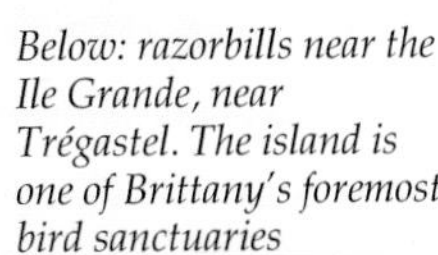

Below: razorbills near the Ile Grande, near Trégastel. The island is one of Brittany's foremost bird sanctuaries

Inland bird-watching Inland, one of the most interesting bird-watching centres is the strange peat marsh called la Grande Brière (see pages 232–3), where coastal species mingle with purple herons, bitterns and rare songbirds. Head for the Parc Animalier near Rosé to watch them. The lonelier uplands of the Monts d'Arrée (see pages 120–1) are home to birds of prey and moorland species. Ospreys even cruise in occasionally on eagle wings. Wooded valleys encourage woodpeckers, owls, warblers and nightingales.

However, as in many parts of Europe, modern agricultural practices and urban development, along with the indiscriminate shooting of migrant birds around the Mediterranean, has severely reduced bird populations.

Neat grey and white houses at Trébeurden provide holiday homes in the summer

▶ St-Quay-Portrieux *71E1*

As was the case with several of the ports along the Goëlo coast, St-Quay once dispatched its menfolk to fish for cod off Newfoundland. Today it has replaced its cod-fishing revenue with scallops, lobsters, mackerel and plaice caught more locally. Most important nowadays, however, is tourism. St-Quay has boomed as an all-purpose resort with a massive new harbour built in 1990 and continues to expand in all directions. To some extent it has outbuilt its natural charms and is not the prettiest or most peaceful place to stay. Its leisure activities, though, are admirable, and it even has some semblance of nightlife with a casino, disco, bars and cafés.

St-Quay has five good beaches to accommodate its crowds, with Mickey Clubs (supervised entertainment for young children) and lifeguards, while an outdoor swimming pool provides calmer waters. Sea-angling trips and cruises to the Ile de Bréhat (see pages 76–7) are available, while the Chemin de Ronde footpath is also popular.

FLOATING STONES
Despite its modern facilities, St-Quay-Portrieux has an ancient pedigree. Its founder was yet another of those Irish monks fleeing from raiding Norsemen. St Ké (or Quay) arrived sometime in the 5th century in a boat laden with stone troughs, used as ballast to steady his craft. Some legends even associate this saint with Sir Kay of King Arthur's court.

▶ Les Sept Iles *70B3*

The seven scraps of land visible from the coast around Perros-Guirec form one of Brittany's most important bird sanctuaries. Half-day boat trips during the spring nesting season offer views of many types of gull, plus oyster-catchers, guillemots, razorbills, cormorants and kittiwakes. Rarer species include petrels and auks, while one island, Rouzic, is noted for a large colony of breeding gannets.

Regular seasonal cruises from Ploumanac'h and Perros-Guirec sail all round the islands, but not all allow time to land. Landings are permitted at only one island, Ile aux Moines, which was once home to a colony of Franciscan friars. An hour's sojourn there allows enough time for a look at the ruined fortress and an old gunpowder factory, and even a scramble up the lighthouse's 83 steps for a glance back at the mainland coast. The islands were once a base for English marauders, hence the fortifications.

Le Père Eternel *has an excellent vantage point of Trégastel from the rocks by the aquarium*

▶ Trébeurden *70B2*

Approached from the west, this is the first village on the Pink Granite Coast proper, and the local rocks suddenly take on a magical hue. Trébeurden is a popular but low-key family resort with facilities for watersports and several good beaches split by rocky piers. Off shore, views of granite reefs and tidal islets add great charm to the setting, though the seafront development is fairly dull. Le Castel and Pointe de Bihit make good viewpoints.

Ile Milliau and Ile Molène (small islands near by) are *sites naturels protégés* (protected areas) with interesting flora and fauna – guided walks are available. The marshland behind the resort (Marais du Quellen) is also a paradise for nature-lovers and provides a grazing patch for a group of Camargue horses.

▶▶ Trégastel *70B2*

The community of Trégastel is split into two sections: *bourg* (town) and *plage* (beach). The resort is obviously the place most visitors head for – a continuation of the scenic rock formations of Ploumanac'h (see pages 86 and 87). Although the beaches are good here the sand is rather coarse. Plage de Coz-Porz is the central beach, with plenty of things to do (children's clubs, watersports and so on). Beneath one of the more dramatic rock clusters a series of caves has been turned into an **aquarium▶** of local and Mediterranean species (*Open* Apr–Oct, daily; for times tel: 02 96 23 88 67. *Admission charge*). The caves were once used as a church, and a clumsy concrete statue of the *Père Eternel* (Eternal Father) stands on top of the rocks.

More intriguing shapes and islets lie near the Ile Renote, and the Grève Blanche to the south. Inland, the 12th-century church in the older Trégastel *bourg* houses the grave of the writer Charles le Goffic. Several megaliths lie scattered in the area: a menhir topped by a cross can be found on the coast road south and there is a dolmen at Kerguntuil. The Ile Grande, 6km south, is linked to the mainland by a narrow bridge, and has an ornithology centre and an *allée couverte* (gallery grave).

OUR LADY OF HOPE
To the south of St-Quay-Portrieux, quieter Etables-sur-Mer is a place of established villas and clifftop views. The chapel of Notre-Dame-de-l'Espérance, built after a devastating cholera outbreak in 1850, has an interior bright with blue stained glass, paintings and tapestry.

Trégastel harbour

ERNEST RENAN (1823–92)
The 19th-century writer and philosopher spent the first 15 years of his life in an old house near Tréguier's cathedral, now a museum to his memory. One room contains his school desk. Renan began to train for the priesthood but lost his vocation and became a free-thinking rationalist, questioning traditional religious views in the light of contemporary scientific discoveries. He appalled the Catholic Church by suggesting in his *Life of Jesus* that Christ, though utterly remarkable, was no more than human. Strong objections were lodged when a memorial statue was erected in the town's main square, but there it remains – the philosopher sits hunched in a chair, lost in thought.

▶▶▶ Tréguier *70C2*

Now usurped by Lannion as the capital of Trégor, this historic town remains one of the most appealing in the whole region. It occupies a hilly site over the Jaudy estuary, where a sheltered inlet provides safe anchorage for many yachts and even some workmanlike cargo vessels.

A couple of tall gateway towers are all that remain of the town's old fortifications. Tréguier's medieval status as a place of art and learning, however, is still echoed in the bookshops and craft galleries that crowd its picturesque half-timbered buildings. The town was founded by a Welsh monk, St Tugdual (or Tudwal), in the 6th century, became an independent diocese 300 years later, and by the 13th century was a place of great significance. This was largely due to the widespread fame of a later saint – Yves, patron saint of lawyers (see page 21), who was then resident in the town.

Tréguier's cathedral, built of pink granite, is its most impressive building – a candidate, indeed, for the prize among any in Brittany. Its piecemeal construction in a variety of styles over several centuries has achieved a pleasing harmony. Most of it is Gothic, though one of its three towers, over the transept, is Romanesque. The great spire at its west end is a masterpiece of the Decorated period, fretted into multi-patterned holes like the shapes from a child's stencil box, to reduce wind resistance. Inside, there is much to enjoy: vaulting, stained glass glowing from nearly 70 windows, Renaissance choirstalls and 15th-century cloisters, where recumbent statues lie in an ambulatory of Flamboyant-style arches on delicate columns. Its most striking feature is the tomb of St Yves, romantically marbled in the 19th century after mindless desecration of the original grave during the Revolution. Votive candles and plaques of thanks stand by his effigy, placed there by generations of grateful lawyers. On the third Sunday in May, the anniversary of Yves' death, a *pardon* is held in Tréguier, when the saint's reliquary is

The cloisters of Tréguier cathedral, with the bishop's palace behind

A quiet corner of Tréguier's old town

wheeled out of the Treasury and carried along the streets to his birthplace down the road at Minihy-Tréguier.

Outside the cathedral lies Place du Martray, a wide square surrounded by lovely old houses, some turned into restaurants and shops. Near the tourist office is Renaud's war memorial, a sculpted woman in Breton dress grieving for lost menfolk.

▶ Trieux Estuary *71D2*

This is best seen by boat (you can sail there on a day trip from Bréhat and Pointe de l'Arcouest), and it is a popular destination for pleasure-sailors, although sandbanks and rapid currents require cautious navigation. The railway line from Paimpol to Pontrieux hugs the banks closely, as does the GR34 footpath. At the river mouth, **Loguivy** is one of Brittany's prettiest fishing ports, where lobsters are a speciality. Lenin chose it as a holiday base in 1902, though not for its beaches – it has none. Further upstream, **Lézardrieux**'s suspension bridge gives good views of oysterbeds and tiny coves, and the local church has an elegant gabled belfry typical of the region.

Some of the boat excursions allow time to visit **Château de la Roche Jagu** on the west bank (*Open* Apr–Oct, daily; Jul and Aug 10–7. *Admission charge*). One of the region's most imposing castles, state-owned now, it was carefully restored to its former glory in 1968. On its wooded eyrie over the Trieux, the castle's 15th-century shell conceals a Renaissance interior of huge fireplaces and fine ceilings. The château makes an imposing venue for summer events, including a jazz festival in August.

Pontrieux commands the original bridging point over the Trieux river, and is a pleasant old port of lovely wood and stone buildings. Once Pontrieux kitted out vessels for the Icelandic fishing runs; now it specialises in shipping *maërl*, a kind of mud used to improve agricultural land.

PRESQU'ILE SAUVAGE

Despite its exciting name, the Presqu'île Sauvage (Wild Peninsula) east of the Jaudy, towards the Sillon de Talbert, is no match for the Plougrescant peninsula west of Tréguier (see page 86), but it makes pleasant pottering if you have time to spare. At Runan is a richly ornate 14th-century church associated with both Templar and Hospitaller knights, containing painted vaults, sculpted altar scenes of the Virgin's life and a lovely east window.

SILLON DE TALBERT

The most striking feature of the Wild Peninsula is a strange 2km-long spit of sand and pebbles trailing north-eastwards into the ocean. The seaweed that collects here is gathered and then processed inland at Pleubian, a research station open to visitors in high season.

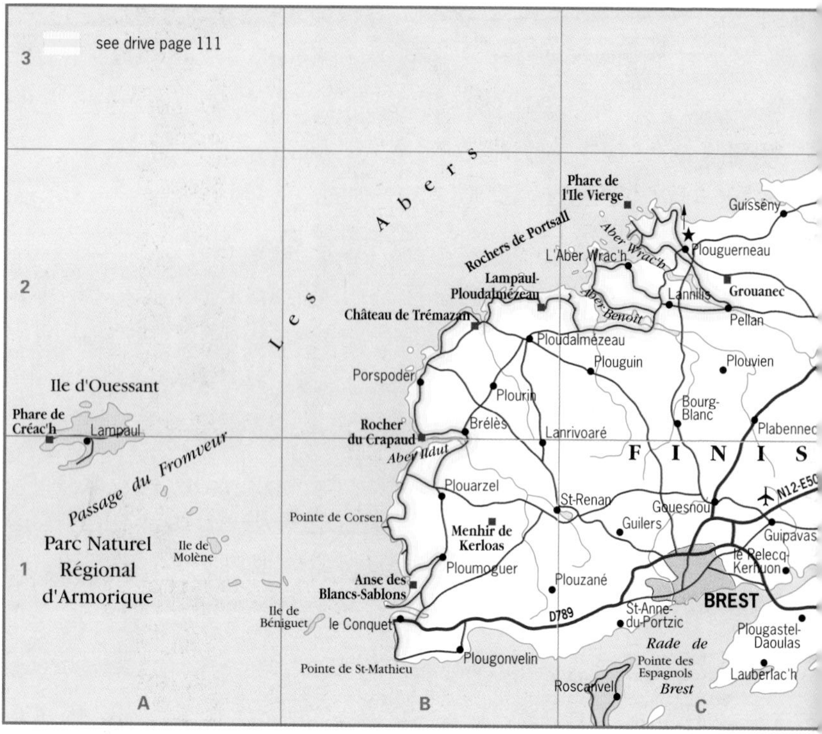

see drive page 111

Smooth granite boulders and soft sand at one of Brignogan-Plages' 10 attractive cove beaches. Several good walks can be taken across the nearby dunes

North Finistère

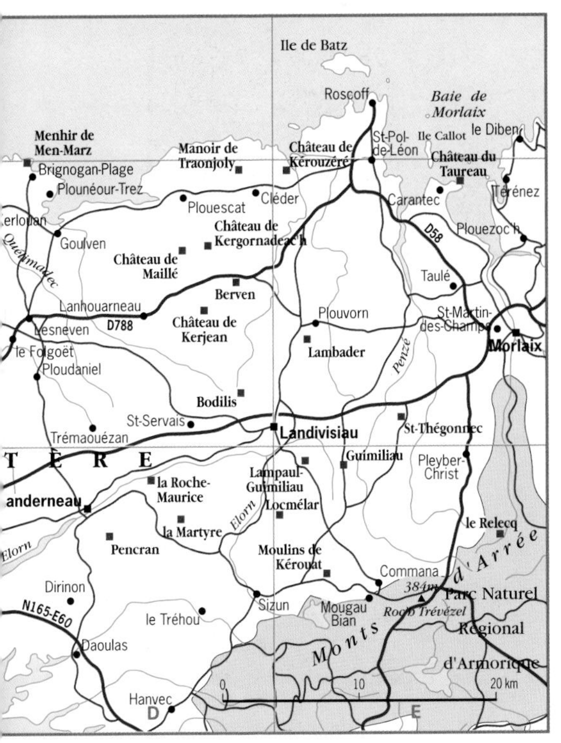

NORTH FINISTERE Most territorial extremities have a romantic fascination, and Brittany's Finistère is no exception. In terms of landscape, however, this tempestuous coast is disappointingly mundane. There are few breathtaking highlights to compare with the jagged, snarling headlands further south or the gorgeous rock and cliff scenery to the east. To enjoy this northern section of Basse Bretagne you must learn to love muddy estuaries, thrive on exposed beaches and appreciate the symmetry of an immaculately tended cabbage field.

In Latin the region's name signified the end of the known world (*finis terrae*). The Celtic Bretons knew the westerly outpost as *Penn-ar-Bed*, 'the beginning of the land' – perhaps a more optimistic way of looking at it. Today the administrative *département* of Finistère covers the whole of western Brittany, and North Finistère is the section between Morlaix and Brest harbour – the old Pays de Léon, once a bishopric based on St-Pol-de-Léon.

REGIONAL COLOUR Finistère is the most Breton of Brittany's regions, deeply imbued with ancient customs and Celtic beliefs. It is the area where you are most likely to hear Breton spoken, and even (though rarely these days) see costumes and *coiffes* worn as everyday garb. Intense religious fervour is mixed with the most far-fetched superstitions – it's a land of priests and a land of pagans, as medieval visitors remarked. Even today, strict morality and pious observance of church services are upheld in the more rural districts. If you happen to visit

Typical half-timbering and granite on a north Breton house

STATISTICS
Despite its lack of scenic highlights, North Finistère has its record-book triumphs for collectors of statistics: it is the home of Europe's biggest aquarium (Brest's Océanopolis), most powerful lighthouse (Creac'h on Ouessant), biggest lift-bridge (Brest's Pont de Recouvrance) and the tallest menhir still standing (Kerloas, near St-Renan).

▶▶▶ REGION HIGHLIGHTS

THALASSOTHERAPY
Many Bretons have perished in the sea, but others testify to its healing powers. Brittany is France's most ardent exponent of sea-water health cures. Sea-bathing first became popular in Louis-Philippe's reign (1830–48), and the first coastal spa was set up in Roscoff by Louis Bagot. Now thalassotherapy centres have sprung up in about a dozen resorts. Here you can bask in sea-water whirlpools, be massaged with high-pressure jets, or smeared with strange seaweed creams in the interests of health, beauty or sheer hedonism. Physiotherapy sessions aim to relieve all manner of aches and pains, including rheumatism and arthritis.

Finistère in early September, be sure to make for the little pilgrimage village of le Folgoët, where one of Brittany's most vivid and evocative *pardons* is held.

HISTORIC LANDMARKS In the 16th and 17th centuries North Finistère grew rich from the grain trade, often exporting it to England and the Low Countries. A large share of the proceeds inevitably went to the local churches, and today the flattish countryside is punctuated with tall and splendid bell towers, pierced with holes to reduce wind resistance. Some of the best of these are at Berven, Bodilis, Goulven and Lampaul-Ploudalmézeau, and the mightiest of all is in St-Pol-de-Léon.

Other signs of prosperity lie in Léon's castles and manor-houses, many of which are frustratingly tucked away down long drives or camouflaged in thickets of woodland. An exception is the Château de Kerjean, south of Plouescat, worth a visit for both the building and its contents. Coastal landmarks include a stately palisade of lighthouses warning shipping off the treacherous reefs. The Phare de l'Ile Vierge, near Plouguerneau, is the tallest in France, and on the Ile d'Ouessant, site of the powerful Phare de Creac'h, there is even a museum about lighthouses.

THE MODERN ECONOMIC SCENE For centuries Finistère's geographical remoteness was a serious handicap. Hampered by poor communications and bad roads, its people looked elsewhere than central France for trading partners. Modern Finistère is now linked by fast *autoroute* and TGV connections to its hinterland, but newly equipped refrigerated container lorries still roll on and off the ferries at Roscoff, laden with early vegetables and prime seafood.

There are no large resorts, but revenue from tourism is important to the region, trickling into the system from a multiplicity of seaside *gîtes*, villas and campsites. Today, the agricultural scene is counterbalanced by the large industrial city of Brest, an important naval base, which since the late 1980s has been a target of large-scale government investment.

TOURING SUGGESTIONS The historic towns of Landerneau (covered in the Armorique section) and Morlaix have much more visual appeal than Brest. None the less, the roadsteads of Brest harbour make a pleasant day out, and the region's best wet-weather destination by far is Brest's impressive Océanopolis. The attractive little ferry port of Roscoff could happily make a base for a night or two, but book accommodation ahead if you intend to visit in high season.

If the region fails to charm, you can easily skate round selectively in a day or two and move on. Don't dismiss it too quickly, though; its peace and small-scale sights may grow on you. Truly glorious beaches take some searching out but they do exist – a stay in the small resorts of Carantec, le Conquet or Brignogan-Plages can be delightful. Many visitors enjoy the *abers* country on the west coast (Welsh-speakers will recognise the Celtic word for a tidal estuary). In fine weather, one excursion is definitely worthwhile – the choppy boat ride to the Ile d'Ouessant off the west coast. This forms part of the Armorique Regional Nature Park, but as it is reached either from le Conquet (about an hour) or Brest (two hours) in North Finistère it is covered in this chapter.

A detail from one of old Morlaix's quaint houses

ILE DE BATZ

If you stay in Roscoff for any length of time, be sure to take a trip to the little Ile de Batz, a 15-minute boat ride off shore – across a treacherous tidal race. Its 750 inhabitants subsist on fishing, seaweed-processing and vegetable cultivation. Increasingly, Batz is a tourist destination, popular for sailing, with sandy beaches and several simple hotels and crêperies. At only 4km long, it is easily walked in less than three hours. A small marine exhibition outlines island life, and its lighthouse can be visited, though be warned, there are 200 steps to climb before you reach the top.

The splendidly embroidered banners normally housed in a small museum near le Folgoët's church make a ceremonial appearance on pardon *days*

BOTANIC GARDENS
Not far inland from the Océanopolis lies the Conservatoire Botanique National de Brest, a fine 22ha botanic garden containing rare and endangered species. The project was set up under the auspices of the Armorique Regional Nature Park and carries out much important research (*Open* daily 9–6, 9–8 in summer. *Admission free*). An exhibition pavilion outlines the ecological challenges to plants in the modern world (*Open* Jul–mid-Sep, Sun–Thu 2–5; Oct–Jun, Wed and Sun 2–5. *Admission free*).

►► Brest *94C1*

History It is hard to imagine that the uncompromising modern architecture of Brest conceals anything historic, but in fact the city dates back to Roman times: a military camp was established here in the 3rd century. Brest expanded in the 13th century when its strategic importance began to take on international significance. The English (invited in to protect the city for Jean de Montfort during the War of Succession) outstayed their welcome for over half a century from 1341, eager to have a toehold in such a useful harbour.

The roadstead (Rade de Brest) is colossal by any measure – over 150 sq km of water between 15m and 20m deep – and, as such, it has determined the fate of the city, for good or ill, since the Middle Ages. The deep-water harbour was valued for its defensive rather than its trading purposes, and so Brest became a naval base, denied the chance to accrue the merchant wealth of Nantes or St-Malo. The naval dockyards were established by Cardinal Richelieu, and those other *ancien régime* strategists Colbert and Vauban also made their mark.

During the German Occupation, Brest became a U-boat base, and thus a target for some of the most ferocious and sustained Allied bombing missions of World War II – 'a storm of iron, steel and blood', as the poet Jacques Prévert put it. Over 165 air raids hit the city in an attempt to prevent German submarines attacking transatlantic convoys. Eventually, General Patton's laconic order, 'Take Brest', resulted in a bitter 43-day siege, ending in hand-to-hand fighting. Before they left, the Germans blew up the docks and as much of the naval installations as they could, and by 1944 Brest was devastated.

Brest is still a bustling naval, commercial and leisure-sailing port

What to see Vast sums of post-war finance have restored the city in a modern, blockish style of spacious boulevards and bleak, tidy plazas – efficient, perhaps, but

scarcely enticing. There is little of the central area worth braving, but anyone who loves ports will want to see the dockyards. You get a good vantage point of the Rade de Brest from the **castle**, which was spared by the bombs. Inside is the **Musée de la Marine▶** (*Open* daily except Tue 10–12, 2–6. *Admission charge*), not an exceptional maritime museum but it does contain a few intriguing oddities, such as a curious manned torpedo from World War II and a 10m wooden boat in which 40 Vietnamese refugees escaped across the South China Sea. Near by is the massive Pont de Recouvrance (Europe's largest lift-bridge) and, opposite, the Tour Tanguy, a 15th-century tower housing another small museum of old Brest. Best of the city's museums, however, is the **Musée des Beaux-Arts (Fine Arts Museum)▶▶**, worth finding for its collection of Pont-Aven School paintings (*Open* except Sun morning and Tue, 10–12, 2–6. *Admission charge; free on Sun*). Look out for Kneipp's *trompe l'oeil* cow with real horns emerging from the canvas.

One of Brest's few interesting buildings is the modern church of **St-Louis▶**, an angular, sharp-edged structure topped by a shallow cupola. Inside, all is space and garish light from its splinter-glass windows.

Best by far in Brest, though, is the **Océanopolis▶▶▶** (*Open* Jun–Aug, daily 9.30–6. *Admission charge*), out on the east side of the port. This is far more than just an aquarium, rather a massive research centre and exhibition of sea-life in all its aspects: ocean currents, algae and seaweed, marine pollution, as well as huge tanks of fish and sea mammals. Labelling is high-tech and in several languages, and there are lots of hands-on activities to entertain children of the video and computer era. There's plenty here for at least half a day, including a section on cooking with seaweeds but, regrettably, there is no decent café or snack bar, only a full-blown sit-down restaurant.

Once a garrison and prison, Brest castle now houses a museum and the offices of the harbour authorities

LA BELLE CORDELIERE
In August 1513 an English fleet was sent by Henry VIII to attack Brest. When it hove into sight of harbour, guests of honour celebrating the Feast of St Lawrence aboard one of Brittany's warships, *La Belle Cordelière* , found their party rudely interrupted by a full-scale alert. The captain, Hervé de Portmuguer, weighed anchor immediately, still with his civilian crew aboard in ceremonial regalia. The Breton fleet commander retreated in panic, but Portmuguer bravely tackled the English flagship to buy time. Both ships caught fire and exploded. All 300 guests perished, exhorted by their captain to 'celebrate the Day of St Lawrence, who died by fire'.

CROSSING THE STONES
The Men-Marz menhir just outside Brignogan-Plages is a good example of a Christianised megalith. Many standing stones were topped with crosses in Celtic times, a painless way of making the transition from the old religion to the new. The crosses quelled, but did not entirely subdue the ancient pagan beliefs, some of which linger on even today in superstitions and festivals.

▶ Brignogan-Plages *95D2*

Though not particularly pink in colour, Brignogan-Plages echoes the coastal drama of the Pink Granite coast further east. Its eight linked beaches are strewn with massive, curiously shaped boulders, some of which dwarf the small grey and white houses scattered unobtrusively around the shallow, curving bay. This is an immensely appealing stretch of seaside, ideal for beachcombing in rockpools, building sandcastles or sheltered sunbathing in private coves. Beyond beach activities there isn't much to do here, apart from visiting the quaint little Chapelle Pol stuck on a boulder with a toytown watchtower, or admiring the tall Men-Marz menhir, depaganised by a cross (see panel). The Castel Régis hotel is an ideal place to relax (see Hotels and Restaurants, page 270).

A few kilometres south-east of the resort, the magnificent belfry of **Goulven▶▶** makes a splendid landmark. The church, which dates from the 15th and 16th centuries, also has fine doorways, carved stoups and an ornate altar depicting the miracles of St Goulven.

▶ Carantec *95E2*

This pleasing little resort occupies a spiky headland jutting into the bay of Morlaix. Sheltered from Atlantic storms by the Roscoff headland, Carantec is an unusually green and lush place, with pines flourishing on the promontories and hydrangeas blooming in large gardens. Its range of clean beaches and its attractive hilly setting make it a fashionable, even slightly exclusive, destination, popular with writers, painters and other celebrities. It has a casino and good facilities for holidaymakers, but despite this it still feels quite unspoilt.

THE ARTICHOKE DRIVE
If you approach Carantec from the Morlaix direction, take the minor D73 road which hugs the estuary – a marvellous drive at high tide, past fishing villages and artichoke fields. During September the crops are just getting to their best, a glaucous expanse of tightly furled, spiky buds on tall, robust stems.

The best beaches are the Grève Blanche, Porspol and the main town beach, Grève du Kélenn. Coastal cliff paths lead to numerous secluded coves. One of the best vantage points is Penn-al-Lann, one of Carantec's antler-like prongs overlooking the island fortress of the Château du Taureau, which was built to guard Morlaix from the marauding English. Another viewpoint is the rocky throne called the Chaise du Curé (Priest's Chair), with panoramas of a wide sweep of Morlaix bay.

Carantec's other coastal protuberance is a 1.5km tidal causeway leading to the Ile Callot, a popular fishing haunt accessible at low tide by car or on foot (environmentally sound notices exhort visitors to walk). On the island is the chapel of Notre-Dame, the scene of an August *pardon* venerating the 16th-century statue inside, followed by a Blessing of the Sea ceremony. *Pardons* are also held in Carantec itself, where the village's parish church houses two

Ile du Taureau's castle was a state prison during the reign of Louis XIV

Le Conquet is best appreciated from the opposite bank of the estuary

valuable processional crosses. A small maritime museum expounds Carantec's briny background, with displays on oyster-farming, seabirds and corsairs.

►► Le Conquet *94B1*

Set on the far west coast, this ancient fishing port is the most attractive holiday base for miles around. Trips to the islands of Ouessant and Molène make an interesting diversion, though local facilities for beach sports are good. Also worth visiting in the main village are a small maritime museum, which documents le Conquet's key wartime role, and its early church, illuminated by a striking mix of 16th-century and sophisticated modern stained glass. A typical Breton representation of Christ, seated and bound, can be seen above the main porch, where 15th-century statues of the Apostles shelter from the elements. Old stone houses line the hilly streets to the port, some with exterior staircases. The only sore thumb is an aggressively modern hotel on the cliffs, La Pointe Sainte-Barbe, and even this is low-rise enough to blend in at a distance (it's also the best place to stay; see Hotels and Restaurants, page 269).

Useful shops and simple eating places can be found in the central streets – check Michel Tromeur's collection of amber jewellery. In the harbour, lobster- and crab-pots lie piled up by the quaysides. At certain high tides the harbour car park may flood, so check before you set off for the islands.

WHITE SANDS

One of Finistère's loveliest beaches is the Anse des Blancs-Sablons, 2km north of le Conquet, a *site naturel protégé* (protected natural site). It's about a 20-minute walk from the harbour via a footbridge. By car it's a longer detour; the road ducks some way inland past marshy pools and grassy dunes. You can walk out on the long nose of the Pointe de Kermorvan past a ruined blockhouse to the lighthouse, with panoramic coastal views. An attractive campsite lies behind the beach.

Left: Carantec's hotels and restaurants take advantage of the coastal panorama

► Le Folgoët *95D2*

The outstanding feature of this small rural community is its massive church, the focus in early September of one of Brittany's largest *pardons* (see opposite). The name of the village means 'Fool's Wood', which refers to the miraculous legend of Salaün (Solomon). Despite his wise name, Salaün was what would have been called the village idiot in crueller times. He lived in woods on the site of the church during the 14th century and could speak only a few words: the Breton for 'Hail, Lady Virgin Mary', which he repeated over and over to himself. He begged for food and drank water at a local spring (now tamed into a fountain by the east wall of the church). When Salaün died in 1358, a white lily sprang from his grave bearing the Latin inscription '*Ave Maria*' in gold letters, and it was widely presumed that he was a saint. News of the miracle soon spread, and Duke Jean IV built a commemorative chapel on the holy site.

The 15th-century rood screen of le Folgoët's basilica is one of Brittany's finest examples of Kersanton stone-carving

Later, the irrepressible Duchess Anne (then Queen of France) made a pilgrimage to Le Folgoët to give thanks for her husband's recovery from a serious illness. She financed a massive refurbishment of the church, a splendid affair with one of Finistère's finest bell towers, Kersanton altars like stone sideboards, and a magnificently knobbly rood screen, most unusually worked in solid granite.

The church was badly damaged during the Revolution and would have been demolished had it not been for the goodwill of a dozen farmers who clubbed together to buy and gradually restore it. Today the huge basilica towers over a sprinkling of modest houses and pilgrim hostels clustered around an enormous green. A small museum of ecclesiastical statuary and Breton furniture is housed in one of the ancient inns.

MIXED BLESSINGS
Devotional practices at Le Folgoët are taken to unusual lengths. Besides the Grand Pardon in early September, it holds another religious ceremony in the last week of July. The *pardon* of St Christopher involves a blessing of motorcars, which raises eyebrows among some traditionalists.

Modern pilgrims continue the ancient tradition of paying homage at Salaün's holy well, which springs from beneath the altar on the east side of le Folgoët's church

Le Folgoët's pardon *is one of the largest and most colourful of the Breton festivals. It is held on the first Sunday in September (or on 8 September if the first day of the month falls on a Sunday).*

Celebrations begin on the preceding evening, with all-night vigils and hourly masses in the church. On the Sunday morning villagers and pilgrims begin to arrive for the grand mass, held at 10.30am. The church is full of votive candles and flowers, while outside, souvenir stalls occupy the huge village green. After the service the local cafés and bars fill up, as pilgrims prepare themselves for a long day. Eventually, the church elders file out across

the green, incongruously bearing crosses past the toffee-stalls and balloon-sellers to a small granite oratory chapel on the opposite side. Another service begins, featuring lengthy sermons and prayers interspersed with stirring Breton hymns. Many canny parishioners bring their own little folding stools or picnic chairs.

After this long service, the crowd disperses for lunch, older villagers speaking Breton as they wander back up the hill from the church. Is it all over? Far from it. At 2.30pm an even bigger crowd assembles for a massive procession of colourful banners and floats, and everyone is decked out in beautiful Breton costumes – women in black dresses with embroidered aprons and lace *coiffes*, men in wide-brimmed felt hats and bright waistcoats. Camera shutters snap again and again as the banners pass, to the accompaniment of a haunting Breton hymn tune repeated many times. Last to arrive is the Black Virgin, a 15th-century statue of Our Lady of Folgoët on her gorgeous dais. Crowd control in this small community is undertaken by one relaxed gendarme and a couple of volunteer Red Cross stretcher-bearers.

In the evening the mood lightens even further, with dancing to Breton music and plenty to eat and drink. For an interesting memory of the *pardon*, buy a cassette of the local hymns.

TROLLOPE AT THE *PARDON*

In medieval times the processions swarmed with beggars seeking alms and sick people hoping for cures. Early visitors to Brittany were repulsed at the sight of such poverty and suffering, and reacted as many Western travellers to India do today. 'Let [the reader] combine every image that his imagination can conceive of hideous deformity and frightful mutilation; of loathsome filth, and squalid, vermin-breeding corruption; of festering wounds, and leprous, putrefying sores...and when he has done this...I feel convinced that he will have but an imperfect idea of what met my eyes at St-Jean-du-Doigt.'
– *A Summer in Brittany*, Thomas Adolphus Trollope (1839).

Above left and below: all generations help to carry the banners at le Folgoët's Grand Pardon

SLEEPING LIKE THE DEAD

If you visit any Breton folk museums, you will certainly see wooden 'box beds', enclosed by sliding panelled doors or curtains, which were used until this century in many rural homes. There is a fine example in the Château de Kerjean. One thing that strikes you immediately is how very short they are – surely not large enough to lie down in comfortably, even allowing for the Breton of less well-nourished times. This is because many Bretons believed that if they lay down like the dead they would never wake again, so they slept propped upright on piles of pillows.

The rood screen at Lambader, south-east of the Château de Kerjean

THE VIRTUOUS FRANÇOISE

One of the rooms in the Château de Kerjean is alleged to be where Françoise de Quelen, a 16th-century lady of the manor, locked up three young noblemen. Her husband, who had left his wife behind at the château while he served at court, accepted a wager with these three men that one of them would manage to seduce her. But Françoise locked them up and set them to work for their supper – if they didn't work hard enough, they didn't get any food. They were only released from their drudgery when the lord of the manor returned. What his wife said to him about his ungentlemanly wager unfortunately goes unrecorded.

►► Kerjean, Château de *95D2*

Open: Jun–Sep, Wed–Mon 10–6 (Jul–Aug, 10–7). Admission charge

Well signposted off the D30 between Plouescat and Landivisiau, this impressive fortified manor house is easier to find than many of North Finistère's grand houses and makes an enjoyable excursion inland. It dates from the 16th century, when Louis Barbier inherited his uncle's wealth and decided to build a château to rival that of the Barbier family's resented overlords at nearby Lanhouarneau. The resulting building was indeed a fine

house, stoutly fortified by a high rampart and wide moat, and fashionably furnished. In 1710 the house was badly damaged by fire, and suffered again during the Terror when the last Seigneur of Kerjean was guillotined. In 1911 it passed into State ownership and has since been thoroughly restored, with appropriate imported furnishings. Visitors are welcomed with an audio-visual presentation and there are regular exhibitions and events, including summer concerts and *son-et-lumière* shows.

The château is set in 20ha of parkland, through which a drive sweeps past a monumental dovecote with 1,200 nesting holes (all, alas, devoid of doves) to the drawbridge entrance where jackdaws caw. Near by is a gallows tree, from which the lord of the manor used to dispatch local miscreants.

Inside the main courtyard, look out for a lovely Renaissance well with Corinthian columns, and the *lunettes* (moon-shaped finials) on the roof dormers – a mark of the local builder. The castle interior contains a museum of Breton furniture, which is set out as it would have been in the original rooms. Box beds, linen presses, grain chests and sideboards are on display – solid, weighty pieces carved with the typical wheel or medallion patterns of the region. You can also visit the vast, high-ceilinged kitchen, cellars reached by steep steps, and a chapel with carved vaulting.

Attractions near by Near Kerjean lies a cluster of interesting churches, worth tracking down if you are touring the area. **Berven►**, to the north-east, has a splendid lanterned belfry and one of Finistère's best examples of a triumphal arch in its close. The interior of the church is just as impressive, with an ornately worked chancel screen and carved shutters in the side-chapel niches which open to reveal statues. **Lambader**, to the south-east, contains a lovely rood screen. **Bodilis▶**, due south, is ablaze with carved beams and a starry blue roof – enough to keep you amused through even the dullest of sermons, though you could end up with a crick in your neck. **St-Servais**, close by, has another impressively balustraded belfry. This village was the home of a local artist, Yan Dargent (1824–99), and a small museum here is dedicated to his works. His most famous painting now hangs in the Musée des Beaux-Arts at Quimper (see page 169). *Les Lavandières de la Nuit* is a highly romanticised canvas depicting the ghostly legend of unfortunate women condemned to return to earth after death to wash their linen eternally on a lonely moor because their loved ones failed to pray for their souls.

▶ Lesneven *95D2*

There is nothing particularly compelling about this cattle-market town and local administrative centre, but if you are passing through (it lies very close to le Folgoët and could make a convenient base for a night), note its fine main square, where there is a distinguished statue of General Le Flô, apparently remembering his stint as France's War Minister in 1871, during the troubled days of Bismarck's expansion of Prussia.

A few venerable 17th- and 18th-century buildings, mellow and creeper-clad, remain in the town centre. Just outside the town on the Ploudaniel road, a German cemetery starkly evokes memories of later Teutonic incursions. A 17th-century Ursuline convent just off the main square houses the Musée du Léon, a local-history collection whose prize possession is a charter signed by Louis XIV.

PAGAN COUNTRY

Lesneven looks a peaceful and civilised little town today, and it is hard to imagine its lawless ancestry as the headquarters of Ar Paganitz (Pagan Country), as Irish visitors in the Middle Ages called the wild northerly parishes around Brignogan-Plages. The locals had a reputation as wreckers, who lured ships on to the reefs and swam out to capsized vessels to bite the ring fingers off drowning women. No doubt some of these tales were apocryphal, but the salvage of wrecked ships certainly made a significant contribution to the local economy. Government attempts to prevent this type of privateering were bitterly resisted.

The Château de Kerjean makes an imposing statement amid regal parkland

THE BITERS BIT
When corsairs sacked Bristol in 1522, Henry VIII sent a fleet of 60 warships to teach Morlaix a lesson. Many of the inhabitants were away at a festival in Guingamp, so the English raiders met little resistance as they ransacked the town. Unfortunately, they discovered Morlaix's well-stocked wine cellars and, having made free with them, staggered away to the nearby woods to sleep off their hangovers. They were thus easily dispatched by the returning townsfolk. Morlaix adopted as its crest an English leopard fighting a French lion, with the motto (a play on the town's name): '*S'ils te mordent, mords-les!*' ('If they bite you, bite them back!')

▶▶ Morlaix

95E2

This fine old town grew up at the head of a large estuary, becoming a strategic bridging point and an important inland port. Once it was Brittany's third city, prospering from fishing, linen, paper, shipbuilding – and piracy. Like St-Malo, Morlaix was a corsair town (see page 68), and the losses of English ships provoked reprisals, notably in 1522. In more peaceful times Morlaix traded extensively with England and the Low Countries, developing strong links through illegal tobacco and, more recently, beer. A couple of French enthusiasts who had tasted real ale in Wales set up a brewery in 1985, producing a beer called Coreff which is now available in many local bars.

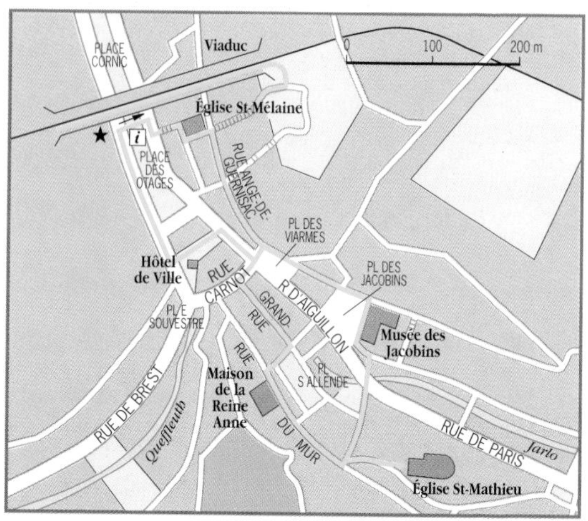

Though the town suffered some war damage, enough of its historic quarter remains to captivate visitors. It is the most appealing large town in North Finistère, with plenty to see and lots of good restaurants. Unfortunately, the hotels are rather lacking in charm, and Morlaix is best visited on a day trip rather than used as a base. Many visit its superior shopping malls to stock up with goods before heading for Roscoff, but there is far more to see than hypermarkets. It is surprisingly easy to find your way round Morlaix: its imposing railway viaduct bestrides it like a colossus, making an instant landmark, and the old town and port lie immediately at its feet, compact and walkable. To find your way out of town again, simply follow either bank of the river downstream, or follow the signposts to the motorway (N12).

Colourful houses in old Morlaix

Above: Morlaix's 58m-high viaduct spans the Dossen valley

Walk

The old town of Morlaix

See map opposite.

Half a day should allow you to see most of the old town, with time to climb its steep hills and meander along quaint alleyways (known locally as *venelles*).

Start by the huge granite **viaduct▶▶**, where you should be able to find a parking place in Place des Otages or by the quayside. The tourist office stands on this square. Through the great arches of the viaduct you can glimpse the canalised port crammed with pleasure craft and an occasional cargo boat, roads running either side.

Head up the steps near the tourist office to the 15th-century church of **St-Mélaine▶**. Outside, an old stone stoup is used as a flower tub. The dim interior is lit by brilliant modern stained glass. Up the steps behind the church a steep path leads to the first level of the viaduct, which you can walk across for excellent views of the town. More steps and alleys at the other side take you back down to Place Cornic, or to hilly walks.

Back behind St-Mélaine again, take rue Ange-de-Guernisac, lined with typical corbelled and half-timbered houses. Join the Grande-Rue near Place des Viarmes, where there are many more picturesque houses. One of the most interesting of these is the 16th-century **Maison de la Reine Anne▶▶** (rue du Mur), a quaintly carved three-storey 'lantern house' with a fascinating interior. A splendidly decorated newel post, carved from a single tree trunk, supports a spiral staircase ascending to a skylight. The Duchess Anne stayed here in 1505, when the town presented her with a live ermine in a diamond collar.

Follow rue du Mur to the church of **St-Mathieu▶** with its square tower. Inside, see the 14th-century hinged statue of the Virgin, which opens up to reveal the Trinity. Finally, the old church on Place des Jacobins houses Morlaix's **Musée des Jacobins▶▶**, with Léon furniture, Breton paintings and a grisly portrayal of Ankou, Brittany's grim reaper.

ISLAND TRADITIONS
The local costumes are not often worn today, though you can see examples in the folk museum. Women used to wear a black outfit with an unusual headdress. They played an important role in social and domestic life (husbands were often away at sea) and even proposed marriage.

Sheep-farming is one of Ouessant's mainstays, and sheep are allowed to roam freely over the unfenced island. Their ears are tagged, each family using a different pattern, so that they can be recognised when they are rounded up. Star-shaped shelters can be seen (for example, near Pointe de Pern) to protect the sheep from the wind.

►► Ouessant, Ile d' 94A2

Anglicised as Ushant, this bare, windswept island lies 20km due west of the Rocher du Crapaud on Finistère's west coast. These are some of the most dangerous waters off the French coast, with lethal reefs and the swiftest currents in Europe. Despite the sterner aspects of the island in bad weather, Ouessant is a popular excursion from North Finistère. The quickest sea crossing is from le Conquet, where ferries roar across in about an hour. There are also boat services from Brest, or you can take a 15-minute hop in one of Finist'Air's light planes from Guipavas Airport in Brest. Although winter storms can be spectacular the climate is mild, with the highest winter mean temperatures in France.

In 1988 this archipelago was designated, somewhat portentously, a *réserve de la biosphère*, and forms part of the Parc Naturel Régional d'Armorique. Ouessant itself is about 7km by 4km, shaped like a clawed crustacean. Ferry passengers arrive at the Baie du Stiff, where a modern lighthouse guards the east side of the island. Next to it is the original structure, built by Vauban (see panel, page 176), and this can be visited and climbed at certain times of day. Ouessant is rather too large to explore on foot, and the best way to travel about is to hire a bike at the quayside. Be

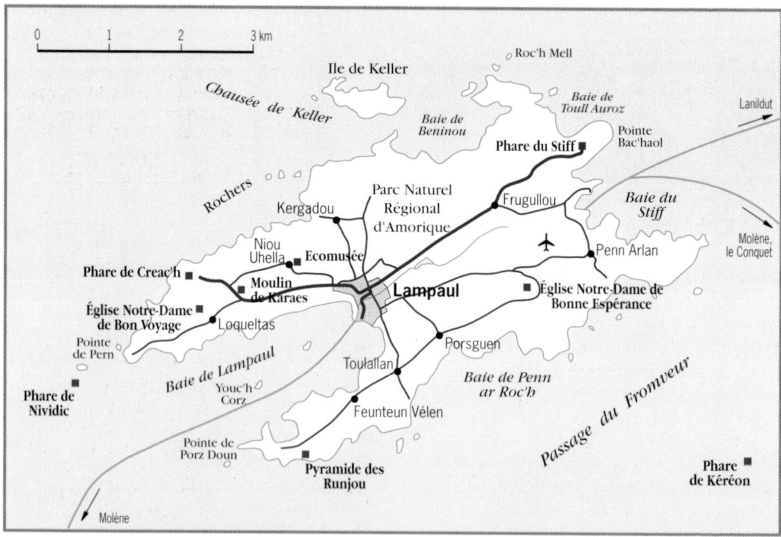

sure to get one with gears: the island may look pancake flat from a distance but when you are cycling against strong winds you'll soon find that it does indeed go up and down. Minibus tours are also available if cycling doesn't appeal.

Time-capsule Ouessant is a fascinating repository of a way of life now fast disappearing in Brittany. Its 1,062 inhabitants now turn to tourism and the scientific cultivation of seaweed rather than to traditional livelihoods like seafaring and farming. Fishing activity has always been limited because there is no good harbour, but many islanders join the

Phare de Creac'h gives a warning to ships off Ile d'Ouessant's treacherous western coast

French naval services, leaving their womenfolk behind to tend fields and raise stock: Ouessant society is still largely matriarchal. Today, most of the land is uncultivated heath, criss-crossed by sheep tracks where a few flocks roam at will. Lampaul is the main village, where you will find cafés, small hotels and a tourist office.

The best way to find out about Ouessant's background is to visit the charming little ***écomusée*▶▶** (*Open* Jul–Aug, daily 10–6; Easter–Jun, Sep, daily 10–12, 2–5; Oct, daily 2–5. *Admission charge*) at Niou Uhella, where two tiny cottages provide space for exhibits of costumes, tools and utensils, as well as furniture made from the timbers of shipwrecks. A section upstairs shows the island way of death – Ankou was a frequent visitor to these seafaring families. One of the cottages is furnished as a 19th-century home, everything as neat and compact as on board ship, and painted bright blue. (The stone houses on the island nearly all have blue shutters and doors – blue being the colour of the Virgin, who protects them from harm.)

The other place to visit on Ouessant is the **Phare de Creac'h▶▶** set on the west side of the island. The lighthouse itself is not open to the public, but there is a lighthouse museum which makes a fascinating introduction to the 50 or so coastal warning systems in Brittany. Find out what a 6,000-watt lightbulb looks like amid the whirling prismatic beams. Labelling is in French only.

PROËLLA CROSSES

The Ouessant custom of mourning the dead lost at sea was observed until only about 30 years ago. Whenever the report of a shipwreck or drowning arrived, sometimes after months of anxious waiting, the island officials would first inform a male relative. He would then break the dreaded news to the mother or widow with the words '*Il y a Proëlla chez toi ce soir*' ('There will be a Proëlla in your house tonight '). A Proëlla, or small wax cross, was placed in the window of the bereaved family's house for the night preceding the funeral, when all the family and friends would keep vigil. After the funeral the crosses were placed in the cemetery mausoleum.

SHIPWRECK

Ouessant and its smaller neighbour Molène frequently lie blanketed in thick sea fogs. Despite all the lighthouses that lie around the rocks, terrible disasters periodically occur: in 1896 the *Drummond Castle* foundered here with the loss of 248 lives. An old rhyme starkly declares the dangers of Brittany's westerly islands for shipping: '*Qui voit Molène, voit sa peine; Qui voit Ouessant, voit son sang; Qui voit Sein, voit sa fin.*' (meaning roughly: 'If you see Molène, you've got problems; if you see Ouessant, you're in bad trouble; if you see Sein, your end is near!')

RUDE GRANITE

In 1967 the town council of Plouescat decided that it could no longer tolerate the existence of a suggestively shaped rock on one of the local beaches. One dark night they blew it up – only to find local artists retaliating against this piece of municipal vandalism by creating even more disturbingly phallic sculptures, which now lie scattered around some of the lonelier shores.

LE GROUANEC

The church and parish close of le Grouanec, about 4km south-east of Plouguerneau, have been restored to reveal a set of typically Breton features – fountain, ossuary, cloisters and gargoyles. The church contains stained glass by the modern master, Max Ingrand, and charmingly carved beams in the south aisle.

▶ Plouescat *95D2*

The most interesting thing about this little town is its magnificent 17th-century covered market building, a forest of oak timbers beneath a slate roof. It still serves its original purpose, and is a good place to buy provisions. A strange seahorse statue stands next to the church opposite the market.

There are lots of quiet beaches near Plouescat – huge expanses of sand dunes and rocks at low tide – and it's a popular place to camp. Inland, the countryside around the town is sprinkled with châteaux, some fortified, others more like the pleasure palaces of the Loire. Among the best of these are the Renaissance **Manoir de Traonjoly** (7.5km north-east), the 15th-century **Château de Kérouzéré** (12km east), the elegant 16th-century **Château de Maillé** (4km south) up a beech and chestnut drive, and the **Château de Kergornadeac'h** (7km south), one of the last fortified houses built in France (1630), with false machicolations and tall chimneys. Not all these are open to the public, but you can get a good idea of their architecture from outside. Greatest of all is the **Château de Kerjean** (see page 104), run by the state and easily accessible to visitors.

▶ Plouguerneau *94C2*

Many holiday homes now expand this village into dull suburbia, threaded by a web of confusing lanes. The reason for the development becomes clear once you reach its coastal attractions – a series of sheltered coves of very fine sand. The village was originally built on an ancient Gallo-Roman camp called Tolente, sacked by the Vikings in AD 875. Some way inland, the old village church contains a collection of wooden statues placed there by thankful parishioners who had escaped the plague. A small museum documents the area's maritime traditions, concentrating more on seaweed collecting than the age-old pastime of looting wrecked ships. On an island just off the Plouguerneau headland stands France's tallest lighthouse, the Phare de l'Ile Vierge, 82.5m high. Trips from Lilia beach take visitors to see it at closer quarters.

A rocky stretch of the Coast of Abers, near Plouguerneau

Above: Finistère's dramatic coast

Drive

Around the *abers*

See map on pages 94–5.

A pleasant and varied 70km drive past beaches, fortresses, lighthouses, dunes and reefs, detouring inland to negotiate wide valleys. Take a picnic; peaceful views are more plentiful than restaurants. Stick to minor lanes near to the sea and allow half a day.

An *aber* (the Celtic word for estuary) is formed when sea levels rise to flood the steep shoulders of a former river valley and its tributaries, resulting in wide fjord-like inlets that are often navigable far inland. Unlike the great tidal estuaries of the Rance or the Dossen on the north coast, the western *abers* are shallow and full of silt. They lack the lush woodlands of those in southern Brittany but the views are broader, with sheets of water mirroring the surrounding heathery moorland. The *abers* are more picturesque at high tide, while the offshore reefs are dramatic at low water.

Start near **Plouguerneau**, detouring around the ragged headlands past sheltered coves and France's tallest lighthouse, the Phare de l'Ile Vierge. Wind upstream along the Aber Wrac'h, the most scenic *aber*, to cross at Pellan. This is particularly beautiful at sunset. Now head back to **l'Aber Wrac'h,** a pretty sailing port and resort. Footpaths through the Ste-Marguerite dunes give views of drying seaweed (processed for fertiliser), the islet-strewn Aber Wrac'h estuary and the Rochers de Portsall where the *Amoco Cadiz* foundered in 1978. South of Aber Benoît, detour coastwards through **Lampaul-Ploudalmézeau**, memorable for its lantern belfry. Between **Château de Trémazan** and **Porspoder** is the most dramatic stretch of coastal scenery. The Aber Ildut is the official boundary between Channel and Atlantic, where the Rocher du Crapaud (Toad Rock) gazes towards Ouessant. Southwards, the Pointe de Corsen is France's true Finistère, the most westerly mainland finger, ending in a tame 50m cliff. Head south via **le Conquet** (see page 101) to Pointe de St-Mathieu (see page 114).

Aber *scenery in north-west Finistère*

ONION JOHNNIES
A street in Roscoff – rue des Johnnies – commemorates these colourful characters, once a familiar sight the length and breadth of the UK as they wheeled bicycles engulfed with strings of Breton onions. Henri Ollivier began the trade in 1828 and it lasted until about 1930, a popular way for Breton farmers to offload their perishable produce at a time when communications with the rest of France were hampered by poor road and rail links. The bar of the Hôtel du Centre, near the old port, displays sepia photos of the Onion Johnnies in their heyday.

Above right: Roscoff produces vast quantities of shellfish; visitors are welcome to look around the viviers *at the east end of the port*
Below right: the belfry of Roscoff's Notre-Dame-de-Kroaz-Batz

ST PAUL AND THE DRAGON
The 19th-century village church on Ile de Batz (a 15-minute boat ride from Roscoff – see panel on page 97) contains the statue of St Paul the Aurelian, who died on the island in AD 573. St Paul is associated with a dragon legend. This 'laidly worm' was alleged to be terrorising the island when St Paul arrived. He wrapped his stole around its neck and cast it into a pit called the Trou du Serpent (Monster's Hole), which is marked by an offshore rock near the lighthouse. The stole (now proved to be an 8th-century oriental textile) is kept in the north transept of the church.

▶▶ Roscoff *95E3*

This town is certainly worth more than the blinkered glimpse many ferry travellers award it, and it is no hardship to spend a first or last night here (book accommodation ahead in season). The deep-water ferry terminal constructed east of the town in 1973 leaves the pretty old fishing harbour unspoilt. The old town, which consists of little more than a single street, runs along the back of the bay, where several concrete jetties erupt from the shore.

Roscoff is really a multi-purpose town. Besides being a popular seaside resort specialising in thalassotherapy, it is one of France's main shellfish ports and a great centre for vegetable export. Roscoff's traditional beret-clad 'Onion Johnnies' (see panel) have been replaced by the huge container juggernauts that whizz artichokes and cauliflowers across the Channel today.

Sights to catch in town include the splendid church of **Notre-Dame-de-Kroaz-Batz▶▶**, with one of the finest of Finistère's belfries. A sundial warns you to *'Craignez la dernière'* ('fear the end'). The exterior is carved with galleons and cannon, signs of its corsair patronage, and all around the church are the lovely 16th- and 17th-century houses of wealthy privateers. The Jardin Exotique, containing 1,500 species of plants from the southern hemisphere, is also worth seeing.

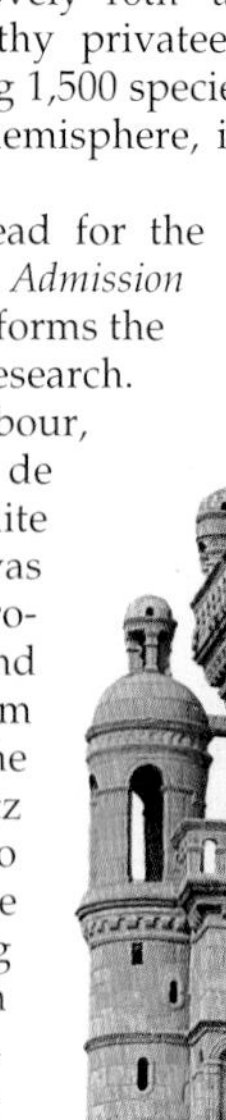

If you want to see fish, head for the **Aquarium** (*Open* Apr–Sep 10–6. *Admission charge*) near the church, which forms the National Centre of Scientific Research. On the other side of the harbour, almost at the top of Pointe de Bloscon, stands the tiny white Chapelle Ste-Barbe (St Barbe was entrusted with the task of protecting Roscoff from pirates and enemies of the Church). From here there are fine views of the town, the harbour, Ile de Batz and Pointe de Primel. Next to the chapel are the ***viviers*▶**, one of the largest open-sea breeding grounds for lobster, crawfish and crab (*Open* Mon–Fri 9–12, 2–5. *Admission free*). Visitors can walk along foot-bridges spanning the ponds, which contain thousands of cubic metres of sea water.

The story of Brittany Ferries, which in just 35 years grew from the original 'Brittany Ferry', a converted tank-landing craft, into a fleet of roll-on, roll-off ships carrying passengers and freight, is a lesson in daring in the great Breton seafaring tradition.

Brittany Ferries

Breton trading links with the UK are ages old, but when Brittany joined with France in 1532 these links were suppressed. Until the early 1980s, roads and railway links between Brittany and the rest of France were poor, and the problem of finding alternative markets ready to accept Brittany's perishable vegetables became acute. During the 1950s and 1960s Breton farmers became increasingly dissatisfied about the lack of government support. Alexis Gourvennec was, at only 24, a leading militant light in his local farming cooperative, which sought to achieve the best possible prices for farmers. For several years they tried unsuccessfully to persuade existing shippers to carry Breton produce to new markets in the UK. Eventually, Gourvennec took the daring initiative of setting up an independent shipping line – the first French-owned cross-Channel operator, and the first scheduled link between Brittany and the UK.

In January 1973 a converted tank-landing craft, laden with freight vehicles, made its first sailing from the deep-water port of Roscoff to Plymouth. It was quickly dubbed 'The Cauliflower Run'. Within a year, the demand for passenger facilities grew, and the company felt confident enough to build a ro-ro ('roll-on, roll-off') ship to carry both passengers and freight vehicles. This first ship was named the *Penn-ar-Bed* – the Breton name for Finistère.

Since those early beginnings Brittany Ferries has proved a runaway success story. Today it is the largest operator on the western Channel, running services from Ireland, Normandy and Spain, as well as Brittany. Besides transporting passengers (and cauliflowers!) across the waves it has blossomed into a fully fledged holiday company, offering the largest number of self-catering *gîte* and motoring holidays of any operator in France or Spain.

ST POL'S BELL

In the great cathedral of St-Pol-de-Léon are the relics of the founding saint, Paul the Aurelian, and his famous bell. When St Pol (Paul) had successfully evangelised the immediate area he planned to take God's word further afield. To help him in his mission he asked Duke Mark for a single item – one of the seven bells used as dinner gongs at the duke's castle – but this request was refused. Soon afterwards a fisherman came to St Pol saying he had caught a huge fish with a bell in its mouth. 'What Mark refused, God has provided,' said the saint.

▶ St-Mathieu, Pointe de *94B1*

'There, the two old enemies are face to face – the land and the sea, humankind and nature,' wrote Michelet in the 19th century in his *Tableau de la France*. On this dramatic spot a Benedictine monastery was founded in the 6th century, allegedly where St Matthew's relics were brought to Brittany from Ethiopia. A great storm blew up and the sailors feared shipwreck, but when they held up the apostle's head the waves subsided and the boat sailed safely ashore.

Today, the roofless abbey church stands gauntly on the windswept headland, a red and white lighthouse tower erupting from the grounds. A newer lighthouse near by is open to visitors, and 163 steps lead to superb views of the Crozon peninsula and the Ouessant archipelago. Down on the dark rocks below the abbey, a memorial pays tribute to French sailors killed in the Great War. Creature comforts are supplied in a smartly modernised little hotel-restaurant overlooking the abbey, the Pointe de St-Mathieu (see Hotels and Restaurants, page 271).

▶▶ St-Pol-de-Léon *95E2*

During the Middle Ages St-Pol was the religious centre of North Finistère, a bishopric founded by St Paul (Pol) the Aurelian. It no longer has a bishop but the cathedral still stands, its crisp twin spires rivalled by the magnificent belfry of the nearby Chapelle du Kreisker, soaring 77m above the town. These two remarkable Norman-style churches apart, St-Pol is best known as an agricultural centre of the immensely fertile Ceinture d'orée (Golden Belt. All around the town early vegetables flourish, particularly artichokes, onions, potatoes and cauliflowers. Refrigerated lorries rumble along the nearby roads, rapidly transporting the produce to appreciative destinations. Aside from its churches and a few pleasant old houses, St-Pol is a working town which regards tourism as a secondary priority. It has few hotels or restaurants, and lacks the charm of Roscoff as a base. If you catch it on a Tuesday (market day) you will see it at its liveliest, doing what it does best.

The **Kreisker bell tower▶▶** is best seen from a distance, when its stately proportions can properly be admired. Despite the vaguely Germanic-sounding name (which is actually Breton and means, prosaically, the church in the town centre), its architecture was inspired by the church of St-Pierre at Caen, which was destroyed during World War II. The spire is pierced with daisy-like shapes, as if by a pastry cutter, to reduce the wind-load. At its base, four smaller, perfectly balanced pinnacles rise from its balustraded balcony. You can climb the tower as far as this balcony for marvellous views.

The interior of the **cathedral▶▶** is more interesting than that of the

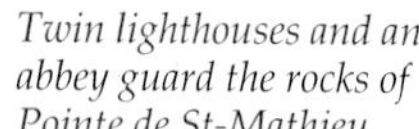

Twin lighthouses and an abbey guard the rocks of Pointe de St-Mathieu

St-Pol-de-Léon's churches offer a scenic backdrop for café visitors

Kreisker (which is now used as a college chapel), but quite a shock after the ubiquitous granite of most Breton churches. A chilling nave of sallow Norman limestone soars above your head ('very harmonious with its thin columns,' says one of the multilingual notices scattered around). Within this lofty space of light and symmetry, fascinating details soon emerge. Over the high altar is a curious snowdrop-like object carved from palm wood, holding the Host. What looks like an old stone bath-tub (a Roman sarcophagus) serves as a stoup, and a little door below the right tower was used by lepers. Lovely old glass tinges the transept walls with warmer colours. The remains of St Paul the Aurelian lie in a gilt reliquary, near a bell rung on *pardon* days to cure headaches and ear disorders.

The best of St-Pol's old houses are in rue Général Leclerc, between the two churches. The Maison du Pilori, where convicts were once put on public display, has a beautiful Renaissance door. Look out for the escutcheoned Maison Prébendale behind the cathedral, a 16th-century canon's house. Champ de la Rive and the Rocher Ste-Anne give good views over Morlaix bay.

Well-kept old buildings in St-Pol-de-Léon

THE KREISKER LEGEND

A dressmaker was working on the day of the Feast of the Virgin when she suffered a paralytic stroke. Healed by St Kireg after she prayed to him, she gave up her house as a chapel to the Blessed Virgin. This was sacked by the English in 1375, but was soon rebuilt. A second misfortune befell the building when its roof was damaged by lightning in 1628. The final spire dates from 1668, and has been copied (with variations) all over North Finistère.

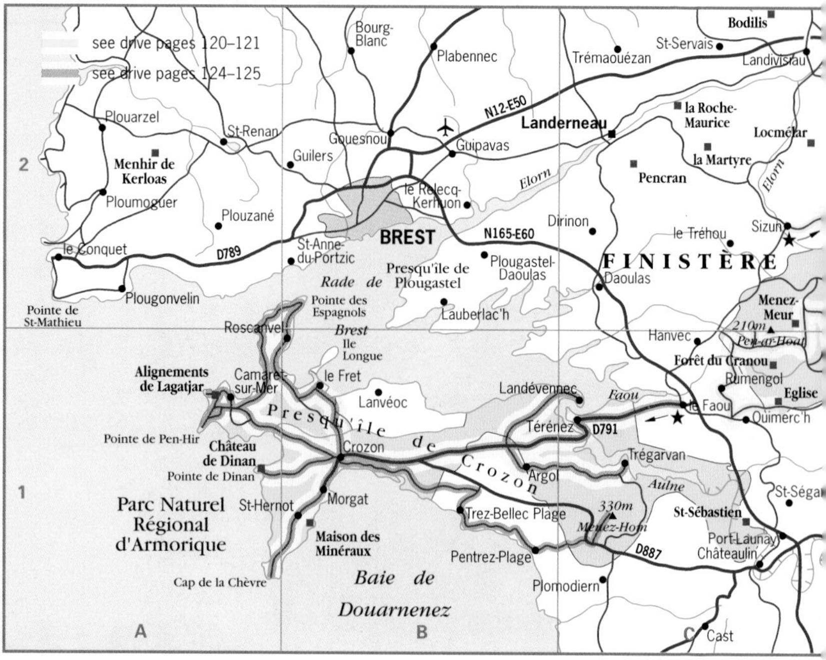

A casualty of the declining fishing industry at Camaret-sur-Mer, which specialises in catching sea crayfish

Armorique

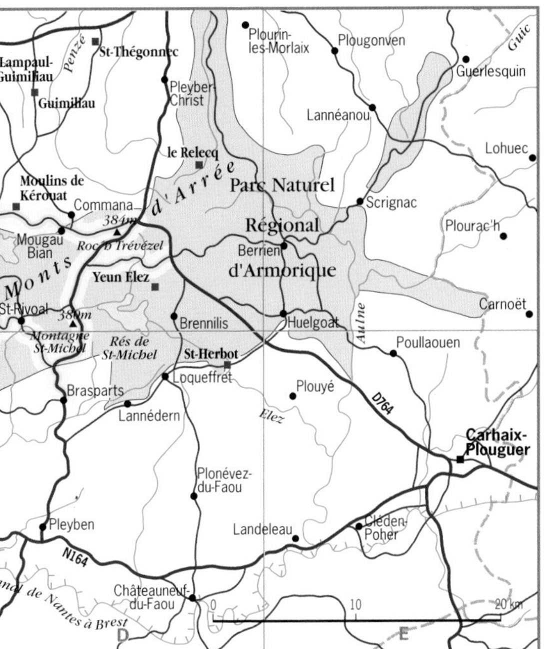

ARMORIQUE The Parc Naturel Régional d'Armorique, to give it its full title, is a slightly odd concept. It is one of 32 regional nature parks in France and was set up in 1969. Geographically confusing, it penetrates waveringly deep into Brittany's *argoat*, or forested heartland, and equally far into the Atlantic to encompass the reef-strewn archipelagos of Ouessant and Sein (both of which are covered in other chapters of this book – see pages 108–9 and 172 respectively). Brittany's highest mountains, the Monts d'Arrée, the lovely Aulne estuary, and some of its best coastal scenery (the Crozon peninsula) are also included within the park boundaries. Its 112,000ha, therefore, represent many typical Breton landscapes. Half as much again consists of islands and open sea, featuring over 300 maritime bird species plus seals and dolphins.

France's regional parks are administered by locally elected delegates whose duties are laid down by charter. The parks' function is broadly similar to that of the national parks: they are conservation areas designed to protect sites of natural and historic interest from inappropriate development or exploitation. But Armorique is not simply a nature reserve; it is an entire ecosystem which, of course, includes its inhabitants. Local residents are encouraged to continue traditional trades, crafts and pastimes, while little museums scattered throughout the region explain various aspects (current or bygone) of rural life. Breton culture is fostered through events and festivals. In practice, lack of funds curtails any very ambitious projects, and the region is becoming ever more dependent upon tourism for its revenue.

Keen walkers, anglers, bird-watchers and cyclists will find plenty to do here, but facilities for the more sybaritic holidaymaker are limited; this is not the place to find

▶▶▶ REGION HIGHLIGHTS

Crozon peninsula *page 124*

Guimiliau *page 129*

Huelgoat *page 130*

Lampaul-Guimiliau *page 132*

Monts d'Arrée *pages 120–1*

Pleyben *page 135*

Parish closes *136–7*

St-Thégonnec *page 138*

The beach at le Pouldu, on Finistère's sunny south coast

gourmet restaurants or suave thalassotherapy centres. Most villages accustomed to visitors will have a *crêperie* or two, however, and increasingly *fermes-auberges* (farm guesthouses) are starting to cater for summer tourists by offering home cooking and regional produce. If you feel like splashing out on serious food, head for St-Thégonnec's splendid *auberge* (see Hotels and Restaurants, page 271).

LANDSCAPES Unlike some areas of Brittany, the Armorique Park is not intensively cultivated (though some parts are afforested). Its landscapes are pleasantly, if unspectacularly, wild, with heather and gorse making ubiquitous ground-cover in unfarmed areas. Much of the countryside is hilly or undulating moorland, erupting in softly contoured pudding-basin domes or outcrops of toothy granite. The hill summits overlook a patchwork of gently hedged fields known as *bocage* country, plaited by a maze of rivers, lakes and streams.

There are no very large towns or resorts in the region; the largest settlements are country markets such as Landivisiau or Carhaix-Plouguer. Industrial intrusions are minimal apart from a little agri-business in the main centres. However, the nuclear power station at Brennilis in the heart of the Armorique Park was a controversial project. Breton nationalists unwisely attacked it with a rocket launcher in 1975 (fortunately without success). Army yomping grounds in the Monts d'Arrée, and the top-secret submarine base on Ile Longue, are similarly unpopular in some quarters.

CLOG-SPEAK

At the beginning of this century, State schools formally discouraged pupils from speaking Breton. A humiliating device called a *vache* (usually a wooden clog) was hung round the neck of any pupil heard talking in Breton, who would then become an object of ridicule. The only way he or she could get rid of the *vache* was to denounce another child, when it would be transferred. In this way many Bretons learned to despise the language they heard in their homes and treat it as a sign of *ruralité*, or uncivilised peasant upbringing. See Trégarvan's Musée de l'Ecole Rurale for more on this (page 125).

PARISH CLOSES Apart from the scenery, coastline and *écomusées*, the main attractions for visitors to this region are the remarkable parish closes, elevated here to a unique and striking art (see pages 136–7). Most of the parish closes are clustered to the north of the region in the Elorn valley. Visitors often speed round them one after the other, clocking them off as if train-spotting, and inevitably cultural overload can soon result. Interesting churches, with or without closes, can be found throughout the area, and it is more enjoyable to intersperse them with other types of sightseeing than to try to squeeze too many of them into a single day.

If you do get hooked on this type of architecture there are over 20 churches worth seeking out in this region alone. At the very least, try to see the 'big three': St-Thégonnec, Lampaul-Guimiliau and Guimiliau, all within a short drive of each other near Landivisiau. The parish closes reveal more about Breton culture than almost any other aspect of the region.

Enjoying the views from Roc'h Trévézel

Stone cottages at Lampaul-Guimiliau

ECOMUSÉES

A useful leaflet available at local tourist offices lists the museums of the Parc Naturel Régional d'Armorique. Especially worthwhile are:

- Domaine of Menez-Meur (animal reserve, horse museum and hiking trails)
- Moulins de Kérouat (restored watermill complex and exhibition)
- Maison Cornec (traditional farmhouse and outbuildings)
- Maison des Minéraux (geology exhibition)
- Musée de l'Ecole Rurale (re-creation of a turn-of-the-century Breton school)
- Maison de la Rivière, de l'Eau et de la Pêche (economy of water and fishing)
- Maisons du Niou (life on the Ile d'Ouessant)
- Musée des Phares et Balises (lighthouse and beacon museum)
- Musée des Champs (agricultural museum)
- Conservatoire Botanique National de Brest (rare and endangered plant species)

Young trout swim in the streams at Sizun's Maison de la Rivière

THE GATES OF HELL
Often shrouded in mists, the lonely and treacherous peat bog known as Yeun Elez near Brennilis is associated with many strange tales of witchcraft and exorcism. If a household was troubled by ghosts, the local priest would carry out a ritual in which the wandering spirit was driven into a black dog, which was then drowned in the bog. Ancient Celtic legends referred to it as the entrance to hell. If the nuclear reactor on its doorstep ever malfunctions, the name will not be inappropriate.

BUCKWHEAT
The classic Breton pancake is made with buckwheat flour. Buckwheat is not a cereal crop, but a plant allied to the sorrel family, with small white flowers. It grows in many parts of the world, particularly the Far and Middle East, hence its French name *sarrasin*, meaning 'saracen', from its discovery during the crusades. Buckwheat was grown extensively in Brittany several hundred years ago, but most of it is now imported. For more information, visit the *éco-musée* Maison Cornec at St-Rivoal in the Monts d'Arrée, where you may see it growing (*Open* Jul–Aug, daily 11–7; Jun–Sep 2–6. *Closed* Sat in Sep. *Admission charge*).

►► Arrée, Monts d' *117D2*

These ancient heights once towered over 4,000m tall. Now, worn down to mere stubs of granite and sandstone, they reach less than 400m. What they lack in altitude, though, they gain in antiquity, for these are some of the oldest rocks on earth. They are still the highest hills in Brittany, forming a desolate stretch of moorland covered with gorse and heather. The hills are either softly domed summits (*menez*) or saw-like, crested outcrops of quartz (*roc'h*) which make tremendous vantage points despite their modest height. Wildlife thrives: deer, wild boar, otters and even beavers can be found in these remote haunts, while kestrels, curlews and buzzards hover overhead. Other signs of life often associated with wild places can also be detected – France's armed forces play wargames here. On the mysterious swampy moor called Yeun Elez, a nuclear power station bathes its superheated toes in the waters of the St-Michel reservoir.

Besides the natural attractions of the Monts d'Arrée, there are several well-presented small museums in rural buildings which trace various aspects of local life. Visits to the fascinating parish closes (see pages 136–7), most of which lie just north of the main Arrée range, can easily be combined with a day's drive through the countryside. Places to stay or eat, however, are in short supply.

Heath and conifers cloak the crests of the Monts d'Arrée

Above: Sizun's triumphal arch

Drive

The Monts d'Arrée

See map on pages 116–17.

This 100km drive incorporates a mix of natural landscapes, old villages and sightseeing, including some parish closes. Allow a day if you want to see the sights and go for a walk as well.

Sizun▶▶ makes a pleasant base for this drive. The village is dominated by a tall church with elaborate panelled vaulting and decorated beams, while the surrounding parish close attracts most attention for its magnificent triumphal arch. Sizun's other attractions are the **Maison de la Rivière▶** (a museum about waterways) in an old mill, and the **Maison du Lac**, an exhibition on river fishing in an annexe, near the Drennec Dam to the south (both are well signposted from the village).

Beyond the **Moulins de Kérouat▶▶** (see page 132) the landscape becomes wilder and the hills higher. **Commana▶** (see page 123) has another fine church and an *allée couverte* (gallery grave), at Mougau-Bian, to the south. The **Roc'h Trévézel▶▶** (384m) is one of the best viewpoints on a clear day, with views as far as Lannion bay. It takes about 15 minutes to scramble up the rocky crest. Head south down the D785 to the **Montagne St-Michel▶**; this is slightly lower than Roc'h Trévézel (380m), and the summit can be reached by car. If you are feeling adventurous, try a detour eastwards across the spooky peat bog of Yeun Elez (see panel opposite). You can walk around the St-Michel reservoir, but stick to the paths carefully – the marshland can be treacherous.

Brasparts has a notable parish close and a fine church (see page 137). The hamlet of **St-Rivoal** contains one of the Armorique's most attractive *écomusées*, the **Maison Cornec▶**, a typical Arrée farmhouse restored as it would have appeared in the 18th century. Note the outdoor stairs, protected by an awning. Barns and out-houses can be explored in addition to the box-bedded, earthen-floor interior.

Wind westwards through the lanes, detouring north to the **Domaine de Menez-Meur** (see page 134), a wildlife park and information centre. Beyond lies the **Forêt du Cranou**, extending over more than 600ha, good for walks and picnics. Nearby **Pen-ar-Hoat** hill can be climbed for good views. The church at **Rumengol** dates from the 16th century. Two *pardons* in honour of Our Lady of Remedies are celebrated here annually. The two splendid altarpieces both date from 1686. The scattered parish of **Quimerc'h** to the south still has the ruins of its church, which fell into disuse after inhabitants found it too remote.

The sheltered harbour of Camaret-sur-Mer

THE FIRST U-BOAT
In 1801 Robert Fulton, an American engineer, tried to demonstrate his brilliant naval warfare invention. This was a submersible craft propelled by oars which could stay underwater for about six hours, during which time it could attach a timed explosive charge to enemy shipping. Fulton intended to use a British frigate at anchor off Camaret as target practice. Unfortunately for him, it weighed anchor at the critical moment and sailed serenely away, unaware that a five-man submarine crew was ploughing frantically beneath the waves to attack it. Disillusioned, Fulton returned to his native America. It was nearly a century before his revolutionary submarine concept was reattempted.

► Camaret-sur-Mer *116A1*

This little lobster-fishing port occupies the most westerly tip of the Crozon peninsula, near some of its most dramatic coastal scenery. Once Camaret was a prosperous place, a popular haunt of artists and writers. Today tourism is increasing, but the fishing industry is severely depressed, and many boats lie rotting on the beach.

The crescent of buildings around the port is pleasantly shabby and unpretentious, with good fish restaurants and a range of serviceable hotels. A long natural bank of silt and pebbles called the Sillon protects the harbour and is the site of a tiny pilgrim chapel, **Notre-Dame-de-Rocamadour►**, restored after fire damage in 1910. At the September *pardon*, a Blessing of the Sea ceremony is held here. The red-brick doll's house **fortress►** at the far end of the Sillon was erected by the military engineer Vauban in 1689. The **Battle of the Atlantic International Memorial** (*Open* daily 10–7. *Admission charge*), sheltered inside a German blockhouse facing the sea, is dedicated to those who died at sea during World War II .

Just west of the town stand 143 stumpy megaliths, the **Alignements de Lagatjar►**, arranged in an indeterminate pattern. The **Pointe de Pen-Hir►►** is the Crozon peninsula's best coastal viewpoint – a natural amphitheatre of 70m-high cliffs overlooking a scattering of rounded boulders in the sea known as the Tas de Pois (Heap of Peas). You can scramble down the cliff path to a grassy platform called the Chambre Verte (Green Room). Several beaches lie below the Camaret headland, but note that the Anse de Pen-Hat is unsafe for swimming.

► Carhaix-Plouguer *117E1*

This former Roman encampment is hardly worth a special detour, but if you are passing through have a look at its most unusual building, the **Maison du Sénéchal►** (now the town's tourist office) in the main street. The exterior of this stone and wooden mansion fizzes with corbelling, slatehanging and strange carved figures.

Today Carhaix-Plouguer is the centre of the prosperous Poher dairy region. The town's large central church, with its square tower, is dedicated to St Trémeur, who bears his head in his hands over the main entrance.

A string of chapels and calvaries scattered around the Montagnes Noires makes an attractive excursion from the town (see page 157); the **Kerbreudeur calvary**, near St-Hernin, is one of the oldest in Brittany.

▶ Châteaulin *116C1*

Steamer trips once made the journey up the Aulne estuary from the Rade de Brest. Today the serpentine river is tidal only as far as Port-Launay, and canalised through Châteaulin. The waterfront scene is still immensely pretty though, reflecting placid water-meadows and steep wooded cliffs. In the spring the water churns with salmon and trout, which leap the lock weirs to reach their upstream spawning grounds. Towpaths by the riverside make good walks or cycle tracks.

The **Chapelle Notre-Dame▶** (above the town on the north bank) has a triumphal arch and a 15th-century calvary; further afield, **St-Sébastien▶**, hidden amid tiny tracks downstream, houses ornate altarpieces. At St-Ségal, just north of the town, is the **Musée des Champs▶** (one of the Armorique Park's regional museums), which traces the changes in local farming since World War II (*Open* Jun–mid-Sep, daily 10–7. *Admission charge*).

▶ Commana *117D2*

This bleak village deep in the Monts d'Arrée offers a few primitive resort facilities and a small tourist office but is visited mainly for its church. Although the parish close lacks the impact of some in the region, it is worth seeing for its triumphal arch and an ossuary containing a small museum of sacred art. Inside the church, three elaborately carved and coloured **altarpieces▶▶** present a masterly array of baroque peasant art.

Just outside the village, in the hamlet of Mougau-Bian, is one of the region's finest prehistoric antiquities, an ***allée couverte*▶**, about 14m long with five horizontal slabs supported on 28 upright stones. If you creep inside the monument you can just make out one or two faint carvings.

LA TOUR D'AUVERGNE

A statue in Carhaix-Plouguer's main square commemorates Théophile-Malo Corret (1743–1800), who was so keen to join the army that he presented false papers when he entered the king's service. He enjoyed a brilliant career and proved valiant and loyal, being wounded many times during the Napoleonic wars. Though ambitious as a youth, he was extraordinarily modest and consistently refused any promotion to a rank higher than captain. He was killed in action on the Rhine in 1800, but is still revered as a hero among French regiments.

The Chapelle de Notre-Dame, Châteaulin

POINTE DES ESPAGNOLS
In 1594, 400 Spaniards occupied this headland for a period of over four years. They had been sent by Philip II in support of the Catholics, at war with the Protestant Henry IV. Elizabeth I of England eventually sent reinforcements to help dislodge the Spaniards, who were finally ousted after a six-week siege. This surprising piece of Anglo-French co-operation was a self-interested manoeuvre to prevent the Spaniards taking Brest harbour, which would have made an ideal base for a much-feared second Armada attack on England.

You can walk out to the rock arch at Crozon's Pointe de Dinan

►►► Crozon, Presqu'île de *116B1*

The Crozon peninsula forms the foaming tongue of Finistère's mad-dog profile. As its regional park status indicates, it has some spectacular coastal cliff scenery, particularly at its westerly capes. The sea laps along large, quiet beaches and reed-filled creeks edged with sea holly. There is little intensive farming and virtually no heavy industry. On the north side there are fine views of the Rade de Brest glimpsed through wooded inlets. Many of the idyllic southern beaches are popular with campers, although those at the tip of the hammerhead can be chilly and dangerous, with shifting sands and currents. Apart from the isolated height of Menez-Hom, the countryside is no more than gently rolling. The best holiday bases are Morgat and Camaret, being good for boat trips, beaches, fishing and watersports. Hotels are mostly simple and seasonal.

Château de Dinan is one of the Crozon peninsula's most dramatic rock formations

Above: reefs and quiet beaches

Drive

The Crozon peninsula

See map on pages 116–17.

A varied 70km drive through quiet villages, bracing headlands and gorgeous beaches to some of Finistère's most exciting coastal scenery. You can easily see most of Crozon in a day, with time for the beach, a clifftop walk or even a short boat trip. Sightseeing is limited, apart from three or four little museums. Camaret is the best lunch stop-off (cheap fish restaurants around the port) – or take a picnic.

Le Faou (see pages 128–9) makes a good starting point. South-west of the town, the road known as the Térénez Corniche (D791) gives lovely views over the Faou and Aulne estuaries and the Rade de Brest. The bridge at Térénez forms a panoramic entrance to the Crozon peninsula. At les Quatre Chemins, you can make detours: northwards to the ruined **Abbaye de Landévennec▶** (see page 133) or southwards to the small village of **Argol▶**, with its cider museum and church with a fine parish close. In summer an organisation called Ar Micheriou Coz arranges demonstrations of traditional crafts (contact the tourist office for details). Near **Trégarvan**, on the south bank of the Aulne, a former school has reopened as the **Musée de l'Ecole Rurale▶**. Visitors are transported back to the early 20th century, with slates, inkwells and old school photos. The museum is interesting – note the attempts to suppress the Breton language – but heavy on documents, for which no translation is provided.

Crozon, the peninsula's main town, has little to detain you except its church, where a peculiar altarpiece commemorates the defeat of a Roman legion. Take the minor road north to **le Fret**, a small, pretty ferry port with views of the Rade de Brest. Continue north towards the **Pointe des Espagnols▶▶** for spectacular views. Vauban fortifications guard the peninsula. To the right you can see the mysterious Ile Longue, a nuclear submarine base. The east road through **Roscanvel** (there is striking modern stained glass in the church) is much lusher than the exposed western side of the headland. Follow the coast through **Camaret-sur-Mer▶** and the **Alignements de Lagatjar▶** to the **Pointe de Pen-Hir▶▶**, Crozon's most exciting viewpoint. Back at Crozon again, head south for **Morgat▶** (see page 135), or take the coast road to the Pointe de Dinan, where the rocky mass known as the **Château de Dinan▶▶** stands beyond a natural rock arch. Down past Morgat the road leads to the **Cap de la Chèvre▶**, where observation posts offer grand Atlantic views. Near St-Hernot, call in at the **Maison des Minéraux▶**, a collection of geological specimens. On the return leg, detours off the D887 lead to lovely long beaches, such as **Pentrez-Plage▶▶**, or the viewpoint of **Menez-Hom▶** (see page 134).

As a French holiday region, Brittany runs the Côte d'Azur a close second. Over 1,000km of sand lie waiting for its visitors – far more than the Riviera offers and much less crowded, even at the height of summer.

SETTING THE TREND
Though sea-bathing was popular throughout the 19th century in the north coast resorts, it took longer to reach more isolated communities. Pierre-Jakez Hélias describes in his autobiography, *The Horse of Pride*, the astonishment the first seaside holidaymakers caused in the Penmarc'h peninsula: 'Little by little, on summer Sundays, we would see families of peasants coming to sit by the sea, first on the grassy clifftops, to watch the half-naked holidaymakers frolicking down below in their one-piece bathing costumes. Then in their turn they would go timidly down to the shore, first to wash their hardened feet, the men first, the women behind.'

Sailing at Bénodet

The variety of coastal scenery in Brittany means that there is some sort of beach for everyone: idyllic sheltered coves or vast wild expanses of shingle; lively resort beaches equipped for any type of seaside sport; or remote hideaways for Crusoe-style solitude. There are island beaches, estuary beaches, beaches strewn with fascinating rock formations, and beaches below awesome cliffs or panoramic headlands. At low tide, a rockpool wonderland emerges from the waves, teeming with hundreds of mysterious crustaceans and seaweeds.

Clean beaches Scoured daily by boisterous Atlantic tides, Brittany's beaches are much cleaner and fresher than those around the soupy Mediterranean. Pollution is rarely a problem except near large centres of population, such as St-Malo, Lorient or Vannes (notices warn against collecting shellfish on some beaches). Many resorts proudly display the EU mark of beach approval – the Blue Flag. If one of these is flying, the water should be cleaner than average. The strong tides bring their own problems, though. At low water, the sea may retreat behind a mournful wasteland of mud, while storms deposit huge quantities of seaweed along the strand.

Keeping warm Squally weather brings its own drama to the Breton coast. The Plage de la Torche (see panel, page 158) in an Atlantic gale is a spectacular sight. Endlessly changing cloudscapes and rainbows compensate for inclement weather, and no enervating *mistral* or *scirocco* winds disappoint, as they may do on the Mediterranean. Water temperatures, though, are a fraction lower on this coast (even in August they rarely rise above 16–17°C), and it may be too cold or rough for young children.

Exciting beach sports such as sand-yachting, windsurfing, waterskiing or parascending provide entertainment for spectators as well as participators. Simpler pleasures like kite flying or *boules* require less organisation – and less expense. Many of the main resorts operate beach clubs (often known as Mickey Clubs in France) where young children are entertained and looked after for a daily charge.

Canoe surfing at Cap Sizun

Beach safety Some Breton beaches are extremely dangerous because of unpredictable currents or strong swell. Large resorts generally provide lifeguard supervision on at least one beach during the main holiday season, though this may not be constant – lifeguards take lunchbreaks too. Many supervised beaches also operate the well-known flag safety system: red means don't swim; orange means that swimming is risky; and green means that swimming is considered safe.

A particular hazard on some of Finistère's west-facing beaches is *baïnes*, or large hollows enclosed by sandbanks. When the tide comes in, the *baïnes* become invisible – bathers may fall into them and soon find themselves out of their depth – and currents may sweep even strong swimmers far out to sea. Noticeboards warn of these on some coasts, and tourist offices provide cartoon leaflets in several languages explaining the dangers. Exposed beaches on the Crozon peninsula, Cap Sizun, Penmarc'h peninsula, and west coast of Quiberon and Belle-Ile can be especially hazardous.

Pick of Breton beaches These are recommended for scenery and interest as well as sand, not all are safe for swimming.
Emerald Coast Dinard; St-Cast-le-Guildo; Sables d'Or-les Pins; Erquy; le Val André.
Pink Granite Coast Binic; Plage Bonaparte; Bréhat; Perros-Guirec; Ploumanac'h; Trégastel-Plage; St-Michel-en-Grève; Locquirec; le Diben.
North Finistère Carantec; Plouescat; Brignogan-Plages; Plouguerneau; Trémazan; le Conquet.
Armorique Camaret-sur-Mer; Morgat; Trez-Bellec Plage; Pentrez-Plage.
Cornouaille Ste-Anne-la-Palud; Baie des Trépassés; Penhors; Plage de la Torche; Bénodet; Beg-Meil; Raguenez-Plage; Port-Manec'h; Guidel-Plages.
Morbihan Quiberon; Carnac-Plage; Ile aux Moines; Houat; Hoëdic; Belle-Ile.
Loire-Atlantique Penestin; le Croisic; Batz-sur-Mer; la Baule; St-Marc.

THE BAIE DES TRÉPASSÉS

The name translates ominously as the Bay of Souls because drowned shipwreck victims often washed ashore here (it is said their souls rise from the surf on All Souls Day). The bodies of dead Druid priests were ferried across this bay in pagan times to their final resting place on the Ile de Sein.

Fun in the sand at Dinard

Medicinal plants, Daoulas abbey

MARY, QUEEN OF SCOTS
Unconfirmed accounts declare one of the figures representing the Three Holy Women on Guimiliau's calvary (the one on the right) to be Mary, Queen of Scots in 16th-century court dress. She was executed in 1587, about the time the calvary was carved.

CATELL GOLLET
A couple of Brittany's most elaborate calvaries (Guimiliau and Plougastel-Daoulas) include horrific scenes of a young girl being torn apart by demons. This is not a biblical tale but a Breton morality story. Catell or Katell (Catherine) loved dancing and other sinful activities, not all of which she confessed to in church. In her fallen state she took a handsome lover and, like many another woman before and since, discovered all too late that he was the Devil in disguise. Her final damnation was to steal consecrated wafers for her lover at mass, and her dreadful punishment is publicised on the calvaries as an 'awful warning' to all bad girls.

Gothic porch at Daoulas church

►► Daoulas — 116C2

Daoulas has been the site of an abbey since the 5th century, when the monks of St Columba arrived. It fell into disuse after being attacked by the Normans but in the 12th century it was rebuilt by Augustinian monks. The abbey flourished for the next 600 years until it was badly damaged during the Revolution. It is now in the care of the local authority, and is imaginatively used as the setting for important summer archaeological exhibitions. At any time of year, though, the charming ruins can be visited, and constitute one of Brittany's best examples of Romanesque architecture.

The ruins stand at the head of the Daoulas creek, which flows into the Rade de Brest. A small town of gold-stone houses huddles below the abbey, the best of which can be seen in the cobbled rue de l'Eglise. An ancient belfried **porch►►** (the former south door), adorned with statues and animal carvings, now provides a triumphal entrance to the parish close. The **church►►** has been restored in Romanesque style but still has its original 12th-century west door. The tranquil abbey grounds near by contain the remains of 12th-century **cloisters►►**, ornamented with foliage and geometric patterns. Only three sides still stand, surrounding a courtyard with a large decorated basin. A few exotic sheep graze in a nearby field, wood pigeons coo, and ducks paddle near a small fountain and oratory with quaint ancient statues, one showing St Thélo riding a stag. To one side is a medieval **herb garden►** containing about 500 species of medicinal plants, each neatly labelled: 'Sage – against gastric and intestinal infections, aches and toothache', or 'Lemon balm – for the stomach, a sedative'. Excavations continue to unearth the old convent buildings and chapter house.

► Le Faou — 116C1

There isn't much to see in this little medieval port, but it is a place of great charm, particularly at high tide when the brimming estuary mirrors the domed church by the waterside. Once the town was a significant timber port; today it has no riverine trade. In the main street 16th-century jettied houses, half-timbered and slate-hung, make a picturesque scene. Not least of le Faou's attractions are its two hotel-restaurants, rivalling each other on

Café scene in le Faou

the main square – both excellent places to stay or eat. The covered market and pleasant streets containing traditional food shops are good places to buy supplies for a picnic.

▶▶▶ Guimiliau *117D2*

This is one of Brittany's star parish closes (see pages 136–7), not to be missed unless you have special dispensation from church visiting. The calvary is one of the most complex and animated in the whole region, with over 200 carved figures from the famed masonic workshops of Landerneau depicting numerous scenes from the life of Christ. The whole assembly, attired in 16th-century dress, looks as theatrical as a Shakespearian play. The knobbly cross in the centre of this wonderful carousel shows the Virgin, St Peter, St John and St Yves with Christ. The thieves, unusually, are absent. More intriguing than these scenes is the vignette of Catell Gollet (Catherine the Damned – see panel opposite).

The church, too, is crammed with busy decoration. A beautifully carved south porch (the creation of Eve is shown on the left inner frieze, and a cat and dog chase each other round the outside) leads into a blaze of timber-panelled vaulting and exquisite woodwork. Notice St Cecilia and David playing a duet on the organ loft, and the superbly carved domed canopy over the font. The pulpit sports sibyls and cardinal virtues; the fine altarpieces represent St Yves the lawyer between the rich man and the poor man, St Hervé with his guiding wolf, and the headless St Miliau. Allow plenty of time to take in all the detail.

A gargoyle grimaces from the church at le Faou

AROUND HUELGOAT
A few local villages are of interest. Scrignac, north-east, is famed for its Breton wrestling champions (contests are still held in nearby Berrien) and its hunting museum, Maison de la Faune Sauvage et de la Chasse, in the old railway station. Brennilis has a lovely 15th-century church (daylight belfry and rich polychrome panels), and a dolmen. At Loqueffret you can visit one of the Armorique Park's little museums, the Maison du Recteur (Priest's House) and a richly decorated church. The next parish church, Lannédern, contains the relics of St Edern, who is depicted on the calvary riding a stag. Beyond Roc'h Trévézel, a short detour north-east takes you to the ruined Cistercian remains of le Relecq abbey.

Above right: mossy rocks in the forest of Huelgoat
Below: the Grotte d'Artus

►► Huelgoat *117E2*

The name means 'high wood' and, appropriately enough, Huelgoat is the main community of one of Brittany's last remaining forests. A decade ago, the forest of Huelgoat was a wondrous place of tangled vegetation, thick with moss and ferns. Then the hurricane of October 1987 smashed many of its ancient trees to matchwood in about

a quarter of an hour. A few timid saplings are beginning to rear their heads above the chaos of uncleared lumber, but in places the woods resemble a fleet of wrecked sailing ships – all stricken masts amid a morass of driftwood and flotsam, now overgrown with brambles and gorse. Some fine old specimens remain, mostly of beech, oak and pine. Newer plantings are often glumly coniferous.

Huelgoat stands by the shores of a large lake, which together with its neighbouring hilly woodland makes it a popular summer resort and excursion centre for activity holidays. Sailing, fishing (carp and perch in the lake; trout in the river), riding, cycling and walking are all catered for locally. The tourist office in the village can provide detailed maps of all the nearby paths, wider and more obvious since the great storm. Car parking areas and picnic sites around the 600ha forest make access possible at many points. The village itself is not particularly interesting, and has a certain mountain-resort dourness, particularly out of season. St Yves stands in the parish church, flanked by the rich man and the poor man as usual (see page 21).

Woodland walks The main walks are well signposted from the village. Paths lead along the banks of the River Argent, which flows out of the lake, or along the canals dug in the 19th century when the silver and lead mines were

Huelgoat looks best from a distance across the lake

worked. Signs of earlier habitation can be found on the hilltops above the valley floor. One strategic defensive site was used by Celtic peoples and became a Gallo-Roman camp after the arrival of Caesar's legions. A small exhibition in a mill, the **Moulin du Chaos▶**, highlights local life and history. Within about 100m of the lakeshore road the name is transposed into Chaos du Moulin in a magical scene of mossy, tumbled boulders, where water-smoothed granite, now softened by vegetation, lines the river valley. A few metres further on is the **Grotte du Diable (Devil's Cave)▶**, accessible down a steep iron ladder. A soldier fleeing the Chouans (see page 179) is alleged to have spent a night here, protecting himself with a pitchfork. When the locals saw his shadow by firelight they had an understandable fright.

In a natural forest amphitheatre near by, occasional cultural events are staged in season. Across the stream, more curiosities include the **Roche Tremblante (Trembling Rock)▶**, a huge oblong stone that will apparently rock on its axis if you push it in the right place, and the **Ménage de la Vierge (Virgin's Kitchen)▶**, a cluster of rocks which a very creative imagination could conceivably convert into pots and pans. At this point the path diverges. The Allée Violette continues by the river-bank towards the road (D769), diverging again around the **Promenade du Fer à Cheval (Horseshoe Walk)** to **Le Gouffre (The Chasm)▶** where the River Argent disappears briefly into a swallow-hole (access via steep steps or a difficult path). The **Sentier des Amoureux (Lovers' Path)** leads uphill to join other paths past the **Grotte d'Artus (Artus's Cave)** and the **Mare aux Sangliers (Boar's Pool)**, to the **Camp d'Artus**, a Gallo-Roman camp consisting of an artificial mound surmounted by oval fortified enclosures – and a lot of dead trees.

South of the River Argent lie **La Roche Cintrée**, a natural belvedere with views over the town, and **Mare aux Fées (Fairy's Pool)** and the old silver mines. The countryside around Huelgoat is a mixture of woodland and open moor, rising to the Monts d'Arrée.

SKETCHERS AND SPORTSMEN

Thomas Adolphus Trollope (brother of the novelist Anthony) remarked on Huelgoat's advantages for 19th-century leisure travellers, whose favourite pastimes were usually drawing and painting or hunting: 'For the first [sketchers], there is an infinite variety of combinations of rocks, wood, and water, with an abundant supply of picturesque figures of both sexes and all ages. For the second [hunters] there are partridges, and hares, and trout, in any quantity he pleases to kill, wolves frequently to be met with, stags sometimes, and boars occasionally.'
– *A Summer in Brittany* (1839)

Right and below: the revived cornmills at Kérouat grind again – at least when visitors arrive

ST MILIAU
Several of the famous parish close churches in Finistère (notably Guimiliau, Lampaul-Guimiliau and Ploumilliau) depict the strange legend of St Miliau, a 6th-century prince of Cornouaille whose jealous brother cut off his head during a quarrel over the succession. Miliau calmly picked up his severed head and let the blood spill over his brother, so proving his guilt for all time. A little boy with clogs and a Breton hat (Miliau's son) adds pathos to the scene. The blameless Miliau was canonised after the miracle and is now the patron saint of the Elorn valley parishes.

►► Kérouat, Moulins de *117D2*

Open: Jul–Aug, daily 11–7; Jun, Sep–Oct 10–12, 2–6. Closed Sep–Oct Sat–Sun am. Admission charge

An abandoned mill village near Sizun, consisting of about 15 buildings surrounded by farmland, has been attractively restored as an *écomusée* by the Armorique Park authorities, and is now much frequented by schoolchildren and coach parties for its educational and entertainment value. The mills, which were built between the 17th and 20th centuries, once belonged to a mayor of Commana, and the living quarters, with their bourgeois furnishings, are those of a well-to-do family. One of the watermills is in working order, and you can see the millstones turning on the gearing mechanism. Explanatory panels in the cottages and outbuildings outline the activities in barns, stables, a tannery and bread ovens.

►►► Lampaul-Guimiliau *117D2*

Though it is usually listed as one of the great Breton parish closes (see pages 136–7), this church is more notable for its interior than its calvary, which is plain and damaged. Before you go in, however, notice the triumphal archway surmounted by triple crosses and the funerary chapel containing an elaborate altar and saintly statues. The stumpy tower of the church is the result of a lightning strike in 1809, and from the outside it does not greatly impress. Inside, however, marvels await.

The decorated rood beam that spans the nave bears a crucifix and statues of the Virgin and St John, while other carvings include fishy dragons on choirstalls and wicked robber faces. A stone stoup dating from the 17th century shows two devils writhing in agony as they touch the holy water. Biblical and mythical scenes are enmeshed in a kaleidoscopic turmoil of high relief on the altarpieces. Annunciation, Passion, Resurrection and Martyrdom slowly emerge amid baroque columns and harvest festival swags. A more sober impression is left by Anthoine's emotive Entombment (1676) in a downstairs chapel.

► Landerneau *116C2*

The one-time capital of Léon stands on the Elorn estuary, a pleasant mix of ancient and modern. Its upmarket shops (see panel), fine restaurants and well-kept accommodation give it a more cosmopolitan feel than most of the towns in this region, and it makes an excellent touring base for a night or two, despite the fact that it lacks seaside attractions.

There are no specific sights within the town except its bridge. The 16th-century **Pont de Rohan▶▶** is one of the few left in Europe with houses built on it. Walk to the north-east side of the bridge for a good view of the stone and slate-hung buildings mirrored in the water.

The most interesting and picturesque parts of the old town lie on the west bank of the Elorn. A wander up the main street and the sidestreets off it reveals a number of antique façades, turreted and ornamented with statues in niches. The Maison de Rohan at the east end of the old bridge has a fine sundial. The town's two historic churches are St-Houardon, with a Renaissance domed tower, and St-Thomas-de-Cantorbéry, with a three-tiered belfry and an adjacent ossuary.

▶▶ Landévennec *116C1*

The main reason to visit this hook-nosed stretch of coast on the Crozon peninsula is to see the Romanesque ruins of an abbey originally founded by St Guénolé in the 5th century. King Gradlon (see pages 18–19) is alleged to be buried here, and some of the abbey's remains show spiral or circular designs of very ancient origin. A museum of monastic history (with an audio-visual show) is housed in a neighbouring 17th-century convent building. A Benedictine community now occupies modern quarters in the village.

Landévennec's location (a *site naturel protégé*) at the mouth of the Aulne estuary is extremely pretty, and its sheltered climate cloaks it in a mass of Mediterranean-style vegetation and lush woodland.

SHOPPING IN LANDERNEAU

Landerneau is especially appealing on market day (Tuesday), when the main square is lively with stalls selling *crêpes* and farmhouse cheeses. If you are looking for souvenirs, try Comptoir des Produits Bretons on Quai de Cornouaille, where beautifully displayed Breton products include books, traditional music cassettes, boat woodcarvings, cider, food and crafts (there is another branch of this shop in Quimper).

The ruins of Landévennec abbey enjoy a remarkable setting

ST ANNE OF BRITTANY
The cult of St Anne, mother of the Virgin Mary, is strong in central Finistère (see page 20), as the statues at Landivisiau indicate. St Anne is sometimes represented in Breton art teaching Mary to read, or in a sort of alternative Trinity with Mary and the infant Jesus.

▶ Landivisiau 116C2

This sizeable cattlemarket town is scarcely riveting, but its mostly modern Gothic-style church is worth a glance (outside at least) for a very large carved porch dating from the 16th century. If you can find a parking place outside, walk down a small side alley (rue St-Thivisiau) to find the fountain of its patron saint, St Thivisiau, decorated with granite panels in low relief. In a cemetery near the tourist office, the little ossuary chapel of Ste-Anne is adorned with caryatids. Inside are a couple of quaint statues of St Anne with the Virgin and St Anne crushing a dragon.

▶ Menez-Hom 116C1

At only 330m high, this gorse-covered peak hardly qualifies as a mountain, but its elevation above the surrounding countryside makes it a popular vantage point. Cars line up at the summit for picnics on clear days in summer, while more energetic folk walk or cycle to the top. Menez-Hom is the final westerly hiccup of the Montagnes Noires, erupting suddenly from a lonely forested landscape. From the top the views extend over the whole of the Crozon and Plougastel peninsulas and Douarnenez bay, with the Noires and Arrée mountains inland. Although it is a peaceful place now, Menez-Hom was a key site in the German defence system during World War II, and was repeatedly strafed. A small chapel at the foot of the hill is dedicated to St Mary.

The sheltered harbour at Morgat is a popular sailing centre

CAP DE LA CHEVRE WALK
The coast south of Morgat consists of rocky heathland scattered with huddled hamlets of white cottages. It is an area of megaliths, with an unusual alignment formation near St-Hernot called Ty ar C'Huré (Priest's House).

▶ Menez-Meur 116C2

Open: Jun–Sep, daily 10–7. Admission charge

At the heart of the Monts d'Arrée, the Domaine de Menez-Meur is a curious mixture of country wildlife park, exhibition and information centre. It covers about 400ha of rolling upland country, through which visitors can stroll along nature trails past enclosures of local fauna such as wolves, wild boar, Highland cattle and Swaledale sheep.

A special exhibition is devoted to the sturdy Breton draught horse, and an adventure playground and bar-restaurant add to the centre's family appeal.

▶ Morgat *116B1*

More genteel than Camaret, the other main resort on the Crozon peninsula (see page 122), Morgat is a popular holiday centre, especially for water-based activities such as sailing and diving, and has an excellent curving sandy beach backed by pine trees. Tuna-fishing boats once set sail from its sheltered harbour; today most of the boats are private yachts or pleasure cruisers taking visitors round the rocky Cap de la Chèvre or to the caves beyond Beg-ar-Gador, remarkable for their vivid mineral colorations. Largest of these is **la Grotte de l'Autel (Altar Cave)▶▶**, 80m deep and 15m high. Tall openings rise from the caves to the cliffs above, where saintly hermits used to rescue shipwrecked mariners. Other, smaller caves are accessible at low tide from local beaches.

In high season a ferry service plies between Morgat and Douarnenez. There are excellent cliff walks down the coast to Cap de la Chèvre (see panel opposite).

▶▶ Pleyben *117D1*

As it is geographically separated from most of the parish closes, Pleyben is sometimes unfairly ignored. But it is one of the finest and largest, and is worth making a special detour to find. The **calvary▶▶** was originally constructed in the 16th century, but parts of it date from later periods and it has an unmistakably neoclassical air about its solid pedestal and triumphal arches. The whole structure bustles with naïve, animated scenes from Christ's life; notice the weeping witnesses of Christ's Passion, and the appetising pie ready for the Last Supper. The whole close is overshadowed by the massive twin-towered church of **St-Germain▶▶**, whose interior boasts some splendid panelling, polychrome statues, stained-glass windows and decorated roof beams.

The town has a prosperous air and welcomes visitors with *crêperies* and souvenir shops. A local confectioner (Chantillot) invites you to watch biscuits and chocolates being made, and stalls on the main square sell honey and *chouchenn* (mead).

WASH HOUSES

Wash-troughs were once a feature of every village, a great source of social interaction and gossip among the womenfolk who undertook this backbreaking task. After soaking the hempen clothes in boiling water and ashes, they took them to the wash house and beat them with paddles. Pierre-Jakez Hélias describes the routine in *The Horse of Pride*: 'When the last piece had been washed, one of the women would strip off all her lower garments and step down into the trough, her skirts tucked up to her hips, to collect the laundry...More than one of them caught their deaths for having ventured into the cold water while in a sweat.' Laundry was washed only twice a year – spring and autumn. There are good examples of wash houses at Landivisiau and Vannes.

Above left: Ankou at Landivisiau's chapel of Ste-Anne
Below: the calvary at Pleyben

The idiosyncratic parish closes of Finistère are quite unique to the region, and one of Brittany's highest forms of art. The best of them are concentrated close to the Armorique Regional Park.

SCULPTURAL THEMES
If you become interested in Breton religious art you will soon spot recurring themes among the regional parish closes. The thieves crucified with Christ, for example, are often sculpted in contorted positions, with their arms and legs wrapped awkwardly around the bars. Christ is sometimes depicted blindfolded and seated with his hands tied in his lap. Many of the ancillary figures on calvaries wear not biblical robes but the elaborate 16th-century dress of the period when the churches were built.

Argol, on the Crozon peninsula, has an exceptional triumphal arch (1659) with a statue of King Gradlon on horseback

The phrase *enclos paroissial* (parish close) refers to the enclosed cemetery around a church. It is usually walled to keep animals out, but pierced with low stiles. The main entrance, through which funeral processions pass, is generally marked by an imposing gateway, often a neo-classical triumphal arch. Inside the close, the most striking feature is the calvary. Breton calvaries are more than mere crucifixes; they are vastly elaborate sculptures detailing many biblical, and sometimes secular, scenes – the Nativity, the Last Supper, and Christ's Passion and Resurrection. These naïve carvings were worked in granite, and most are now softened by time and weathering, and covered with lichen. In the days when many parishioners were illiterate, the stone carvings provided a vivid pictorial subtext to the Church's teachings. They also reinforced the association that was ever-present in Breton society between the living and the dead – the link between generations, and the hope of resurrection amid the despair of mortality.

The typical Breton close also includes an ossuary, or charnel house. Such was the pressure on these patches of hallowed ground in times of plague or famine that every five years or so old corpses were exhumed to make room for the new ones. The bones were then placed in the ossuary, and when that in turn was full all the bones were given a grand ritual burial in a common grave. Ossuaries look like small chapels, some with a skeletal

Ankou outside to remind the living that their turn will come. Today very few still contain bones; instead they have been turned either into souvenir shops or treasury museums.

During the 16th and 17th centuries parts of Finistère grew rich on sea trade and linen, and parishes began to spend their newly acquired wealth on churches and calvaries. The most famous parish closes date from this period. Some villages became rivals, each anxious to have the biggest and best, and the most skilful masons and wood-carvers could set a high price for their work. Church interiors blossomed with baroque altarpieces and coloured statues, while beams and vaults sprouted carvings and paintings, particularly on the side beams (purlins) and on the rood, or glory, beams spanning the naves.

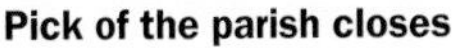

Pick of the parish closes

Brasparts St Michael slays his dragon on the calvary; lovely baroque altarpiece with blue and gold barleysugar columns decorated with vines, snakes and birds.

Guimiliau (see page 129) Vast, ornate calvary in 16th-century dress; Catell Gollet scene; altarpieces, porch, pulpit and domed baptistery.

Lampaul-Guimiliau (see page 132) The church interior is the place to look – glory beam, choirstalls, stoups and altarpieces glow with vivid detail; lovely Entombment sculpture.

Locmélar Less well known but enjoyable; cross-barred calvary, altarpieces and banners, painted beams and ceiling.

La Martyre One of the oldest closes; ossuary, triumphal door, carved porch.

Pencran 16th-century ossuary, carved porch, balconied belfry.

Pleyben (see page 135) Elaborate, very large calvary; twin-towered church with carved beams and altarpieces.

Plougastel-Daoulas (see page 138) Large, elaborate calvary and plague cross; carvings of Catell Gollet.

La Roche-Maurice Classical ossuary with Ankou figure; twin-galleried belfry; splendid rood beam.

St-Thégonnec (see pages 138–9) Triumphal arch; superb calvary; inside the church, magnificent pulpit and a life-size Holy Sepulchre sculpture.

Sizun Triumphal arch with coffin rest; ossuary; rich panelling and vaulting.

Others parish closes worth seeing Guéhenno, Lanrivain, Kergrist-Moëlou, St-Jean-du-Doigt, Argol, St-Herbot, Cléden-Poher, Lannédern, Brennilis, Pleyber-Christ, Bodilis, Berven.

CHARNEL HOUSES

Although hardly any ossuaries contain bones today, in former centuries the piled bones inside would have been clearly and horrifyingly visible. In some parish closes the skulls were kept in small boxes fixed to the ossuary walls. After 25 years or so they were taken out and added to the rest of the bones, which were recycled regularly to make room for fresh corpses.

Left: St-Thégonnec's calvary
Below: detail, Pleyben calvary

▶ Plougastel, Presqu'île de *116B2*

The ragged tatters of land that jut into Brest harbour were very isolated until the modern Albert-Louppe bridge was constructed over the Elorn estuary in 1930; even today, they are not much visited by tourists. Most of the region consists of dull countryside devoted to market gardening – particularly the luscious early strawberries that are celebrated throughout Brittany and exported in vast quantities. Strawberry growing, though, is not a spectacular activity, and most of it goes on invisibly behind hedges and plastic cloches. Other products of this mild, fertile area are shallots, tomatoes and hothouse flowers.

A few scattered chapels make focal points for excursions down the long lanes to the waterfront, from which there are attractive, but hardly obligatory, views of Brest and the Crozon peninsula. Lauberlac'h is a pretty fishing port, but there are no real resorts or good beaches here. The village of Kersanton may ring a bell; this is where much of Brittany's best monumental granite comes from – malleable, but hardening over time.

The history of the region is more interesting than its landscapes, and the best place to learn about it is in **Plougastel-Daoulas▶** itself. Most of the town is fairly dull, but the early 17th-century **calvary▶** is justly famous for its impassive granite tableaux of over 180 figures. Christ steps from his tomb, as though from a bath; the thieves' souls are greeted, one by an angel, the other by a devil; and as at Guimiliau (see page 129), poor Catell Golett is torn asunder for her sins. The calvary was built in memory of a terrible epidemic which ravaged Plougastel in 1598, and the bumps on the cross-shaft are said to represent the blisters of the plague, not the stumps of branches as on other calvaries.

PLOUGASTEL-DAOULAS MUSEUM

The Musée du Patrimoine et de la Fraise, housed in a modern building near the church, provides an absorbing and well-presented introduction to the history of this insular community, which has developed its own customs through the centuries. Farming, seafaring, local costumes and furnishings are featured, with special emphasis on the strawberry (introduced from Virginia in the 17th century) scallop-dragging and the Breuriez apple festival (*Open* Jun–mid-Sep, Mon–Sat 10–12.30, 2–6.30, Sun 2–6. *Admission charge*). Plougastel found itself uncomfortably close to Brest in World War II: its bridge was bombed and the town suffered many losses.

▶▶ St-Herbot *117D1*

The unusual square-towered church stands proudly in a wooded dell, a sheltered oasis in otherwise desolate countryside deep in Brittany's *argoat*. Outside, a lichen-mottled calvary and a Renaissance ossuary catch the eye, but the church is more interesting inside. Carved saints whirl round the main door at the top of the horseshoe staircase. A superb wooden screen surrounds the chancel, topped by a crucifixion scene where angels bear Christ's arms up, and skulls are piled on rocks below the crosses. Tufts of hair from cattle tails lie on the plain granite tables by the chancel, an offering to St Herbot, the patron of horned beasts. Lift up the choirstalls for some lovely misericords, and notice the saint's tomb, a simple block with low-relief carving.

▶▶▶ St-Thégonnec *117D2*

St-Thégonnec was one of Brittany's richest parishes in the 17th century and its close is one of the highpoints of this curiously specialised form of Breton art. Through its massive triumphal arch stands a complete set of parish close accoutrements. The multibranched **calvary▶▶▶** is one of the later versions, constructed in 1610. The biblical scenes are vividly captured. Christ's tormentors set about their sadistic work with gusto (one of them is alleged to be the Protestant king, Henry IV), angels mop up the Redeemer's blood, and the little-known St Thégonnec puts in an appearance on a low niche. Legend has it that when a wolf ate his donkey, St Thégonnec tamed it and harnessed it to his cart, where it looks like a little dog. The funerary chapel in the close contains a poignant piece of sculpture by Jacques Lespaignol – an oak-painted **Entombment▶▶** scene.

The church interior is equally sumptuous, with statues adorning every nook and altarpieces bustling with detail. St-Thégonnec's pride, however, is its **pulpit▶▶**, a *tour de force* in wood, encrusted with saints, angels, evangelists, cardinal virtues and God himself, giving Moses the tablets of stone inscribed with the words of the Ten Commandments. After this, anything else in the village is an anticlimax, except perhaps the food at its celebrated *auberge* (see Hotels and Restaurants, page 271).

WOLF COUNTRY
The story of St Thégonnec, whose donkey was eaten by a wolf, is made a little more credible by a local stationmaster in the late 19th century who mentioned the wolves which visited the village in winter – 'one of which has killed my favourite dog'. Until this century wolf-hunting was a popular and necessary sport in Brittany from October to January, when hungry wolves were a real threat to local communities.

HENRY THE APOSTATE
The Protestant King Henry IV was the archetypal pragmatist. His cynical conversion to Catholicism in 1592 ('Paris is worth a Mass') gained him little respect among the villagers of St-Thégonnec, where he is immortalised on the calvary as one of the principal tormentors of Christ. But Henry's expediency averted national insurrection, and when the Edict of Nantes was signed two years later, the debilitating Wars of Religion came (at least temporarily) to an end (see pages 38–9).

Details on the calvary at St-Thégonnec: Christ Reviled (above) with Roman soldiers and (below) the Deposition scene

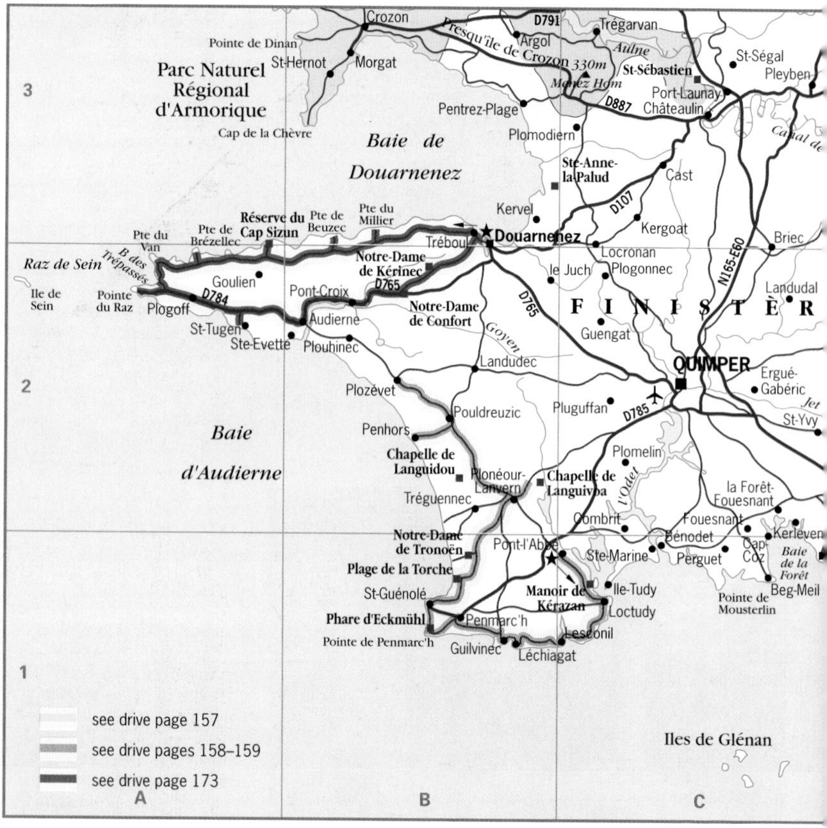

see drive page 157
see drive pages 158–159
see drive page 173

Breton costumes proudly worn at Pont-l'Abbé, one of the most traditional of all the Cornouaille towns

Cornouaille

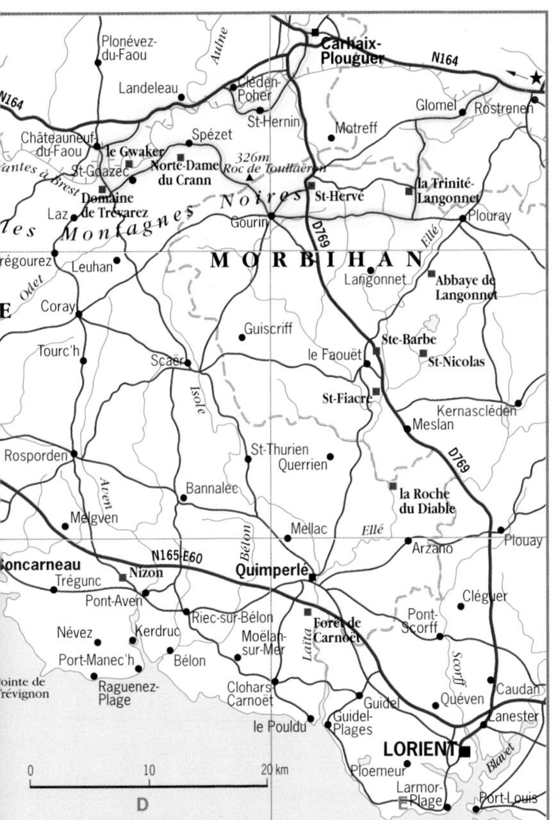

CORNOUAILLE Cornouaille is in many ways the most typically Breton part of Brittany and its natural and cultural features contribute to its immense popularity as a holiday destination. With a south-westerly maritime location, it is alternately soothed by the mild Gulf Stream and battered by Atlantic storms, and its landscapes offer both bleakness and welcoming havens. Its Celtic heritage, the most apparent and carefully preserved in Brittany, and the strip of coastline between Pont-l'Abbé and le Pouldu attract vast numbers of holidaymakers during the season.

Inland, the large town of Quimper acts as regional headquarters and is well worth a day's exploration. On a smaller scale, Locronan and Quimperlé shouldn't be missed. A tour of the Montagnes Noires, which straddle the borders of three *départements*, makes an interesting picnic outing. Aside from these, Cornouaille's interior is unexceptional, and its attention focuses steadfastly on the sea. A blend of idyllic sheltered beaches, picturesque wooded estuaries, apple orchards and quaint fishing towns gives this area its distinctive charm. The Sizun and Penmarc'h peninsulas add more rugged ingredients to coastal excursions, though their relative lack of creature comforts makes them less suitable as resort bases. Beaches, too, can be dangerous on these exposed shores and are less than ideal for children or anyone who is a weak swimmer.

▶▶▶ **REGION HIGHLIGHTS**

Cap Sizun *pages 172–3*

Concarneau *page 148*

Locronan *page 156*

Montagnes Noires *page 157*

Pont-Aven *page 162*

Quimper *page 168*

THE GLÉNAN DAFFODIL
St-Nicolas, one of the Glénan islands (see page 154), claims the smallest nature reserve in France, a tiny plot of land protecting one of Europe's rarest flowers. Le Narcisse de Glénan was allegedly brought to the island by Phoenician sailors, and first identified as a unique species in 1903. It is a tiny plant, so fragile that it is easily swamped by more rampant vegetation. A flock of sheep therefore grazes the reserve, and visitors are asked to keep dogs on a lead. Though a host of silvery flowers can be seen blooming in April and May, picking them is, of course, strictly forbidden.

Fishing boats take on a festive air at Douarnenez, one of Brittany's major fishing ports

LIVING FROM THE SEA Cornouaille has an ancient and venerable pedigree. It was once a kingdom – according to legend the seat of King Gradlon, whose great city of Ys lies beneath the waves in the bay of Douarnenez (see pages 18–19). When Ys was submerged, Gradlon set up his court in Quimper, which is still the regional capital. During the Middle Ages, Cornouaille was a Duchy whose boundaries stretched as far north as Morlaix. After the union of Brittany and France, the region's importance diminished, and it suffered economic decline and isolation over the following centuries. Its people retained their fiercely independent streak, however, and stood their ground bravely against the monstrous taxes imposed by Colbert to finance the Sun King's extravagance. Linen-weaving and the manufacture of hempen sailcloth made the merchants of Locronan wealthy for a while, but even these industries eventually slid into sharp recession.

Fishing alone remains a great staple, and even today Cornouaille's ports are among the foremost in France – notably Douarnenez and Concarneau. These are unpretentious working towns that still earn their living from the sea, as generations have done before them, albeit with state-of-the-art technology these days. To find out more about fishing, visit the excellently presented museums in each of these towns (Musée du Bateau and Musée de la Pêche) and, if possible, an early morning *criée* (fish auction) by the harbour, where the night's catch is sold and distributed to markets throughout France. Tourists are welcome at these events, but *criées* these days are businesslike affairs in modern sheds rather than picturesque market scenes. Keep your wits about you or you may be bowled over by a crate of haddock on a fork-lift truck. Local seafood, needless to say, is excellent, complemented by rich dairy produce from the interior and the best Breton cider, produced mostly around Fouesnant.

LOCAL TRADITIONS Cornouaille is the most Celtic region of Brittany, and culturally it is enormously rich. Here,

A HEAD ABOVE THE WAVES

In his book, *The Horse of Pride*, Pierre-Jakez Hélias recounts a fascinating anecdote from the 1930s, when Brittany was opening up to seaside tourism in a big way: '...one day, mark my words, a girl wearing a tall Bigouden *coiffe*, dressed all in black velvet bordered with glass beads, arrives by the jetty. When a moment later she gets out again, she is wearing a black bathing costume, but she has kept her *coiffe* on her head. She runs to the sea, plunges into it and begins to swim. And it's an astonishing sight to watch the girl's *coiffe* sailing lightly on the bright swelling sea.'

Quimperlé and its church of Notre-Dame-de-l'Assomption

particularly in the Pays Bigouden (Penmarc'h peninsula), you can find traces of a rural lifestyle that is centuries old, epitomised most memorably in the remarkable *coiffes*, or headdresses, of the region, which are exaggerated here into enormously tall towers of lace. These *bigoudènes* are increasingly rare nowadays, and are seen mostly in museums or at festivals to impress tourists. In remoter byways, though, you may still glimpse older women wearing them behind net curtains as everyday garments. Such hats are said to be character-forming, and indeed, keeping them on in anything above the lightest breeze must require great ingenuity.

For a detailed look at the folk history of the region, visit Pont-l'Abbé's castle museum, followed by a tour of Penmarc'h. Quimper also encapsulates much local Breton culture (see the departmental museum and, if possible, the Festival de Cornouaille in July). For more background, track down Pierre-Jakez Hélias's autobiographical account of his Bigouden childhood near the village of Plozévet, *The Horse of Pride* (Yale, 1978). A rich social tapestry woven against a canvas of backbreaking labour and poverty brings this region to life more forcefully than any museum bonnet collection.

Cornouaille's culture is not all *coiffes* and costumes, however. In the late 19th century it fostered the famous Pont-Aven School of artists, whose most talented exponent was Gauguin. To follow the artists' trail, visit Quimper's Musée des Beaux-Arts, followed by Pont-Aven and le Pouldu. Local people and landscapes were the main sources of inspiration for these painters, as they are for many resident artists and craftworkers today.

The charming houses of Pont-Croix are well worth exploring

MOELAN-SUR-MER
The quiet, scattered hamlets around the Bélon estuary attract an increasing number of visitors. The countryside is deeply rural, with low-lying, sometimes waterlogged pastureland divided by screens of elms. The village of Moëlan (no longer *sur mer*) acts as the regional centre. It has some useful food shops and a helpful tourist office which freely dispenses guides to local walks, antiquities and other places of interest. Glance at the 15th-century calvary in the chapel of St-Philibert if you are passing through. The region boasts an unusually good selection of seafood restaurants (all, of course, offering oysters), and one exceptional hotel, Les Moulins du Duc (see Hotels and Restaurants, page 271).

Audierne's picturesque harbour

▶ Audierne *140B2*

The Goyen estuary meets the sea at Audierne, a fishing port sheltered from the open sea by an obliging triangular headland, the Pointe de Lervily. Audierne's extensive river frontage gives it breathing space and the town spreads itself handsomely along the west bank beneath a wooded hill. Moored boats blend appropriately with the wealthy shipowners' houses ranged along the quayside. The main beach is some way downstream at Ste-Evette.

Audierne's prosperity was built on fishing, and there was once a thriving tuna fleet here which sailed as far as Africa. Douarnenez's modern port facilities attract the deep-sea fishermen now, and today Audierne's daily catch is more likely to consist of langoustines, lobsters and crab, conveniently available in the local ***viviers*** (enclosed fish-breeding tanks). These form one of the largest fish farms in France, and visitors are welcome.

Audierne's other place of interest is **La Chaumière (The Thatched Cottage)▶** (*Open* Apr–Oct, daily 10–1, 2–7. *Admission charge*) directly opposite the fish farm on the corniche road to the south. An ancient mariner will show you round his 17th-century ancestral home, a splendid re-creation of a Breton family house that is full of fascinating details and space-saving storage ideas. Wooden spoons are stacked in a circular holder above an ingenious sliding table, and you can almost see the populous family of the sepia photographs tucking hungrily into fish soup around this dining table, or clambering into the box beds.

You can walk beside the wooded Goyen, but there are no boats upstream. From Ste-Evette, however, there is a regular boat service to the Ile de Sein (see page 172). The chapel of **St-Tugen▶**, 4km west of Audierne, is a Gothic

building renovated in the 17th and 18th centuries, with an elegantly traceried south porch and a fountain dedicated to its patron. St Tugen can also be found in the chancel in sculpted form, bearing his miraculous keys to keep rabid dogs at bay. During the Middle Ages, pilgrims paid handsomely for copies of these leaden keys, hoping the saint's blessing would work the same magic. Notice the chimney and firedogs in the baptismal chapel, and the strange catafalque bearing statues of Adam and Eve.

▶ Beg-Meil *140C1*

This peaceful resort is immensely popular with families who eschew the brighter lights of Bénodet. Many visit regularly enough to remember with regret the stately pine trees that graced the promenade before the great storm of October 1987. Today Beg-Meil seems well established but slightly underdressed, though its setting is undeniably pretty – a placid postcard scene of sandy coves, dunes and rockpools. It occupies a corner site, one aspect facing the sheltered bay of Concarneau, the other looking towards the open sea. Bright boats bring lobsters ashore, but there is nothing much else to distract from the simple pleasures of the seaside.

Paddling in the shallows at Beg-Meil, an ideal family seaside resort

You can sail and dive here, or take boat excursions to the Iles de Glénan (see page 154), across the bay to Concarneau, or up the Odet river. Footpaths follow the wooded shoreline northwards towards Cap-Coz, a sandy nose jutting a kilometre into the Baie de la Forêt, where houses and simple hotels are shaded by a promenade of surviving pines.

▶ Bélon *141D1*

The main reason to search for this tiny hamlet scattered over the wooded mud flats of the Bélon estuary is to eat oysters, which outnumber the human population by an astronomical factor. It's a confusing place, spanning both banks of an unbridged and serpentine river. To find the oysterbeds, head for the north bank via Riec-sur-Bélon.

Bélons are the original native flat oysters, farmed here from their spat stage to supply the beds of Cancale on the Emerald Coast (see pages 50–1). Gourmets should seek out the deceptively simple bar-restaurants which specialise in local molluscs, such as Chez Jacky or La Cabane. Several smart hotels tucked into leafy hideaways cater for sophisticated tastes.

One of Cornouaille's smartest and most comfortable hotels is at Audierne

THE OYSTER PRINCE
Maurice Sailland, a celebrated gourmet and *bon viveur* who wrote several gastronomic tomes under the pen-name of Curnonsky, adopted the little hamlet of Riec-sur-Bélon as a wartime retreat between 1914 and 1918. He is believed to have attended over 4,000 public banquets during his life, and his appearance in any French restaurant commanded hushed respect and terror among the kitchen staff. At Riec, however, he enjoyed the relaxed hospitality of Madame Mélanie Rouet, who had the reputation of being the best cook in Brittany, possessing special ways with oysters.

SUNSET STRIP
Bénodet faces due west and enjoys spectacular sunsets from its sheltered location. A late stroll by the river beside the lighthouse and the port when some of the summer crowds have dispersed is one of the best ways to appreciate the resort.

▶▶ Bénodet *140C1*

Bénodet has undeniable advantages, though its popularity and fashionable image perhaps lead it to think rather more highly of itself than it deserves. It lacks the friendliness and good value of less sought-after Breton resorts, and the promotion of its tourist facilities is unusually pushy. In summer, expect large crowds.

Boat trips galore Apart from its natural setting and an odd scrap of fortress, Bénodet has no sights or historic buildings. However, for seaside activities it is hard to beat. There are tennis courts and swimming pools, a public golf course a short distance inland at Clohars-Fouesnant, clean Blue Flag bathing beaches (see page 126), and a magnificent sailing school at le Letty, in the tidal lagoon sheltered by a strange long dune. You can windsurf or canoe, rent bikes or horses, and take a bewildering range of boat trips. One excursion not to miss is a trip up the Odet river, confidently trumpeted in Bénodet's tourist literature as the prettiest estuary in France; artists have frequently considered its green shores and clear water a worthy subject. The best bit is the wooded gorge-like scenery around les Vire-Court (literally 'short-tack') where sailboats must weave skilfully back and forth to avoid the banks. About half a dozen river cruisers leave Bénodet each day during the high season, these taking about an hour and a quarter to reach Quimper.

Above and below: there is no shortage of summer activities at Bénodet

By day, the charm of Bénodet's setting is best admired from the **Phare de la Pyramide (Pyramid Lighthouse)**. If you can manage the 191 steps, the balcony near the lantern rewards you with a fine panorama of the bay of Concarneau and the Iles de Glénan, plus the Odet estuary inland. St-Gilles Point to the south and the viewpoint on the Avenue de Kercreven over the port also make good camera angles.

Even after dark there are places to go in Bénodet (nightlife is a rare commodity in Brittany), including a couple of night-clubs and a

casino. None of the resort's activities could be described as rowdy, however, and it still retains something of a village-like air despite much speculative tourist development. Accommodation is generally unremarkable and overpriced (including its cramped campsites), but there are a few good places to eat, particularly the attractively cottagey Ferme du Letty out near the sailing school (see Hotels and Restaurants, page 280).

Escaping the crowds To escape the crowds, take the graceful modern road bridge (Pont de Cornouaille – excellent views) or the little shuttle ferry across the Odet to the picturesque backwater of **Ste-Marine▶▶**, a tranquil scene of old cottages, pine-clad rock and sand beaches, and small fishing boats. There is one simple but charming shuttered hotel on the waterfront, and a serious restaurant called L'Agape (see Hotels and Restaurants, page 280). A glorious pale sandy beach (Plage du Teven) of almost tropical beauty stretches west towards Ile-Tudy. Other long beaches stretch out towards the **Pointe de Mousterlin▶**, where camping is popular and there are extensive views of the whole bay. Inland, the little 12th-century chapel of Ste-Brigitte at **Perguet** has an excellent example of Finistère's typical church architecture: an exterior roof staircase leads up to the belfry.

Nature and tradition The **Parc botanique de Cornouaille**, a 3.5ha natural park off the D44 road, between Pont-L'Abbé and Combrit, is a continuous feast of colours from April to September as its camellias, rhododendrons, magnolias, azaleas, heather and rosebushes flower in turn (*Open* daily 10–7; Apr, Sun only. *Admission charge*). Near by, in the village of Combrit, the **Musée du Cidre Bigouden** has guided tours in English, ending with a visit to the workshops, where cider is turned into brandy, and free tastings (*Open* mid-May–mid-Sep, Mon–Sat 10–12, 2.30–7. *Admission charge*).

Bénodet, at the mouth of the Odet estuary

ENGLISH LOCUSTS

'No Egyptian ever dreaded the approach of a swarm of locusts more than the native residents of the little towns of France do the settling down of a flight of English. For the result in both cases is the same – scarcity and dearness of every article of consumption...I met, in the remoter parts of Britanny [*sic*], three or four old Englishmen, many years resident in the country, who constantly retreat before the advancing flood of their countrymen like the squatters, those pioneers of civilisation in the western forests of America, knowing that to live cheaply they must find some part of the country where English gold has not yet penetrated.'
– Thomas Adolphus Trollope, *A Summer in Brittany*, shows that mass tourism is nothing new. He wrote this in 1839 about Dinan; today it could apply to Bénodet.

CRIÉES
Concarneau's celebrated fish auctions, or *criées*, are held by the Arrière-Port in the early morning. The fishing boats unload their catches between midnight and 6am, after which they are rapidly sold to the highest bidder. Don't expect any *folklorique* fishwives crying cockles and mussels on the quayside; fish auctions are a serious and highly competitive affair these days, and the proceedings resemble an anglers' stock exchange. Visitors are welcome to the large modern sheds (there are even guided tours a couple of times a week in July and August). Arrive before 7am if you want to see any action.

Concarneau takes on a festive air in high season

►► Concarneau *141C1*

This is still one of France's most important fishing ports, on the east flank of a deep bay where shipping takes refuge from Atlantic storms. Whales and sardines have all figured in its former prosperity; although West African tuna still appears, at today's *criée* (fish auction) a huge variety of sea creatures gasp their last in crates of ice. Concarneau combines its piscatorial role with tourism now, offering boat trips up the Odet or to the Iles de Glénan (a 25-minute hydrojet service) and capitalising on the sandy beaches that lie both north and south of the town in the sheltered Baie de la Forêt. These are not Brittany's best: the town beaches such as the Plage des Sables Blancs look a bit tired in high season, and others near the Pointe du Cabellou to the south can be covered in seaweed at certain times.

Island stronghold The best part of Concarneau is its lively old port. The **Ville Close►►**, or walled town, separates the pleasure craft in the marina from the serious business of the inner harbour. This charming citadel measures little more than a kilometre across, and can easily be explored in an hour or two.

Like St-Malo's *intra muros* quarter (see pages 66–7), Concarneau's Ville Close is on an island, linked to the rest of the town by a fortified bridge and gateway. Concarneau was first fortified in the 11th century, then steadily beefed up by the Normans until, by the 14th century, it was considered impregnable. The English held it for over 30 years after the War of Succession, when they occupied it in support of Jean de Montfort. Even the mighty Du Guesclin (see pages 34–5) had to besiege it three times before it fell and the English were driven out. During Louis XIV's reign the military strategist Vauban altered and strengthened it still further, lopping the tops off its towers and erecting the great ramparts that protect the Ville Close from maritime invasion. Although it was restored in the 19th century, the Ville Close looks much the same today as it did in Vauban's time.

The fortified entrance has a friendlier aspect today. Sundials and tubs of geraniums decorate the clock-tower gate, and the cannon are now merely ornamental. Today, the invading hordes of tourists who cram into the picturesque narrow alleys during summer are bombarded more seductively with handmade chocolates and biscuits. Less welcomingly, the town charges an entrance fee to climb the ramparts, but access at the far end is free of charge, and gateways piercing the walls give satisfying glimpses of the port beyond. There is one smart (and expensive) hotel-

LA FÊTE DES FILETS BLEUS
In late August Concarneau holds its famous Blue Nets Festival. Originally set up in 1905 to help the families of distressed sardine fishermen whose catches were failing, the mix of music, parades and folk events is similar to many summer festivals held in Brittany. The nets used for Concarneau's sardine fishing fleet were traditionally blue, hence the name, but modern nets are usually brown.

The fortress entrance gate to Concarneau's walled Ville Close

restaurant within the walls, Le Galion (see Hotels and Restaurants, page 272), but plenty of fast food and ice-cream among the souvenirs.

Fishy business Do not miss the excellent **Musée de la Pêche▶▶** (*Open* Jul– Aug, daily 9.30–7.30; Sep–Jun 10–12, 2–5. *Admission charge*) in the Ville Close, housed in the former arsenal on the main street. Every kind of net, line, block and tackle seems to be on display, along with some ancient sardine tins and model fishing craft. In general, the museum's presentation is very good, though labelling is only in French. Wood-and-leather clog-wellingtons, giant scooping nets and a monster coelacanth enliven informative displays on the movements of fish stocks through the oceans, and the operation of drag nets. Slide shows complete the visit. Outside, spry visitors can explore an old 34m trawler moored by the walls – not exactly a comfortable or luxurious workplace.

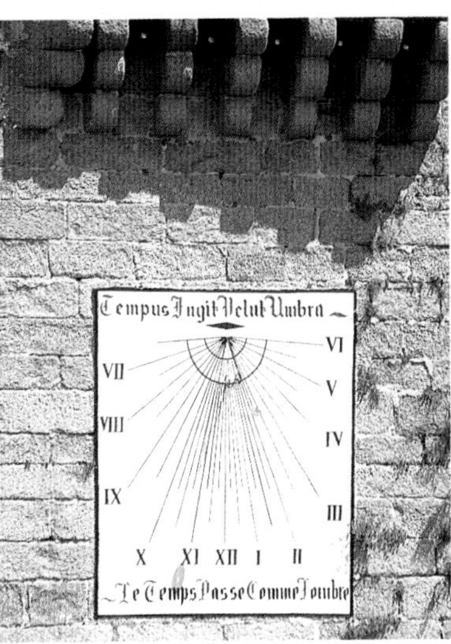

Above: Concarneau does a brisk trade in matelot *gear*
Left: the sundial on Concarneau's walls reminds visitors that time flies

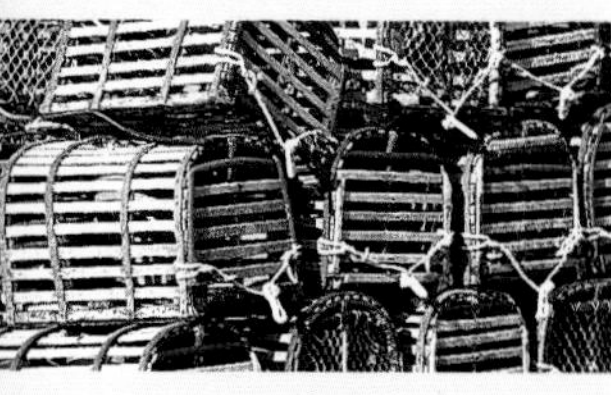

Brittany is still France's most important fishing region, but where former generations braved the eternal perils of storm and shipwreck, today's fishing communities face less tangible threats – the depletion of fish stocks and competition from foreign imports.

A DANGEROUS LIVING
The *Terre-neuvas* (Newfoundlanders) and *Islandais* (Icelanders) brought prosperity to north Breton shores from the end of the 15th to the 19th centuries. The fleets left Brittany in early March and returned in August via the coast of Gascony, where they sold their fish for a good price and replenished their stocks of salt. Life on board was hard and dangerous, and whenever a shoal of cod was discovered sleep was abandoned and the crews worked day and night without pause.

Business or pleasure Fishing is both a serious, hazardous industry and a pleasurable pastime in Brittany. For centuries a large proportion of the region's inhabitants have made a living from the sea, setting sail from their homes, sometimes for six months of the year, to face terrible dangers and hardships. Less riskily, whole families spend happy Sundays ferreting through rockpools with hoes and trowels in pursuit of edible molluscs and crustaceans. Others sit patiently on riverbanks waiting for bobbing floats or twitching lines. Cradle nets dangle from bamboo poles attached to stilt-huts on the Rance and Vilaine, and in the Grande Brière marsh-eels are harpooned from flat-bottomed barges. Altogether, Brittany has about 9,600km of river bank and shoreline for recreational fishing. Fishing for pleasure is immensely popular throughout the region, and discarded tackle can be a minefield for wildlife and leisure sailors.

Deep-sea fishing Until the beginning of this century, hundreds of boats from North Brittany worked the rich fishing grounds around Iceland and Newfoundland. Pierre Loti's novel *Pêcheur d'Islande* (see panel on page 81), gives a flavour of Paimpol's fishing industry in the late 19th century; today, only St-Malo still sends vessels to trawl the cod and haddock banks of the North Atlantic. From Cornouaille, summer fleets head south, chasing tuna, mackerel and sardine shoals around West Africa and the Azores. In winter the boats are used for other types of fishing. Today only a handful of fleets are truly ocean-going. Most deep-sea fishing from Brittany is done in the Bay of Biscay or the Irish Sea. To compete effectively, boats must be rigged out expensively with the latest refrigeration equipment and computerised navigational aids.

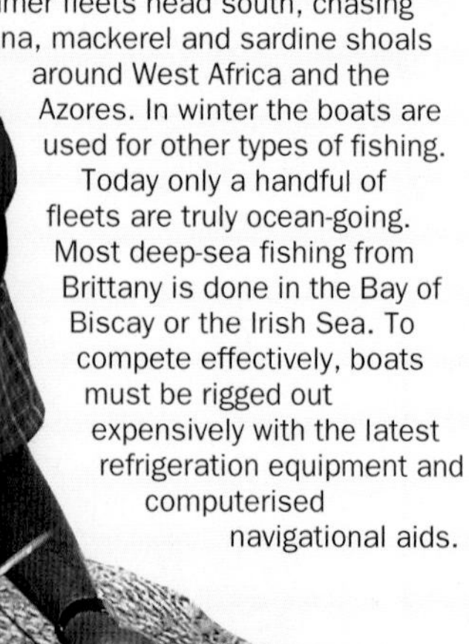

Net-mending is still done the old way in some of Brittany's fishing ports

Both salt- and smoke-curing have given way to ice as a method of preservation. The catch is graded, filleted and packed for market on board, and then swiftly distributed in efficient containerised transport as soon as it is landed. Concarneau, Douarnenez, Lorient and St-Malo are Brittany's largest fishing ports, though there are many smaller fishing towns all around the Breton coast, whose fleets hug inshore waters for sole and turbot, mullet and skate. About 12,000 Bretons earn their living by fishing, or in associated shore-based industries such as canning and processing. About two-thirds of France's canned fish is produced in Brittany.

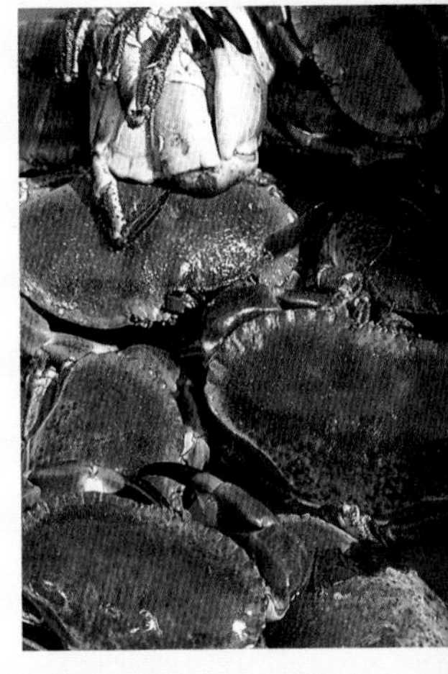

Breton shellfish is often farmed today

Dispatching the fish The best way to get a feel of this vital industry is to visit the fishing harbours when the boats arrive, and attend one of the *criées* (fish auctions – see panel on page 148). The night catch is unloaded very early in the morning and sold from about 6.30am onwards in large warehouses by the quayside. Plastic crates overflow with all kinds of grotesque sea creatures, and forklift trucks dart everywhere. The auction process is fast and furious, with loudhailers and frantic telephoning. The best and biggest *criées* are held at Concarneau and Douarnenez, and the excellent fishing and boat museums in these towns provide further background. Other Penmarc'h fishing towns (Guilvinec, Lesconil, Loctudy and Audierne) also hold *criées*, some in the afternoon.

Colourful boats

Fish farming Increasingly, fish farming satisfies the voracious appetites of the restaurant trade. Oysters now spend their lives preparing for the table in sacks of plastic mesh, while mussels attach themselves guilelessly to conveniently accessible ropes hung from wooden posts. Salmon and trout no longer swim oceans and leap waterfalls, but flap listlessly in overcrowded ponds. If you enjoy Brittany's glorious variety of seafood (and there are few who do not), try visiting a *vivier* (fish farm) to see what goes on behind those *cotriades* and *assiettes de fruits de mer.* Cancale, Roscoff and Audierne have some of the largest artificial breeding grounds in France for oysters, lobsters, crab and *langoustines.*

WHALING

Breton whalers ventured into the northern seas from the 15th to the 17th centuries. 'Whaling was not then the safe, mechanised slaughter it has since become: the harpoon was hand-thrown at close quarters, with considerable risk to life and limb... The Bretons were renowned for their endurance and quiet determination, though at times of danger they were capable of sublime eccentricity,' wrote Jules Michelet in the 19th century.

The Ile Tristan, just off Douarnenez

►► Douarnenez

140B3

Ranking just after Concarneau in France's fishing port league, Douarnenez has a similarly workmanlike atmosphere. The older, pinkish-beige buildings around the Port du Rosmeur give it some character, though it lacks any picturesque old quarter to rival Concarneau's Ville Close. It has a significant sardine fleet, but also specialises in lobster and deep-sea fishing. The port's prosperity soared in the latter half of the 19th century, after François Appert invented a technique of preserving food by sterilising and hermetically sealing it in tins. Today, canning factories surround the quays, where a *criée* (fish auction) is held early in the morning.

The drowned city The modern facilities of the Nouveau Port attract trawler fishermen from afar, but Douarnenez is a very ancient town, pre-dating even Roman times when it was a famous production centre for *garum* (fermented fish oil), an important ingredient in Roman cuisine. In the Dark Ages, the town became associated with King Mark and the Tristan legend. It was also one of the disputed sites of Brittany's mythical Atlantis – the Lost City of Ys, drowned by King Gradlon's daughter (see pages 18–19). As in most of these tales, church bells ring beneath the waves of Douarnenez bay for those with ears to hear them. There may be a grain of truth in the legend somewhere, for sea levels certainly did rise sharply in this part of Brittany at some stage around the 6th century.

Boats and beaches As with most of Brittany's seaside towns, Douarnenez puts in a bid for its slice of the tourism trade. The resort area lies in Tréboul across the Port-Rhu river, linked by a 24m-high steel bridge. Tréboul is a renowned sailing centre with a large, modern marina, and also offers thalassotherapy. Sea-fishing trips and excursions round the bay leave from Rosmeur in the summer, when a ferry service also links Douarnenez with Morgat on the Crozon peninsula (see page 135).

Douarnenez has comparatively few sights, though the **Musée du Bateau►►►**, a maritime complex on the old harbour of the Port-Rhu river, is definitely worth a

ST TUTUARN'S ISLAND

One explanation of the origin of Douarnenez's name is that it is a corruption of *Tutuarn-Enez* (St Tutuarn's island), after a 6th-century hermit who lived on the offshore rock known as Ile Tristan.

DAHUD

The legend of Ys (see pages 18–19) is really a Christian morality tale. Douarnenez was sacred to the Celtic horse-god Marc'h, a Druidic deity. King Gradlon's daughter, Dahud, had apparently remained faithful to the old pagan beliefs while her father had been converted to Christianity by St Guénolé. Dahud's downfall symbolises the conquest of paganism in Cornouaille.

detour. This vast museum, which occupies the whole harbour area, has a wonderful collection of sailing and fishing craft moored on the banks. Some of these boats can be visited in summer: steam tugs, sand dredgers, tuna boats – even a Thames barge and a lightship. Many maritime events, regattas and ship-handling demonstrations are organised, and the floating harbour of Port-Rhu welcomes historic ships. Around the museum, many craftsmen contribute to Les Ateliers de l'Enfer, an apprenticeship centre devoted to traditional shipbuilding, woodcarving (including figureheads) and the art of making models. Unusually, this Breton museum also caters to the inner man, woman or child: a suitably nautical-looking *crêperie* dishes up sustenance on the quayside.

The entrance charge to the **Musée du Bateau** also admits you to the indoor **boat museum**▶▶ (*Open* mid-Jun–Sep, daily 10–7; Oct–Dec, Feb–mid-Jun, Tue–Sun 10–12.30, 2–6. *Closed* Jan. *Admission charge*), housed in a handsome old canning factory where all kinds of boat-building techniques can be watched. Here, dozens of genuine old boats are imaginatively displayed, from simple Severn coracles and flat-bottomed Brière barges to a 19th-century clipper.

Douarnenez bay has many beaches, but some of them are dangerous for swimming. Tréboul's main beach is the Plage des Sables Blancs. A pleasant footpath, the Sentier des Plomarc'h, leads from the old harbour 2km eastwards to the Plage du Ris, backed by pinewood cliffs. Ile Tristan, at the mouth of the Port-Rhu river, is the subject of many legends and was the haunt of the 16th-century bandit, La Fontenelle (see panel). The suburbs and surrounding villages have a number of arresting churches, such as **le Juch**, with its quaint statue of St Michael slaying his dragon, and some fine old glass.

LA FONTENELLE

This vicious bandit terrorised the Pays Bigouden from his lair (Ile Tristan) in the late 16th century, using his Catholicism as an excuse to attack the mainly Protestant population of the Penmarc'h peninsula. He killed over 5,000 peasants and carried off 300 boatloads of booty. At first Henry IV dealt with him surprisingly leniently, demanding only that his private army should be disbanded, but eventually he was accused of plotting against the king and broken on the wheel in 1602.

Above: traditional sailing boats can still be seen occasionally on the Breton coast, sometimes restored as pleasure craft, sometimes in maritime museums

Left: Douarnenez harbour combines business with pleasure – sailboats in the marina, fishing smacks in the port

FOUESNANT
This is a pleasant enough town, though it has little of great interest except its 12th-century church, where a modern war memorial by the Breton sculptor, Quillivic, depicts a woman in local costume mourning for the dead. Fouesnant is in the centre of a very fertile fruit-growing region. Apples and cherries are its speciality, and it is reputed to produce the best cider in Brittany. If you turn up in summer you may get a chance to taste the produce at the pardon of Ste Anne at the end of July, or, in mid-July, at the Fête des Pommiers (Apple Tree Festival) , when religious ceremonies merge into bibulous celebrations.

WET-WET-WET
Les Balneïdes, on the Beg-Meil road out of Fouesnant, is a well-designed indoor water park with the longest water-slide in Brittany. If there's too much water outside, try this aquatic paradise, maintained at a comfortably steady 30°C. Saunas, whirlpools, cascades and waterchutes provide a range of both gentle and exhilarating fun for the whole family.

▶ La Forêt-Fouesnant *140C2*

Smart yachts clank their rigging in the vast 1,000-berth marina here at the end of a beautiful wooded inlet, the fjord-like creek of the St-Laurent river. At high tide the water forms a spectacularly scenic looking-glass, inverting boats and trees with sharp-edged perfection; at low tide it disintegrates into a snake of mud. Needless to say, the marina is a Mecca for keen sailors, the old fishing port seeming dead in contrast. Campers also flock here, though the best beach is at Kerleven, about 2km away.

In the village of Fouesnant itself, the 16th-century **church▶** has an unusual calvary with four corner pilasters. Local walks and drives along the wooded coast road make for attractive tours, and there are boat trips to the Iles de Glénan and up the River Odet.

▶ Iles de Glénan *140C1*

The Glénans are famous for their birdlife (terns, cormorants and the like) and for a prestigious sailing school based around three of the islands. You can see this compact archipelago on clear days from most of Cornouaille's south coast, and it makes enough of an impact to attract 2,000 visitors a day in high season. The island group consists of some nine islets ranged around a lagoon of calm water called La Chambre, about 18km south of Concarneau. Several resorts run regular boat services to the islands, allowing a day, or half a day, to explore. Concarneau's hydrojet service whisks you here in 25 minutes; longer boat services ply from Bénodet, Beg-Meil, Loctudy, Quimper, Ste-Marine and la Forêt-Fouesnant. Since facilities on the islands are limited, it is a good idea to pack a picnic. Visitors can land at St-Nicholas only, which can be explored on foot in half an hour.

A poignant war memorial by the Breton sculptor Quillivic at Fouesnant's old church

Very little wine is produced in Brittany today. Muscadet, the wine of the Nantes region, now comes officially from the Pays de la Loire. Brittany's more authentic tipple is cider, which makes an excellent accompaniment to crêpes.

Cider and other drinks Cider in shops is sold in corked bottles as *cidre bouché*, and may be still or sparkling. In more traditional bars or restaurants you may be offered local rough cider from a bowl (beware: it can be extremely strong). Pear cider (*poiré*) is made in small quantities around Pontivy, and a fierce cider brandy (*lambig*) is distilled in some areas. The best cider is alleged to come from around Rennes and the Rance valley, or Fouesnant in Cornouaille. Several cider producers have opened little exhibitions or museums on cider-making (at Pleuhiden, la Forêt-Fouesnant and Argol).

Beer is also a local drink. The traditional brew was Cervoise, a barley beer. Now real ale is produced in Morlaix, which visitors are invited to inspect and sample at the Coreff brewery (see page 106). Mead, or *chouchenn*, also known as *hydromel*, is a sweet, honey-based drink, best served chilled. Various local *eaux-de-vie* (fruit-flavoured spirits) are also available, perhaps the most unusual of which is a strawberry liqueur that is produced in the Plougastel region.

Cider is still made in traditional presses in a few places; this one can be seen in the Rance valley

Wines A few truly Breton vines still struggle on the Rhuys peninsula, as they have done since Roman times. The resulting wine, however, doesn't match the standard of the wines produced in the 12,000ha of vineyards near Nantes. Best of these is the AOC Muscadet de Sèvre et Maine, a crisp, dry, white wine ideal with seafood. Look for the words '*sur lie*' on the label, meaning the wine is fermented 'on the lees' (in other words, on the grape pips and skins, which produces a much better flavour). Lesser wines of the Pays Nantais include ordinary Muscadet, Muscadet des Côteaux de la Loire, Côteaux d'Ancenis (white, red or rosé) and the widely available white VDQS Gros Plant, an undemanding companion for dishes such as shellfish or *galettes*.

Muscadet de Sèvre et Maine

THE HARD STUFF
Cynics say that you need three people and a wall to help you drink the potent wine from the Rhuys peninsula: one to pour it out, one either side to stop you keeling over, and the wall behind to prop you up as you collapse backwards!

SHOPPING IN LOCRONAN
Several of the old buildings on the main square now house craft shops and studios offering tasteful souvenirs. The Maison des Artisans, next to the church, is the most obvious of these, with local linen (fashioned into napkins and tablecloths nowadays rather than galleon sails), ceramics, wood-carvings and woollens ranged on three floors of a splendidly antique house. Flax and wool are spun and woven here, while other residents make a living from tea shops, antique trading or health foods. A glassworks can be visited on the Châteaulin road.

▶▶ Locronan *140C2*

Some claim that this is the prettiest town in Brittany. Roman Polanski thought it evoked Thomas Hardy's Wessex, and used it as a film-set for his mud-spattered version of *Tess of the d'Urbervilles*. The 'old town' is actually very small, confined mainly to a magnificent cobbled square surrounded by a perfectly preserved assembly of Renaissance merchants' mini-mansions, all pedimented dormers and lopsided timbering.

Locronan's prosperity derived from sailcloth manufacture. It cornered the market in the 17th century, supplying not only the French navy but also Spanish and English merchant shipping. However, when Louis XIV abolished Locronan's monopoly on hempen sailcloth the town's economy soon collapsed, leaving it fossilised in its glamorous heyday like an insect in amber.

The small **museum▶▶** (*Open* Jun–Sep, daily 10–6.30. *Admission charge*), outlines the town's history and its artistic associations (Yves Tanguy, the Surrealist painter, lived in rue Lann). Today, Locronan has recovered something of its affluence through tourism; crowds flock to the town and are requested to leave their cars outside and walk. A select handful of hotels and restaurants make Locronan an attractive, if pricey, touring base.

Traditional wood carvings on sale in Locronan

The **church▶▶** is the most striking building on the square – a stalwart 15th-century construction in a style known as Ogival Flamboyant. It is dedicated to St Ronan, an Irish missionary who converted much of the local area during the 5th century. The lively carved pulpit inside the church depicts many scenes from his life, and his tomb lies in the 16th-century Chapelle du Pénity, built on the south side of the church. After St Ronan's death, Locronan became an important place of pilgrimage – even St Yves paid homage here; the local *pardons* (called *troménies* in Locronan) continue the tradition (see panel).

Rue Moal (the old weaving quarter) leads to a smaller but equally charming church, **Notre-Dame-de-Bonne-Nouvelle▶**, which has a calvary and 17th-century fountain, and a Christ Reviled, inside.

THE *TROMÉNIES* OF LOCRONAN
Every year the locals of Locronan celebrate their patron, St Ronan, by re-enacting his daily penitential climb up the hill near the town. This is known as La Petite Troménie. Every sixth year, however, there is a longer 12km Grande Troménie right round the hill, stopping at 12 points representing the Stations of the Cross. The next Grande Troménie takes place in July 2001.

DOMAINE DE TRÉVAREZ

The extensive grounds of the Château de Trévarez have been turned into a country park, with rose gardens, shrubberies and forest walks. The ruined 19th-century mansion was commandeered by German U-boat crews during the last war and bombarded by the RAF, but now the grandiose architecture of the Belle Epoque château is steadily being restored.

Many of Locronan's old mansions now house shops and restaurants

Drive

The Montagnes Noires

See map on pages 140–1.

A 90km inland tour through green, rounded escarpments along the course of the Nantes–Brest canal. Wayside chapels and calvaries and quiet country towns are the main focal points. Allow the best part of a day, with a picnic or lunch-stop in Châteauneuf-du-Faou.

The Montagnes Noires (Black Mountains) are gentler and greener than the parallel Arrée range to the north. Wooded paths lead by streams and houses of dark slate; every so often the locks and sluices of the Nantes–Brest canal appear.

Starting at the little town of **Rostrenen**, first see the castle chapel of Notre-Dame-du-Roncier (porch and fountain), site of a miraculous ever-flowering hawthorn bush where a statue of the Virgin was found. Then head for **la Trinité-Langonnet▶**, a Flamboyant church with Renaissance beam decorations. **Gourin** is an old slate-quarrying town, now an agricultural centre with dairy and stud farms. Its 16th-century church has a polychrome *Pietà*. Detour north briefly to the chapel of **St-Hervé**, in Flamboyant Gothic, then across to the **Roc de Toullaëron▶**, at 326m the highest point in the Montagnes Noires. Continue via **Spézet** and the chapel of **Notre-Dame du Crann▶▶** with its 16th-century stained glass and shuttered wooden altarpieces.

Follow signs for St-Goazec, deviating to the canal at the **Ecluse de Gwaker** (lock), where a waterfall tumbles into a pool. Retrace your steps to the D36 to the **Domaine de Trévarez▶** (see panel above).

Châteauneuf-du-Faou▶ is a pleasant canal town on a wooded ridge, famous for salmon fishing and home to a good restaurant (see Hotels and Restaurants, page 272). The church contains frescoes by the Pont-Aven artist, Paul Sérusier. Continue towards **Carhaix-Plouguer** (see page 122), calling at the parish closes of **Cléden-Poher▶** (16th-century altarpieces and calvary) and **St-Hernin▶** (calvary with St Michael and the dragon, and the thieves being cruelly punished).

The tall bigoudène coiffe *is one of the most striking in Brittany*

PENMARC'H BEACHES
The notorious Plage de la Torche is best seen in a gale – nothing stops those breakers. Skilled windsurfers practise here, but it is a fantastically dangerous beach and cannot be recommended for swimming – warning notices abound. The long rocky nose of Pointe de la Torche separates the beach from neighbouring Plage de Pors-Carn, a more welcoming but still hazardous crescent of sand.

►► Penmarc'h, Presqu'île de *140B1*

This desolate Cornouaille extremity was once a prosperous and populous region. Over the centuries, economic disasters struck in the shape of a vicious bandit called La Fontenelle (see panel, page 153), the disappearance of the cod shoals from its shores, and periodic tidal waves which threatened to engulf the whole low-lying region. Today, Penmarc'h seems a grim place to earn a living, the vast shingle beaches of the bay of Audierne exposed to the full brunt of Atlantic storms. Scattered white houses lie like spilt sugarcubes over the bleak farmland, and dour little fishing ports stud the south coast. However, despite the absence of local cod, Penmarc'h is still a significant fishing region.

Crêperies, galette shops and potteries are steadily proliferating to cater for tourism, though Penmarc'h is not the place to find luxurious lodgings or restaurants. Sheltered Loctudy most closely resembles a seaside resort, offering boat trips to the Iles de Glénan and up the Odet river. Although it may lack visual appeal, Penmarc'h is, however, full of interest. Marketed keenly by the tourist authorities as the Pays Bigouden, it is one of the most tenacious repositories of Breton culture. Here you will still see old-fashioned methods of farming and spot the older women wearing their curious tall *coiffes*.

Pont-l'Abbé is the regional centre, and is a good place to find detailed touring information. Sightseeing is classic Breton fare – churches, megaliths, calvaries and lighthouses. The wildlife scene is more unusual; visit the **Maison de la Baie d'Audierne►** to discover the ecology of the dunes and brackish lagoons behind the shoreline (*Open* Jul–Aug, daily 11–7; Sep–Jun, daily 2–6. *Admission free*).

Lace makes popular souvenirs, although much is mass-produced by machine these days

Drive

The Penmarc'h peninsula

See map on pages 140–1.

This is a quiet, pottering 50km drive through a cultural time-warp of fishing ports, salt marshes and sand dunes. Pont-l'Abbé is the most convenient base. Allow about half a day.

Start in Pont-l'Abbé (see pages 166–7) with a visit to the tourist office to pick up leaflets. Head south, stopping off at the **Manoir de Kérazan**, a furnished château set in parkland with a fine art collection. **Loctudy▶** stands at the mouth of Pont-l'Abbé's lakelike estuary, almost bridged by the curved sandy causeway of Ile-Tudy. The church is its finest feature, hiding a beautiful Romanesque interior behind a nondescript 18th-century façade. Good beaches lie west of the port.

Lesconil is the next real port, with an evening *criée* (fish auction). Several large beaches lie to the west. The twin ports of **Léchiagat** and its much larger sibling, **Guilvinec**, form France's fourth fishing port, a scene of bustling commerce with boats tightly packed in the harbour. **Penmarc'h**, further west, is a scattered parish with a fine late-Gothic church (St-Nonna). Notice the ships and fish carved on the porch, signifying the church's patronage. Right at the tip of the peninsula, the **Phare d'Eckmühl** (lighthouse) beams its signals over 50km from a granite tower (worth climbing for the views). **St-Guénolé**, an unlovely sardine-canning centre, has a long beach and a reef of black rocks where the sea pounds. The town's **Musée de la Préhistoire▶** is a muddled affair, but helps to put some of the local antiquities into perspective. Menhirs and reconstructed dolmens stand outside; inside are dusty displays of skulls, flints, fossils and early tools.

Near by stands one of Brittany's most venerable calvaries, **Notre-Dame de Tronoën▶▶** (1450), now striped with lichen. The biblical and secular mingle, with unusual scenes of cudgelling dimly discernible to the south, and Mary (who has very long arms and hair) to the north. North Penmarc'h is scattered with interesting churches, notably at **Languivoa**, **Languidou▶** (ruined) and Plozévet. Penhors is the scene of a famous September *pardon*.

Above: dangerous coastline

Calm water at Loctudy

The embroidered aprons and starched lace caps of traditional Breton costume become so familiar from postcards and tourist literature that it takes a while to realise hardly anyone actually wears them any more. Sadly, the buckles and bows of yesteryear are now mostly consigned to folk museums or festival days.

Costumes appear on high days and holidays now, especially in Cornouaille

Out of fashion It is hardly surprising that few people in Brittany dress traditionally today. The cost, in time and money, of making and maintaining these costumes, trimmed extravagantly with lace, velvet or satin, has simply become too great for modern practical lifestyles. A Breton wedding outfit used to take about three months to make; there are other things to do on dark winter evenings these days. Besides, as Pierre-Jakez Hélias bluntly remarks in his autobiography, *The Horse of Pride*, local costumes of this type are 'a typical feature of peasant civilisations' – and hence something that modern Bretons may prefer to forget about. None the less, the sentimental tourist may lament the loss of these colourful garments, and those who market Brittany lose no opportunity to squeeze them into the picture somewhere in the glossy brochures they produce.

Regional variety You will still have plenty of opportunity to see traditional costumes if you attend any of Brittany's many summer folk festivals or *pardons*, and just occasionally you may spot one or two of the older women wearing a *coiffe* at mass or on market day. Virtually any *écomusée* or museum of local history contains a few examples, and there are extensive collections in Quimper, Rennes, Guérande, Nantes, Dinan and Pont-l'Abbé. Cornouaille generally had the most cheerful costumes, and is still the region where you are most likely to come across them.

The Pays Bigouden (Penmarc'h peninsula) has one of the most striking *coiffes* of all, a tall tower of starched linen, supposedly representing a menhir. Fixing these hats on to the head was an amazingly complex performance – and keeping them on in a high wind even more so, though they are pierced like Finistère steeples to allow the wind through. Until comparatively recently, the *bigoudène* was an unexceptional *coiffe*, but between 1880 and 1950 it gradually increased in size to its present height of 32cm. Wearing these coiffes was alleged to show strength of character, but they are scarcely flattering garments for most apple-cheeked Breton faces.

Other regional *coiffes* show a remarkable variety of shapes and sizes: some with ribbons and streamers, others with starched wings, peaks and lacy edgings. Men generally wore short, dark jackets with broad lapels and bright waistcoats, and wide-brimmed black felt hats trimmed with buckles and ribbons. Trousers or breeches (known in Breton as *bragonbras*) were usually extremely baggy.

Vive la différence The traditional costume dates back to the 16th century, when Breton clans developed subtler ways of expressing their differences than banging each other over the head. This was born from the same spirit that produced the great parish closes of the region, built at about the same time – an ostentatious statement of rivalry and one-upmanship.

About 70 distinct styles of costume eventually developed, signifying membership of a particular regional group or family. The richness of the costume revealed individual status or wealth within that group, and many

Traditional costumes from all over Brittany can be seen at Pont-l'Abbé's annual Fête des Brodeuses (embroidery festival)

fine distinctions were made about the precise number of skirts a woman should have in her multi-tiered dress. Costumes began to represent a significant proportion of a family's assets, and were often inherited or passed on at marriage. Richer families would have several complete outfits, for weddings, funerals and the like.

More often than not, plain black was worn for everyday dress, but ceremonial costumes were highly elaborate and richly embroidered. Over the years these have inevitably been modified, and modern versions are worn with shorter skirts and fashionable shoes. But the *coiffe* used to be *de rigueur* at all times, in all weathers: fixing it on was the first thing a woman did in the morning, and removing it was the last thing she did at night.

CLOGS

The local *sabotier*, or clog-maker, was once a pillar of society in every Breton community. To see one of the original clog workshops, visit the tourist office in the village of la Chapelle-des-Marais in la Grande Brière. A short film shows a clog-maker working at his skilled craft using the tools on display.

Sabots *(clogs) were once everyday wear in Brittany*

THE GORSE-FLOWER FESTIVAL

Painting was not the only art that Pont-Aven fostered. The poet and song-writer, Théodore Botrel (1868–1925), was born here in a red-tiled house near the main square. In 1905 he founded Brittany's first folklore festival, La Fête des Ajoncs d'Or, which is still held annually on the first Sunday in August. Many other towns have developed their own festivals along very similar lines.

►► Pont-Aven 141D1

Mills in the landscape *'Pont-Aven, ville de renom; quartorze moulins, quinze maisons'* goes the rhyme ('Pont-Aven, that famous town; 14 mills and 15 houses'). The mills can still be seen today, though only one of them is still working. One has been transformed into a celebrated hotel-restaurant, while others are occupied by art galleries, with which the town is now overburdened in memory of the famous colony of painters, among them Gauguin, who settled here in the 1880s.

Despite its sometimes wearisome commercialisation and the summer crowds, Pont-Aven is a remarkably attractive place, still recognisably the scene captured in so many well-known wood and water landscapes of the late 19th century. The tumbling river rushes past the mills over granite boulders, some of which form slippery stepping-stones. Cambry, an 18th-century writer, wrote: 'The noise of the river, the roar of twenty waterfalls deafen the traveller.' Riverside walks lead away from the madding crowds past wash houses and ruined mills to Pont-Aven's pretty port, once used for shipping oysters and wine. Those keen on watersports can hire canoes and kayaks from the port.

Pont-Aven is a good place to look for souvenirs. Worthwhile art may be discovered among the mass-produced tourist tat, and imaginative ceramics as well as the ubiquitous Quimper *faïence*. Toothsome *galettes de Pont-Aven* (biscuits) are a local speciality, along with cider and *chouchenn* (mead), *kouignamann* (a delicious butter cake with caramel topping) and canned fish. The Gauguin connection is well-mined, and prints and T-shirts featuring his works abound. Staying or eating locally can be either memorable and expensive – for example, at the Moulin de Rosmadec (see Hotels and Restaurants, page 273) – or unmemorable and expensive, so always choose your billet with care!

Pont-Aven's art museum attracts visitors from all over the world

Art and artists The tourist office provides full details of the local walks and painting trails. Don't miss the walk through the Bois d'Amour, a popular artist's spot in the beech and chestnut woods above the village. The charming **Chapelle de Trémalo►►** contains the rugged inspiration for Gauguin's *Christ Jaune* (now in the Albright Art Gallery in Buffalo, US), a vividly carved sallow crucifix in the nave. The lopsided eaves of this woodland chapel nearly touch the ground; inside, the roof is propped with buttresses, the beams studded with decorative bosses and curious beasts. At nearby **Nizon**, the calvary provided another of Gauguin's models, this time a *Christ Vert*. Bright, modern glass splashes the dark interior, where a wooden Christ suffers patiently above a Golgotha of skulls.

To see more works of the Pont-Aven School, be sure to visit Pont-Aven's **museum►►** (*Open* Jul–Aug, daily

You are never far away from the sound of running water in Pont-Aven; the town's only working watermill is now carefully preserved as a tourist attraction

10–7; Sep–Jun, daily 10–12.30, 2–6.30. *Admission charge*) where four galleries house grainy old photos of the town and its bohemian visitors in a startling array of headgear. Pont-Aven's most glittering star, Gauguin, is represented by a mere couple of canvases, *La Crique* and *Le Sabotier*, which are heavily protected behind toughened glass. None the less, the museum has some interesting paintings: for instance, Paul Sérusier's *Ramasseuses de Fougères* (*The Heather-gatherers*) and Monet's *Falaises à Ouessant* (*Cliffs at Ouessant*). Returning fishing fleets, *pardons* and country folk dressed in traditional Breton costume provided an endless source of inspiration for the resident artists. There are also some 20th-century works on display, and temporary exhibitions are held at the museum.

Sailing downstream Downstream from Pont-Aven, the River Aven is one of the most beautiful in Brittany, winding through wooded banks past picturesque villages. You can see it best by boat (perhaps in *La Belle Angèle*, a replica 19th-century coastal vessel known as a *caboteur*, used off Pont-Aven between 1877 and 1930, which can now be hired for excursions: for more information apply to Pont Aven tourist office or tel: 02 98 95 32 33). Alternatively, try a drive down the west bank on a fine evening. **Kerdruc** presents a delightful scene, with views east towards the white yachts of **Rosbras**' sailing school on the opposite bank. **Névez**, a little way to the west, has some quaint painted wooden statues in its Ste-Barbe chapel (tucked away from the centre among old stone houses).

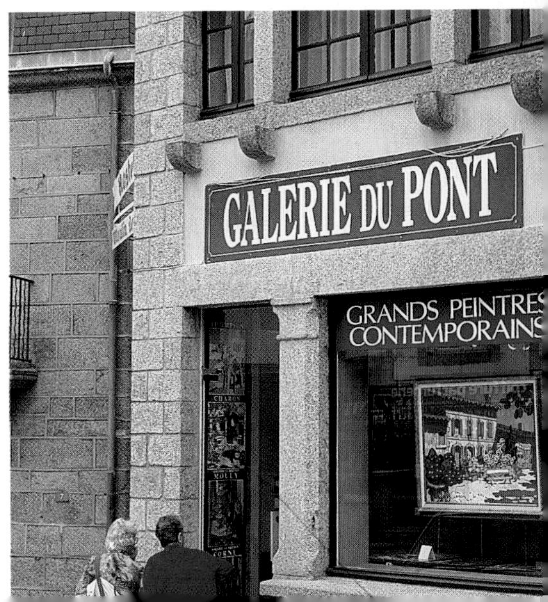

Pont-Aven's rich artistic heritage is conspicuous in the high street

Brittany's cultural heritage shows such clear evidence of creative talent, particularly in its church architecture and furniture-making, that it seems odd so few artists were known by name until the 19th century. Even then, most of them were not native to the region but hailed from outside.

CAREER MODELLING
The Pont-Aven School artists found no great difficulty in obtaining subjects for their paintings: 'The peasants, both men and women, are glad to sit for a franc for the greater part of a day; it is only at harvest time, when field labourers are scarce, that the demand may be greater than the supply, and recruits have to be found in the neighbouring fishing villages. Once or twice a week in the summer, a beauty comes over from Concarneau in a cart, her face radiant in the sunshine, the white lappets of her cap flying in the wind.'
– Henry Blackburn, *Breton Folk* (1880).

Gauguin was one of the more famous exponents of the Pont-Aven School

The Pont-Aven School Brittany's most famous group of artists is known as the Pont-Aven School, whose most illustrious exponent was Paul Gauguin (1848–1903). But these were by no means the first painters to be inspired by the Breton landscape and inhabitants. Writers and artists had trampled through Brittany since the late 18th century, and several books about the region achieved popular acclaim and helped to put it on the Victorian map. One influential travelogue was *A Summer in Brittany*, written in 1839 by Thomas Adolphus Trollope, brother of the novelist Anthony Trollope. A later book, *Breton Folk* (1880), by Henry Blackburn, described the already burgeoning artistic scene in Pont-Aven in the 1870s: 'Its inhabitants in their picturesque costume have learned that to sit as a model is a pleasant and lucrative profession... On approaching Pont-Aven the traveller notices a curious noise rising from the ground and from the woods around him. It is the flickering of the paint brushes on the canvases of the hardworking painters who come into view on leafy nooks and shady corners.'

Gauguin and the Synthetists Gauguin first arrived in Pont-Aven in 1886, where he discovered an established coterie of artists, many of whom were English or American. Their reasons for choosing Brittany were not simply a love of the landscapes and an everlasting supply of biddable local models; they could also live very cheaply there, and the Pension Gloannec in the main square was soon colonised by a bohemian clientele. Most of their talents were modest, and Gauguin soon tired of their derivative outpourings. But the artist did find Brittany unexpectedly congenial for his work: 'When my clogs strike the granite underfoot, I hear the dull, matt, powerful tone that I'm after in my painting.'

In 1888 a kindred spirit arrived at Pont-Aven in the shape of Emile Bernard, who was experimenting with an innovative technique called *cloisonnisme*. Together, Bernard and Gauguin developed an earthier, less naturalistic style that became known as Synthetism. Their techniques involved abandoning conventional perspective, and instead painting from memory in a bold, bright, two-dimensional manner with heavy outlines. Religious subjects gave their work a spiritual and emotional depth – for example, Gauguin's

Christ Jaune, based on the sculpture in the Chapelle de Trémalo at Pont-Aven (see page 162).

In 1889 Gauguin abandoned Pont-Aven for a quieter life in le Pouldu, where a band of like-minded followers (Sérusier, Filiger and Bernard) soon joined him to develop their artistic ideas still further: 'Paint what you see, not what is there!' was their motto. A few years later Gauguin left Europe for the South Seas, where he endured great

hardship and poverty. But he never forgot Brittany; when a heart attack mercifully curtailed the final ravages of syphilis, the last painting on his easel was *A Breton Village Under Snow*, now in the Louvre.

Other artists Gauguin overshadows the rest of the Pont-Aven School. Disappointingly little of his work remains in Brittany, but his fellow-artists are much better - represented, and provide a fascinating insight into Brittany as it used to be. The major collections are in Pont-Aven, Quimper, Rennes, Nantes and Brest. Vannes' La Cohue museum and Morlaix's Musée des Jacobins also have good art sections, and le Faouët displays works by little-known 20th-century Breton artists. Two native artists who deserve a mention are: Mathurin Méheut (1882–1958), whose animated paintings, drawings and ceramics feature animal scenes; and Emmanuel de la Villéon (1858–1944), an Impressionist. Their works are on display in their home towns of Lamballe and Fougères.

ANNA THE JAVANESE
Gauguin's time in Brittany was not entirely happy. When he lived in Pont-Aven he kept an Indonesian mistress who always had a tame monkey on her shoulder. When Gauguin tried to prevent children from taunting and throwing stones at her in Concarneau, he became involved in a brawl with some drunken sailors, who kicked him savagely with their wooden clogs: 'My leg is broken level with the ankle, and the bone has pierced right through the skin,' he wrote. While he was recovering, his mistress plundered his Parisian studio and made off with all she could find.

Little of Gauguin's work can now be seen in Pont-Aven

EMERALD EYES
An artists' trail along the Emerald Coast has been prepared by the tourist authorities, pinpointing the exact locations various artists chose for landscape paintings. The locations, mostly between Dinard and Cap Fréhel, include scenes by Picasso, Renoir and Emile Bernard. Bernard wrote of his artistic summers in St-Briac: 'We all had a debt to pay to Brittany. It was she who lit up our youth, she who brought us so many poetic emotions and kindled Faith and a love of Art. It is wonderful to think that she will never forget us.' Ask for the explanatory leaflet called 'Emerald Eyes' at local tourist offices.

Pancake-making is a fine art in Brittany

► Pont-Croix

140B2

The Goyen river, which meets the sea at Audierne, ceases to be tidal at Pont-Croix, a pretty inland port of medieval gold-stone houses and narrow streets. Its most interesting building is the church of **Notre-Dame-de-Roscudon►►**, which has three beautiful lacy gables over its south porch. Inside, the weighty nave distorts some of its massive lozenge-shaped pillars. Notice the remarkable woodcarving of the Last Supper in the chapel behind the altar, and the fine old glass intermingled with more modern windows.

► Pont-l'Abbé

140B1

The capital of the Pays Bigouden commands a strategic bridging point at the head of a complex inlet where the River Pont-l'Abbé joins the sea. The town was established by the monks of Loctudy and fortified in the 14th century. Its castle houses a **museum►** of local history with a fine collection of *coiffes* and costumes. Other exhibits include Breton furniture and model ships, which you must visit on a guided tour (*Open* Jun–Sep, Mon–Sat 10–12, 2–6.30. *Admission charge*). A brighter note of the tour is a visit (on the same ticket) to the **Maison du Pays Bigouden►►** (*Open* Jun–Sep, Mon–Sat 10–12, 2.15–6. *Admission charge*) (2km south-east), a traditionally furnished farmhouse of limewashed stone. The outbuildings and agricultural tools give it an earthy reality sometimes lost among endless displays of box beds and linen presses. While in the town, see the domed 14th-century church of **Notre-Dame-des-Carmes►** (once the chapel of a Carmelite monastery) and its colourful rose window.

Aside from this, Pont-l'Abbé's attractions are limited, though it does have one or two good-value hotels which make it worth considering as a touring base. It is a busy market town and the main shopping centre for a large area (Thursday is market day). The local tourist office

CHAPELS NEAR PONT-CROIX

Notre-Dame de Confort, 6km east of the town, is a 16th-century church with a galleried belfry. The glass is particularly fine, especially the Tree of Jesse in the chancel. On the final arch in the nave is a carillon wheel with 12 bells, traditionally rung to restore speech to dumb children. The calvary outside was restored in 1870. Notre-Dame de Kérinec, a little further north-east, was struck by lightning in 1958, but its lovely 17th-century bell tower has been rebuilt in the same style.

Pont-Croix's hilly streets contain some well-restored old buildings

The striking south porch of Pont-Croix's church dates from the late 14th century, though parts of the rest of the church are even older

(also in the castle) supplies information about the whole Penmarc'h region. If you catch the town in July you may be lucky enough to see the Fête des Brodeuses, celebrating Pont-l'Abbé's speciality – embroidery. Doll-making is another local craft.

► Port-Manec'h *141D1*

This tiny resort stands at the mouth of two lovely estuaries, the Aven and Bélon. Though somewhat overwhelmed by a crassly designed modern hotel on the waterfront, the setting is undeniably pretty. A private château shares an eye-catching span of pine-strewn coast with a small beach in a sandy cove. The beach-huts date from Belle Epoque days, when Port-Manec'h became a chic watering hole. Paths lead from the beach to the port, where watersports are well catered for at the Centre Nautique. You can also walk from the lighthouse along the cliffs to **Raguenez-Plage►**, a little hamlet straggling down to an unspoilt sandy beach punctuated by a tidal island. Still further west, the **Pointe de Trévignon** offers more coastal views, on clear days extending as far as the Ile de Groix.

► Le Pouldu *141E1*

The last resort on Finistère's south coast, le Pouldu has expanded greatly with characterless holiday homes and campsites in recent years, and has lost some of its former fishing-village appeal. Its long beaches look south, sheltered by low grassy cliffs. Some way from the sprawling beach development, le Pouldu's port on the pretty Laïta estuary offers boats for hire.

Gauguin retreated here in 1889 along with a select band of talented artists (see pages 164–5). They all lodged at a local inn which is now the Café de la Plage. Near by, the **Maison Marie Henry►** has been carefully re-created with period furnishings and copies of the paintings the artists left behind on the walls in lieu of rent (*Open* Jul–Aug, daily, guided tours only 10.30, 11.30, 3.15, 4.15, 5.15 and 6.15; Jun–Sep, except Wed 3, 4 and 5. *Admission charge*).

GAUGUIN'S MORTGAGE
When Gauguin decided to quit French shores for the warmer climes of Polynesia he could not (as usual) raise the rent he owed his landlady, Marie-Henry. Instead, he left her a few paintings as a surety against his debt. When he returned out of the blue some years later, his reputation firmly established, he somewhat meanspiritedly demanded his pawned canvases back, and even started legal proceedings to retrieve them. Today the pictures are scattered worldwide in famous art collections, and a single one of them would raise many times the 300 francs that Gauguin originally owed.

QUIMPER *FAIENCE*
An abundance of fresh water, fuel and suitable clay made Quimper a centre of the pottery industry over 300 years ago. Quimper pottery is now sold all over Brittany in a distinctive blue and yellow *paysan* design of flowers, birds and costumed figures. True Quimper ware is all hand-decorated and individually signed before firing, though many cheaper imitations are mass-produced these days. Good-quality seconds can be purchased in a shop near the factories. The most famous and oldest *faïencerie* is the factory set up by HB Henriot, which still produces traditional styles (it offers guided tours). More modern designs can be found at the Keraluc workshops.

►►► Quimper *140C2*

One of Brittany's most charming cities, Quimper is not to be missed if you are anywhere in Cornouaille. Its only serious weakness is a lack of pleasing old-town hotels, which makes it less than ideal as a touring base. For a day trip, however, Quimper will entertain you royally as it is excellent for shopping, strolling, eating and sightseeing. The old quarter, near the junction of the Odet and Steir rivers, is quite compact and easy to explore on foot. Leave your car near the cathedral if you can, or by the tourist office on the south bank of the Odet. To visit the pottery workshops, walk or drive downstream to Locmaria.

Continued on page 170.

Market day in Quimper

The old town of Quimper

See map opposite.

A saunter through the old city in the shadow of St-Corentin's twin spires. Allow half a day, including visits to museums. Add an extra hour or two if you wish to do justice to the *faïence* potteries at Locmaria.

Start by the tourist office in Place de la Résistance, a well-stocked regional information centre. Rising sharply behind are the wooded, landscaped slopes of Mont Frugy, worth the 80m climb for a city overview (and a good place for a picnic). Cross the river, heading for the cathedral spires in the old quarter. The **Cathédrale St-Corentin▶▶** dates from the 13th to 15th centuries, though its lacy steeples were erected only in 1856, now blending well with the original fabric. Restoration is improving the gloomy interior, whose nave is oddly out of true with the 13th-century chancel. Stained-glass windows and works of art line the aisles and side-chapels, and St Corentin's life is carved on the pulpit. From the pleasant gardens behind, you can survey the cathedral's Gothic exterior.

Next door in the bishop's palace is Quimper's history museum, the **Musée Départemental Breton▶▶**, containing a great selection of costumes, pottery, worm-eaten sculpture and furniture. Notice the fine spiral staircase in the Rohan tower. Quimper's other central museum is the **Musée des Beaux-Arts** (**Fine Arts Museum**)**▶▶** in the town hall, with samples of the Pont-Aven School and local artists Pierre de Bellay and Max Jacob.

After this, wander westwards through the pedestrianised old town past quaint stone and timber mansions, such as the ornately decorated **Maison des Cariatides▶** in rue Guéodet (now a popular *crêperie*). Traces of the ramparts can be seen in rue des Douves and the boulevard de Kerguélen. The modern covered market (*halles*) by rue Astor replaces one destroyed in a fire in 1979. Bridges over the Steir give good views of old flower-decked buildings. The **Place Terre-au-Duc▶**, by the southernmost bridge, has one of the best concentrations of Quimper architecture, and the church of **St-Mathieu▶** at the west end of the walk has a fine 16th-century chancel window.

Now head south, over the Odet, and follow the river a few hundred metres downstream to Locmaria (off the map). Visit the Romanesque church, with its glory beam, and the earthenware ***faïence* factories▶** (see panel opposite). The **Musée de la Faïence▶▶** contains a fascinating display of Quimper ware and ceramic techniques through the ages.

An overview of the town and the spires of St-Corentin

Water rushes through the lower town of Quimperlé

ST CORENTIN'S FISH
Corentin was King Gradlon's first bishop in Quimper, and founder of the city's great cathedral. He was alleged to have lived by means of a miraculous immortal fish which swam in the pool near his hermitage. Whenever Corentin was hungry he would simply catch the fish and carve a chunk off it, then toss it back into the water where, unharmed, it instantly renewed itself ready for the next meal.

THE GLASS CEREMONY
A statue of King Gradlon on horseback stands between the spires of Quimper's cathedral. In the past, a July festival honoured the town's royal founder. An official would climb up to the statue and drink a toast of wine to the king; then he would throw the glass down into the square below, where the assembled citizens would try to catch it. Anyone who could deliver the glass intact to the mayor would receive a hefty prize of gold coins. No one ever managed it, though a good many hands were cut trying!

Continued from page 168.

Once Quimper was the capital of the ancient kingdom and medieval Duchy of Cornouaille, whose boundaries stretched as far as Morlaix. It became the legendary seat of Gradlon's court after Ys sank beneath the waves (see pages 18–19), and developed into a place of influence and prestige. After Brittany's union with France, Quimper was largely eclipsed, even serving as a place of exile in Louis XIII's reign. In World War II the town was a hub of Resistance, but was fortunate enough to avoid most of the destruction that savaged other Breton cities.

For centuries, poor communications hampered economic development, but Quimper now has an international airport and greatly improved road and rail links. There is some industry on its outskirts, but it functions mostly as a market and tourist centre. Quimper is the most overtly Celtic city in Brittany, and market days still attract stallholders in *sabots* and *coiffes*. Its three-day July folk festival (Festival de Cornouaille) is enormous, rallying visitors from all over Europe, especially its Gaelic fringes. A month later, the annual Seminaires Musicales attract a more classical following.

South-east of the town centre in Ergué-Armel is the **Musée de l'Alambie**, where there is a fascinating display of stills and apple-presses. A detailed commentary describes the 300-year-old brandy-making tradition in Brittany, with free tastings and the chance to buy brandy made on the premises (*Open* daily 10–12.30, 2–5.30. *Admission charge*).

▶▶ Quimperlé *141E1*

The name of the town comes from the same Breton root as Quimper (*kemper*, a meeting of rivers). In Quimperlé the fast-flowing rivers Ellé and Isole converge noisily to form the Laïta. A steep hill divides the split-level old town.

In the Ville Basse, or lower town, the church of **Ste-Croix▶▶** makes a prominent, squat, grey statement on its island setting, surrounded by rivers and bridges. It has a most unusual cruciform design, based on the circular church of the Holy Sepulchre in Jerusalem. Like the rest of Quimperlé, Ste-Croix is on two levels, the arcaded chancel raised on a sort of dais. The crypt and apse comprise some of Brittany's best surviving Romanesque architecture and date from the 12th century, but the remainder of the church was rebuilt after structural damage a century ago, when the original bell tower collapsed. The new bell tower stands apart from the rest of the church. In the older sections the Celtic carvings and capitals are worth close examination. Other points of interest are the Renaissance stone altarpiece by the entrance and a 16th-century Entombment scene.

The streets near the church contain some venerable houses, particularly rue Dom-Morice, where the **Maison des Archers▶** contains a local history museum (*Open* Jul–Aug, daily 10.30–6.30; Jun and Sep, Wed–Mon, 1–6.30. *Admission charge*). There are more fine half-timbered and corbelled houses in rue Brémond-d'Ars, along with the ruined church of St-Colomban and an interesting exterior staircase on the old law courts (Presidial) at No 15 *bis*.

In the upper town, the church of **Notre-Dame-de-l'Assomption▶** (also known as St-Michel), makes a complete contrast to its Ville Basse neighbour. This is solid, four-square Gothic in the main square, but perilously constructed on a steep slope, using adjacent buildings as props. In places it is crumbling badly, and its fine porch carvings are weathered. Inside, the nave is gaunt and lacking an aisle, while Our Lady of Good Tidings stands woodenly in the chancel.

QUIMPERLÉ EXCURSIONS

Quimperlé itself has relatively few diversions, but a couple of good picnic expeditions lie within easy driving distance. About 12km north-east is the Roches du Diable, a rocky platform overlooking a steep, cliff-lined valley where the Ellé foams far below. Access is free – it's a short walk through pretty woodland from the car park to the viewpoint. South of the town, along the attractive Laïta valley, the Forêt de Carnoët extends over 750ha. Tracks lead in from the woodland road, and from there you can drive around parts of the forest, or park in clearings and walk beyond the barriers that prevent vehicular access.

Quaint back alleyways in Quimperlé reveal many interesting old buildings

The Chapel of Ste-Anne, focus of pardons

KENTOC'H MERVEL
During World War II every able-bodied male on the Ile du Sein volunteered to answer General de Gaulle's call to arms. The women and children were left behind singing the 'Marseillaise' from the quayside. After the war, de Gaulle visited the island in person to present its citizens with the Croix de la Libération, the highest honour for services rendered in wartime. A local war memorial captures the spirit of the Senans with the Breton inscription '*Kentoc'h Mervel*' – 'Better to die'.

POINTE DU RAZ
The Pointe du Raz is one of Finistère's most dramatic headlands. Intense visitor pressure has eroded the landscape, but on windy days it is unforgettable. An ambitious restoration programme has encouraged the vegetation to grow again. Technically it is not Brittany's most westerly promontory, but sailors remark that the climate and temper of the sea seem to change once it is rounded.

Right: a much-venerated statue at Ste-Anne-la-Palud

▶Ste-Anne-la-Palud *140B3*

St Anne, mother of the Virgin Mary, is the patroness of Brittany and in certain areas has a great cult following (see page 20). The *pardon* held at this tiny place on the bay of Douarnenez for three days over the last weekend in August is an indication of her importance; pilgrims hail from far and wide to pay homage to a painted granite statue dating from 1548, while torchlit processions celebrate mass at a chapel in fields near the beach. The chapel is not particularly old (19th century), and stands inland from the original site founded by St Guenolé in the 6th century, which was swamped by the sea. Everyone dresses up, and this is one of the best opportunities to see Breton costumes. At other times of year Ste-Anne is a peaceful place of quiet beaches, dunes and a wooded headland.

▶ Sein, Ile de *140A2*

Barely visible above the waterline, Sein presents yet another challenge to mariners navigating the west coast of Brittany. *'Qui voit Sein, voit sa fin'* ('Who sees Sein, sees his doom'), goes the rhyme, and a chain of lighthouses backs up the warning.

The island lies about 8km off the Pointe du Raz, measuring only about 1.8km long at its maximum. It is rather like an iceberg, at times virtually submerged, but its reefs and sandbanks trail far beyond the shore. A lethal tidal race runs between the straits, amply justifying Sein's feared reputation.

In pagan times the island was one of the last refuges of the Druids, who were buried here. Later, its only inhabitants were wreckers preying on lost ships; the bodies of the drowned often washed up on the mainland Baie des Trépassés. Eventually, the Senans developed a more public spirit and they are now renowned for their intrepid sea-rescue services. Tourists may visit the island by boat from Audierne (a one-hour journey), though there is little to see but birds and lighthouses.

▶▶▶ Sizun, Cap *140A2*

The jagged finger of Sizun stretches far into the Atlantic, ending dramatically at the Pointe du Raz. The best scenery lies to the north. Sensible footwear is essential if you want to explore as the paths can be slippery. Take binoculars if you are keen on birds.

Sizun is full of legends: Tristan and Isolde shared their star-crossed love at Douarnenez, and King Gradlon's beautiful city of Ys lies somewhere beneath the waves. Farming and tourism are the mainstays of the local economy. Apart from the fishing ports of Douarnenez and Audierne, there are no large towns, and few settlements exhibit much character (Pont-Croix is a pleasing exception). The cultivated scenery inland is unexceptional and not worth detailed exploration.

Pointe de Raz, a dramatic, unforgettable headland on Cap Sizun

Drive

Cap Sizun

See map on pages 140–1.

This 100km drive requires repeated cul-de-sac detours from the main coast road and some walking. Allow at least half a day.

Starting from **Douarnenez** (see pages 152–3), head along the north coast road (D7), ducking northwards first at **Pointe du Millier▶**. A few minutes' walk to the point offers a splendid view of the bay. **Pointe de Beuzec▶** (accessible by car) has similar views.

The Réserve du Cap Sizun▶▶ is a bird sanctuary, best visited in the nesting season between April and mid-July. Further west, **Pointe de Brézellec▶** offers a magnificent vantage point of serrated rocks and cliffs. Still further along, the **Pointe du Van▶▶** requires a lengthy walk to a desolate headland, less spectacular than Pointe du Raz but less crowded. The cliffs here are dangerous. Southwards is the sweeping crescent of the **Baie des Trépassés▶▶**. Currents here are strong. **Pointe du Raz▶▶▶** is undoubtedly the highlight of the journey (see panel opposite).

Return on the D784 via St-Tugen, Audierne and Pont-Croix (see pages 144 and 166), calling *en route* at **Notre-Dame de Confort▶** and **Notre-Dame de Kérinec** chapels (see panel on page 166).

Notre-Dame-des-Naufragés (Our Lady of the Shipwrecked), Pointe du Raz

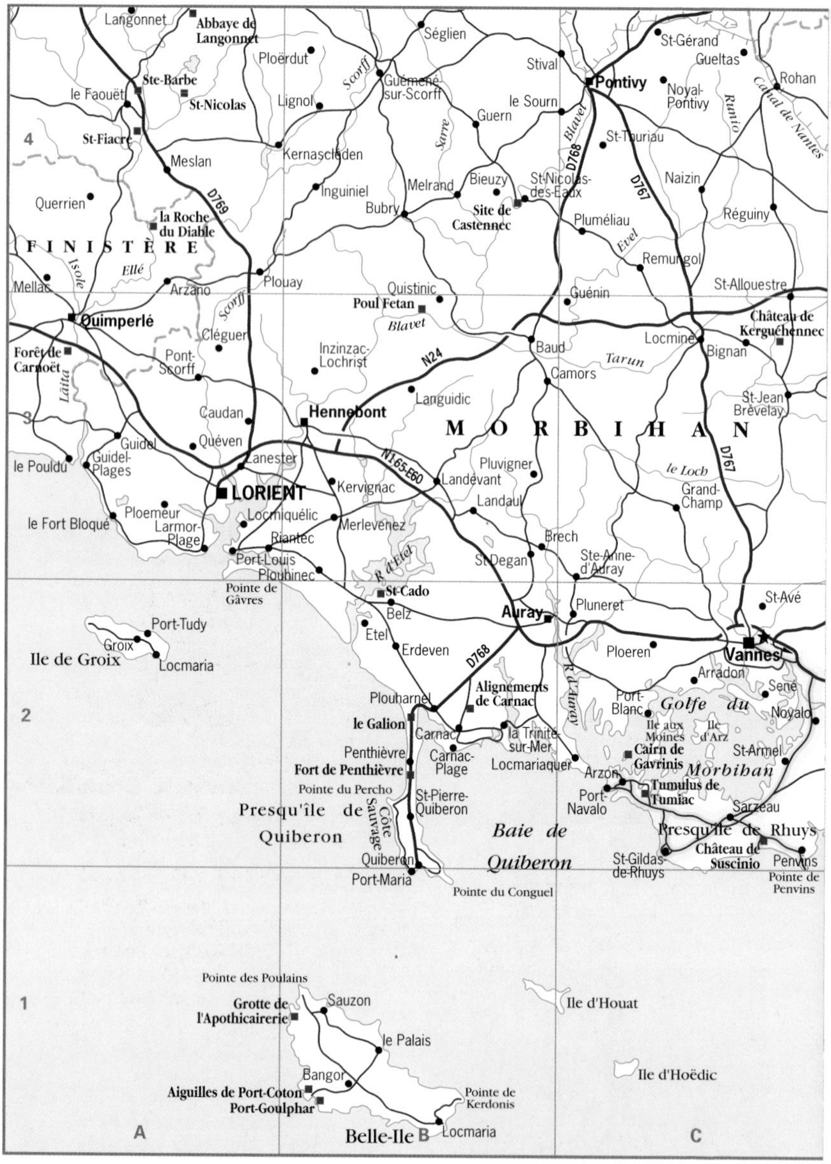

Langonnet
Abbaye de Langonnet
Ploërdut
Séglien
Stival
St-Gérand
Gueltas
Rohan
Canal de Nantes
Pontivy
Noyal-Pontivy
Runio
le Faouët
Ste-Barbe
St-Nicolas
Lignol
Scorff
Guémené-sur-Scorff
le Sourn
Guern
Sarre
Blavet
St-Thuriau
4
St-Fiacre
Kernascléden
D768
D767
Meslan
Naizin
Melrand
Bieuzy
St-Nicolas-des-Eaux
Querrien
D769
Inguiniel
Bubry
Site de Castennec
Pluméliau
Réguiny
la Roche du Diable
Evel
FINISTÈRE
Isole
Ellé
Remungol
Mellac
Arzano
Plouay
Quistinic
Guénin
St-Allouestre
Poul Fetan
Quimperlé
Scorff
Blavet
Château de Kerguéhennec
Cléguer
Baud
Locminé
Bignan
Forêt de Carnoët
Pont-Scorff
Inzinzac-Lochrist
N24
Tarun
Laïta
Camors
Languidic
St-Jean Brévelay
3
Caudan
Hennebont
MORBIHAN
Guidel
Quéven
D767
le Pouldu
Guidel-Plages
Lanester
N165-E60
Pluvigner
le Loch
Landévant
Kervignac
LORIENT
Grand-Champ
Landaul
le Fort Bloqué
Ploemeur
Locmiquélic
Merlevenez
Larmor-Plage
Riantec
Brech
Port-Louis
R. d'Etel
St-Degan
Ste-Anne-d'Auray
Plouhinec
Pointe de Gâvres
St-Cado
Pluneret
St-Avé
Belz
Auray
Port-Tudy
Etel
Groix
Ile de Groix
Locmaria
Erdeven
D768
Ploeren
Vannes
Arradon
Alignements de Carnac
Séné
Plouharnel
R. d'Auray
Port-Blanc
Golfe du
2
le Galion
Ile aux Moines
Ile d'Arz
Noyalo
Carnac
la Trinité-sur-Mer
Penthièvre
Carnac-Plage
Cairn de Gavrinis
St-Armel
Fort de Penthièvre
Locmariaquer
Arzon
Morbihan
Pointe du Percho
Tumulus de Tumiac
St-Pierre-Quiberon
Port-Navalo
Presqu'île de Quiberon
Côte Sauvage
Sarzeau
Baie de Quiberon
Presqu'île de Rhuys
Château de Suscinio
Quiberon
St-Gildas-de-Rhuys
Penvins
Port-Maria
Pointe de Penvins
Pointe du Conguel
Pointe des Poulains
1
Grotte de l'Apothicairerie
Sauzon
Ile d'Houat
le Palais
Ile d'Hoëdic
Bangor
Aiguilles de Port-Coton
Pointe de Kerdonis
Port-Goulphar
A
Belle-Ile
B
Locmaria
C

The cobbled old town quarter of Rochefort-en-Terre

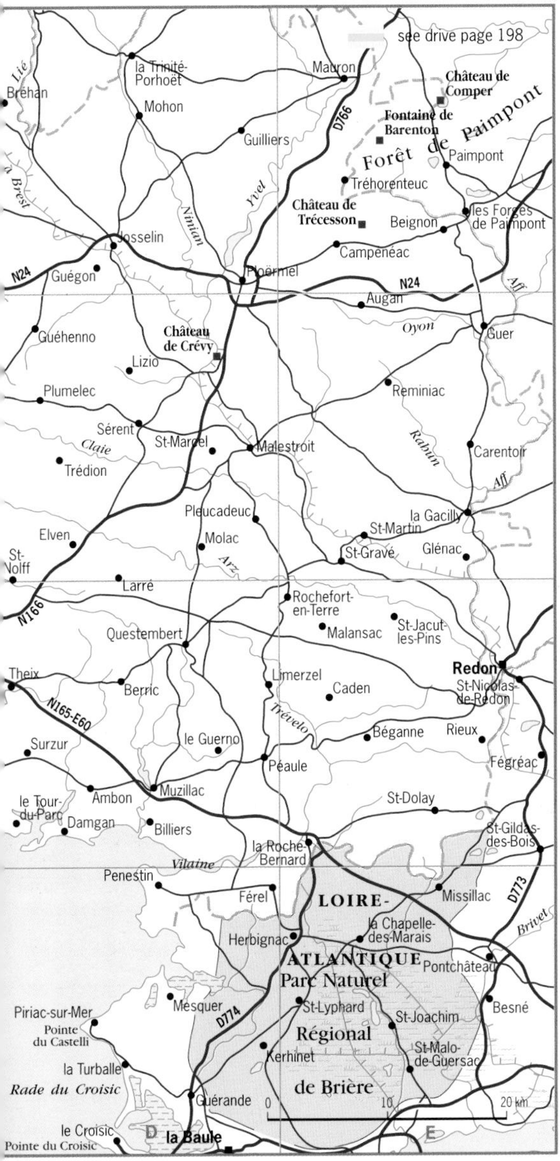

see drive page 198

Morbihan

▶▶▶ REGION HIGHLIGHTS

MORBIHAN Morbihan is the only one of Brittany's *départements* with a specifically Breton name. It means 'Little Sea', a reference to its most striking geographical feature, the vast, mud-rimmed tidal lagoon known as the Golfe du Morbihan. This strange, landlocked maze of creeks and islands provides a splendid breeding and overwintering ground for enormous numbers of seabirds and wildfowl, and its sheltered microclimate and varied habitats produce a rich, almost Mediterranean plant life.

In summer the gulf hums with excursion cruisers and flurrying sails, as countless boats weave in and out of complex channels that run between pine-topped, grassy

VAUBAN (1633–1707)
One of the great military engineer's finest achievements, the citadel at le Palais, can be seen on Belle-Ile in Morbihan. Sébastien le Prestre de Vauban rose against all odds of class and birth to become Marshal of France. A gallant soldier, he demonstrated early in his career an uncanny flair for siege warfare, and created an innovative ring of superbly designed fortresses all over France for his master, Louis XIV. Vauban's politics were by no means undilutedly Royalist. He became increasingly uneasy about the lot of the poor, and foresaw the Revolution. He died, out of royal favour, in 1707. Despite his remarkable achievements, rapid developments in military strategy rendered many of his fortifications obsolete by the time he died.

hummocks, and past chapels, ruined villas and the extraordinary prehistoric cairn at Gavrinis. In 56 BC the Golfe du Morbihan witnessed a crucial battle when Julius Caesar defeated the Veneti and confirmed Roman rule in Armorican Gaul (see pages 32–3).

HOLIDAY OPTIONS Morbihan is an important holiday area, and in summer the local population swells to many times its resident size. Sandy beaches and calm muddy estuaries where oysters thrive characterise much of the coast. Beachcombers and yachting folk are prominent visitors, while Quiberon and Carnac, the liveliest resorts, offer thalassotherapy treatments. Messing about in boats is a particularly popular pastime. The apparent gentleness of the seaside scenery may deceive, however: strong currents make some beaches extremely dangerous, especially along the west coast of Quiberon and around the Morbihan gulf.

Right: a lively palet *match in Pontivy's town square*

Seawards, Morbihan incorporates several islands, including Brittany's largest and most beautiful, Belle-Ile. The mainland coastline is generally low-lying and less dramatic than north or west Brittany, but its warmer and more sheltered climate may make summer seaside holidays a more attractive option. Less welcome are the increased humidity, and a large crop of mosquitoes encouraged by brackish expanses of sheltered water.

The whole tempo of this Breton riviera is slightly more Mediterranean, more French, than elsewhere in Brittany – the locals even produce wine on the Rhuys peninsula. But the season is still short; expect the shutters to come down soon after the school summer holidays end.

The region extends far inland through plateaux of heathy schist and woodland carved by many rivers, and is more or less bounded on its northern fringes by the course of the Nantes–Brest canal. Hedged fields, trout

Old schooner at Auray, now a museum

streams and small copses (the last remnants of once-vast forests that cloaked Brittany's interior until medieval times) make for pleasant but not very remarkable scenery.

LOCAL INTEREST The only really large coastal town is Lorient, one of France's most important commercial and fishing ports. For most visitors, smaller ports such as Locmariaquer or Port-Louis, or the historic old city of Vannes, hold many more attractions. Inland, other towns of architectural interest include Josselin, Auray, Rochefort-en-Terre, la Roche-Bernard and Pontivy. The relative prosperity of places able to capitalise on tourism disguises a sadder aspect of Morbihan's declining rural economy. Some of those picturesquely fossilised little *éco-musées* are all that remain of once-flourishing villages whose livelihoods have vanished.

Historically, however, the whole of the Morbihan area is packed with interest, from its famous collection of neolithic monuments around Carnac to grand ducal castles and ancient *villes fleuries*. Many aspects of regional life are traced in a selection of excellent modern museums. Specifically Celtic or Breton culture is less apparent than, say, in Cornouaille or North Finistère: you will rarely find *coiffes* or costumes worn here, and there are fewer Breton-speakers. But the religious element still dominates, with dozens of healing fountains, wayside chapels and calvaries, and the most important pilgrimage centre in all Brittany at Ste-Anne-d'Auray.

The most haunting memories of Morbihan are provided by its oldest monuments – the mysteriously ordered menhirs of Carnac. In high season traffic crawls past the metal fencing protecting thousands of standing stones, neatly arranged in *alignements* (rows). Overrun by tourists during the day, the menhirs seem diminished, almost mundane. But if you see them quietly and in solitude – in an early morning mist, or perhaps by moonlight – the ancient magic returns. At these times the stones seem to stand guard over the landscape like a petrified army, defying all attempts to explain them away.

LEST WE FORGET
In every village, war memorials commemorate the fallen of the Great War, some of them touching portrayals of personal grief: an old Breton couple mourn their lost sons; an infantryman leans disconsolately on his rifle. On many, a jaunty cockerel symbolises a new dawn. Monuments erected after World War II testify to the horror of hideous atrocities and mass executions committed in retaliation for Resistance sabotage. Not all war crimes were carried out by the Gestapo; Vichy agents were also responsible for some. To find out more about wartime Brittany, visit the Musée de la Résistance Bretonne at St-Marcel, near Malestroit (see page 192).

The wash houses (lavoirs) by the ramparts of Vannes

Waterfront cafés in St-Goustan

BENJAMIN FRANKLIN
A gale forced a ship carrying the famous American, then serving as ambassador to France, to take refuge at Auray in 1776. Franklin was on his way to Nantes, hoping to enlist France's help against the English in the American War of Independence. He spent the night at No. 8 Place St-Sauveur (now a popular *crêperie*) and travelled on to Nantes overland.

THE MIRACULOUS VISION
In 1623 a ploughman, Yves Nicolazic, saw a vision of Ste Anne telling him to build a church in a place she would show him. The good ploughman unearthed an ancient statue which he took to be a sign from heaven. The church was duly built, and soon became a great place of pilgrimage. The sacred statue was burned by a Revolutionary mob as a graven image, but fragments of it remain inside the base of the present 19th-century version. Nicolazic's alleged house in Ste-Anne-d'Auray can be visited (free).

Modern pilgrims, Ste-Anne-d'Auray

►► Auray *174B2*

This ancient place illuminates several periods of Breton history. It seems peaceful now but has witnessed some bloody scenes, including the last battle of the 14th-century War of Succession and a terrible massacre of Chouan counter-Revolutionaries in 1795 (see panel opposite). Auray is said to have been the last place Julius Caesar reached in his conquest of Gaul. The Romans set up camp in what is now the St-Goustan quarter, still the oldest and most picturesque part of the town. A small cluster of harmoniously timber-framed 15th-century houses decorates the quayside Place St-Sauveur and the hilly streets behind. From the opposite bank (reached over a picturesque medieval stone bridge), the promenade du Loch, by the remnants of the old castle, gives an excellent view. The restored schooner moored on the waterfront contains a small local history museum. Up the hill in Auray's main centre, the church of **St-Gildas►** has a fine Renaissance porch and a marble altarpiece (1664).

Ste-Anne-d'Auray►►, to the north-east, commemorates the feast of Brittany's patron St Anne (on 26 July), when thousands of pilgrims gather for one of the region's most spectacular *pardons*. The church itself is of no great interest; a ponderous 19th-century basilica now replaces the original. In the vast cathedral precinct, the **Scala Sancta►** is a disembodied double staircase which the faithful climb on their knees. Various museums are housed in the church buildings: a treasury of relics and religious sculpture (including a relic of St Anne offered by Anne of Austria), a costume museum and a diorama of the pilgrimage in medieval times.

More stirring than any of this commercialised religiosity is the vast **war memorial►►**, raised by public subscription to the 250,000 Bretons who died serving in World War I. Walls over 200m long inscribed with the names of the dead enclose a space of paved walks and lawns. Outside the town, a Franco-Belgian cemetery contains row upon row of neat plain graves.

The French Revolution dashed Breton hopes of independence. Far from promising liberté, égalité *and* fraternité, *the actions of the Revolutionary leaders seemed to spell repression, discrimination and intolerance.*

As the excesses of the Revolution worsened, the Breton language was threatened with abolition, churches were vandalised and people everywhere suffered terrible hardships. In Nantes, the infamous Jean-Baptiste Carrier began a personal Reign of Terror, drowning thousands of suspected Royalists in the Loire. Breton traditionalists responded by banding together in a secret society called the Association Bretonne, popularly dubbed the Chouans (from *chat huant*, the cry of the screech owl, which they used for night signalling).

In Morbihan the Chouan cause rallied around a local farmer, Georges Cadoudal, who had been appalled at witnessing mass executions in Rennes. Dispossessed aristocrats, many in exile in England, latched on to the Chouans in the hope of retrieving their former power and wealth. In 1795 an expeditionary force of French exiles, backed by the British Navy, landed on the Quiberon peninsula, hoping to team up with the Chouans and stage an insurrection. But their numbers were much smaller than expected, and their cause had been betrayed to the Republican commander General Hoche (see panel on page 197). He trapped the invading force at the tip of the peninsula and took nearly 1,000 prisoners. Some were executed immediately, while others were taken to Vannes and Auray for interrogation and then shot.

George Cadoudal, leader of the Chouan cause

The last hero Cadoudal himself got away and lived to fight another day. Again he was defeated, escaping to England in a fishing boat. Impressed by his courage, Napoleon offered him a free pardon and high office but Cadoudal refused, and staged an even more reckless scheme – to kidnap the newly proclaimed emperor. The plot was thwarted, and this time Napoleon showed Cadoudal no mercy. The last Chouan was shot by a firing squad in Paris in June 1804. His body rests in a little mausoleum overlooking his family farm on the outskirts of Auray (see panel).

CHOUAN SHRINES
On the western outskirts of Auray, a glum neo-classical mausoleum contains the tomb of local hero, Georges Cadoudal, the last Chouan. More Chouan history can be traced just north of the town, where a chilling black and white reliquary chapel in the Carthusian monastery pays homage to the 953 exiled Chouans who were executed in Auray after their failed Royalist uprising. The original collegiate church near by was built in 1364 to commemorate Jean de Montfort's victory in the final battle of the War of Succession (see page 34), and his dead adversary and brother-in-law, Charles de Blois. The Champ des Martyrs, just up the road, was where the Chouan rebels were actually shot.

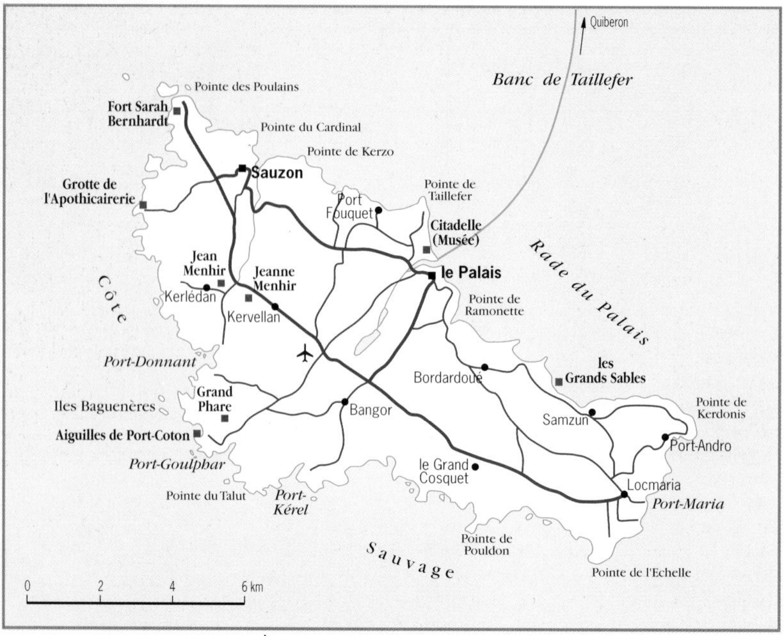

Quiberon
Banc de Taillefer
Pointe des Poulains
Fort Sarah Bernhardt
Pointe du Cardinal
Pointe de Kerzo
Sauzon
Grotte de l'Apothicairerie
Pointe de Taillefer
Port Fouquet
Citadelle (Musée)
Rade du Palais
Jean Menhir
Jeanne Menhir
le Palais
Côte
Kerlédan
Kervellan
Pointe de Ramonette
Port-Donnant
les Grands Sables
Bordardoué
Grand Phare
Iles Baguenères
Bangor
Pointe de Kerdonis
Samzun
Aiguilles de Port-Coton
Port-Andro
Port-Goulphar
le Grand Cosquet
Locmaria
Pointe du Talut
Port-Kérel
Port-Maria
Pointe de Pouldon
Sauvage
Pointe de l'Echelle
0 2 4 6 km

HOUAT AND HOÊDIC
Trips to these two smaller, more peaceful islands (whose names mean 'Duck' and 'Duckling' in Breton) east of Belle-Ile are also advertised from Quiberon. Journey time is about an hour.

▶▶▶ Belle-Ile *174B1*

Of all Brittany's islands, Belle-Ile perhaps has most to offer. It is the largest, at 17km by 10km, has attractively varied scenery, and is rich in history. Access to the island is easy, with regular boat services in season making the 45-minute crossing from Quiberon.

Boats dock at Belle-Ile's capital, **le Palais▶▶**, a small bustling port with hotels, shops, cafés and restaurants. Above the harbour looms a mighty star-shaped fortress, originally built in the 16th century and strengthened by Vauban (see panel, page 176). The citadel now houses a **museum▶▶** outlining Belle-Ile's history in photographs, documents, sardine tins and seaweed pictures (*Open* daily 9.30–7 in summer. *Admission charge*).

Leaving Quiberon for Belle-Ile

The sheltered port of Sauzon has a delightful setting

The island consists of four parishes, named after its four principal settlements. (One is called Bangor, indicating early occupation by Welsh monks.) After successive waves of Celts, Romans, Saxons and Normans passed through, the island passed to the abbey of Redon in 1006. Later it was owned by Louis XIV's ambitious finance minister, Nicholas Fouquet, who strengthened Belle-Ile's defences mightily and even stationed his own navy here. Unsurprisingly, the king saw him as a threat, and had him arrested by the Three Musketeers in 1661. English and Dutch forces repeatedly attacked the island and the English held it for two years from 1761, after which it was swapped for Menorca.

The interior of the island is a plateau of fertile schist, cut by many valleys in which white houses cluster, sheltering from the wind. Moorland alternates with hedged arable fields, vegetable plots and cattle pastureland, and the climate is mild but windswept. The east coast has several safe sandy beaches: les Grands Sables is the largest, with facilities for watersports. Another sheltered beach is at Port-Kérel on the south side, the only safe bathing on the Côte Sauvage. The scenery on the west side is much more dramatic. **Port-Goulphar▶▶**, where coach parties are usually dropped off for lunch, overlooks a fjord-like inlet with preternaturally blue-green water. Further north, an obligatory photo stop at **Port-Coton▶▶** provides a splendid view of the sea-gnawed Aiguilles (Pinnacles) rock stacks, which Monet is alleged to have painted 38 times. The lighthouse on this coast is one of the most powerful in Europe, with a beam of 120km. **Port-Donnant▶▶** has a beautiful but dangerous beach.

At a road junction inland, two menhirs known as Jean and Jeanne are alleged to be the petrified remains of lovers punished for pre-empting their wedding night. The **Grotte de l'Apothicairerie (Apothecary's Cave)▶▶** lies in a bleak headland of silver-green rocks and gets its name from cormorants' nests, which look like chemist's jars. A dangerous path leads down the cliffs. **Sauzon▶▶**, on the north-eastern side, is the prettiest place on the island, a charming fishing port of lobster pots, colour-washed cottages and bright flowers.

THE CANADIAN CONNECTION

In 1763 Belle-Ile (then in English hands) was exchanged for Menorca in the Treaty of Paris. Another condition of this treaty was the expulsion from New England of French settlers who refused to submit to English rule. About 80 of the original French-Canadian families moved to Belle-Ile in 1766, bringing with them the potato, a new crop which had not yet found its way to mainland France.

GOOSE BARNACLES

In winter, locals on Belle-Ile, roped like mountaineers, clamber down the perilous cliffs of the Côte Sauvage in search of a strange delicacy called *pouce pied*, a large, rudely shaped barnacle which grows on the rocks by the waterline. The French aren't very keen on these salty things, but they achieve a high price in Spain and are mainly exported there (where they are known as *percebes*, a popular snack with drinks).

Carnac's evocative Alignements de Kermario are best seen from a viewing platform at the eastern end of the site

PREHISTORY MUSEUM
Finds from Carnac's megalithic sites are displayed in the Musée de Préhistoire, founded in 1881 by a Scottish archaeologist, James Miln, and enlarged by his local collaborator, Zacharie Le Rouzic. A visit to the museum helps to put the megaliths in context (borrow the English explanatory notes as you walk round). The presentation is streamlined and chronological, from earliest paleolithic (450,000 years ago) to early medieval times, obviously with the main emphasis on the neolithic period (4000–1500 BC) to which Carnac's megaliths belong (*Open* Jul–Aug, Mon–Fri 10–6, Sat–Sun 10–12, 2–6; Jun and Sep, Wed–Mon 10–12, 2–6. *Admission charge*).

▶▶▶ Carnac *174B2*

Thousands of visitors invade Carnac every year in order to see the extraordinary and baffling array of megaliths just outside the town (see pages 184–5). Apart from these and the explanatory **museum▶▶** (see panel), Carnac's only building of interest is its **church▶**, dedicated to St Cornély, patron saint of farm animals, whose statue can be seen on the façade between two oxen. Inside, the panelled vaulting is covered with paintings.

Carnac's seaside resort, **Carnac-Plage▶**, occupies a long, gently shelving beach of fine sand, extensively developed with modern hotels, beach and yacht clubs and thalassotherapy. Smaller, quieter settlements near by specialise in oysters. Carnac's summer crowding has increased accommodation prices and lowered standards.

▶ Etel Estuary *174B3*

On the map this complex estuary looks even more extensive than Lorient's bustling roadsteads to the west. Once you reach the declining fishing port of Etel at the mouth of the inlet you soon see why the Etel river is left mostly to oysters. A deadly sand-bar almost blocks the entrance to the estuary.

The Etel is not Brittany's prettiest river, but for drivers exploring local megaliths the quiet access lanes to points on its trailing shores make good picnic spots, overlooking grassy islands and oysterbeds. The best place to make for is picturesque **St-Cado▶▶** (see panel opposite).

▶▶ Le Faouët *174A4*

The most striking feature of this attractive little town, watered by rivers from the Montagnes Noires, is its splendid 16th-century covered **market hall▶** in the main square. A small **museum** near by houses a collection of early 20th-century art on Breton subjects (*Open* Jun–Sep, daily 10–12, 2–6. *Admission charge*), while on the town's northern edges is an excellent apiary exhibition

called **L'Abeille Vivante►** (*Open* Jul–Aug, daily 10–7; Apr–Jun, Sep–Oct, daily 9–12, 2–6. *Admission charge*), showing the honey bee in action through glass cases. Lots of honey-based products are on sale.

Other places of interest lie scattered around the town and could be strung into a pleasant half-day tour. About 3km to the north is **Ste-Barbe►►**, a chapel in Flamboyant style shoehorned into a rocky crevice in a wooded hillside overlooking the Ellé valley. Legend states that the chapel was built by a knight caught in a terrifying storm, who prayed to Ste Barbe for protection. Pilgrims today toll the bell by the custodian's house for Ste Barbe's blessing (you have to be strong to make any sound). If you want to see the interior (less compelling than the setting) you must wait for the guardian. Inside is an unusual carved 'lord's gallery' and some good stained glass.

St-Fiacre►►, the same distance south-east of Le Faouët, is essential viewing if you are at all keen on Breton churches. Inside, a brightly coloured **rood screen►►** dating from 1480 depicts some of Brittany's liveliest and laciest Flamboyant-style woodcarvings. Above athletic angels, who seem to be practising as trapeze artists, the seven deadly sins assume human forms – sloth is a man playing the bagpipes, theft an apple-scrumper, gluttony someone being spectacularly sick.

Another fine rood screen can be seen in the **Chapelle St-Nicolas►** some distance east. Continuing north past St-Nicolas, you reach the mostly modern Cistercian abbey of **Langonnet►**, a retreat for priests. The chapter house is original, dating from the 13th century. South of le Faouët lie the **Roches du Diable (Devil's Rock)►**, a popular beauty spot overlooking the Ellé. Paths from a woodland car park lead to a rocky platform where steep cliffs drop down to the surging river below.

The interior of St-Fiacre chapel at le Faouët

ST-CADO

This is a particularly idyllic spot on the Etel estuary, a circular islet anchored to the shore by a slim causeway. On it stands a pretty village of stone fishing cottages. Its Romanesque chapel is dedicated to the island's patron, a mysterious Celtic monk able to cure deafness in all who place their ears to his stone bed. St Cado's fountain stands below the east end, overlooking the shore. A legend tells how St Cado persuaded the Devil to build the bridge linking the island to the mainland in return for the first soul to travel across. When it was finished, St Cado sent a cat across before anyone used it. A dog-lover, obviously.

St-Fiacre's unusual gable-belfry has three slim spire turrets

Prehistoric monuments exist in many parts of the world, but nowhere are they so numerous as in Brittany. Even the words used to describe them – dolmen (table stone), menhir (long stone) and cromlech (curved stone) – are Breton.

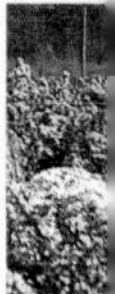

VISITING THE STANDING STONES

Until 1991 the standing stones were freely accessible, but now the main groups near Carnac are fenced off to protect them from damage. Visitors can see them (no charge) from a raised viewing platform called an Archéoscope (information centre with a film show), which gives a clear picture of the rows (you can't see them very well from the roadside). This conservation measure – understandable but regrettable in some ways – is rather belated. For many centuries the stones have been dug up, removed, reshaped, defaced, and perhaps mistakenly restored until it is impossible to know precisely their original positions, or even how many there were.

The Menhir de Champ Dolent, near Dol-de-Bretagne

Enigma variations Most of Brittany's archaeological wonders are clustered in and around Carnac and the Morbihan gulf. Estimates of their numbers vary widely, from 2,500 to over 5,000. Of the two main types the most numerous are the menhirs, or standing stones. You find these all over Brittany, but nowhere are they as dramatically organised as in Carnac, for instead of being isolated totems they are arranged in curious lines (*alignements*), some terminating in curved formations (cromlechs).

The other type is the group consisting of dolmens, cairns, *allées couvertes* and tumuli. These are less numerous, and to some extent less mysterious in that they are clearly burial chambers, presumably for important people such as priests or chieftains. They are generally flat-topped, table-like constructions made of stone slabs, and sometimes covered with mounds of earth (see also pages 30–1).

Current knowledge of the people who built the megaliths is very scanty, but they were clearly sophisticated folk capable of organising vast amounts of manpower and time for these weighty projects. Most of the stones were erected between about 4500 and 1800 BC, though some may be even older than this, pre-dating Mediterranean antiquities such as the Egyptian Pyramids or Crete's Palace of Knossos.

Mixed views Many archaeologists regard Carnac as the most important prehistoric site in Europe. Not everyone is equally impressed, however. The Breton stones are numerous but they lack the awesome scale and solitary impact of, say, Stonehenge in the UK. Perhaps the most remarkable thing about them is that they are still there, when virtually all other traces of the civilisation that built them (and many subsequent civilisations) have passed away. Some find the absence of conclusive evidence about their purpose fascinating; others are disappointed to discover that one megalith looks pretty much like another. All sorts of theories abound as to what exactly the stones were for – from some sort of astronomical observatory designed to predict times for planting crops, to temples of sun worship or fertility rites.

At some megaliths there is an entrance charge, while others can be explored for free. A torch is useful to see the interiors of burial chambers properly; wear robust footwear, as the areas around and in the chambers can be slippery and muddy after rain. Finds from the sites are displayed in regional museums, the most illuminating of which are in Carnac (see panel on page 182) and in Rennes (see page 221).

Pick of the Megaliths

Carnac Menhirs: three main groups of *alignements* just north of the town (free access) – **Ménec▶▶▶** (11 rows of about 1,100 stones that stretch for 1km); **Kermario▶▶▶** (982 stones set out in 10 rows); **Kerlescan▶▶▶** (540 stones set out in 13 rows, with a cromlech at one end). Dolmens: **Crucuno▶▶** (a 40-tonne capstone); **Mané-Kerioned▶** (has engravings). Tumuli: **Kercado▶▶** (a mound covering a large carved dolmen, topped by a menhir – open daily); **Tumulus de St-Michel▶** (a 12m-high burial place with several chambers – guided tours; good views from the top).

Locmariaquer Grand Menhir Brise▶▶ (see panel); **Table des Marchands▶▶** (decorated dolmen protected by a tumulus. Dolmens: **Pierres Plates▶**, **Mané-Lud, Mané-Rethual, Mané-er-Hroech** (free access).

Golfe du Morbihan Cairn de Gavrinis▶▶▶ (impressively decorated burial chamber on island; see panel, page 193).

Near Morlaix Tumulus de Barnenez▶▶ (11 burial chambers with approach galleries in massive cairn).

Near Rennes La Roche aux Fées▶▶ (20m covered gallery of purple schist; see panel on page 213).

Many other menhirs and dolmens are sprinkled all over Brittany. There is an important concentration at St-Just, near Redon, and more *alignements* at Lagatjar, Morgat (Crozon peninsula) and Quiberon.

GRAND MENHIR BRISE

This monument in Locmariaquer is the largest-known standing stone. Or at least it would be if it were not in several pieces – it is now on its side, broken into four sections (a putative fifth piece is missing). Experts believe the 20m-high menhir must have been subjected to some natural calamity such as lightning or earthquake several hundred years ago. The task of manhandling such a colossal piece of granite is truly awesome: over 12,000 people and 125 teams of oxen would have been required to shift it. (*Open* Jun–Sep, daily 10–7; Apr–May, daily 10–6. *Closed* lunchtime. *Admission charge*).

THEORIES ON MENHIRS

Over the centuries the standing stones of Carnac have spawned an amazing number of explanations. 'Carnac,' said Flaubert, 'has had more rubbish written about it than it has standing stones.' Most experts attribute some sort of religious or ritual element to them, but several go for military theories. Were they perhaps the tentpegs of Caesar's army, or anti-tank devices set up by the Germans during the Occupation (as one apocryphal US Marine is supposed to have concluded during the Liberation of Brittany)? Or were they Roman soldiers, miraculously turned to stone to save Carnac's patron saint, Cornély, as he fled for his life from Rome in the 3rd century?

You can still walk round some of Carnac's monuments, though many are now fenced off to prevent damage to the stones. To get a better impression of the lines, see them from the Archéoscope viewpoint

Notre-Dame-de-Paradis, Hennebont

► Groix, Ile de 174A2

A popular excursion from Lorient, this island takes about 45 minutes to reach by boat. You can take a car but many visitors prefer to explore by bike. The island measures about 8km by 2km and has about 3,000 inhabitants, most of whom live in the capital, Groix, or its pretty harbour town, Port-Tudy.

Ile de Groix is a raised plateau fringed by steep cliffs, most dramatic on the north and western sides, where the coastline is deeply indented and pierced with blowholes. Safe havens and bathing beaches can be found on the more sheltered eastern side, notably the convex Plage des Grands Sables.

Parts of the island are cultivated, but most of the inhabitants live on fishing and, increasingly, tourism. Once Groix had an important tuna fleet, the largest in France up to the 1930s. A sign of these times can be seen in the tuna-fish weather vane on Groix church, but now the industry has declined and its canning factory in Port-Tudy houses an ***écomusée*►** displaying many aspects of island life (*Open* Jun–Sep, daily 9.30–12.30, 3–5; Oct–May shorter hours and closed Mon. *Admission charge*). Groix's last fishing boat, the *Kenavo*, lies at anchor in the harbour.

Groix favours the self-sufficient visitor. Geologists find the island fascinating for its unique selection of rare minerals, while ornithologists head to the western tip for resident seabirds and passing migrants.

TUNA-FISHING IN GROIX

In his book, *The Six Sailors of Groix*, the Breton novelist Henri Queffelec describes the tuna-fishing scene during the 1930s: 'The boats were crammed in, gunwhale to gunwhale... Oh, the wonderful confusion of mooring ropes, which crossed over each other, got tangled up in tillers and grappling-hooks, and plunged beneath the keels!'

► Guéhenno 175D3

If an exhaustive tour of Finistère's parish closes has not drained you completely, seek out this charming calvary 10km south-west of Josselin. It dates originally from 1550, but was badly damaged in the Revolution. The local masons demanded such high fees to restore it that the parish priest and his assistant decided to have a go at it themselves, which explains the charmingly naïve carvings. A cock crows on a column in front of the cross, symbolising Peter's denial of Christ. The ossuary behind represents Christ's tomb, guarded by soldiers.

►► Hennebont *174B3*

Only a small section of this once-proud feudal town remains. Its iron-smelting industry and its proximity to the U-boat pens in Lorient (see page 191) made it a target for heavy attacks in World War II. For all that, Hennebont is not without interest.

The pepperpot towers of the 14th-century **Porte Broërec►** (much restored) define its earlier fortifications. As well as the small museum within the barbican (containing costumes and the like), the massive belfry and carved porch of the 16th-century church of **Notre-Dame-de-Paradis►** demand attention at the top of the hill. The botanic gardens of **Parc de Kerbihan►** make a pleasant stroll, and also within the town is one of Brittany's most important stud-farms, or ***haras*►►**, with around 70 stallions palatially housed. Guided tours are available (*Open* mid-Jul–Aug, guided tours 10, 11, 2.15, 3.15, 4.15; Sep afternoons only. *Admission charge*).

Out of town, the industrial suburb of Inzinzac-Lochrist on the banks of the River Blavet once had a thriving iron foundry, and during the wars it played a significant role in munition manufacture. Despite innumerable strikes and protests, the foundry finally closed in 1966, and an **industrial museum►►** now occupies the old smelting works. A short distance upstream is an annexe of the industrial museum, the **Musée de l'Eau►**, which examines the role of the waterway through all manner of fishing tackle and an aquarium of river fish (*Open* Mon–Fri 10–12, 2–6; Sat–Sun 2–6. *Admission charge*).

Still further up the Blavet, the abandoned village of **Poul Fetan►** (another victim of rural economic decline), has been turned into an *écomusée* of traditional thatched cottages furnished in period style, with complexes of crafts shops and cider-presses incorporated. Former inhabitants put on as good a show as they can for the trooping visitors. The village is well sign-posted from neighbouring roads (*Open* Jun–mid-Sep, daily 10–7, guided tours in the morning. *Admission charge*).

LA FORÊT DE TREMELIN

This 750ha expanse of mixed woodland north of Hennebont makes a pleasant place for a stroll. Crisscrossed by footpaths and trails, it contains many species of wildlife, including badgers and deer. The barrage lake of Ty-Mat makes a good picnic site.

A well dating from 1623 is one of the earliest surviving examples of Hennebont's wrought-iron industry

▶▶ Josselin 175D4

Josselin's mighty **castle▶▶** (*Open* Jul–Aug, daily guided tours 10–6; Jun–Sep 2–6; Apr, May, Oct, Wed, Sat–Sun 2–6. *Admission charge*), mirrored in the waters of the Oust, is an impressive sight and lingers long in the mind's eye. Its walls rise sheer from the rocky riverbanks, culminating in three circular towers topped by witches-hat turrets. Beyond the forbidding exterior, however, the living quarters shelter behind a gloriously delicate façade of Flamboyant Gothic tracery.

The River Oust, canalised at Josselin, is one of the best places for boating in central Brittany

The town was founded in about AD 1000 by a nobleman who bestowed on it the name of his second son. In about 1370 the original fortress was superseded by the present version, which was constructed by Olivier de Clisson (Du Guesclin's successor as Constable of France). De Clisson married Marguerite de Rohan, widow of Jean de Beaumanoir, who commanded the victorious side in the heroic Battle of the Thirty during the War of Succession (see panel). Subsequently Josselin passed into the hands of the powerful Rohan family. The Renaissance screen was added between 1490 and 1510.

Twice the castle was partially dismantled, once in 1488 and later on Richelieu's orders in 1629. The building was abandoned after damage in the Revolution and then finally restored in the 19th century. Descendants of the original Rohans still live in the castle. The grandly furnished rooms on the ground floor are open to the public. One of the castle's prize possessions is the table on which the Edict of Nantes (see page 238) was signed in 1598. The former stables house the **Musée des Poupées▶▶**, containing over 500 Rohan dolls dating from the 18th century to modern times. Smiling *babuschkas* from Russia and snake-charmers from Asia mingle with modern blue-eyed Barbie dolls, in pottery, wood, wax and plastic. Tickets for the castle include entrance to the museum (opening times for the two are the same).

The old town of well-kept timber-framed houses lies behind the castle around the 12th-century basilica of **Notre-Dame-du-Roncier (Our Lady of the Brambles)▶**. Most of it is in the Flamboyant style, with wondrously elongated

THE BATTLE OF THE THIRTY

In March 1351 the leaders of the opposing sides in the War of Succession, weary of siege warfare, staged a chivalric fight to establish ascendancy. Each side supplied 30 hand-picked knights, and the contestants met halfway between their two camps at Josselin and Ploërmel, where they fought on foot. The English-backed supporters of Jean de Montfort were commanded by John Bemborough, while the French contingent from Josselin (supporting Charles de Blois) was led by Jean de Beaumanoir. The day was won by the French leader. Over eight knights lay dead, including Bemborough, and the rest were captured (in true chivalric style they were treated well). Beaumanoir won the battle but not the war, which grated on for another 13 years, culminating in the Battle of Auray (see page 178).

gargoyles and a fretted spire (which you can climb). Inside lies the tomb of Josselin's former lord and master, Olivier de Clisson. From the opposite side of the river the picturesque Ste-Croix quarter and the **Chapelle Ste-Croix▶** provide good vantage points of the castle.

▶ Kerguéhennec *174C3*

Open: Tue–Sun 10–6. Admission charge

This extensive estate of wooded parkland and a lake surrounding an 18th-century château is now owned and administered by the Morbihan local authority, which has turned it into an imaginative outdoor gallery for modern sculpture. European artists of international renown exhibit works here, and visitors wander through the grounds as though on some treasure hunt, spotting weird and wonderful *objets trouvés* amid the trees. Strange red plastic forms float in the lake; concrete slabs or circular patios of crazy paving erupt on grassy promenades; a broken skiff dangles in a tree. Check the greenhouse for Jean-Pierre Raynaud's red flower pots (1986). The château's grand *salons,* which were restored in the 19th century, can be visited in summer.

▶▶ Kernascléden *174A4*

The extraordinary church that dominates this small village was built by the Rohan family, lords of Josselin and Pontivy. Both inside and out, the mid-15th century building is full of interest. Its lichen-mottled exterior is much carved and ornamented with slender crocketed pinnacles and sculpted balustrades, and there is a splendid set of Apostles in one of its porches.

The church's real claim to originality, however, lies inside, where frescoes adorn the walls and vaulting. Some are damaged, but all remain vivid and colourful. Scenes from the Virgin's life decorate the chancel, an angelic orchestra plays soundlessly in the north transept, and Christ rises serenely from his tomb. Startling Bosch-like visions of hell disturb the south transept – eyes are put out and demons bake the damned in cauldrons or barrels turned over raging fires.

THE *PARDON* OF THE BARKING WOMEN

Josselin's Whitsuntide *pardon* is named after the miraculous Virgin found in a bramble bush (Notre-Dame-du-Roncier), which now takes pride of place in the church. A strange legend is associated with it. One day a ragged beggar woman asked for a drink of water at the pump, but the local women drove her off with dogs and harsh words. Immediately their curses changed to a dog-like howl, for the beggar was the Virgin in disguise sent to try their charity. Every Whitsun, the women of Josselin must ask the Virgin for forgiveness or the barking curse will take hold again.

Josselin's mighty castle guards the waterfront approach to the old town

►► Locmariaquer *174C2*

After Carnac, this small oyster port is the most important site in Brittany for megaliths. Its most dramatic prehistoric remains lie in a single fenced compound just north of the village, near an information centre (see page 185).

Locmariaquer's charms are not confined to the nearby ancient monuments: it is a pretty place, with less suburban development than Carnac and a friendlier, more genuine atmosphere. The beaches aren't as good, but they are in a pleasant setting behind pines or dunes (there are also several decent walks). At low tide you can join a host of local families hunting for shellfish among the rocks. In the village centre, old stone cottages and a pretty church stand around the harbour, where rival boat companies advertise tours of the Golfe du Morbihan.

Good-value accommodation and eating places also score over Carnac. Locmariaquer's double-aspect location commands both gulf and bay views, including an excellent sighting from the Pointe de Kerpenhir of the strange grassy tumulus on **Gavrinis** in the Golfe du Morbihan (see panel on page 193).

La Trinité-sur-Mer, between Carnac and Locmariaquer, consists of a modern yacht marina serviced by chandleries and smart boutiques. Though well-equipped for the sailing fraternity, it has no more charm than a purpose-built ski resort, and has few advantages to recommend it as a touring base.

THE MAST POND

The black poles you may spot emerging at low tide from the River Scorff near St-Christophe bridge are the remnants of a mast pond, where wood used for boat building was stored in waterlogged sand to prevent it rotting. It was first started in 1826.

► Lorient *174A3*

Brittany's fourth largest city is almost entirely modern, a blockish place of angular white buildings and functional port facilities. During World War II it was repeatedly pounded by Allied bombs until over 85 per cent of its

The attractive centre of Locmariaquer

Antiques and bric-à-brac on sale at a street market in Lorient

PONT-SCORFF

Just north of Lorient, comfortably away from the urban tentacles, a zoo on the woodland banks of the River Scorff keeps a collection of big game and other animals in moderately natural settings (*Open* daily 9.30 or 10–nightfall. *Admission charge*).

buildings lay in rubble. The Germans held out here long after there was any military point in doing so. Ironically, the main target of the attacks, the concrete U-boat pens, survived almost intact. Used by the French navy for the past 50 years, they are now open to visitors (guided tours in summer).

French nationals only are allowed to visit the Arsenal (naval dockyard), but the rest of the port is easily accessible from the new town: the massive cargo wharfs at the Kergroise docks; the vast modern fishing port of Kéroman (one of the best equipped in France); and the pleasure marina of Kernevel. The fishing port is liveliest in the mornings but, unlike other Breton ports, the businesslike daily *criée* (fish auction) is not open to the general public except on limited guided tours in summer (ask at the tourist office for details).

The ***Victor Pleven*** is the last and largest of French trawlers, known as *Terre-Neuvas* because they sailed as far as the coast of Newfoundland in search of cod and haddock banks (*Open* daily 10–12, 2–6. *Admission charge*).

Lorient's name (*l'Orient* means the East) echoes its purpose: it was once the headquarters of the Compagnie des Indes (India Company), founded here by Colbert, Louis XIV's naval minister, in 1666 when its predecessor across the water in Port-Louis failed. This southerly site was chosen to avoid the hazards faced by Channel shipping during the 17th century because of English pirates. It thrived for a century, then declined rapidly after the loss of India and the French Revolution.

Lorient offers little else for visitors, apart from boat trips around its three roadsteads and excursions to Ile de Groix (see page 186), plus a summer international Celtic festival, the Festival Interceltique, which attracts visitors and participants from far and wide. Dreary suburbs extend inland up the twin estuaries of the Blavet and Scorff, and local pollution makes it no place for a beach holiday. The modern concrete church of **Notre-Dame-de-Victoire▶** (usually known as **St-Louis**) stands in the new shopping area. It is an angular, brutalist structure roofed by a shallow dome, with a dramatically stark interior illuminated by bright, jagged splinter glass. The murals and Stations of the Cross may appeal to visitors with modern tastes.

LARMOR-PLAGE

Lorient's nearest resort at the mouth of the estuary is also a naval base. Larmor-Plage's parish church dates from the 12th century and has a number of interesting features and a fine interior. Traditionally, any warship leaving Lorient on active service would fire a three-gun salute as it passed Notre-Dame-de-Larmor, and in reply the priest would hoist a flag, ring the church bells, and give the ship a blessing. On the Sunday closest to 24 June, Midsummer's Day, a Blessing of the Waters ceremony is held in the town.

A rock-strewn beach at Pointe du Percho, Golfe du Morbihan

ILE AUX MOINES
This straggly lump of land measures about 7km at its longest. It is the most populous – and popular – island in the gulf, thronged with day-trippers in summer. The quickest ferry journey is from Port-Blanc (five minutes). Woods and heaths make up most of the interior, and lush plants fill the gardens of stone or thatched houses. You can explore its innumerable paths and lanes on foot or by bike, heading for scattered megaliths or a stepped calvary. The beach near the port is one of the best in the gulf.

Strange and humorous carvings decorate the old houses around Malestroit's main square

▶▶ Malestroit 175D3

This ancient baronial town sits at the junction of several major roads, and is also on the Nantes–Brest canal. Its historic core is around Place du Bouffay and the church of St-Gilles (12th to 16th centuries) – a delightful assembly of slate-hung Gothic and Renaissance houses which repay close inspection for their bizarre carvings: a man in his nightshirt beats his wife; a hare plays the bagpipes, and a sow threads a distaff. Edward III of England and Philip VI of France signed a truce in Malestroit during the Hundred Years War, giving England a 40-year foothold in Brittany.

Apart from pleasant walks along the canalside there isn't a great deal to see or do in the town itself, but at **St-Marcel**, a short distance west, the **Musée de la Résistance Bretonne**▶▶ (*Open* mid-Jun–mid-Sep, daily 10–7; mid-Sep–mid-Jun, Wed–Mon 10–12, 2–6. *Admission charge*) is essential viewing for anyone interested in local history. It stands on the site of a significant wartime operation in June 1944, when the local Maquis (French Resistance) successfully diverted many German troops from the Allied landings in Normandy.

The first room re-creates Brittany under the Occupation, with the buckled engines of a shot-down American bomber amid propaganda posters and ration cards. In subsequent rooms, Resistance sabotage, the black market and an account of the battle of St-Marcel are covered, while the tune of 'Lili Marlene' trickles relentlessly into the visitor's brain for the rest of the day. The presentation is generally good, but pick up the English translation at the desk and follow the numbering system carefully. Local monuments and war memorials show how vividly (and bitterly) memories of war continue to linger in this area.

▶▶▶ Morbihan, Golfe du 174C2

The 'Little Sea' which gives its name to the region was formed quite recently in geological terms – between 2,000

and 4,000 years ago, when land levels fell. Over 20km wide and 15km from north to south, the gulf is an area of great natural and historic interest. It has the largest concentration of seabirds on the French Atlantic coast, and a great variety of wildlife habitats: dunes, mud flats, oysterbeds, salt marshes, lagoons, islands, creeks, estuaries, reed beds, heaths and pinewoods. Mediterranean vegetation flourishes in the mild climate of the area.

There are no real seaside resorts on the gulf, apart from Locmariaquer (see page 190), whose main beach faces the open sea and is therefore rather exposed. The small settlements along the shore catering for holidaymakers offer sailing centres, boat trips and watersports rather than bathing beaches. A handful of hotels, restaurants and campsites provide the necessary facilities for quiet waterside sojourns. Fresh seafood, needless to say, is excellent – oysters are a speciality.

For all its sheltered location away from ocean storms, the gulf is fiercely tidal, its waters ripping in and out of the narrow neck near Locmariaquer like fizzing champagne. Currents can make its beaches very dangerous for swimming. At low tide the water generally retreats beyond acres of mud or weed, and pollution can be a problem in the built-up area around Vannes. The state of the tide – and the weather – can make a huge difference to the appearance of the gulf.

One of the best excursions in Morbihan is a boat trip across the gulf, possibly stopping at one of the islands *en route*. There are over 300 of these islands, some no more than grassy hummocks barely emerging from the waterline, others much larger and inhabited; some are even privately owned by film stars or other celebrities. Tourists who use public transport may land on only three islands: the **Ile aux Moines▶▶** (the largest and most varied of the islands – see panel opposite); the **Ile d'Arz** (with a good hotel-restaurant, L'Escale; see Hotels and Restaurants, page 281), and the **Ile de Gavrinis▶▶** (see panel). Several centres offer a bewildering variety of boat trips, notably Vannes, Locmariaquer, Port-Navalo and Auray. Larmor-Baden operates monopoly sailings to Gavrinis. If you have your own boat you can explore at leisure, weaving among the disorientating landmasses and lagoons.

ILE DE GAVRINIS
If you have time for only a brief exploration of the gulf, head for Gavrinis and the most ornately decorated prehistoric tomb in Brittany. It is buried beneath a grass-topped stone cairn, easily visible as you approach the island. Many of the stones composing the burial chamber display ritualistic or realistic shapes of snakes, sun-rays, chevrons and spirals. The pressure of visitors is eroding the site, and at some point in the future tourists will probably be excluded (*Open* Apr–Oct guided tours daily; tel: 02 97 57 19 38. *Admission charge*).

Carvings from the porch at Ploërmel

LIZIO
This pretty place was once a halt for pilgrims on the long journey through France to the Spanish medieval shrine of Santiago de Compostela. The skill of the local stone-cutting industry shows through in the perfectly bonded masonry of its mellow buildings. Weaving was another important industry in the community.

▶ Ploërmel *175D4*

Ploërmel's finest hour was probably in the 14th century, when the Montforts, who held the town at the time, won the War of Succession and became medieval Dukes of Brittany. It is now the market centre of the prosperous Porhoët farming region, and a popular touring base for the Forêt de Paimpont to the north-east (see pages 216–17). The local reservoir (Etang au Duc) caters for fishing and watersports enthusiasts.

On 27 March 1351 the famously chivalric tournament known as the Battle of the Thirty was fought half-way between Ploërmel and Josselin (see panel on page 188). The town was damaged during World War II, and comparatively little of the old medieval hunting town remains, apart from the Flamboyant Gothic church of **St-Armel▶**, where the local patron slays a dragon and Dukes Jean II and III stand in a side chapel. Notice the carvings on the north door; among more biblical scenes, one shows a clogmaker sewing up his nagging wife's mouth.

Just a few picturesque houses line Ploërmel's older streets, notably the **Maison des Marmousets▶** on rue Beaumanoir, but a few sights lie south of the town: **Lizio** has an **Ecomusée des Vieux Métiers▶**, with over 10,000 farm- and craftworking implements on display (*Open* daily 10–12, 2–7. *Admission charge*). The crumbling 14th-century Château du Crévy, just off the N166, contains a marvellous **costume museum▶▶** with fashion from the 18th century to the present day. Guided tours take about an hour, past Worth evening gowns, minute Chinese shoes for bound feet, and naughty underwear (*Open* Jul–Aug, 10–6 guided tours. *Admission charge*).

▶ Pontivy *174C4*

Like Josselin, Pontivy was a seat of the Rohan family. Its squat fortress of rusty schist at the north-east end of town dates from about 1485, with pepperpot bastions guarding a deep, dry moat. Now the castle is used for temporary exhibitions (the tourist office stands just outside).

Pontivy splits sharply into two architectural styles: higgledy-piggledy half-timbering in the old town (shown here) and Napoleonic order in the new town to the west (shown opposite)

The town hall at Pontivy, a formal public building typical of the Napoleonic era

Pontivy's old town around the Place du Martray looks more or less contemporaneous with the castle. The main square is busiest on Tuesdays, which is market day. Quaint old half-timbering characterises the narrow streets near **Notre-Dame-de-la-Joie**, where a revered statue answered local prayers during an outbreak of bubonic plague. Less overtly picturesque but equally interesting is the newer sector to the south-west of the town, which was built by Napoleon. Pontivy's Republican sentiments appealed to the Consul-cum-Emperor, and he modernised the town in formal neoclassical style with wide, grid-like boulevards, landscaped parks, and grandiose administrative and military buildings. Later, Pontivy fitted in neatly with Napoleon's ambitions to create a canal linking Nantes and Brest that was far away from coastal marauders. The townsfolk rechristened the town Napoléonville in his honour, but it reverted to its original name when Bonapartism fell out of favour.

Pontivy makes a pleasant enough touring base for a day or two. Several villages to the south lie within a brief drive. **St-Nicolas-des-Eaux▶** stands placidly on the Blavet, its older nucleus of thatched cottages much expanded by modern grey-white holiday homes. Just south of the village the river executes a dramatic loop, and at the encircled knoll known as the **Site de Castennec▶** an excellent view can be had from a roadside belvedere. **Bieuzy▶** has an attractive church with a knobbly Renaissance chevet. Next to it is an unusual war memorial – not the banner-waving type, but an ordinary soldier leaning casually on his rifle. An old well, communal bread oven and fountain can also be seen.

Melrand, down the road, has granite houses and an unusual calvary encrusted with gold lichen, its shaft ornamented with the heads of the Apostles. A **Ferme Archéologique (Archaeological Farm)▶** dating from about AD 1000 has been excavated and reconstructed as a tourist sight, complete with thatched dwellings, rare breeds of sheep and a medieval-style herb garden (*Open* Jun–Aug, daily 10–7; Sep–May, daily 11–5. Closed mid-Dec–mid-Jan. *Admission charge*).

THE VENUS DE QUINIPILY

The humdrum little town of Baud (some 20km south of Pontivy) has just one claim on visitors' attention, a *jolie laide* statue known as the Venus de Quinipily, which can be found in the grounds of the Château de Quinipily 2km south-west of Baud. Originally discovered at Castennac, the statue is of uncertain provenance, some declaring it to be Roman or Egyptian. Thus suffused with curious pagan legends, the image became the object of various unspeakable practices, and was several times thrown into the Blavet by order of the Church (whereupon it was instantly retrieved). Eventually the local lord of the manor had the statue decently resculpted, with some clothing and a less ample posterior, and placed her on her present dignified plinth.

THE BRETON LEAGUE
One of the more confusing patches of Brittany's history occurred during the Wars of Religion in the late 16th century. The Duke of Mercoeur (then Governor of Brittany) plotted against the succession of the Protestant French king, Henry IV. The duke's Catholic supporters, the Breton League, enlisted the help of Philip II of Spain, and in 1590 a force of 3,000 Spaniards arrived at Port-Louis, which they occupied for eight years. A similar Spanish garrison was set up on the Crozon peninsula (see panel on page 124). The insurrection ended in 1598 when Henry signed the Edict of Nantes, which granted freedom of religion to Protestants (mainly Huguenots) throughout France, thus ending the Wars of Religion.

▶▶ Port-Louis *174A3*

The history of this sea-port at the mouth of the Blavet estuary is inextricably bound up with Lorient, its huge sibling across the water (see pages 190–1). As the fortunes of one town waxed, the other's waned.

The fortified citadel at the entrance to the roadstead was founded in 1591, when Port-Louis was under temporary Spanish occupation (see panel). It was subsequently reinforced in 1616 and 1641, and used as a prison, barracks and arsenal. Port-Louis was the original headquarters of the Compagnie des Indes (India Company), set up by Cardinal Richelieu in Louis XIII's reign (when the town took his name). The venture was not a success. Despite the port's previous experience of trade with Africa and Madagascar, it had become corrupt and gangster-ridden, and soon the first Compagnie des Indes failed. It was resurrected in Lorient in 1666 to challenge English and Dutch trading supremacy in the Far East.

Port-Louis achieved minor prosperity from sardine- and tuna-fishing in the 19th century, and is now an attractive little resort. Ironically, it is Port-Louis, not Lorient, that now displays the history of the Compagnie des Indes in the **museum complex**, within the ramparts: **l'Arsenale**, with model ships and naval documents; the **Poudrière** (Powder Factory), focusing on naval armaments, mines, torpedoes and the like; the **Musée de Bateaux** (Boat Museum), about sea-rescue services; and the **Musée de la Compagnie des Indes (India Company Museum)▶▶**, with exotic imports from the Orient, along with documents, maps and models (*Open* Apr–Sep, 10–7; Oct–Mar 1.30–6. *Closed* Tue except Jul–Aug. *Admission charge*). Walks along the ramparts offer excellent views of the Blavet roadsteads, and near the car park is a gateway that leads to an attractive, quiet beach of sand and rock. Just

The rocks off the Quiberon coast are a peril to shipping

Port-Louis is still a thriving tuna-fishing port

south of the town, the enclosed Mer de Gâvres presents a mournful scene of mud flats and ducks.

▶ Quiberon, Presqu'île de *174B2*

This curious protuberance from the Morbihan coastline is reached by a causeway of tidal sediment in places scarcely wider than the road. Plouharnel, at the top of the peninsula, offers two unusual attractions: ***le Galion*▶**, a mock galleon filled with shell pictures of extraordinary elaboration, and the **Musée de la Chouannerie▶** (*Open* Apr–Sep, 10–12, 2–6. *Admission charge*) recounting the story of the Chouans (see page 179). The main road along the Penthièvre isthmus leads past piles of blown sand and windblasted conifers, with a massive exposed beach on the west side. Eastwards the sands of Sables Blancs look inviting at high water.

At the **Fort de Penthièvre**, which guards the neck of the peninsula, a monument commemorates 59 Resistance members who were executed here in 1944. To the west the Atlantic beats wildly at the Côte Sauvage, a coast of cliffs, caves, crags and chasms. There are beaches here too, but the undertow is treacherous, as testifed by an awesome list of drownings. Head west to **Pointe du Percho▶**, and walk to the end for views of rocks fractured and wave-sculpted into sea-caves. **Beg-er-Goalennec** makes another good belvedere for this exciting coast.

Quiberon▶ is one of Morbihan's liveliest resorts, its harbour area throbbing with shops, restaurants, bars and hotels. Traffic queues form in summer as over 100,000 visitors annually converge, most bent on visiting Belle-Ile (see pages 180–1). Beyond the bustling *gare maritime* at Port-Maria, the long beach curves past a massive modern thalassotherapy centre towards the low-lying **Pointe du Conguel**. The east coast consists mostly of low-key holiday development and amorphous little resorts. **St-Pierre-Quiberon** is the largest, with rows of megaliths (22 in all) on rue des Menhirs. Sheltered from prevailing winds, the bay of Quiberon is smooth and calm. Marinas and Beg-Rohu's national sailing school cater for the local passion.

THE BLAVET VIRGINS
A tale from Port-Louis' period of Spanish occupation relates how a group of 40 young girls tried to evade capture by Spanish forces. They set sail in a ship but were pursued. To prevent themselves being seized they joined hands and leapt into the sea, where they all perished.

SHELL PICTURES
Le Galion, a modern replica of an 18th-century vessel built from an old barge, lies beached in Plouharnel at the north end of the Quiberon peninsula. It has an extraordinary display of elaborate shell pictures, including depictions of the Piazza San Marco in Venice, a Japanese pagoda and a Loire château (*Open* Jul–Aug, 9.30–7, Apr–Jun. Sep shorter hours. *Admission charge)*.

GENERAL HOCHE
A crucial turning point of the Chouan rebellion (see page 179) took place in Quiberon in 1795, when General Hoche massively defeated the straggling invasion fleet of exiled aristocrats and their supporters from England. He wrote to his chief of staff: 'The Anglo-French Emigré Chouans are trapped like rats on Quiberon, where the army has hemmed them in. I hope we shall be rid of them in a few days.' This happened more literally than he intended. The 900 beleaguered Chouans surrendered, were taken prisoner and, to Hoche's horror, were all shot without trial at Auray. He protested at this atrocity, but to no avail.

Above: market, St-Gildas-de-Rhuys

Drive

The Rhuys peninsula

See map on pages 174–5.

The Rhuys peninsula is the arm of land cradling the southern side of the Golfe du Morbihan. From its tip, the Locmariaquer headland is only 2km away; by road, it is a 60km drive via Vannes and Auray. Allow three hours or so from Vannes.

The Rhuys peninsula enjoys an unusually mild microclimate. Figs, camellias and pomegranates flourish, and there are even vines, producing a heady wine of legendary potency.

Starting from Vannes, follow the main gulf road (D780) round to the south-east, skirting the waterfront. Sarzeau is the main community on Rhuys, though it has little to interest visitors aside from a couple of fine Renaissance houses near the church and a regional tourist office. South of the main road, a signposted turning leads to the peninsula's most interesting sight, the **Château de Suscinio▶▶**, restored in 1995. Dating from the 13th century, it stands in lonely marshes – partly roofless now – but was once moated by the sea. The castle used to be a summer residence of the Dukes of Brittany, and the Duc de Richemont, final victor of the Hundred Years War, was born here.

Further west, another detour from the main road leads to **St-Gildas-de-Rhuys**, where a dour abbey church attracts pilgrims for its associations with Peter Abelard (see panel on page 199). Inside, notice the carved capitals, model ships and the tomb of St Gildas, a 6th-century saint.

To the right of the main road near **Arzon**, a small hillock erupts from the low-lying surroundings. This is the **Tumulus de Tumiac▶**, known as Caesar's Mound, a neolithic monument from which Julius Caesar is said to have watched the naval battle in which the Veneti were defeated in 56 BC (see page 33). The tip of the peninsula is quite extensively developed, the little resort of **Port-Navalo** now covered with holiday homes. **Port du Crouesty** is a modern marina complex of apartments and boutiques.

►► La Roche-Bernard *175E2*

Originally this attractive town was a Viking foundation. During the Wars of Religion it was a Protestant centre, and its fortunes grew after the Edict of Nantes in 1598, when religious tolerance was granted. Its ship-building industry flourished, and the great warship *La Couronne* was commissioned in 1634. Riverine trade also prospered; cargo boats sailed up and down the Vilaine, bearing grain, wine, timber, salt and spices. This aspect of the town's history is covered in the **Musée de la Vilaine Maritime►►** (*Open* Jul–mid-Sep, daily 10.30–12.30, 2.30–6.30. *Admission charge*), housed in the Château des Basses-Fosses on the west bank. During the Revolution, la Roche-Bernard was a Republican town, but the Chouans overcame the few stalwarts defending it. They ordered the mayor, Joseph Sauveur, to shout 'Long live the King', but he shouted 'Long live the Republic' instead and was shot dead.

Since the Arzal dam was built, the river is no longer tidal, and pleasure craft are the only vessels to reach the town. The massive suspension bridge spanning the river replaces an earlier one accidentally destroyed during World War II, when lightning struck an ammunition dump belonging to the Germans. In its day, the earlier bridge was the longest ever built, and its supporting pillars can still be seen from the new bridge.

A by-pass speeds traffic past the town, leaving the centre relatively peaceful. The old quarter around place du Bouffay is far less grim today than it was in 1793, when a guillotine stood here. The town hall displays a gun from an English warship, the *Inflexible*, which sought refuge here after a battle.

La Roche-Bernard has an excellent range of accommodation and restaurants, and makes a good touring base. On the way to Vannes lies the **Moulin de Pen-Mur**, an old mill where you can watch paper being made in the traditional way (*Open* Apr–Sep, Mon–Sat 10–12, 2–6, Sun 2–6; Oct–Mar, Sat 10–12, 2–5.30, Sun 2–5.30. *Admission charge*).

ABELARD'S EXILE

The sad affair of Héloïse and Abelard in the 12th century is one of the great love stories of all time. Abelard was forced into exile as abbot at St-Gildas-de-Rhuys, 'a wild country where every day brings new perils', he wrote. When his fellow monks attempted to poison him he managed to escape down a secret passage, and eventually returned to Paris. The lovers were finally reunited in death and now lie in the same grave in Paris. A museum at Abelard's birthplace, le Pallet near Nantes (just outside the area covered by this book), documents Abelard's life.

Cannon watch over the estuary at la Roche-Bernard, once an important naval dockyard

►► Rochefort-en-Terre 175E2

Winner of many 'best-kept village' competitions, Rochefort-en-Terre is instantly and conspicuously appealing. It stands high on a spur of schist jutting into the Arz valley, and is surrounded by plunging slopes of woodland and babbling brooks. The old town is best explored on foot. Aristocratic stone mansions, much embellished with carvings and windowboxes, line the cobbled main streets, and some have been turned into shops and restaurants catering for well-heeled visitors.

The church, **Notre-Dame-de-la-Tronchaye►►**, is a delightful building with an unusual gabled façade and a delicate three-tiered calvary standing outside. Inside, interesting features include Renaissance altarpieces of white stone and a wrought-iron font. The revered statue of Our Lady of la Tronchaye, discovered in the 12th century apparently hidden from Norse invaders in a tree, stands in the south transept behind a wrought-iron grille. A *pardon* takes place on the Sunday after Assumption Day.

Rochefort-en-Terre's old centre is best savoured on foot

Near the top of the town stands a castle. The original fortress was damaged in 1488 and finally destroyed during the Revolution, but at the turn of the 20th century two American artist brothers, Alfred and Trafford Klots, decided to restore and rebuild it, using stone salvaged from various local châteaux. Today the castle belongs to the town, and is open to the public. It is furnished in 16th- and 17th-century style, embellished with tapestries, paintings by the Klots brothers, and a collection of Quimper porcelain madonnas. A small museum of popular folklore stands in the grounds, and the terrace commands excellent views of the surrounding countryside.

A couple of contrived tourist attractions can be found close to Rochefort: a **Parc de Préhistoire** at Malansac relates an everyday story of cavemen in lifesize tableaux (*Open* Apr–mid-Oct, daily 10–8. *Admission charge*), and an exotic tropical garden flourishes at St-Jacut-les-Pins – but the local scenery beats both hands down.

Pricey *chambres d'hôtes* seem to be the only accommodation option in town, but to the north-west the Château de Talhouët promises an unusual and delightful stay (see Hotels and Restaurants, page 275).

Prehistory comes alive at Malansac

SLATE QUARRIES

The terrain around Rochefort-en-Terre shows much evidence of quarrying. The Lac Bleu, just south of the town, makes a pretty spot for a picnic, its waters eerily blue with suspended particles, and the long-disused slate galleries are inhabited by unusual fauna (blind butterflies and long-eared bats).

Watching the world go by in Vannes

►►► Vannes *174C2*

Vannes is one of Brittany's best-looking towns, livelier and more cosmopolitan than many and with a Gallic rather than a Celtic air. It has a long and prestigious pedigree and has played an important role in Breton history. The name stems from Veneti, the Celtic tribe that Caesar vanquished. Vannes shared the honour of being the Breton capital with Nantes and Rennes throughout the Middle Ages, finally signing away its status by the Act of Union with France in 1532.

There is plenty to see here and Vannes also makes a good excursion centre, particularly for boat trips on the Golfe du Morbihan. The river is canalised and used by pleasure craft, which moor outside the old town. Near the *gare maritime* a leisure complex offers several wet-weather attractions: an aquarium (overshadowed now by better versions at Brest and le Croisic), a butterfly park and a museum of mechanical dolls. Like several otherwise appealing Breton towns, Vannes suffers a conspicuous lack of pleasant central accommodation.

THE ELVEN TOWERS

Largoët castle, north-east of Vannes at Elven, is an impressive feudal ruin in extensive wooded parkland. It once belonged to the Marshal de Rieux, tutor to Anne de Bretagne. In 1488 the castle was burned down by the king of France, Charles VIII, and now the ruins make an atmospheric setting for summer *son et lumière* presentations. During the day visitors are welcome to wander through the woods from the lodge to the gaunt ruins. Two mighty towers and a gateway with a drawbridge over the moat are still intact (*Open* Jun–Sep, daily 10.30–6.30; guided tours in the afternoon. *Admission charge*).

One of Vannes' picturesque old houses

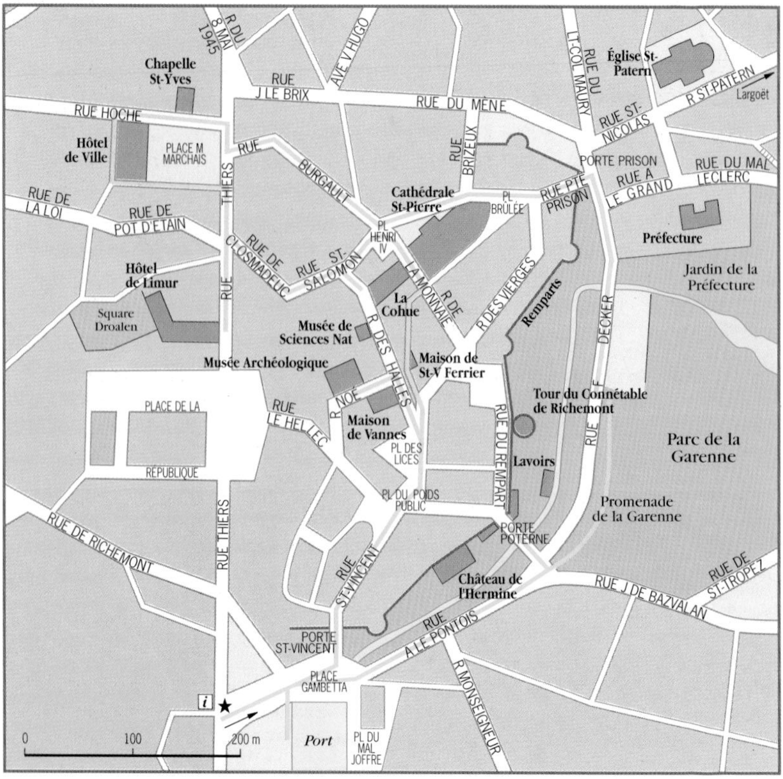

The old town of Vannes

Vannes escaped serious wartime damage, and much of its delightful walled old town remains intact. This stroll round the scenic area surrounding the cathedral offers an agreeable mix of museums and architecture, covering the period from prehistory to the present day.

Vannes' ramparts confine traffic to the outskirts of the old town, where it screeches around confusing one-way systems in search of parking places. Try Place de la République or the area by the port, then approach the walled town on foot. **Porte St-Vincent** at the southern end is a good place to start, and you can visit the tourist office *en route*. Nearby **Place Gambetta** consists of a terraced crescent of 19th-century buildings, its cafés and bars especially lively in the early evening.

Beyond the walls, virtually every street or square has some buildings of interest. On a fine day, old Vannes is remarkably photogenic. **Place des Lices** used to be a medieval tilt-yard where jousting tournaments were held. Just off it, on a corner of rue Rogue, is the Maison de Vannes, an old house adorned with carved wooden statues of a jolly rustic couple known as **Vannes and his Wife**. Near by is the small but interesting **Musée d'Archéologie du Morbihan**, in the 15th-century Château Gaillard, once the Breton parliament. The lacklustre display doesn't do justice to the contents, which include finds from Morbihan's important megalithic sites on the first floor.

The **Cathédrale St-Pierre▶▶** is unmissable, an eclectic muddle of architecture from the 13th to the 19th centuries, trailing through Romanesque, Gothic and Italian Renaissance styles. Inside the unusual Rotunda chapel lies the tomb of St Vincent Ferrier, the town's patron, and there are pictures and tapestries depicting his good works. This Spanish saint, a Dominican monk, achieved great fame as a preacher and performed many miraculous cures. He travelled widely and played a role in ending the Papal schism between Rome and Avignon. Less benevolently, his flamboyant oratory was the cause of anti-Semitic riots in the Spanish city of Toledo, when many Jews were flung over the cliffs to their deaths. When the saint died here in 1419, the people of Vannes refused to give up his body to Spanish or Dominican authorities, and it was laid to rest in the cathedral, where it still lies. Be sure to see his house at 17 Place Valencia, marked by a niched statue. The **cathedral treasury**, housed in the old chapter house, contains a fine collection of religious gold plate.

Virtually opposite the cathedral is **la Cohue▶▶**. This medieval covered market has served many purposes over the years, and once housed the law courts. Today it contains museums of art and the history of the Golfe du Morbihan, interspersed with temporary exhibitions.

Wander west to rue Thiers in the newer town to glance at the imposing 19th-century **Hôtel de Ville▶**, with its fine equestrian statue, and the **Hôtel de Limur**, a 17th-century town house. Then walk back through the machicolated Porte Prison and meander past the **ramparts▶▶**, their stern defensive towers softened by brilliant flowerbeds and a passing stream. You get a good view of these from the **promenade de la Garenne**, a raised walk by well-tended public gardens. Notice Vannes' most picturesque buildings: the medieval ***lavoirs* (wash houses)▶▶** near the Porte Poterne, a photogenic assembly of slate roofs and flower-decked dormers.

Beautifully kept municipal gardens add cheer to the forbidding ramparts enclosing the old town

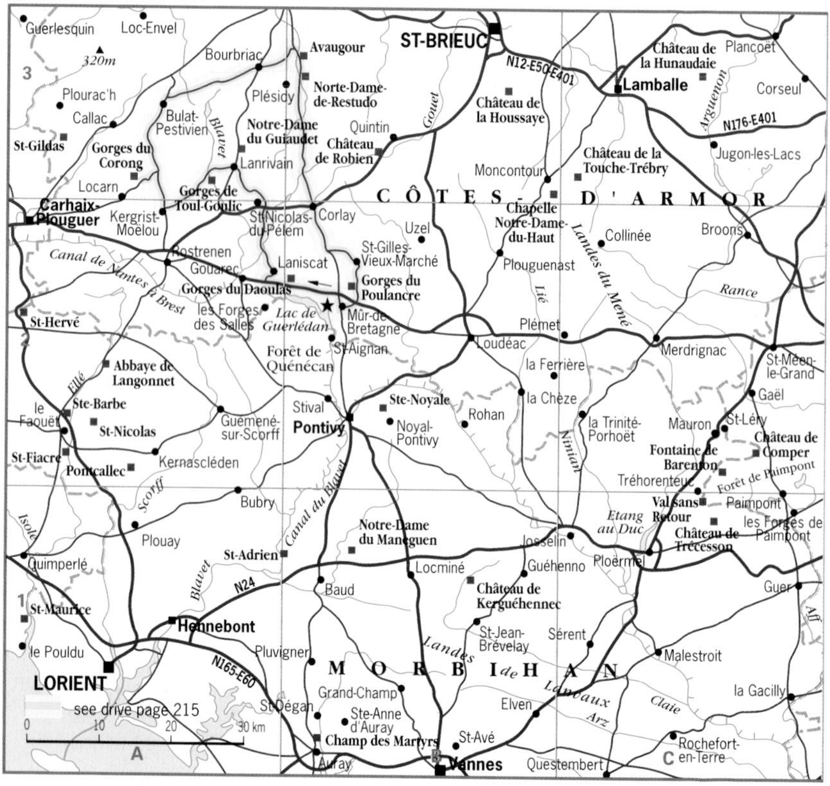

The castle at Combourg, where the writer François-René de Chateaubriand spent two emotionally charged years of his adolescence

Inland Brittany

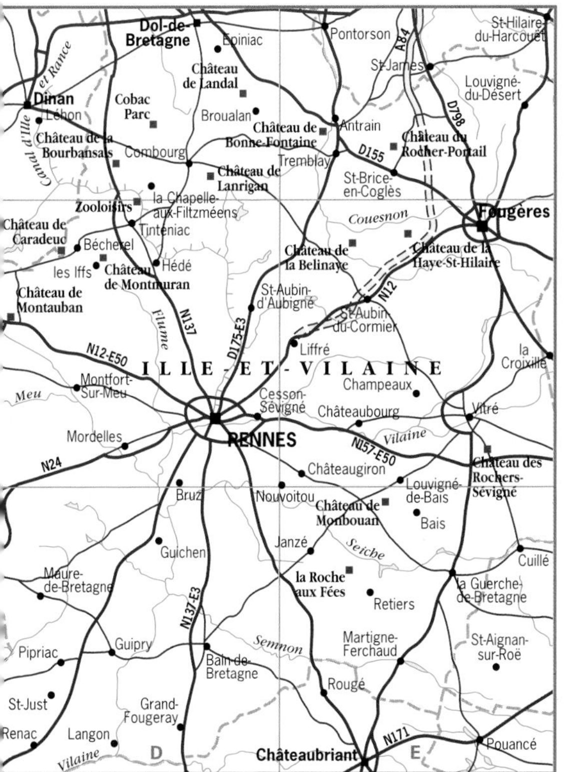

INLAND BRITTANY Compared with Brittany's overtly attractive coastline, the interior of Haute Bretagne (the easterly section closest to the rest of France) has little charisma. Mostly it is an uneventful 'managed' landscape given over to agricultural pursuits and interspersed with low hills, stands of woodland and sluggish waterways. Mighty fortresses punctuate the marches that once severed Brittany from neighbouring France, yet at first sight there seems little to distinguish this region from the lush farmland of Normandy or the Loire Valley – there are few of the *coiffes*, *pardons* or parish closes that characterise the far west. The lonely plateau villages north of Mûr-de-Bretagne have preserved more of their traditional culture, and here Breton is still spoken in a few places.

HISTORIC INTEREST Historically, though, Haute Bretagne's hinterland offers rich pickings, from the great bastion towns of Fougères and Vitré to the present provincial capital of Rennes, one of Brittany's most cosmopolitan cities. Rennes is often undersold because of its unattractive industrial sprawl, but its museums and historic centre amply repay a day's exploration. Smaller fortified towns such as Montfort-sur-Meu and Quintin are more easily accessible destinations.

Touring the countryside is not unrewarding, whether by boat along its canal systems, by road through the lonely lakes and gorges north of Pontivy, or on foot through remnants of the virgin forests that once cloaked Brittany's

▶▶▶ REGION HIGHLIGHTS

Fougères *page 208*

Gorges around Mûr-de-Bretagne *page 215*

Forêt de Paimpont *page 216*

Rennes *pages 218*

Vitré *page 224*

A SALMON A DAY
In 17th-century Brittany, salmon was very much part of the staple diet. Over 4,500 tonnes of it were eaten every year, and it was no special treat. At one time it was regarded as such dull fare that servants in the great houses of central Brittany made their masters sign contracts promising not to give them salmon more than three times a week!

argoat. Most evocative of these woodlands is the Forêt de Paimpont, the Brocéliande of Arthurian legend.

UNCROWDED RESORTS Apart from in the obvious tourist centres, accommodation and restaurants are scarcer inland than on the coast, and may be geared to commercial travellers. Tourism is big business throughout Brittany and if you choose a base carefully (perhaps in one of the *stations vertes* – country tourist centres – now promoted as inland resorts) you should have little difficulty in finding somewhere to stay, even at the height of the summer season when coastal resorts are crammed to capacity. Increasingly, farmhouses and private châteaux provide interesting alternatives to conventional hotels. Fougères, Mûr-de-Bretagne and Combourg make pleasant town bases, and there are a couple of excellent hotels conveniently and peacefully located between Vitré and Rennes.

Grey granite dominates at Combourg

ANIMAL MAGIC
If you have children to amuse, the Combourg area offers several possibilities. The Château de la Bourbansais (12km west) makes an impressive statement of turrets and pavilions across velvety lawns set with classical statuary, but its contents (Aubusson tapestries and oriental porcelain) may appeal less to younger visitors than the menagerie of wild animals roaming through the park. Cobac Parc at Lanhélin (10km north-west) also has over 200 animals among many other amusements (water park, boat rides and mini golf). Zooloisirs at Québriac near Tinténiac (8km south-west) offers an unusual mix of rose gardens, mild-mannered livestock (llamas, wallabies and the like) and an extensive collection of stuffed beasts.

Wherever you go in Fougères, you can't avoid the hills

The stately château at Caradeuc

► Bécherel *205D2*

A thriving linen industry once kept this pretty old hill town prosperously afloat on its granite ridge. Now Bécherel's sobriquet is *cité du livre* (city of the book), and second-hand bookshops of all types occupy many of its charming stone houses. A book market is held on the first Sunday of each month, and a major book fair takes place in spring.

A few sporadic castle ruins are left in the town, for Bécherel was once fortified. More noteworthy, though, is the **Château de Caradeuc►**, 1km west. Only the landscaped park and gardens are open to the public (*Open* Easter–mid-Sep, daily 10–7. *Admission charge*).

Bécherel stands in attractive wooded walking country, with good views over the Rance valley to the north. If you have time you could make a short tour east towards Hédé (see page 212). Pause at the Gothic church of **les Iffs►**, with its beautiful stained glass and unusual sculpture, and at the **Château de Montmuran►** (*Open* Easter–Oct, daily 2–7, Sat 2–5. *Admission charge*), where Du Guesclin was knighted in 1354 (see pages 34–5).

► Combourg *205D3*

Massive towers with conical roofs and spiky finials pierce clumps of trees above the town's grey roofscape by the lakeshore. These belong to Combourg's mighty feudal fortress, first founded by an Archbishop of Dol in the 11th century. It underwent many modifications during the Middle Ages and was once owned by Du Guesclin.

In 1761, the **castle** (*Open* Jul–Aug, daily 11–12.30, 1.30–5.30; Apr–Jun, Sep, Wed–Mon 2–5.30. *Admission charge*) was bought by Count Chateaubriand, father of one of France's most famous Romantic writers. The young François-Réné spent his childhood imprisoned with his sister Lucile behind these gloomy walls. Downstairs his parents lived in reclusive melancholy, his father pacing the drawing room in silence and his mother incapacitated by hypochondria and religious mania. Chateaubriand later wrote vividly of these formative experiences in his memoirs. Visitors are taken to see his haunted bedroom in the Tour du Chat (Cat Tower), the chapel and the archives, and along a parapet walk with a good view of the town.

THE MASTER OF CARADEUC

The fine Regency-style Château de Caradeuc was once the home of a fiery public prosecutor, the Marquis de Caradeuc de la Chalotais, whose pamphlet advocating the dissolution of the Jesuits (a powerfully conservative influence on local government) caused a political stir in 1762. Louis XV opposed his views and had La Chalotais arrested, but the Rennes parliament took his side – and won. Many historians believe this clash of wills was a significant spark in the events leading to the French Revolution.

Statuary in the grounds of Caradeuc

THE MARQUIS DE LA ROUERIE
Fougères has seen its share of conflict. The Chouan movement (see page 179) was founded by the Marquis de la Rouërie (1756–93), a minor scion of Fougères nobility. Instead of fleeing into exile like many of his peers, he organised a form of guerrilla resistance in the Breton countryside, stowing caches of arms and drumming up supporters. However, he died early on in the struggle, which dragged on in Brittany for a further decade. Fougères was used as the setting for both Victor Hugo's *Quatre-vingt-treize* (*Ninety-three*) and Balzac's *Les Chouans*, the classic novels of this period.

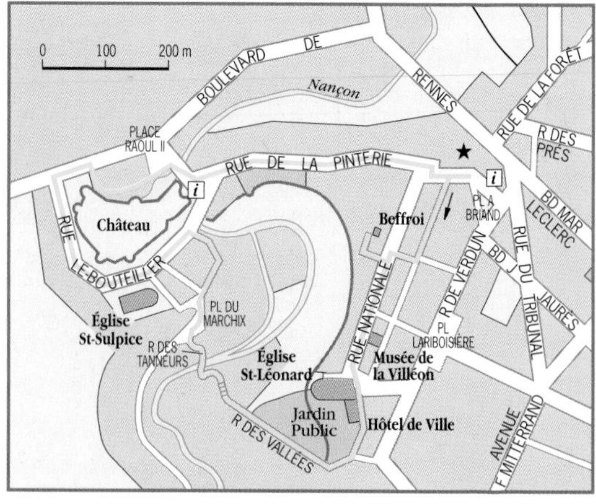

▶▶▶ Fougères 205E2

Fougères is a frontier town, once capital of the marshlands dividing France and Brittany. Duchess Anne dubbed it 'the key to my royal treasure'; for Victor Hugo, Fougères was 'the Carcassonne of the North'. Its promontory setting above a tight loop in the River Nançon is a classically defensible location, though unusually its massive fortress was constructed *below* the town, not above it. The rocky spurs above the castle walls cradle the upper town of mostly 18th-century buildings. Precipitous steps and alleys lead from the back of the church of St-Léonard down to a much older sector around the Place du Marchix, where tanneries and mills can be seen among an enchanting cluster of 16th-century houses, focused by the slender pencil spire of St-Sulpice.

Like many Breton towns, Fougères grew wealthy on the textile trades of wool and hemp. Later it turned its ancient cattle market and tanning business to good use in a new enterprise – shoe manufacture – supplemented after post-World War II recession by ventures into electronics and robotics. Beyond the modern suburbs a state forest of beech, spruce and chestnut extends north-east, shading megaliths and 12th-century cellars used as hiding places in times of war.

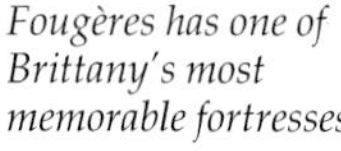
Fougères has one of Brittany's most memorable fortresses

Walk

The old town of Fougères

See map opposite.

If you start at the top of the town you get an overview of its huge fortress before you explore inside. Allow half a day and try to see the local art museum (Musée de la Villéon).

Head for the upper town and park in one of the squares near the tourist office. From here, walk along the pedestrianised rue Nationale. Don't miss the elegant 14th-century ***beffroi***▶ (belfry) behind the covered market. Continue along rue Nationale until you reach **Musée de la Villéon**. This museum, housed in a picturesque 16th-century house, is dedicated to the Impressionist painter Emmanuel de la Villéon (1858–1944), a native of Fougères.

The church of St-Léonard stands near the Renaissance town hall, its grey austerity lifted slightly by vivid stained glass (ancient and modern) and an ornate north façade. Behind the church, neatly kept municipal gardens give a splendid vantage point over wooded chasms, the Marchix quarter and the tremendous fortress beyond. Using these as your target, thread your way down the stepped alleys and across the river via the rue des Tanneurs. The streets around the Place du Marchix contain many ancient buildings. The Flamboyant-style church of **St-Sulpice**▶ has as much grace inside as its exterior suggests. Fine woodwork and granite altarpieces catch the eye, as does a 12th-century statue of the Virgin (Notre-Dame-des-Marais) suckling a Child who looks rather too old for such things.

Above: the Marchix quarter, as seen from the upper town

Visit the **castle**▶▶ next. This is one of the largest and most imposing in France and is the town's main tourist attraction. The original fortress dates from around AD 1000, and despite its stalwart defences it was frequently attacked and often changed hands. Festivals are sometimes held in the extensive grounds. A walk outside the walls is almost as impressive as a tour inside, where you can investigate the tower rooms and walk the ramparts. Notice the foundations of the keep (destroyed in 1166) and the waterwheels by the gatehouse.

Return to the upper town via rue de la Pinterie, a steep climb. More gardens give you a chance to catch your breath, and a final overview of the castle and river.

St-Léonard's church and gardens

After centuries of living with the threat of sea raids or invasion by the kings of France, it is scarcely surprising that Brittany bristles with fortresses, watchtowers and walled towns. Most of them, naturally, stand along the coastline, or on the region's eastern borderlands.

PICK OF THE FORTRESSES

- Walled towns: Vannes, Vitré, Guérande, St-Malo, Concarneau.
- Military citadels: Port-Louis, Belle-Ile.
- Medieval castles: Josselin, Fougères, Dinan, Nantes, Châteaubriant, Hennebont, Pontivy, Kérouzéré, Montfort, Trécesson.
- Coastal fortresses: Fort la Latte, Suscinio, Brest, Fort National (St-Malo).
- Evocative ruins: Largoët, Hunaudaie, Tonquédec, Ranrouët, Coatfrec, la Groulais (Blain).
- Furnished châteaux: Kerjean, Combourg, Roche Jagu, Rochers-Sévigné, Rosanbo, Bienassis, Quintin, Kérazan.
- Parks and gardens: Bourbansais, Trémazan, Kergrist, Kerguéhennec, Caradeuc.

Castles through the ages Compared with the stately pleasure domes of the Loire or the doughty strongholds of the Dordogne, Brittany's castles are mostly in a minor league. The Breton nobility were relatively poor, and what resources they had were devoted mainly to spiritual buildings such as churches and parish closes rather than grandiose defensive structures.

Scarcely anything remains of Brittany's earliest fortifications, though a few vestiges of Gallo-Roman hill-camps can be seen here and there. The wooden motte and bailey forts of the early Middle Ages have also mostly vanished. Not until castles were constructed of stone did they stand much chance of surviving the test of time, and Brittany's abundant building material, granite, was ideal for the purpose. Islet citadels were built at Port-Louis, St-Malo and Concarneau, while Vannes, Vitré and Guérande were substantially enclosed by walls. Through the centuries, fortress designs changed as methods of warfare advanced from lengthy sieges to sophisticated artillery attacks. Du Guesclin, hero of the 14th century, fought very different battles from Vauban, Louis XIV's military engineer in the late 17th century.

Gradually, castles began to be built for purely domestic use, with more comfortable interiors, aesthetic façades and decorative flourishes, and landscaped parks or gardens. Wealthy merchants and corsairs formed a new breed of gentry in Brittany, and there was a sudden spate of country manor houses in the 17th and 18th centuries, particularly near St-Malo and Morlaix. During the 19th century a craze for the medieval past produced a wave of neo-Gothic edifices, sprouting fake battlements and arrowslits at every turret.

Fort la Latte's romantic seacliff setting on the Emerald Coast

Destruction and restoration Many castles and manor houses have succumbed through the ages to military onslaughts, or the slower incursions of time and the elements. Cardinal Richelieu ordered a good many Breton fortresses to be demolished, or at least reduced in size, to dissuade the truculent Duchy from any notions of insurrection. Revolutionaries took great delight in destroying the grand houses of the *ancien régime*, or the hideouts of Chouan Royalists. More recently, World War II added its share of mayhem. Ironically, it was Brittany's allies rather than its enemies who did most of the damage in their attempts to drive out the Nazi occupying forces. The towns of St-Malo, Brest, Lorient, Hennebont and St-Nazaire – all fortified in their heyday – were pulverised.

What you see of Brittany's fortifications today is generally a piecemeal reconstruction rather than the original medieval buildings. Some are mere ruined shells, or are still in private ownership and not open to visitors. A few château owners happily accept paying guests into their homes, and these provide a fascinating alternative to conventional hotels.

No longer practical for their original purpose or as converted dwellings, plenty of castles are used as museums, tourist offices, exhibition centres, backdrops for pageants or *son et lumière* shows, amusement or wildlife parks, and grand hostelries. Many are open to the public and can be visited during the summer. You are free to look around most of them by yourself, although a few insist on guided tours (ask about foreign-language tours). The tourist authorities suggest several touring routes linking major castles, such as the Route des Ducs de Bretagne, the Route du Léon et du Trégor or the Route des Marches. Look out for the leaflets in local tourist offices.

Pepperpot towers adorn the restored castle of Combourg

STAYING IN CHATEAUX

If you want to try a taste of château hospitality, look out for the brochures produced by several like-minded consortia – *Bienvenue au Château, La Vie de Château, Château Accueil* – available in many tourist offices.

A detail from the ramparts of St-Malo

CHÂTEAU DE MONBOUAN
This 18th-century castle, reflected in the still waters of its moat, stands in the centre of a lovely park. The castle was restored in the 19th century and the rooms now open to the public (particularly the drawing room) give a good idea of interior decoration in the reign of Louis XV. In the entrance hall there is an imposing staircase adorned with a beautiful wrought-iron railing (*Open* mid-Jul–Aug, 9–12, 2–6. *Admission charge*).

▶ La Guerche-de-Bretagne *205E1*

Du Guesclin (see pages 34–5) was once the seigneur of this feudal manor, now grown to a small town famed for its cider. A cluster of half-timbered houses with porches can be seen near the church, an unusual building with a triple-sided apse and a stoutly buttressed Romanesque tower. The quaintly carved misericords under the choirstall seats are worth a look.

▶ Hédé *205D2*

Woods and water are the lasting impressions of this hill village. Streams, cascades and ponds gleam all around, and lush, terraced gardens almost hide the crumbling stone houses and castle ruins perched on an outcrop of rock. The Romanesque church contains an alabaster statue of the Virgin and a 17th-century wooden altar. In the surrounding grounds modern bronze memorials commemorate heroes of war.

Just north of Hédé, at the tiny village at la Madeleine, the Ille-et-Rance canal passes through a magnificent staircase of 11 **locks▶▶**, with a drop of 27m.

Tinténiac▶, another pretty canal village to the north, also has an interesting church with lots of curious architectural features. An old wooden grain store by the side of the canal houses the **Musée de l'Outil et des Métiers▶** (*Open* Jul–Sep, 10–12, 2–6.30. *Closed* Sun morning. *Admission charge*), a collection of craft tools and machinery in working order belonging to former blacksmiths, cartwrights, saddlers, cobblers, coopers and so on.

Trees cloak the buildings in the pretty village of Hédé

▶ Loudéac *204B2*

The town itself is of no great interest, merely a spider's web of main roads at the centre of an intensive agricultural region. It holds several large markets and is also well known for horse-racing. About 10km to the south-east lies **la Chèze**, an attractive village with resort facilities and a museum devoted to country crafts, the **Musée Regional des Métiers▶**, which is housed in an old stone tannery on the banks of the River Lié (*Open* Jul–Aug, daily 10–12, 2–6; May, Jun, Sep afternoons only. *Admission charge*). The village was once a Rohan stronghold and the remains of

The old quarter of Moncontour

its 13th-century castle are still visible. **La Ferrière**, 16km south-east, has a large 14th-century church with fine stained glass and statues.

▶ Moncontour *204B3*

This sudden granite spur between two valleys makes an obvious fortification site. Most of the town walls were destroyed in 1626, though a château was reconstructed in the 19th century on a hill to the north. The historic quarter of hilly alleys and old houses huddles round a fine church, **St-Mathurin▶**, whose splendid windows date from the 16th century.

About 3km south-east of Moncontour, near Trédaniel, stands the **Chapelle Notre-Dame-du-Haut▶**, which contains the wooden statues of seven healing saints, typically Breton in style. St Mamertus cures intestinal disorders; St Yvertin deals with headaches; St Léobinus treats eye diseases; Ste Eugénia helps with labour pains; St Hubert tackles rabies; St Méen's speciality is madness; and St Houarniaule soothes irrational phobias.

The castle of **la Touche-Trébry**, 6km to the east, dates from the late 16th century and was once the home of the governor of Moncontour (*Open* Jul–Aug, 2–7, guided tours. *Closed* Sun. *Admission charge*).

▶ Montfort-sur-Meu *205D2*

The unusual purplish-red colour of the local stone immediately marks Montfort out from its grey neighbours. One of the town's claims to fame is that it is the birthplace of Louis-Marie Grignion (1673–1716), a missionary saint canonised in the 20th century; his birthplace at 15 rue de la Saulnerie is open to the public. Montfort's most imposing building, however, is the 14th-century **Papegaut tower**, the last vestige of its baronial castle. This now houses the small but charming **Ecomusée du Pays de Montfort▶** (*Open* daily 9–12, 2–6. *Closed* Sun mornings. *Admission charge*), whose dolls, *coiffes* and old-fashioned wooden toys is genuinely delightful. Traditional games like skittles can be practised in the courtyard. *Papegaut*, which gives the tower its name, is an archery game (the target is a cockerel on a pole). A film on the legends of Brocéliande is shown in the top room of the tower.

LA ROCHE AUX FÉES
Fifteen kilometres west of la Guerche-de-Bretagne lies one of Brittany's largest and most striking megalithic monuments: 42 slabs of purplish schist, each weighing up to 45 tonnes, form what looks like an *allée couverte* (gallery grave), though there is some doubt whether it was ever used as a burial place. You can walk inside easily without crouching. It is a popular trysting place for lovers, and engaged couples traditionally walk around the monument in different directions, counting the stones. If their calculations differ by more than a couple of stones, the marriage is doomed!

Lac de Guerlédan, near Quintin

LAC DE GUERLÉDAN
Away from the dam, the lake is most attractive, its glittering surface a constant flurry of boats and windsurfers. To the south stands a last bit of *argoat*, the natural woodland that once covered most of inland Brittany, in the shape of the Forêt de Quénécan – an ideal spot for walks and picnics. Focal points for exploration include St-Aignan, south-west of Mûr-de-Bretagne, which has a lovely old church, and les Forges des Salles, a picturesquely fortified hamlet at the far west side of the lake. Beau-Rivage is the most popular leisure centre along the shoreline, while the main watersports base is at le Rond-Point.

▶ Mûr-de-Bretagne *204B2*

This popular inland resort attracts visitors for its leisure facilities and surroundings rather than tourist sights. The tourist office's label for the area, *'la Suisse bretonne'* (Breton Switzerland), is absurdly extravagant, but overall this region has more to offer in terms of scenery than most of inland Brittany.

In the village itself there is little to see apart from the oak-shaded chapel of Ste-Suzanne to the north, once a haunt of the noted landscape painter Camille Corot (1796–1875). Mûr-de-Bretagne stands on the artificial Lac de Guerlédan, a sinuous, multi-branched reservoir which stretches 11km from a massive concrete dam across the Blavet, built in the 1920s. This makes the Nantes–Brest canal unnavigable as far as Carhaix by anything larger than a kayak. The advantages of hydro-electric power are more pressing today than British threats to French shipping (the *raison d'être* for the canal in Napoleonic times). Nowadays, pleasure boating has taken the place of heavily laden barges.

Lac de Guerlédan provides ideal conditions for many watersports

The gorges around Mûr-de-Bretagne

See map on pages 204–5.

A 130km tour of the lonely schist plateau north of Mûr-de-Bretagne, exploring calvary villages and hidden churches in wild countryside. Take a picnic and walking shoes for visiting gorges. Allow most of the day.

From Mûr-de-Bretagne, head west past the lakeshore, turning north via the **Gorges du Daoulas▶**. Much of the woodland that once clothed this valley was damaged by a storm in 1987, and spindly birch is beginning to replace it on the steep, gorse-covered slopes. The swift Daoulas river races along the narrow valley floor to join the Blavet.

St-Nicolas-du-Pélem▶ is a quiet village and an increasingly popular *station verte* (hotel and campsite). The 15th-century church contains a bell which the faithful ring before praying to ensure heavenly attention. The church at **Lanrivain▶**, on a large central square, still has fresh flowers on its melodramatic war memorial. The calvary near by consists of large stone figures (about two-thirds life-size) looking rather like Snow White and the Seven Dwarfs in nightcaps. Through the open slats of the ossuary chapel, paper-thin skulls and wafery femurs glimmer faintly.

West lie the **Gorges de Toul-Goulic▶**, which can be reached via a steep path down through the woods. Here the River Blavet disappears beneath mossy boulders in a deep cleft. **Kergrist-Moëlou▶**, south-west again, has a fine aristocratic 16th-century church containing the crests of the Rostrenen family and a barrel-vaulted ceiling painted with curiously secular figures. The parish close, gloomy with ancient yew trees, contains a two-tier calvary of about 100 carved figures in blue granite. These were badly damaged during the Revolution and replaced haphazardly on an octagonal plinth. A memorial by the post office commemorates lost heroes: '*A la Mémoire des Aviateurs Américains James Stubblefield, William A Monson...*'

Further north-west, on one of the emptiest parts of the plateau, the **Gorges du Corong▶▶** make another scenic detour. This is a fairly long walk (half an hour each way), but a spectacular one. A tributary of the Hyère river flows through a rocky chaos of waterfalls in thick woodland.

Head north via **Bulat-Pestivien▶**, where the church has ornate porches and a strange sacristy frieze. Notice the lectern with a peasant in local costume, and the sacred fountains scattered through the village. **Bourbriac▶**, to the north, has yet another worthy church with an ancient pillared crypt and a tower in a mix of Gothic and Renaissance styles. The sarcophagus of St Briac lies inside. **Avaugour**, eastwards, offers more chapels, one with statues of the Apostles, the other (**Notre-Dame-de-Restudo**) with 14th-century frescoes. Head southwards via Plésidy (noting the **Manoir de Toul-an-Gollet▶**) and Corlay, deviating to the *village fleuri* of **St-Gilles-Vieux-Marché**, which nestles in the Poulancre valley, before returning to Mûr-de-Bretagne.

The main square, Bourbriac

ELUSIVE BROCÉLIANDE
The Forêt de Paimpont is periodically colonised by droves of New Agers claiming Druidic beliefs. They are allegedly responsible for removing many of the signposts directing visitors to the wonders of Paimpont and thus, they claim, preserving some of its mystery. After much fruitless searching for sacred fountains and places of enchantment, modern visitors may well sympathise with Robert Wace, author of *The Romance of the Rose*, who wrote in about 1160: 'I went thither on purpose to see these marvels...but I found none. I went like a fool, and so I came back..and found myself a fool for my pains.'

►► Paimpont, Forêt de *204C2*

This 7,000ha forest is a pale echo of the woodlands that once covered this part of Brittany, and much has been commercially replanted since any Arthurian knights could have roamed here. But the Brocéliande of ancient legend recounted by the troubadour poet Chrétien de Troyes still exerts a whimsical tug on the imagination. Every year thousands of visitors arrive not simply to explore the forest's prosaic hiking trails and picnic sites, but in vague, half-serious hopes of experiencing a touch of Merlin's magic, or perhaps of gaining a fleeting glimpse of the Holy Grail itself.

The village of Paimpont stands in the centre of the forest, and acts as its main resort. It dates only from the Revolution, and is an unusual place with an enclosed centre of purplish-grey terraced stone houses. Near by is a large lake with pedalos and passing waterfowl. The 11th-century abbey church (belonging to a monastery that once stood beside the lake) conceals within its plain interior a silver reliquary of St Judicaël and an ivory crucifix (carefully locked away, but you may ask to see them). A surprisingly jolly Virgin relaxes near the altar.

The tourist office by the church (open summer only) can provide maps and guides through the forest. If you propose to track down any Arthurian secrets, detailed instructions are essential. Otherwise, simply enjoy the pleasant woodland walks through bracken and wildflowers, past numerous pools.

None of the forest sights is spectacular, and most of them are more fun for their legends than in themselves. The **Fontaine de Barenton►**, where a spring bubbles up, is where Merlin fell prey to the beautiful enchantress Viviane and was imprisoned in a circle of air. It is said that if water is sprinkled on the slab next to the fountain (known as the Perron de Merlin, or Merlin's Stone), a great storm will be called up and a mysterious horseman in black armour will appear. This magic has apparently been invoked to end droughts in recent times.

A sacred site in the Paimpont forest – Merlin's Stone

Another popular destination for romantics is the **Val sans Retour** (**Valley of No Return**), where a steep path leads to the **Rocher des Faux Amants** (**Rock of False Lovers**), a trap set by the evil sorceress Morgan le Fay to ensnare men who have betrayed their lovers. Only Lancelot, ever faithful to his Queen Guinevere, managed to break the spell.

There are two castles in the forest. The **Château de Comper►** is a mostly 19th-century structure housing the **Centre de l'Imaginaire Arthurien**, which presents lectures and film shows about the Arthurian legends. The **Château de Trécesson►** is more satisfactorily medieval, in red schist with a turreted gatehouse (though it is not open to the public).

The church at **Tréhorenteuc▶** combines Christianity with King Arthur, and contains a stained-glass window and frescoes depicting the Holy Grail and the Knights of the Round Table. An entrance fee is charged.

▶ Quintin *204B3*

The terraced houses of this attractive old town stand above the Gouët river. Quintin was once famed for its fine linen, used for Breton *coiffes*, collars and veils, and before the Revolution was entirely dependent on weaving.

Amid Quintin's attractive old quarter of 16th- and 17th-century half-timbering stands the town's main building of interest, its basilica. This contains a holy relic of the Virgin's belt, alleged to have been brought back from Jerusalem in the 13th century. Other notable features inside are the statue of Our Lady of Safe Delivery (much revered by mothers-to-be), and the holy water stoups made of giant Javanese shells. Below the east end of the church is the Porte-Neuve, the last vestige of the ramparts that once encircled the town. The **château** in the town centre dates from the 17th and 18th centuries and houses a museum of local history, displaying linen, porcelain and fans. The cellars and kitchens of the castle can also be visited (*Open* mid-Jun–Sep, daily 10.30–12.30, 1.30–6.30. *Admission charge*).

THE HOLY GRAIL
This was the legendary cup from which Christ drank at the Last Supper. After the Crucifixion, his disciple, Joseph of Arimathea, collected a few drops of Christ's blood in the Grail, and carried it away from Palestine, landing first in Britain and then in Brittany, where he settled in the Forest of Brocéliande before vanishing mysteriously. On hearing of the Grail, King Arthur and 50 of his truest knights set out to find it. Only the purest in heart would be successful, the prize going to Sir Percival.

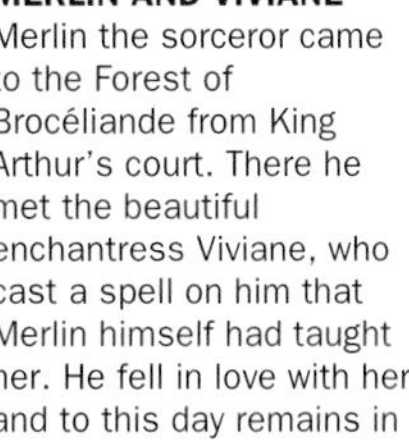

MERLIN AND VIVIANE
Merlin the sorceror came to the Forest of Brocéliande from King Arthur's court. There he met the beautiful enchantress Viviane, who cast a spell on him that Merlin himself had taught her. He fell in love with her and to this day remains in her thrall, willingly caged in a magic circle of air.

Left: Quintin
Below: the Robien Château, near Quintin

CLOUDED MEMORIES
The Panthéon, a large room in Rennes' town hall, salutes the memory of those Rennais who fell in World War I, and the ceiling is studded with the names of the military heroes of that conflict. One name, however, is obliterated by a strip of paper. Maréchal Pétain, the traitor of Vichy, is despised in Brittany for his collaboration with the Germans.

▶▶▶ Rennes 205D2

Many regular visitors to Brittany cold-shoulder its capital. Rennes stands some distance from the sea, in a swathe of low-lying countryside where the Rance and the Vilaine converge. Apart from a few appealing stretches of the Vilaine valley and some patches of deciduous woodland north-east of the city, the surrounding scenery can best be described as uninspiring. If you are touring the Breton marches, the old borderlands between France and Brittany, however (in particular the magnificent castles of Fougères and Vitré), give Rennes a day of your time.

Inside its modern industrial carapace, the old centre has a lively charm and several genuinely worthwhile museums that place Brittany's historic and cultural significance admirably in context. Driving and parking within the city centre can be a nuisance, but good transport links

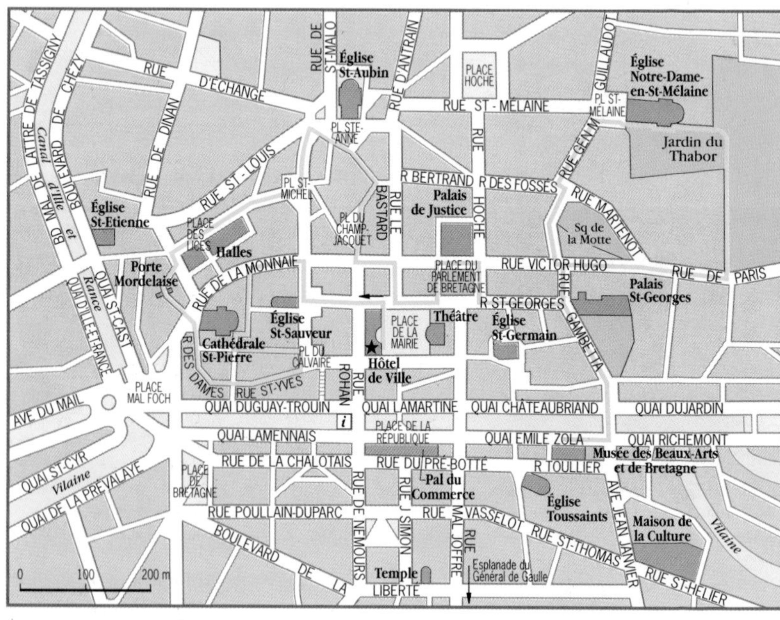

Dramatic half-timbering in Rennes

with other towns in Brittany make it quite feasible to visit Rennes on a day excursion from another base (there are direct bus and train services to St-Malo, Vitré, Fougères, Dinan, Nantes and so on).

History The Romans developed the town from a Gaulish settlement, and it became a strategic hub of important military highways. During the Middle Ages, Rennes shared parliamentary power with Nantes and Vannes, but it became the undisputed Breton capital during the time of the Duchess Anne. It was at Rennes that the duchess first met Charles VIII, with whom she made her momentously tactical match (see pages 36–7). From then on Rennes was to play a significant role in Brittany's political upheavals, including the uprisings against the monstrous taxation imposed during Louis XIV's reign, the Revolutionary Terror, and the German Occupation during World War II.

Above: peaceful Jardin du Thabor

Walk

The old town of Rennes

See map opposite.

The Breton capital's stripy old houses and grand civic architecture make a pleasant half-day tour, although you could spend longer browsing in its excellent museums. There is a vast free parking area at esplanade du Général de Gaulle, south of the river, or you may be lucky in Place des Lices, a shorter walk.

The imposing Hôtel de Ville on Place de la Mairie is a good starting point, one of Jacques Gabriel's most confident municipal statements after the great fire of 1720. The huge clock tower known as 'Le Gros' connects two curving side-wings. Officials will show you round for no charge. Opposite stands the frothy theatre; to the south is the massively ponderous Palais du Commerce.

Thread westwards now through a maze of old streets lined with picturesque houses around two churches. **St-Sauveur▶** is built in a rococo style. Inside, Our Lady of Miracles is depicted as a pretty woman in a red and gold robe. She saved Rennes from the English in 1357 and is still well patronised. **St-Pierre▶**, Rennes' cathedral, forms a graceless, lumpish 19th-century building in Roman style with a colonnaded apse of red marble. The rich, sombre interior contains one splendid work of art – a 16th-century Flemish altarpiece of gilded wood behind glass in a side-chapel by the south transept. Find the light switch to enjoy its amazing three-dimensional effects.

On the edge of the old town, the **Porte Mordelaise** is the last remnant of the 15th-century ramparts. It was through this entrance to the city that the Dukes of Brittany passed for their coronations. Close by is the **Place des Lices▶**, where jousts were once held. Two art-nouveau *halles* (market buildings) now dominate the square, continuing a market tradition that first began in 1622. East of here lies another cluster of half-timbered buildings which survived the fire; the most eye-catching group stands in Place du Champ-Jacquet, a mass of tall, stripy façades dating from the 17th century.

The **Palais de Justice▶▶** is the former seat of the Breton Parliament, and also predates the fire (1618–55). Somewhat ironically, it was severely damaged by fire in 1994 and, for a while, it was feared that the intricate timber-framed roof and beautiful coffered ceilings were too badly damaged to be repaired. Fortunately, restoration has begun and, if work goes to plan, the building will reopen to the public for the new millennium.

A stroll in the **Jardin du Thabor** makes a pleasant change of pace. These large, varied gardens once formed the grounds of a Benedictine abbey (the church of **Notre-Dame-en-St-Mélaine** still stands). Finish the walk on the south bank of the river at the twin museums.

Above: house detail
Right: some of Rennes' restaurants have antique settings

STEPPING BACK IN TIME
Some way out of town (follow rue Maréchal-Joffre 8km southwards – a bus route) is the Ecomusée du Pays de Rennes at Bintinais farm, which traces the evolution of agricultural life in Brittany. There is an educational trail and rare breeds of farm animals are kept on the premises (*Open* Mon–Fri 9–12, 2–6, Sat 2–6, Sun 2–7. *Closed* Tue. *Admission charge*).

HERO OR TRAITOR?
Breton feelings towards Bertrand Du Guesclin (see pages 34–5) are mixed. While he takes pride of place on horseback in Dinan's main square (the scene of his heroic duel with Sir Thomas of Canterbury), his statue in Rennes was blown up by Breton nationalists in 1946. Some extreme separatists have never forgiven him for taking the French side against the Breton Duke Jean IV during the War of Succession.

Cosmopolitan culture Rennes' population has doubled since World War II to nearly 250,000, which makes it by far the largest city in Brittany apart from its old rival Nantes (which now belongs technically to the region of Loire-Atlantique). It is mainly preoccupied with administrative, commercial and industrial concerns. The Citroën headquarters lie just outside the city, and many of Rennes' more transient occupants are students attending its two universities or its prestigious medical school. Economic mainstays include electronics and telecommunications, the construction industry and the manufacture of transport equipment.

Compared with other Breton towns Rennes feels atypically urban, even cosmopolitan, and more French than most. Breton culture, however, is well and truly alive here, from the destructive antics of political separatists to the more creative aspects of its great July arts festival, Les Tombées de la Nuit. Encouraged by its young student population, French rock and jazz musicians congregate in the city.

Museums Rennes has two major museums, the **Musée de Bretagne▶▶** and the **Musée des Beaux-Arts▶▶**, which were housed in the same building along the embankment, south of the river. However, lack of space has prompted change. The Musée de Bretagne's permanent collections, including the best archaeological finds from different parts of Brittany, displays on the corsairs and traditional Breton life with audiovisual presentations, will be on show in the city's Nouvel Espace Culturel from 2005. During the transition, the museum holds temporary exhibitions in its present premises, renewed every four months. The Musée des Beaux-Arts will gradually acquire more exhibition space for its expanding collections (*Open* Wed–Mon, 10–12, 2–6. *Admission charge*).

The Musée des Beaux-Arts (Fine Arts Museum) contains one of Brittany's most important collections of paintings, ranging from 14th-century primitives to Impressionists and members of the Pont Aven School. Works to look out for include an **Etude de Draperie** (*Drapery Study*) by Leonardo da Vinci, Rubens' weltering wildlife scene *La Chasse au Tigre* (*The Tiger Hunt*), Georges de la Tour's *Le Nouveau-Né* (*The Newborn*), and Gauguin's *Nature Morte aux Oranges* (*Still Life with Oranges*). An emotional 19th-century canvas by Luminais depicts the legend of Ys, with Dahut slipping into the waves from King Gradlon's galloping horse. Twentieth-century artists such as Picasso and Tanguy are also represented, along with many minor Breton painters.

THE GREAT FIRE

One event that changed the face of Rennes for ever was a disastrous fire in 1720, apparently started accidentally by a drunken carpenter. The fire raged for almost a week, and nearly 1,000 houses were destroyed, though luckily very few lives were lost. Eventually a rainstorm extinguished the flames. Rennes' inflammable timbers were subsequently replaced with the dignified, spacious stone buildings that give the centre its present chilly elegance.

Left: more elaborate façades in Rennes

The Musée de Bretagne and Musée de Beaux-Arts. The Musée de Bretagne is in the process of moving and its museum premises are open for temporary exhibitions only until 2005.

Brittany has changed dramatically since World War II. The land of coiffes *and* lits clos *has been supplanted by a progressive, forward-looking society that is eager to cast aside its peasant lifestyle. Ironically, tourism – a prime source of revenue for the region – encourages a new remembrance of things past.*

Collectable items Brittany is still economically deprived compared with some parts of France, and those who make their living directly from the land or the sea, as generations have done before them, know that times can be hard. But the laboriousness of everyday life and the humiliating anguish of poverty that Pierre-Jakez Hélias described in his autobiography, *The Horse of Pride*, have largely disappeared. With them went many of the symbols of earlier times – the furniture and costumes, craft tools and kitchen utensils. Most young Breton couples setting up home in Brittany nowadays would probably find a washing machine more useful than a carved oak linen press. To the Bretons' surprise, however, affluent Parisians are flocking to snap up their box beds and old dressers. Breton furniture is highly collectable, sometimes fulfilling new functions as hi-fi units, drinks cabinets or bookshelves.

Tourists, too, seem eternally fascinated by these vanishing bygones. Today, Brittany bursts with folk museums, all anxious to reveal the wholesome qualities of traditional rustic life. The most successful of these *écomusées* add an authentic flavour to the region and are genuinely informative about local lifestyles (see panel opposite for a selection of some of the best museums).

LITS CLOS
'Ah, those *lits clos*, what a good buy! I have found some that have been converted into a coat-cupboard in the hall, a library in the study, a buffet or drinks cupboard in the living-room, a music-box combining pick-up, radio and television. I have even seen one that functions as a toilet, to the great satisfaction of its users.'
– Pierre-Jakez Hélias, *The Horse of Pride*.

Furniture The solid, dark-wood furnishings of traditional Breton homes often show a high level of craftsmanship, but above all they are intensely practical. Everything had a specific purpose, and was designed to fit into as compact a space as possible. The constraints of a small cottage, usually housing a large family, meant that its contents had to be skilfully stowed away. Indeed, the reconstructions of Breton interiors you see in the museums are often reminiscent of a ship's galley.

Stock items were usually built to a set

A particularly elegant and refined example of a double-decker box bed at the Ecomusée du Pays de Rennes. This must have belonged to a well-off family

pattern and turned out in great numbers. Decorations were ornate, though repetitive – circular medallions, religious motifs, flower garlands or geometrical patterns are commonly seen, sometimes interspersed with copper studs.

The most characteristic item found in all respectable households was the box bed (*lit clos*), like a cupboard with a sliding door or curtain. Some were double-decker affairs with bunks for children and a bar where a cradle could be hung and rocked. In poorer homes the bedding would be a layer of broom, the quilts stuffed with oats. A bench chest (*banc-coffre*) or blanket box was often used as a step to climb into the bed. The table (*table-huche*) was another essential piece of family equipment, often constructed with sliding panels so that it would take up less space when not in use. A circular contraption to hold spoons or cutlery could be moved up and down, Heath Robinson-fashion, over the table at mealtimes. Marriage chests (to hold trousseaux), dressers, linen presses, grain chests, wardrobes and long-case clocks were other customary items in more well-to-do homes. Comfortable chairs were reserved for heads of households.

Domestic architecture Many Breton towns display a remarkable number of beautiful half-timbered old houses, often jettied or partly slate-hung. Houses that are not timber-framed are still nearly always built of granite, though this may be disguised by whitewash. Dormer windows and turreted gables are common features, and many buildings are decorated with quirky carvings of animals or human figures. Frequently, an exterior stairway leads to a loft or roof.

Houses in the north and west tend to be lower, often only one storey, with small windows and doors carefully placed to reduce the effects of rain and wind. In dryer Morbihan or Loire-Atlantique, thatch was once a common roofing material, especially around the marshlands of the Grande Brière.

PICK OF THE FOLK MUSEUMS

- Moulins de Kérouat, Sizun.
- Ecomusée de Niou Uhella, Ouessant.
- Ecomusée du Pays de Rennes.
- La Chaumière, Audierne.
- Musée Départemental Breton, Quimper.
- Musée Bigouden, Pont-l'Abbé.
- Château de Kerjean.
- Maison Cornec, St-Rivoal (Monts d'Arrée).
- Musée d'Art Populaire du Pays de Lamballe.
- Musée du Patrimoine, Plougastel-Daoulas.
- Musée de la Vilaine Maritime, la Roche-Bernard.
- Musée de la Cohue, Vannes.
- Ecomusée du Pays de Montfort, Montfort-sur-Meu.

Breton interior reconstructed in the Ecomusée du Pays de Rennes

VITRÉ MUSEUMS
Several museums can be visited in and around Vitré on a combined ticket. Most worthwhile are the museums in the castle: sculpture and plans of the château in the Tour St-Laurent, and a weird assortment of pickled reptiles, insects and frogs in grotesquely anthropomorphic poses – playing billiards, fencing, on crutches – in the Tour de l'Argenterie; see also the Limoges enamelled triptych in the chapel of the Tour de l'Oratoire (*Open* Jul–Sep, daily 10–6. *Admission charge*). About 7km south-east lies the Château des Rochers-Sévigné, a fine Gothic manor with witch-hat turrets, once the home of Madame de Sévigné. The grounds, designed by Le Nôtre of Versailles fame, feature lawns etched with scroll patterns (*Open* Jul–Sep, daily 10–6. *Admission charge*).

▶▶▶ Vitré *205E2*

The best view of old Vitré can be had from the north-east, as you approach from the Fougères direction. Closer to the town, a hilly belvedere by the banks of the Vilaine known as **Tertres Noirs▶▶** gives a splendid silhouette of bristling turrets, drum towers and ramparts. Within the walls, the town seems just as carefully preserved as distant glimpses promise, and half-timbered, slate-hung houses lurch in all directions on hilly, cobbled streets.

Needless to say, Vitré's prettiness attracts many sightseers, and much of the old town's commercial activity now caters expressly for tourists. In former years Vitré's prosperity sprang from the textile trade (hemp, sailcloth, wool and cotton stockings), and today it still makes clothes and remains a market centre. Varied agricultural and industrial enterprises are based in the modern sector to the south of the railway line. The railway station is conveniently close to the historic centre, should you decide to visit the town by train.

The memorable parts of Vitré perch on a promontory overlooking the Vilaine, guarded by a massive triangular fortress at the western tip. The town's strategic location on the frontier between France and Brittany made it a constant target during the struggles of the Middle Ages. During the Hundred Years War, English forces camped for several years in the sector to the north-west until the siege-weary inhabitants paid them a ransom to go away. The present suburb is called **Faubourg du Rachapt▶** (meaning 'repurchased'). Its renovated stone cottages, once considered slums, now form an attractive part of the town.

Vitré backed the right horse (the king of France) in the years before the Union, and its prosperity grew rapidly. Many rich merchants settled in the town, and it is their fine mansions that give Vitré its classy architectural stamp. During the 15th and 16th centuries the town became a Huguenot (Protestant) stronghold, and was besieged by Catholics during the Wars of Religion. Some gratitude for these leanings is perhaps expressed in Henry IV's famous compliment to the town: 'Were I not King of France, I would be a citizen of Vitré.'

A brick and slate corner turret on a house in old Vitré

Walk

The old town of Vitré

See map opposite.

Start at the **castle**▶▶, Vitré's unmissable attraction. The gatehouse entrance admits you to a triangular courtyard surrounded by towers and curtain walls. Two of the towers contain small museums (see panel opposite), while in the centre of the courtyard stands an incongruous town hall built in 1913.

The **rue Beaudrairie**▶▶ (which takes its name from the leather-workers who once plied their trade here) contains the greatest concentration of old houses, now tastefully restored. The church of **Notre-Dame**▶ dates from the 15th and 16th centuries. It has a daisy-pierced spire and a fine interior, but its most interesting feature is a pulpit on an outer wall from which a Catholic priest harangued the unfortunate Huguenot Coligny family who lived opposite.

If you walk through the Poterne St-Pierre near the church you can follow a well-preserved section of the ramparts (those on the southern side have mostly disappeared) as far as the

Above: restored houses along rue Beaudrairie

Tour de la Bridolle▶ on Place de la République. Rue Sévigné, rue Poterie and rue d'Embas all contain quaint old houses. Notice No. 9 rue Sévigné, where Madame de Sévigné once lived, and the turreted Hôtel de la Botte Dorée at 10 rue d'Embas. Beyond the city walls, the church of **St-Martin** is also worth a glance – inside is a forest of candelabra and Romanesque arches.

Vitré castle

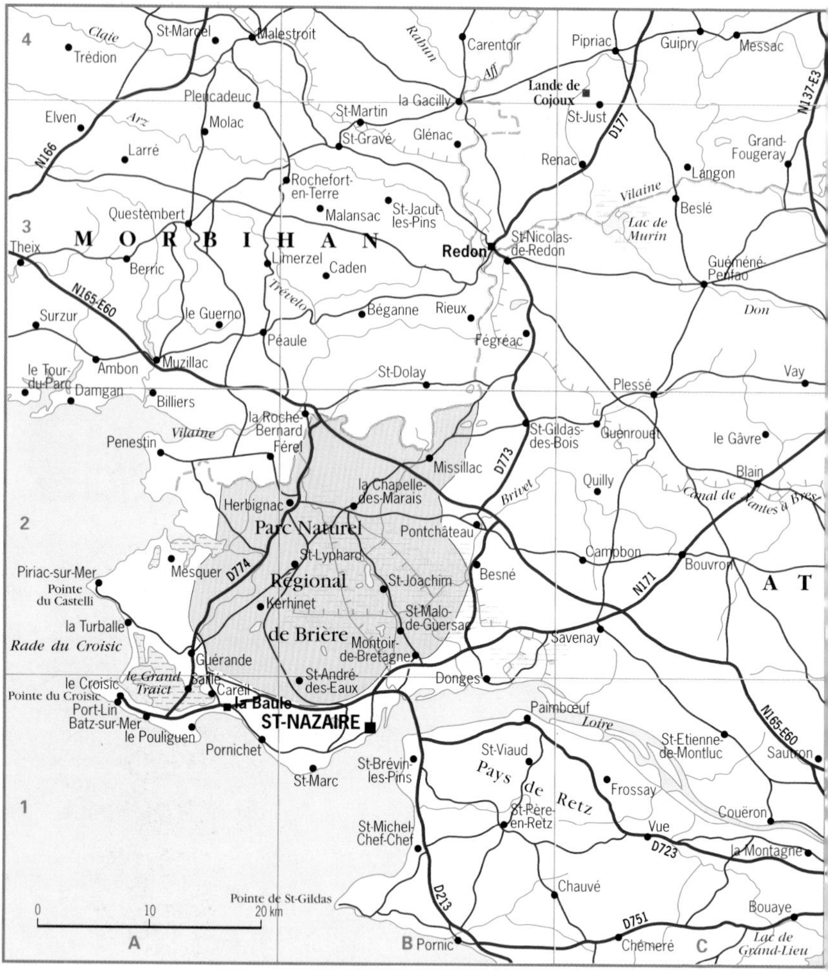

A peaceful stretch of the Nantes–Brest canal

Loire-Atlantique

LOIRE-ATLANTIQUE An administrative reshuffle in 1973 severed this south-easterly *département* from Brittany and attached it to the neighbouring region, Pays de la Loire. In doing so it snatched away one of Brittany's biggest and most fashionable seaside resorts, la Baule, and its historic capital of Nantes. But Bretons pay little heed to Parisian bureaucrats. For them the logical boundary of Brittany is still the stately River Loire, which flows past Nantes and St-Nazaire on its final reach to the sea, forming a climatic and cultural watershed. North of it are the grey slate roofs and granite churches of the Breton landscape; southwards lie the red clay tiles and soft tufa stone of warmer climes, where apple orchards and vegetable plots give way to vineyards and fields of sunflowers, and the language and local ways are unmistakably French.

WATERY PLEASURES Most of the area's attractions lie on or near the coast. Beach-lovers have plenty of choice: the vast stretch of sand at la Baule is outstanding in any

The seafront at la Baule

REGION HIGHLIGHTS

terms, but if small, quiet resorts are more your style you may prefer to head for the Croisic peninsula, or perhaps St-Marc, that archetypal little place near St-Nazaire where Jacques Tati's classic 1950's film comedy *Monsieur Hulot's Holiday* was set. If you are looking for completely unspoiled seclusion, make for the sands around Pénestin. The Plage de la Mine d'Or is one of the best of these undeveloped beaches.

Inland, Loire-Atlantique is most interestingly explored by boat – a pleasure cruiser up the Erdre from Nantes, a canal boat around the maze of waterways at Redon, or the traditional *chaland* (flat-bottomed punt) used in the Grande Brière. Unfortunately, the River Loire itself is drearily industrialised for most of its length between St-Nazaire and Nantes; for better views of it, head upstream towards the town of Ancenis.

La Baule's attractive holiday villas lie behind the seafront road

UNUSUAL LIFESTYLES Coastal Loire-Atlantique is a typical Breton flatland, which the sea and the Loire have periodically smothered in thick strata of silt and sand. Alluvial deposits and huge beaches trapped the marshlands behind, and the water-covered vegetation decomposed forming another layer – peat. The Grande Brière is perhaps the most spectacular of these ancient bogs, and the regional park of which it forms part is one of the largest wildlife reserves in France. Now drained and tamed with canals, it is still largely inaccessible except by boat. The traditional lifestyle of the people living in the Grande Brière revolved around cutting peat, eel-trapping, gathering reeds for thatch and hunting the marshland ducks. However, many Briérons now head for the dockyards of St-Nazaire for their livelihoods, and tourism plays an increasing part in their insular existence.

The salt marshes around Guérande form one of Loire-Atlantique's strangest physical features. Aerial photographs show them as an exquisite mosaic of variously sized lagoons and rectangular pits fringed with white, crystalline heaps. Salt extraction by evaporating sea water is another ancient mainstay, practised since Roman times. Today the industry is less important than it was when Brittany revelled in exemption from the hated *gabelle*, or salt tax, imposed on the rest of France. Looming over the salt marshes are the tall belfry of Batz-sur-Mer and the intact stone ramparts of medieval Guérande.

THE ANCESTRAL HEART Loire-Atlantique has no mean share of fortresses. Châteaubriant guards the marches – another link in the chain of border castles fending off incursions from the east. Grand-Fougeray, just over the *département* border in Ille-et-Vilaine, retains only its keep. Colourful legends haunt both these castles, imbuing them with more charisma than the ruined stones alone. Meanwhile, Ancenis and Nantes mount watch over the Loire, Brittany's natural southern moat.

If you are touring Loire-Atlantique, one place that certainly shouldn't be ignored is Nantes. Brave its discouraging suburbs and make for the old quarter by the castle and cathedral. Modern Nantes may look south and east for its new-found role as capital of Pays de la Loire, but its ancestral spirit is as Breton as the great Duchess Anne, who was born here, married here for the second time to a reigning French king, and whose heart (at least until the chaotic upheavals of the Revolution) rested here in a golden casket.

THE HEART OF BRITTANY
When Anne died, her funeral ceremony was hugely elaborate. She was buried in the traditional last resting-place of all French monarchs – St-Denis, near Paris – but her heart was placed in a golden casket in Nantes cathedral. Courtiers present as it was removed from her body marvelled at its exceptional size, and the casket is inscribed: '*En ce petit vaisseau de fin or, pur et munde, Repose ung plus grant cueur que oncque dame eut au munde*' ('In this small vessel of pure gold rests the greatest heart any lady ever had in the world'). During the Revolution the heart (or its ashes) vanished, but the casket can still be seen in Nantes' Palais Dobrée (see page 240).

The Chateau des Ducs de Bretagne in Nantes

DU GUESCLIN'S AXEMEN
Little remains of the castle at Grand-Fougeray, now a small market town but once a strategic frontier fortress. During the Hundred Years War, the Breton warrior Bertrand Du Guesclin captured Fougeray by disguising himself and a band of 30 of his best soldiers as woodcutters. Once inside the castle defences, they dropped their log bundles and drew arms. The entire English garrison was slaughtered.

A windmill on the salt marshes at Batz-sur-Mer

THE BURNING BUSH
Behind Batz-sur-Mer's church are the ruins of another – Notre-Dame-du-Mûrier. The story goes that Jean de Rieux, lord of Ranrouët castle in the 15th century, was sailing home in bad weather, fearing shipwreck at every moment. He prayed for heavenly guidance and saw a strange flickering light above one of Batz's safe beaches, then when he reached the shore he found a mulberry bush (*mûrier*) had mysteriously burst into flames. He built the Gothic chapel in gratitude for this miracle. The granite gable shows a fine example of a turreted staircase.

►► Batz-sur-Mer *226A1*

At first sight the only thing that marks out the small town of Batz is the striking spire of **St-Guénolé►**, which towers 60m above the low-lying salt marshes of the Guérande peninsula. Inside, the church is memorably charming, from the large-handed madonna at the door to the off-centre chancel draped with fishing nets. Carved bosses catch the eye, one decorated with the torments of the damned. Also in the village centre is the **Musée des Marais Salants (Salt-Marsh Museum)►►** (*Open* Jun–Sep, daily 10–12, 3–7. *Admission charge*), a museum dedicated to the local salt-working trade (see panel on page 234).

Batz has several good sandy beaches which are quiet enough to contrast pleasantly with the massive jet-set resort of la Baule to the east. A cliff-path from St-Michel beach has good views of the rocky coastline. Balzac stayed in Batz and set his novel *Béatrix* here.

►► La Baule *226A1*

This huge, purpose-built resort is the largest and most glamorous in Brittany, the nearest it gets to the Côte d'Azur. Less than three hours from Paris by high-speed train, it makes a popular weekend playground for affluent city-dwellers in search of a breath of sea air. Bronzed jetsetters flock here for its excellent facilities and a magnificent beach – 'the most beautiful in Europe', according to the tourist authorities. Stretching for 7km, the crescent of golden sand shelves so gently that you can walk out about 100m and still be well within your depth. Behind it, modern hotels and apartment blocks line the seafront road with all the charm of a shelf of detergent packets. Here and there, however, the soulless rectangles are leavened by more imaginative architecture: look for a spirited wedding-cake villa encrusted with mermaids, pink roses and plaster urns.

Thalassotherapy centre, la Baule

The history of the resort dates back a mere 100 years. Before that, the seafront was entirely undeveloped apart from an old fishing village called Escoublac. Over the centuries several great storms engulfed it in Loire silt and shifting sand, until in 1840 belts of pine trees were planted to help stabilise the dunes and protect the coast from gales, and a more favourable microclimate developed. Escoublac was relocated inland and in 1879 the seaside pleasure palaces began to appear.

The west end of the resort is the older and more dignified section, with several massive Belle Epoque hotels and a casino. Behind the seafront wall of modern buildings lies a belt of elegant Edwardian chalet villas in shady gardens. Eastwards stretches the 1930s development of la Baule-les-Pins, a genteel residential district. The hilly Parc des Dryades offers a peaceful haven, its cheerful flower-picture beds interspersed with more naturalistic landscaping. Here you can pay homage to la Baule's founder, Louis Lajarrige, commemorated in statue form.

OXBLOOD FURNITURE
Traditionally *paludier* (saltmaker's) furniture is painted a rich dark red, reflecting the odd colour the salt pans assume at a certain critical salinity just before the salt crystallises. Typical examples can be seen in the local museums at Batz-sur-Mer, Guérande and Saillé.

What to do Thalassotherapy centres, marinas and every conceivable leisure or seaside activity are available at la Baule. A constant round of events and entertainments is programmed throughout the season – tennis, golf, riding, bridge, sailing, windsurfing – including 'Breton Weeks' (festivals celebrating all things Breton), reminding visitors to these anonymous and artificial surroundings where they are. The main shopping and restaurant area lies behind the beach on avenue du Général de Gaulle, and here too is the main tourist office, on Place de la Victoire. Campsites are mostly situated inland. The older resorts of **Pornichet** and **le Pouliguen**, at either end of la Baule's long promenade, offer a more traditional, less flashy atmosphere.

Smart pleasure craft line the marina at la Baule

In summer fast hydrojet boats ply to Belle-Ile (see pages 180–1) and other Morbihan islands from Pornichet. Le Pouliguen's *port de plaisance* (pleasure-boat harbour) lies in a sheltered channel which links the ocean with the salt marshes around Saillé. Its buildings date from a more gracious age, and even the Garage de la Plage presents a stylish façade of swirling curlicues.

PEAT-CUTTING
The ancient turbary, or peat-cutting rights, of the Brièrons represented a significant part of their income at one time. The writer Alphonse de Châteaubriant vividly describes in his classic novel *La Brière* (1923) how the local people set to work on the precious few days of the year when they were permitted to extract turf: 'They hurled themselves on the treasure. Bearded men with darting eyes, women with calloused ankles – in teams, in families, in clans, they settled to their 50 square feet and turned over the soil, dug it, rummaged in it, carried off the strips of sward.'

►► Brière, Parc Naturel Régional de *226B2*

Created in 1970 and covering a total of about 40,000ha, this marshland park (one of 32 regional nature parks in France) enjoys similar status to the Armorique Nature Park (see pages 117–19) in Finistère. About a sixth of it is known as the Grande Brière, and before the last Ice Age this low-lying basin was thickly wooded. When the sea level rose it flooded and all the vegetation died, forming a layer of peat. Gradually the sea retreated, however, and the marshes were drained.

Duke François II, father of the Duchess Anne, granted the 21 communes of the Brière joint ownership of the marshlands in 1461. The Brièrons developed their own way of life, jealously guarding these ancient rights and resentful of outside interference. Their traditional economy was based on hunting and fishing. They used the local reeds for thatching their cottages and weaving wicker fish traps, and found their way through the waterlogged terrain on flat-bottomed punts. A vital source of revenue came from peat, which they were allowed to cut for just nine days each year (see panel).

Inevitably, the 20th century brought great changes to the marshlands as the coastline developed, new roads were built and tourism consequently increased. Many Brièrons forsook the marshes for city life and higher pay in the shipyards or factories of St-Nazaire.

Following the creation of the park, the future of the marshes has been assured. Steadily the secretive, inaccessible Brière is opening up to leisure pursuits such as

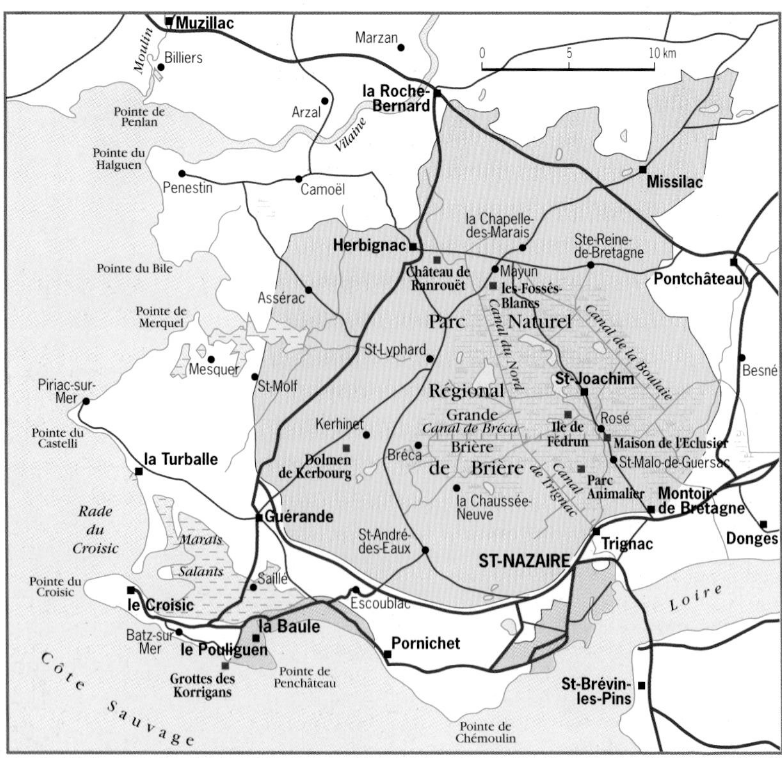

Reeds are still used for thatching in the Brière Regional Nature Park

fishing, riding and boating. *Gîtes*, hotels and campsites discreetly emerge around the edges of the marshes, little museums spring up in old cottages, and in season every back garden *curée* (canal) seems to have a *blin* or *chaland* (barge) moored, ready to ferry passengers.

Exploring Embarkation points are easy to find (for example, Bréca or les Fossés-Blancs). You can explore on your own – although it's easy to get lost or stuck in the reeds – or take a short guided tour. If you prefer to explore on foot, the GR3 footpath crosses the eastern marshes (known as les Marais-des-Donges).

A circuit of the roads by car takes about a day. Call at **Kerhinet▶**, a tidily restored hamlet of reedthatch. One cottage has been converted into a little *écomusée*. **St-Lyphard▶** church spire offers a panoramic view over the marshes, and **la Chapelle-des-Marais** has the park's main information centre. The town hall contains a fine example of a *morta*, or fossilised tree trunk.

Ile de Fédrun▶▶, a granite islet village set amid the marshes, is connected to the main road by two bridges. Several of its cottages have been turned into museums, including the **Chaumière Briéronne (Thatched Cottage)▶**, with another typical interior (*Open* Jun–mid-Sep, daily 10.30–1, 2.30–6.30. *Admission charge*), and the **Maison de la Mariée (Bride's House)▶**, displaying a collection of wax bridal flowers (see panel). **Rosé▶**, further south, contains the **Maison de l'Eclusier (Lock-keeper's House)▶**, now a tiny museum of marsh animals and local history (*Open* Jun–Sep, daily 10.30–1, 2.30–6.30. *Admission charge*). Near by is the **Parc Animalier▶**, a nature reserve with hides and information panels to help visitors identify species (*Open* May–Oct).

MOCK ORANGE
The making of bridal flower ornaments from wax became an important cottage industry for the women of the Brière during the 19th and early 20th centuries, and the products were exported worldwide. The centre of the industry was St-Joachim. The Maison de la Mariée in Fédrun shows how elaborate these wedding accoutrements were, and how carefully they were preserved in glass globes (*Open* Apr–Sep, Tue–Sun 9–12, 2–7. *Admission charge*).

Visitors explore la Brière in traditional style

Brittany, the land by the sea, reaps a rich harvest from its maritime location. The fruits de mer *are not always shelled or finned, but also include less obvious products such as salt and seaweed.*

MORE INFORMATION
To find out more about seaweed, visit Brest's magnificent Océanopolis. You can also look round Algoplus in Roscoff, north Finistère, where seaweed is processed for use in foodstuffs and cosmetics. Roscoff, home of the first thalassotherapy centre, founded by Louis Bagot, also has an exhibition on seaweed. For more on salt extraction, visit the museums at Batz-sur-Mer, Saillé and Guérande.

Seaweed gathering When the tide retreats on many Breton beaches, especially after storms, vast piles of seaweed are left behind. Tractors and trailers converge to scoop it away, but the clearing-up exercise is not carried out merely to remove the smelly substance from the tourist's gaze. Seaweed (*goëmon* in Breton) is a valuable commodity in Brittany. For centuries it has been collected and dried to use as fertiliser, particularly in Finistère and on the western islands. The rich, vegetable-growing soils of the Ceinture d'orée (Golden Belt) near St-Pol-de-Léon owe their productivity largely to seaweed. Specially equipped boats sail out towards Ouessant to collect the tangles of drifting weed on a rotating screw-like device called a *scoubidou*. Certain species are even farmed, thereby removing the local's dependence on the tide and its rather haphazard seaweed retrieval.

Most of the seaweeds washed up on Brittany's beaches belong to the *Fucus* family, and are usually brownish with air-sacs or vesicles that enable them to float, sometimes over huge distances. However, if you peer into rockpools and explore the foreshore carefully you will find many kinds of all shapes, sizes and colours. Hundreds of species occur on the Breton coast and about 90 per cent of France's total production comes from the region. When washed and dried they are decorative enough to frame – seaweed pictures are a local art form.

Today, seaweed is known to contain a huge range of hormones, vitamins, trace elements and proteins, and its range of uses has expanded rapidly as a whole new field of scientific research has opened up – for example, soda and alginates are extracted for use in foodstuffs, cosmetics and pharmaceutical products. Thalassotherapy treatment centres have sprung up all over Brittany in recent years, specialising in sea-water cures. Many health and beauty treatments are based on seaweed extracts, and you can have the seaweed plastered over you, eat it or bathe in it. How effective these 'cures' are is much debated, but medical research is certainly taking seaweed seriously now, and top chefs are using it in new styles of cooking. Its potential as a source of protein for malnourished people in poorer parts of the world is colossal.

Salt extraction Brittany's salt industry stems back to Roman times. Salt was a precious commodity needed for preserving food, and by the 13th century it had become much prized. A high tax was levied on it, known as the *gabelle*, but for many years Brittany was exempt. *Marais salants*, or salt marshes, are found in several parts of Brittany, especially around the bay of Mont-St-Michel, on the Golfe du Morbihan and near la Baule. Because the climate is more favourable in the south, the salt-extraction plants lie mainly around la Baule. Sheltered, low-lying bays where the tides are easily controllable, with a high incidence of wind and sun, are most productive.

Today, the uses of salt are more limited, and Brittany's production is only a tiny fraction of the huge quantities produced in Mediterranean pans. However, Brittany's salt is prized for its purity. Salt extraction takes place only during the summer, when there are about 30 to 40 so-called 'harvests'. The winter is then spent repairing the salt-pans and canals.

The most dramatic salt-pans can be seen around the Guérande peninsula, a surreal landscape of pools and ponds connected by a complex network of sluicegates and drainage channels. Egrets and wading birds explore the pans, stepping through pink tassles of salt-tolerant glassworts and sea lavender. Purified salt is sold by the roadside all over the marshes and makes a popular, inexpensive regional souvenir.

THE SALT CRYSTALLISATION PROCESS

Sea water is allowed to flood gently into the larger lagoons at high tide, and from these reservoirs it trickles gradually into smaller, shallower pits, which are clay-lined to prevent the water draining away. As the water evaporates the salinity increases, until eventually the salt crystallises out at a concentration of about 250g per litre. Fine white crystals of table salt (*fleurs de sel*) are raked off the surface of the water, while the coarser greyish crystals that form below the waterline are more suitable for industrial uses or cooking. Each *oeillet* (salt-pan) produces about 70–90kg of salt at every 'harvest'.

Salt-pans near Guérande

CARRIERE DES FUSILLÉS
A monument by Châteaubriant's gates commemorates 27 hostages executed by the Nazis on 22 October 1941 in reprisal for the assassination by the Resistance of Colonel Holtz, commander of the German forces based in the town. All local Resistance suspects were rounded up and shot in a quarry west of the town. The monument stands on a pigeonholed plinth containing earth from the execution site.

DYING OF JOY
One of the legends about Châteaubriant's castle tells how a 13th-century lady, Sibylle, was so overcome when her knight husband returned safely from a Crusade in 1250 that she died of happiness after running to embrace him.

►► Châteaubriant *227D3*

Set well inland amid lake-strewn woods, Châteaubriant stands guard on the Anjou border, part of the line of fortified bastions protecting Brittany from invasion. Its church, **St-Jean-de-Béré►**, is of some interest (the oldest parts of red sandstone date back to the 11th century).

Most visitors, however, make for Châteaubriant's **castle►** (*Open* mid-Jun–mid-Sep, guided tours 10.30, 2, 3.30 and 5. *Closed* Sun morning and Tue. *Admission charge*), partly feudal, partly Renaissance in style. The keep is the oldest section; the Seigneurial Palace was built by Jean de Laval, Count of Châteaubriant, and several rooms are associated with the sad story of Françoise de Foix (see panel opposite). A balcony at the top of the central staircase overlooks the gardens of the Court of Honour (*Open* daily 9–6).

►► Le Croisic *226A1*

This fishing village resort occupies a bulbous headland on the shores of the Grand Traict lagoon. The harbour faces north towards the salt marshes, where three islands joined by bridges to the mainland form separate basins. The original town lies immediately behind, slightly shabby but pleasantly genuine. The oldest (17th-century) houses lie near the lantern-towered church, sporting dormers, shutters and wrought-iron balconies.

If you are an early riser (5am) you may be in time to catch the fish auction in a new building on one of the islets – a visitor's gallery overlooks the bidding floor. On the opposite (ocean) side of the peninsula, Port-Lin acts as le Croisic's resort. Drive right round the headland for a panoramic view of the dark crags. The low hills near the port are man-made – the residue of ballast unloaded by cargo ships in the 18th and 19th centuries.

The port at le Croisic

Le Croisic's aquarium, the **Océarium►►**, is ideal for a wet day but worth a visit in any case. Arranged in five informative and interestingly themed sections, the

building takes the form of a starfish. Both Atlantic and tropical species are displayed. Exhibits include baby eels and fingernail-sized infant turbot, mussel-farming on *bouchots*, and gurnards gulping gently at their spectators. The tanks are large and beautifully seascaped; the biggest (containing sharks, congers and skates) even has a transparent walk-through tunnel (*Open* Jun–Aug, daily 10–7; rest of the year closed lunchtime. *Admission charge*).

►► Guérande *226A2*

Guérande's 15th-century ramparts completely encircle the town, and are studded with six towers; four gateways provide access. The finely turreted church of **St-Aubin►**, at the heart of the old town, contains a mix of features from many different periods, including a Merovingian sarcophagus, Romanesque columns, and superb stained glass of vivid blues and roundels.

One of the fortified gatehouses (St-Michel, the governor's house) contains a fascinating local **museum►►**. Many displays are connected with the salt industry, including furnishings, tools, costumes and so on (*Open* Apr–Sep, daily 10–12.30, 2.30–7. *Admission charge*).

South of Guérande lies a weird landscape of neatly kept salt-pans, where egrets fish. Roadside vendors sell bags of purified salt and pickled samphire, one of the few plants that can survive the briny conditions. To find out more about the salt-extraction process, visit two small museums: the **Maison des Paludiers►** at Saillé, 3km south of Guérande (*Open* Mar–Aug, daily 10–12.30, 2–6. *Admission charge*), and the **Musée des Marais Salants►►** at Batz-sur-Mer (see page 230). North of Guérande the coastal road leads through the lively sardine-fishing town of **la Turballe** to Pointe du Castelli (with fine views) and the pretty old village of **Piriac-sur-Mer►** (which has some 17th-century timbered houses).

Châteaubriant's castle was founded in the 11th century

FRANÇOISE DE FOIX

Jean de Laval remodelled Châteaubriant's castle in the early 16th century as a fitting home for his child-bride, Françiose then only 11. As she grew up, news of her beauty and intelligence spread, and eventually François I requested her attendance at court. The jealous count made excuses, arousing the king's curiosity even further. François bribed a servant to tell him the signal Jean de Laval used to communicate with his wife, and thus managed to arrange a meeting with her. Dazzled by the splendour of court life, Françoise became the king's mistress, but when he tired of her he sent her back to Châteaubriant, where her husband locked her away in a dark room. After 10 years Françoise died, murdered, some say, by Jean de Laval, who never forgave her.

THE DUCHESSE DE BERRY
The bourgeois monarchy of Louis-Philippe (1830–48), faced a minor rebellion in 1832 when the Duchesse de Berry staged an abortive rising in Brittany in a bid for the throne. She arrived in Brittany disguised as a peasant and hid in a house in Nantes. The police arrived and, finding the house chilly, started a fire in the grate. Eventually several soot-covered, spluttering figures landed ignominiously in the hearth. The duchess and her loyal followers had spent 16 hours up the chimney.

▶▶▶ Nantes *227D1*

The industrialised outskirts of Brittany's historic capital do not entice, but once you manage to abandon your car safely in the old town Nantes suddenly becomes a much more enjoyable place. The central areas are compact enough to explore without developing blisters, but if you should tire an excellent network of buses and trams cuts down the walking (day passes and *carnets* are available).

Orientation Exploring all the city sights takes at least a day, and if you decide to stay on there is plenty to do in the evenings or in wet weather. If you choose Nantes as a base for a short break, the surrounding area also offers lots to see and do. Nantes' crowning glory is its cathedral, though its art collections rival any elsewhere in Brittany. Of its dozen-plus museums, few are essential viewing but most have a quirky charm. Monday and Tuesday are bad days for sightseeing (several museums close).

The charm of Nantes lies in its atmosphere and variety rather than any set-piece sights. Its shops and stately buildings have touches of Parisian sophistication, and its youthful university population gives it plenty of cultural energy and evening entertainment, yet it has all the down-to-earth practicality and good sense of provincial France. Today it is a great commercial centre and ranks as France's seventh largest city.

The church of St-Nicolas, Nantes

History Nantes goes back a long way, to a Gaulish tribe called the Namnetes, who gave the city their name. After the Romans came and went, the Breton Celts fought off successive waves of invading Franks and Norsemen until AD 939, when Alain Barbe-Torte (Crookbeard), a heroic leader, finally drove out the Vikings and became Brittany's last king, choosing Nantes as his capital. After the wars and confusion of the Middle Ages, the Dukes of Montfort restored peace and order. Anne de Bretagne was born in the castle and completed the construction begun by her father. In 1598, the castle witnessed another historic event when Henry IV signed the Edict of Nantes, which granted freedom of worship to the many Protestant Huguenots and ended the religious wars that had torn France

apart. The edict brought peace for a century, until its revocation by Louis XIV in 1685.

In the great trading years of the 16th to 18th centuries Nantes prospered – firstly from sugar and slaves (the notorious 'ebony' trade with Africa and the Caribbean), later from shipping and sardines. When the Loire silted badly, shipping moved downstream to St-Nazaire, and Nantes hastily diversified into food processing and other light industries. Dredging techniques now keep the Loire free enough to allow modest cargo vessels as far inland as Nantes, and its quays are still lively with grain silos and derricks. After serious damage during World War II, Nantes' grand townscape of the 18th and 19th centuries around the Place Royale has been restored.

Main sights The **Château des Ducs de Bretagne▶▶** was built by Duke François II in 1466 and used first as a ducal palace, then as the Breton governor's residence. It has been much restored and the moat refilled. The courtyard and ramparts can be visited free of charge.

A vast restoration programme, launched in 1994, is due to be completed in 2008. The aim of the project is to create a modern museum devoted to the history of Nantes and its region, the restored castle being the first and main exhibit of the museum. Phase 1 was completed in 1998 with the reopening of the 18th-century *harnachement* (saddlery) building, which now holds major temporary exhibitions on themes such as *Nantes–St Nazaire, The History of a Port* and *The Edict of Nantes*.

The cathedral of **St-Pierre▶▶▶**, a glorious church of dazzling white tufa, is an amazing *tour de force*, its deceptively simple lines giving the impression of limitless height and space. The best thing in it is the splendid marble tomb of François II and his wife (parents of the Duchess Anne), carved by the master sculptor Michel

Some of Nantes' older quarters make appealing, traffic-free places to stroll

BEAUJOIRE

This large park some way north of Nantes by the banks of the Erdre is the site of France's biggest flower show, the Floralies Internationales. Plants from all over the world are exhibited here, with many countries taking a stand. You can reach Beaujoire easily from Nantes town centre by bus or boat.

MINOR MUSEUMS
The Musée Jules-Verne at 3 rue de l'Hermitage (near quai de la Fosse) celebrates a local son, born in Nantes in 1828 and perhaps Brittany's best-known writer outside his native land. Memorabilia and portraits illustrate Verne's imaginative life and writings (*Open* daily 10–12, 2–5, except Sun morning and Tue. *Admission charge*). Also on this stretch of quayside is the *Maillé-Brézé*, an escort ship launched in 1957 and taken out of service in 1988. It is now docked permanently on the Loire, and visitors are welcome to look round the living quarters, anti-submarine and anti-aircraft weapons and detection systems (*Open* Jun–Sep, daily 2–6. *Admission charge*).

Colombe. Just outside stand the **Porte St-Pierre**, a 15th-century gateway, and la Psalette, another turreted structure from the same period, now part of the sacristy.

Housed in a palatial 19th-century building, the **Musée des Beaux-Arts (Fine Arts Museum)▶▶** contains a wide range of French and European art, from Italian Primitives and Dutch still life to Impressionists, 20th-century abstracts and modern exhibitions (*Open* Wed–Mon 10–6, Fri 10–9. *Admission charge, free on Sun*).

The **Palais Dobrée▶▶** is an eccentric Romanesque mansion, the former home of a Nantes shipowner, Thomas Dobrée (1810–95), whose patchy collection of art and antiquities is now displayed inside. On the same ticket you can see the **Musée d'Archéologie Régionale▶▶** with a vast array of local and faraway finds from neolithic times to the Viking raids, including Egyptian sarcophagi, Greek and Etruscan ceramics, jewellery etc. (*Open* Tue–Sun 10–12, 1.30–5.30).

Nantes' natural history museum, the **Musée d'Histoire Naturelle▶▶**, is a curious, enthusiastically managed collection. The most bizarre item is the stretched skin of a soldier whose dying wish was to be made into a drum. Unfortunately, his skin was too thick to offer any beatable resonance, so here it hangs for all to see (*Open* Tue–Sun 10–12, 2–6. *Admission charge*).

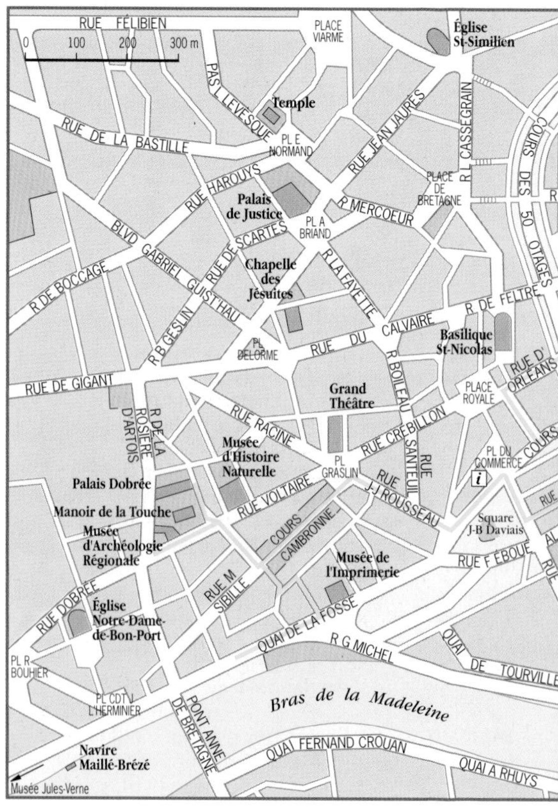

Walk

The old town of Nantes

A walk around Nantes' well-restored centre. Allow a full day, including museum visits and a lunch-stop or drink at the magnificent art-nouveau brasserie, la Cigale.

Start at the top of the town, and after visiting the main sights here (castle, cathedral and fine arts museum), relax in the **Jardin des Plantes▶**. Go back along rue de Richebourg, deviating briefly to the late-Gothic **Chapelle de l'Immaculée**. Head for the delightful **Ste-Croix district▶▶**, where 15th- and 16th-century houses line the streets (explore rue de la Boucherie, rue de la Juiverie and rue Bossuet). Most of the nearby Place Royale was destroyed in the last war but has been faithfully restored.

Further west, lies the **Ancienne Ile Feydeau▶**, once embraced by the arms of the Loire, but now no longer an island. Many of the houses of rich shipowners can be seen here. **Passage Pommeraye▶** is worth a glance for its elegant covered 19th-century shopping centre. **Place Graslin▶** has a mix of 18th- and 19th-century buildings, best appreciated from the tables outside the **brasserie la Cigale▶▶**.

Cours Cambronne▶ is another fine collection of 18th- and 19th-century houses. Head for the **Musée de l'Imprimerie▶**, an interesting museum of printing, and the quai de la Fosse. Finish at the Musée d'Archéologie, Manoir de la Touche and Palais Dobrée.

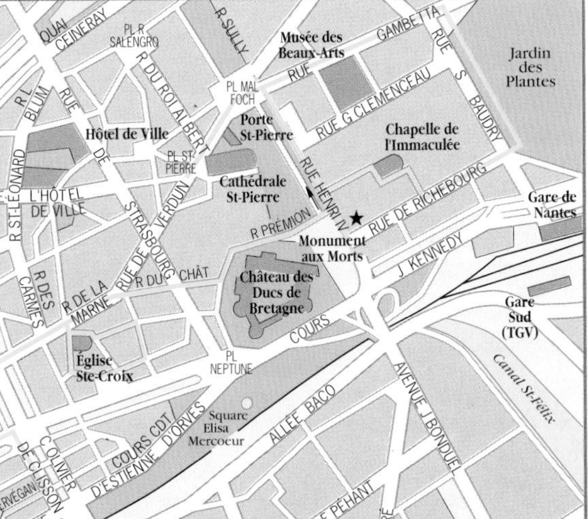

East end of Nantes cathedral

Over 650km of navigable rivers and canals cross Brittany, and the network provides one of the most enjoyable ways of exploring the interior. Many companies hire out suitably equipped craft for boating holidays, and excursion cruisers ply from many waterside centres.

RIVER TRIPS
Not all canal boats are suitable for the stronger currents of the tidal estuaries, and navigation can be tricky. To enjoy these stretches, therefore, you may prefer to let someone else take the helm unless you are an experienced boat-handler. The Rance, Aulne, Odet, Auray, Aven and Trieux all offer regular boat trips in season. Pick up tariffs and timetables at any tourist office.

History Brittany's canal system was not designed for holidaymakers: its original purpose was much more earnest. The aim was to provide a safe overland passage for freight vessels, which were constantly harassed by enemy ships on the open seas. A scheme to link St-Malo and Brest via inland waterways was first proposed in 1627, but it took the ambition and foresight of Napoleon to implement it. By this time naval tension between England and France was so acute that a cross-country link became an urgent priority.

The Nantes–Brest canal was begun in 1810, linking the Loire with the Aulne and thus providing access to the open sea via the Rade de Brest. The project took 26 years to construct and represented a fantastic cost in human and economic terms. It was initially very slow to recoup capital expenditure, but by the end of the century its time had come and it enjoyed a brief heyday of shunting coal, slate and fertiliser across the province.

After World War I, improved rail and road connections caused a sharp decline in canal trade, and by 1928 cargo barges were rare. The construction of the Guerlédan dam half-way along its course effectively severed the Nantes–Brest link, and afterwards the central section between Pontivy and Carhaix-Plouguer was navigable only by kayak. In 1945 the last freight barge sailed through Châteaulin, and today the canal is used exclusively for tourism.

Waterways today Brittany's inland waterways fall into three main sections, each a combination of river and canal. The Ille-et-Rance section flows south across eastern Brittany, linking St-Malo with the Atlantic via Rennes and Redon. The canalised stretch between Dinan and Rennes (49 locks) joins the River Vilaine for the southern part of the journey. It is a popular route for yachts and cabin cruisers cutting through from the Channel to the

The canalised River Oust runs through tranquil scenery near Josselin

Atlantic, avoiding the perilous seas of west Finistère. Some of the most picturesque sections lie near Hédé, with its remarkable staircase of locks, and around Redon. The final section down to la Roche-Bernard and the Arzal dam is also interesting.

Two east–west sections are all that remains of the broken-backed Nantes–Brest canal. One of these links Nantes and Lorient via Pontivy and the River Blavet

Flower-decked locks at Redon

(135 locks); the other joins Carhaix with Brest via Châteaulin and the Aulne estuary (35 locks). On the eastern section the stretches of Oust around Rochefort-en-Terre and Josselin are perhaps the prettiest, and on the Blavet the section around St-Nicolas-des-Eaux. Westwards, the calm loops of the Aulne estuary are attractive for most of the journey from Carhaix-Plouguer, but particularly scenic around Châteauneuf-du-Faou.

Hiring a boat Fully equipped boats (cabin cruisers or narrowboats) can be hired at various centres along all these routes for varying lengths of time – a day, a weekend or longer – and you can choose whether to sail back to your starting point or take a one-way trip. Canoes can be hired on certain stretches, though Brittany's waterways favour the placid paddler rather than the whitewater enthusiast.

The maximum draught allowable on the canal system is 1.2m, and the maximum speed limit is 6kph. Off-season rates are very much lower than July and August charges. Moorings, waterpoints and chandlery services are available *en route*. Bikes can often be hired to take with you on board, and can add a useful and enjoyable dimension to the holiday. Towpaths accompany the routes in some places, though not continuously.

MORE INFORMATION
La Roche-Bernard's Musée de la Vilaine Maritime, Redon's Musée de la Batellerie and Hennebont's Maison de l'Eau make interesting ports of call for more information about canals and rivers. French Government Tourist Offices (FGTOs) abroad, or any local office, can provide a list of contact numbers to hire boats, or you can ring the Comité des Canaux Bretons (tel: 02 99 71 06 04). Main hire centres include Châteauneuf-du-Faou, Josselin, Redon, Hédé, Pont-Coblant, Rohan, Baud, Malestroit and Nantes.

Negotiating a lock on the Nantes–Brest canal

LA GACILLY
The attractions of this small town north of Redon – pretty enough just to look at – are enhanced by its local perfume factory. La Gacilly is the headquarters of Yves Rocher's cosmetics empire, which is based on biological plant products rather than synthetic laboratory concoctions. The factory here employs over 1,000 workers. Visitors can see the **Végétarium**, an original museum entirely devoted to the vegetable world (*Open* Apr–mid-Nov, daily 10–6.45; mid-Nov–Mar, Tue–Sun 2–6.15. *Admission charge*). Needless to say, Yves Rocher products are also on sale in town, along with many arts and crafts.

►► Redon *226B3*

Not only roads, railways and waterways converge at Redon, but also three *départements* and two regions – Brittany and Pays de la Loire. This well-kept and attractive little town once served as Rennes' seaport; today it is an important agricultural centre with a Monday market. Various light industries (computers, children's clothes) have been established in the newer parts of the town.

Pleasure craft have taken the place of the cargo barges that once plied along the River Vilaine, but you can still take river trips with Vedettes Jaunes, going downstream as far as the Arzal dam or upstream to Beslé. Under your own steam you can follow the Nantes–Brest canal, which crosses the Vilaine at Redon in a complex series of locks, bridges and sluicegates. The Oust adds its own tortuous course to this watery complexity, waveringly joining up with the canal to the north of the town. Houseboats, pleasure cruisers, canoes and sailboats all converge on Redon throughout the year.

Floral town For most of the year Redon proudly keeps up its reputation as a *ville fleurie*, with a profusion of window-boxes, hanging baskets and flower tubs to give it a constantly festive appearance. Bars with live music, good-value restaurants and even a summer theatre provide diversions for its visitors, and it makes a pleasant base for a day or two, with many attractive excursions and walks, especially along the waterfront. Central hotels tend to cluster around the railway station (not the prettiest part of the town), but there are one or two attractive alternatives in more rural settings (see Hotels and Restaurants, page 277). At the end of October the Foire Teillouse festival celebrates the local chestnut harvest with music, dancing and crafts, while the town's chefs cook up imaginative nutty dishes.

Pleasure cruisers line up for river and canal trips at Redon

Old Redon The oldest and most interesting part of the town lies north-west of the cross formed where the canal meets the river. The church of **St-Sauveur▶▶** is the most prominent landmark, an ancient abbey church with a Romanesque tower emerging from its splayed Gothic buttresses. The Gothic belfry near by was separated from the original church by a fire in 1780, and the adjacent 17th-century cloisters now house a college. One of the best views to be had of the church is from the raised walk of chestnut trees on the other side of rue Richelieu. In the autumn a mini-army of municipal workers arrives on this esplanade with large vacuum cleaners to clear up leaves and fallen conkers. A tidy place indeed.

The main street, **Grande Rue**, takes you through the heart of the old town. If you need picnic provisions, this is a good place to buy them (look for chestnut specialities in season). On the way you will pass some of its quaintest houses, some corbelled or frescoed. Several old salt-houses can be seen on rue du Port. Down on quai Duguay-Trouin stand the later elegant homes of wealthy shipowners, who were once able to watch their vessels pass by from their living-room windows. Intricate wrought-iron balconies decorate the façades. An inscription on one of these houses reads: *'Je suis de 1782, mes voisines de 1783'* ('I date from 1782, my neighbours from 1783'). A few scraps of the town's original ramparts remain around quai St-Jacques. On the river you may see an unusual method of fishing, whereby large cradle-like nets are suspended on long poles from a boat.

For more information about the local waterways, visit the **Musée de la Batellerie de l'Ouest▶▶** (*Open* mid-Jun–mid-Sep, daily 10–12, 3–6. *Admission charge*) on quai Jean-Bart by the pleasure-boat harbour, its entrance marked by two massive oak lock gates. The exhibition traces the history of the port and its waterborne traffic from earliest times to its decline this century, with an aquarium of river fish and a film show to supplement the models, photographs and documents that are on display.

COJOUX COUNTRY
North of Redon, the countryside west of the village of St-Just (known as the Lande de Cojoux) is liberally sprinkled with megaliths. In fact this part of Brittany has the densest concentration of prehistoric remains outside Carnac. It is poorly documented in tourist literature, but there are guided tours on Sundays in July, August and September. Alternatively, visitors can follow a signposted path that leads across the moor. Among the monuments, the Alignements du Moulin (13 blocks of quartzite) and the Demoiselles de Cojoux (three menhirs, one on its side) are perhaps most impressive.

Left: Redon's Grande Rue

Above: old Redon

MONSIEUR HULOT'S HOLIDAY

Film buffs may like to make a short pilgrimage to the little resort of St-Marc, just west of St-Nazaire, where Jacques Tati made his classic film in 1953. The Hôtel de la Plage is still there, facing the sands from an enticing rocky coast topped with prim villas on wooded cliffs. The film achieved only modest success in its native land, and today the French are still mystified by its enormous popularity among English-speakers, who are the butt of so much its gentle ribbing.

▶ St-Nazaire 226B1

This unfortunate place took such a pounding during World War II that it has comparatively few tourist attractions. Like Brest and Lorient it has been rebuilt in a bleak, blockish style using vast amounts of concrete. If you enjoy dockyard scenes, however, it has something to offer, and its past is very interesting. To learn more about this, head straight for the port to visit the **Ecomusée de St-Nazaire▶** (*Open* Jun–Aug, daily 9.30–6.30; May, Sep and Oct, Wed–Mon 10–12, 2–6. *Admission charge*), which documents the history of the town from earliest times to the present day, concentrating particularly on wartime bombardment and the subsequent reconstruction. The most interesting section of the museum can be seen in the submarine exit, a covered lock which enabled German U-boats to slip out of the harbour in secret. It now houses the French submarine *Espadon*, which sailed beneath the polar ice-cap; a tour of the submarine's interior is included in the museum ticket.

In 1840 St-Nazaire was the postal station handling mail bound for Mexico and the Antilles. In former days, however, St-Nazaire's connections with the Caribbean were less innocent; it participated in the notorious 'ebony' (slave) trade which made Nantes prosper. Shipbuilding has long been one of its main industries. It took up the slack when the Loire silted so badly that deep-draughted shipping could no longer reach Nantes. The Blue Riband liners *Normandie* and *France* were built here, and in 1988, the *Sovereign of the Seas* – at the time the largest cruise liner in the world – was launched from its docks. Its shipyards, which suffered badly during the recession, are picking up again and associated industries such as oil-refining and petrochemicals help to keep the town going.

St-Nazaire's most striking architectural feature is its massive suspension bridge (3,356m long) over the Loire, a graceful curve topped with red and white pylons. For a stiff toll, it provides a fast link to the south of France.

The docks at St-Nazaire

Travel Facts

Arriving

Getting there

By air From Paris the choice of Breton destinations is wide: **Air Inter** and **Air France Europe** serve Quimper, Brest, Rennes, Nantes and Lorient. Other airlines serve Dinard, Lannion, Vannes and St-Brieuc. There are also direct flights from the UK, Ireland and the Channel Islands to several airports in Brittany with **BritAir** (UK tel: 01923 502044; France tel: 02 98 62 10 22), **Air France** (UK tel: 0181 742 6600; France tel: 08 02 80 28 02) or **Jersey European Airways** (CI tel: 0990 676676) – some only in summer.

Some airport cities, such as Nantes and Quimper, are firmly on the European 'weekend break' list. If you are travelling from the US or Canada it is probably best to make your way to Paris and then travel onwards from there; Australasian visitors may find it cheaper to get to Brittany via London.

By sea Brittany Ferries (UK tel: 01705 827701) operate direct sailings to St-Malo and Roscoff from Portsmouth, Plymouth and Cork. Services operate all year round. Check brochures carefully for special excursion rates and cheaper sailings. Crossings take between 7½ and 9 hours from Britain (longer from Ireland).

From the eastern Channel ports you have a choice of other ferry operators (P&O, Sealink Stena, Sally Line, Hoverspeed) – and of course the Channel Tunnel. Against apparent gains on shorter crossings you must balance the time and cost of motoring through northern France (including petrol, *autoroute* tolls, meals and overnight accommodation).

By train The advent of the TGV (*Train à Grande Vitesse*) has revolutionised travel within Brittany. You can now reach Rennes in 2 hours from Paris (Gare Montparnasse); St-Brieuc or Vannes in about 3 hours; and Brest, Lorient or Quimper in 4 hours. Through-fares are available from Britain or Ireland via the Channel ports or Paris (including good-value air/rail deals). By prior

The modern architecture of the airport at Rennes, also well served by the TGV

A P&O ferry heads for Calais

arrangement, you can take a bike with you on SNCF, the French state railway (UK tel: 0345 300003 for more information).

By road Excellent motorway links (A11 and A81) connect Brittany with Paris and the rest of the French road network. A fast dual carriageway runs via all the major centres around the Breton coast and up through Rennes. There are no toll roads (*péage*) in Brittany. Coach operators will take you to the ferry ports from the UK; on arrival in Brittany you must find your way by local buses.

Customs regulations

Since 1 January 1993 there has been virtually no restriction on duty-paid goods taken from one EU country to another, provided that the goods are carried personally and intended for personal use. Guide limits have been issued stating what is considered suitable for personal use (10 litres of spirits, 90 litres of wine, 110 litres of beer, 800 cigarettes) and if you exceed these you may be questioned closely. Goods bought in duty-free shops (at airports and on ferries) are still subject to restrictions.

Visitors arriving from outside the EU must abide by much tighter regulations when they enter France (currently 200 cigarettes or 50 cigars; 1 litre of spirits or 2 litres of fortified wine or 4 litres of table wine; 60ml perfume and 250ml toilet water).

Travel insurance

Adequate insurance cover is essential for peace of mind (motoring insurance is covered on pages 252–3). Many of the policies available are similiar, but read the small print carefully to see if any exclusions would affect you. Certain credit cards provide insurance for cardholders and their family when tickets are bought with their card.

All EU citizens are in theory entitled to reciprocal health care, provided they take form E111 issued by local health authorities, but reimbursement can be a time-consuming and bureaucratic procedure and may leave you out of pocket. Check to see whether your existing house contents or health insurance covers you for losses abroad. If you do suffer a loss report it to the police within 24 hours (you need to obtain a copy of your statement for any insurance claim you make). Collect receipts for all expenses incurred.

Visas

All visitors to France require a valid passport or excursion document. European, North American and Japanese visitors require no visa for stays up to three months, but Australian and New Zealand nationals must have one. Check entry requirements with your nearest French consulate if you hold a non-EU passport. Several types of visa are available – allow plenty of time to apply (two months is advisable).

Essentials

When to go

Brittany's tourist season is short and intense. In July and August beaches, campsites and *gîtes* burst at the seams, but by the end of September a great many resorts may already be closing. In winter not much happens on the tourist scene: hotels and all but the largest museums and attractions are closed, and very few boat trips or sports activities take place. Festivals and events are nearly all geared to the summer season between Easter and October.

If you have a choice, try to avoid visiting in the peak school holiday season, when prices are high and resources are stretched. May/June and September are good times to go, neither crowded nor moribund, although the sea is still cold. The weather is always unpredictable.

Climate

Brittany's climate is maritime, like the south-west coast of Britain, but a little warmer and drier in summer, and wetter in winter. Be prepared for rain at any time of year. Winter sees few extremes of temperature, and frost and snow are rare. Average daytime temperatures in summer are about 21°C, a little warmer and drier on the south coast than in the north. Near the sea there is usually a breeze, which may blow up to storm force occasionally on the exposed ocean coast. High winds have wreaked havoc with Brittany's native woodlands in recent years.

National holidays

- **New Year's Day** 1 January
- **Easter Sunday**
- **Easter Monday**
- **Labour Day** 1 May
- **VE Day** 8 May
- **Ascension Day**
- **Whitsun** (and following Monday)
- **Bastille Day** 14 July
- **Assumption Day** 15 August
- **All Saints' Day** 1 November
- **Armistice Day** 11 November
- **Christmas Day** 25 December

Time differences

France is on Central European Time – one hour ahead of GMT for most of the year, six hours ahead of US Eastern Standard Time, nine hours ahead of Pacific Standard Time and nine hours *behind* Sydney. French summer time begins on the last Sunday in March and ends on the last Sunday in September.

Money matters

Currency The French franc (FF) is made up of 100 centimes. There are coins of 5, 10, 20 and 50 centimes and 1, 2, 10 and 20 francs. Banknotes come in denominations of 20, 50, 100,

Quiberon's Côte Sauvage

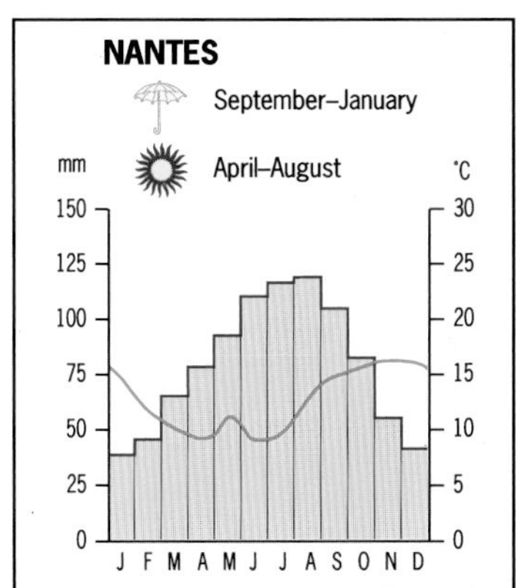

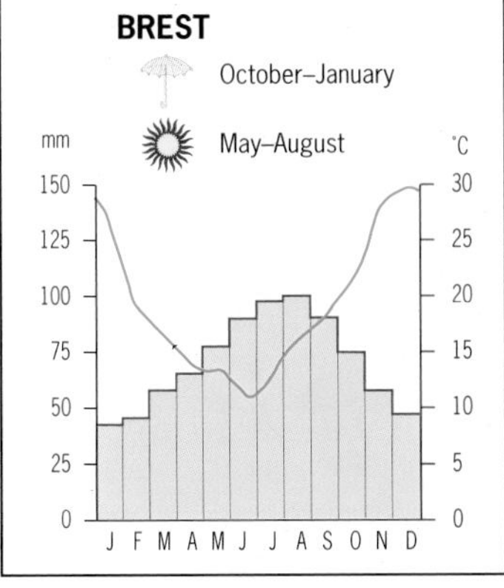

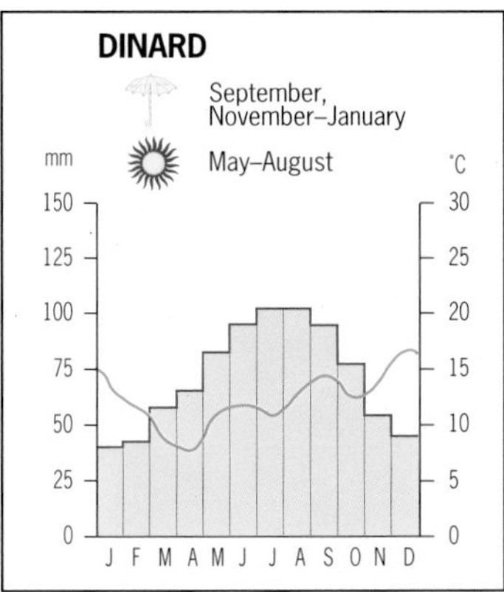

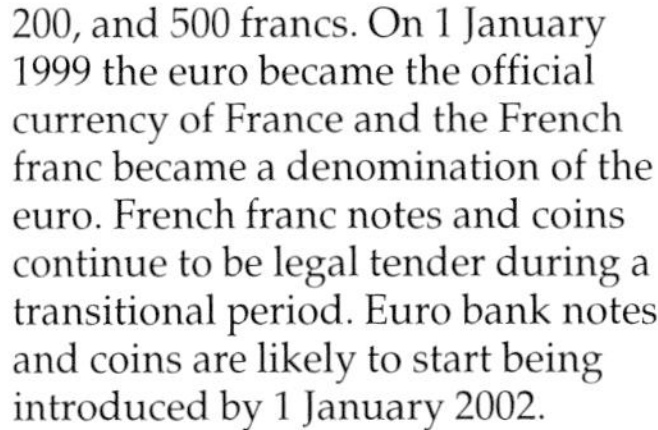
200, and 500 francs. On 1 January 1999 the euro became the official currency of France and the French franc became a denomination of the euro. French franc notes and coins continue to be legal tender during a transitional period. Euro bank notes and coins are likely to start being introduced by 1 January 2002.

The safest way to carry large amounts of money is in traveller's cheques, or Eurocheques if you have a European bank account and the appropriate card. Ask for some small denominations when you order cheques and when you cash them (500F notes can be difficult to change). Banks with a *Change* sign usually give the best exchange rate, though many shops and hotels also offer exchange facilities. Banque de France, Banque Nationale de Paris and Crédit Lyonnais generally offer reasonable exchange rates and fairly low commissions.

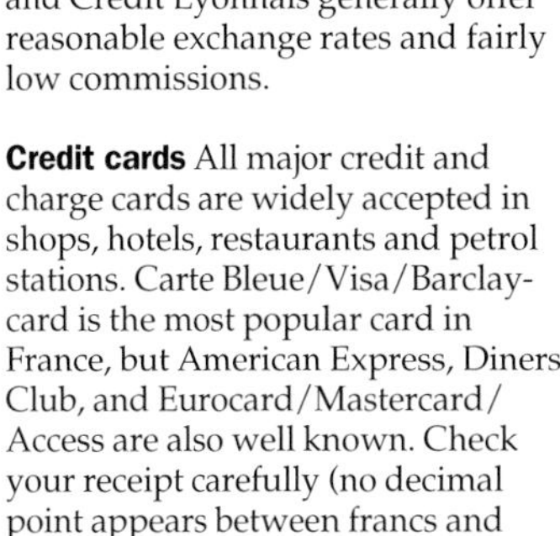
Credit cards All major credit and charge cards are widely accepted in shops, hotels, restaurants and petrol stations. Carte Bleue/Visa/Barclaycard is the most popular card in France, but American Express, Diners Club, and Eurocard/Mastercard/Access are also well known. Check your receipt carefully (no decimal point appears between francs and centimes; a comma appears instead).

Some retailers are reluctant to accept credit cards for amounts below 100F. Many banks now have multilingual cash dispensers for customers with credit cards, but you must have a PIN (personal identification number). Alternatively, you can draw cash advances at any bank that displays the Carte Bleue (Visa) or Eurocard (Access) sign.

Driving

Car rental

Except for very short breaks, hiring a car in France is unlikely to be cheaper than bringing your own vehicle across the Channel or from elsewhere in Europe. However, some inclusive holiday packages offer good value and may be worth considering. It is probably cheaper to fix up a car-hire deal before you travel, but all the major international car-hire firms have desks at airports, ferry terminals and main railway stations. Some companies insist that drivers should be at least 21 years old. If you don't have a credit card you will have to produce a substantial cash deposit when booking. Make sure you sign for collision damage waiver when you take out a contract. You will only need to take out personal accident insurance if it is not covered by your general travel insurance.

Accidents and breakdowns

If your car breaks down, try to move it off the main highway and flash your hazard warning lights or place a red triangle 30m behind your car. Emergency phones (*postes d'appel d'urgence*) linked to the local police station are placed at 4km intervals on main roads and every 2km on motorways. If you have an accident, you must call the police (tel 17 – which also summons an ambulance if necessary). You must also complete and sign an accident statement and exchange insurance details. If possible, try to enlist witnesses at the scene of an accident.

Motor insurance

Check before leaving your own country that you have comprehensive insurance, and extend your cover if necessary. Many companies offer breakdown cover abroad, including the AA's 5-Star cover, which gives great peace of mind. It is advisable, though no longer legally required, to carry a Green Card with you, which will provide automatic evidence that you are fully protected if you have an accident. Check your policy with your travel agent if you are booking a package holiday.

Driving regulations

To drive in France you must be at least 18 years old and carry a full valid national driving licence (not a provisional licence). If you are taking your own car, you must have the vehicle registration document (plus a letter of authorisation from the owner if the car is not registered in your name), insurance documents and a car nationality sticker. Seat belts must be worn by the driver and all passengers. Children under 10 must sit in the back unless in a specially fitted backward-facing seat.

Driving is on the right, and headlamp beams must be adjusted on right-hand-drive cars. Carry a red warning triangle in case of breakdown. Drink-driving limits (0.5g/litre) are strictly enforced by the police; if you fail a breath test, expect a heavy fine or driving ban.

Fines

Hefty on-the-spot fines may be imposed for contravening French traffic regulations. If you don't have cash you may be able to proffer vouchers if you have insurance cover. If you consider yourself innocent, you can opt to pay a deposit (*amende forfaitaire*) and the police will issue a receipt.

Priority
Priorité à droite (priority to traffic coming from the right) still causes confusion on French roads, not least among France's own nationals. The rule is still (officially): in built-up areas you must give way to anyone coming out of a side turning from the right. Signs may indicate that you have right of way (*passage protégé*) on a major road. On roundabouts *priorité à droite* no longer applies and you must give way to any car already on the roundabout. Watch for the signs '*Vous n'avez pas la priorité*' and take great care. If an oncoming vehicle flashes its lights at you this means the driver thinks he or she has priority and you should give way. It's safest to do so!

Roads
There are three types of roads: A stands for *autoroute* (motorway); N is a *route nationale* (main road); D is a secondary road (most roads in Brittany are D roads, even those that seem quite big). Speed limits are 130kph on toll motorways, 110kph on dual carriageways, 90kph on other roads and 50kph in towns (lower in wet or foggy conditions).

Parking
Don't park where kerbs are marked with yellow paint. Major towns often have *zones bleues* where parking discs must be used (obtain one from the tourist office). Elsewhere there may be meters (2F coins are useful) or complicated signs indicating *Côté du stationnement, jours pairs/impairs* (meaning you can park on one side of the road on alternate days of the month – in other words, odd or even). In towns, multi-storey car parks may be the answer.

Fuel
There are four basic grades of petrol: *gazole* (diesel), *super* (98 octane), *sans plomb* (95 octane unleaded) and *super sans plomb* (98 octane unleaded). The cheapest place to buy petrol is usually at big supermarkets.

Route planning
In high season (July and August) main coastal routes in Brittany can

Cruising along on the open road

get very congested. The Automobile Association can tailor-make routes for you or provide advance recorded information on traffic situations in Europe.

Maps showing the *Bis* network are available free from roadside kiosks or tourist offices. *Bis* means *Bison Futé* (wily buffalo), a government scheme recommending fast through-routes for holiday traffic.

Road signs
International European traffic signs are steadily replacing the older ones in Brittany, though you may still find old-fashioned place-name signs hewn from granite or set in concrete.

Chaussée déformée – uneven road surface
Gravillons – loose chippings
Nids de poules – potholes
Déviation – diversion
Rappel – watch your speed (literally, reminder)
Cédez le passage – give way
Absence de marquage – no road markings
Ralentir – slow down
Route barrée – road closed
Passage protégé – right of way
Priorité aux piétons – pedestrian right of way
Sens unique – one-way street
Sens interdit – no entry
Toutes directions – route for through traffic

Public transport

Rail

A good network of railways runs east–west, connecting all Brittany's main centres. North–south travel is rather more complicated. The flagship trains are the high-speed TGVs, for which a reservation is needed. There are also *rapide* and *express* trains, and slower local services.

Good deals are available for visitors who wish to travel by train. **EuroDomino Rover** tickets (available in Europe, but only outside France) allow unlimited travel on three, five or 10 days during a one-month period. The **France Railpass** (available in North America) gives similar travel limits. These passes are for tourists only and must be purchased from SNCF in your own country:

- **Canada** 1500 rue Stanley, Montreal PQ H3A 1R3.
- **UK** 179 Piccadilly, London W1V 0BA (tel: 0891 515 477).
- **US** 610 Fifth Avenue, New York NY 10020 (tel: 212/582 2110).

Bus

Buses cover a far wider network of places than the railways and are generally cheaper. They are mostly useful for short hops rather than long hauls. The main bus station in a town is usually next to the railway station, and some coach services connect with trains. Tickets should be bought on the bus and cancelled (*compostés*) in a machine near the driver.

Boat

Trips to Brittany's islands are highly recommended, as are cruises along its estuaries. The following companies operate regular summer services:

- **Emeraude Lines** (tel: 02 99 40 48 40) Rance Valley, Chausey islands, Channel Islands and Fréhel coast from St-Malo and Dinard.
- **Condor** (tel: 02 99 20 03 00) Channel Islands from St-Malo and Dinard.
- **Vedettes de Bréhat** (tel: 02 96 55 86 99) Trieux estuary and Ile de Bréhat from Erquy, le Val-André, Port Dahouet, Binic, St-Quay-Portrieux and Pointe de l'Arcouest.
- **Les 7 Iles en Vedettes** (tel: 02 96 91 10 00) the Pink Granite Coast and the bird sanctuary of les Sept Iles from Perros-Guirec.
- **Vedettes de l'Ile de Batz** (tel: 02 98 61 79 66) Ile de Batz from Roscoff.
- **Vedettes Armoricaines** (tel: 02 98 44 44 04) Rade de Brest and Crozon peninsula from Brest and le Fret.
- **Compagnie Maritime Penn ar Bed** (tel: 02 98 80 24 68) Ouessant and Molène islands from Brest and le Conquet; Ile de Sein from Audierne.
- **Vedettes Rosmeur** (tel: 02 98 92 83 83) bay of Douarnenez and Crozon peninsula from Morgat and Douarnenez.
- **Vedettes de l'Odet** (tel: 02 98 57 00 58) Odet estuary from Bénodet, Loctudy, Beg-Meil, Port-la-Forêt, Concarneau and Quimper.

Trams are the best means of transport in Nantes

Queuing for a cruise boat on the Emerald Coast

• **Vedettes Glenn** (tel: 02 98 97 10 31) Odet estuary and Iles de Glénan from Concarneau.
• **Vedettes Transrade** (tel: 02 97 33 40 55) Ile de Groix from Lorient and Port Louis.
• **Compagnie Morbihannaise de Navigation** (tel: 02 97 31 80 01) Belle-Ile, Houat and Hoëdic from Quiberon; Ile de Groix from Lorient.
• **Navix** (tel: 02 97 46 60 00) Golfe du Morbihan from Vannes, Ile d'Arz, Ile aux Moines, Port-Navalo, Locmariaquer, le Bono, Auray; Belle-Ile from la Trinité-sur-Mer.
• **Izenah** (tel: 02 97 26 31 45) Golfe du Morbihan from Port-Blanc and Ile aux Moines.
• **Vedettes l'Aiglon** (tel: 02 97 57 39 15) Golfe du Morbihan and Auray estuary from Locmariaquer.
• **Compagnie des Iles** (tel: 02 97 46 18 19) a grand tour of the Golfe du Morbihan from Vannes.
• **Vedettes Blanches Armor** (tel: 02 97 57 15 27) trips from Larmor-Baden to Ile de Gavrinis (Golfe du Morbihan).

Student and youth travellers
A valid International Student Card may entitle you to discounts on travel, accommodation, admission charges and so on. Enquire at a travel agent about reduced rail or coach fares (Transalpino, Inter-Rail, Eurail) if you are under 26. The **Union Française des Centres de Vacances** (8 rue du Dr Francis Joly BP256, 35005, Rennes Cedex; tel: 02 99 67 21 02) organises many cultural, leisure and sporting activities for young people. Contact the **Association Bretonne des Auberges de Jeunesse** (41 rue Victor Schoelcher, 56100 Lorient; tel: 02 97 37 11 65) for information on youth hostels. *Gîtes d'étape* are large country hostels, usually with dormitory-style accommodation, designed for younger people on activity holidays. A booklet called *France Youth Travel* is available from the French Government Tourist Office (free, but enclose a stamped addressed envelope).

Communications

Media

Foreign newspapers are available in most tourist centres during the tourist season. *Le Monde* and *Le Figaro* are France's biggest national dailies, but the most widely read regional newspaper in France is the *Breton Ouest-France*, which gives details of local events, listings and the other goings-on. *Télérama* lists French radio and television programmes.

Besides French national stations such as France Inter (1829m long wave; English-language news bulletins in summer on weekdays at 9am and 4pm) or Radio France Bretagne Ouest (93FM; English holiday news at 10am and 5pm), the BBC's Radio 4 and World Service can be received in most parts of Brittany.

Catching up with the news

For Voice of America, try FM. Some of the larger, more expensive hotels are equipped with satellite dishes offering a variety of foreign television channels.

Post offices

Bureaux de poste can be recognised by the initials PTT or just *Poste*. Correspondence marked *poste restante* may be addressed to any post office in France and collected on proof of identity (passport) for a small fee. You can buy stamps (*timbres-poste*) at tobacconists (*tabacs*) as well as post offices. Post boxes are yellow (free-standing or set into a wall). Use the *département étranger* slot for foreign mail. Many post offices have photocopying and fax machines. (See also Opening times on page 263.)

Telephones

Public call boxes in France are generally very efficient and fully operational. There are very few coin boxes left and most booths now operate with a *télécarte* (phone card) available from post offices, railway stations, *tabacs* (newsagents) and tourist offices in 50 or 120 units, costing around 40F and 98F respectively. In rural areas look for a blue sign saying *téléphone public* on private houses. If you use a phone in a café or restaurant you will probably be surcharged, and if you make a call from a hotel room you will pay a hefty premium.

Telephone numbers in France are usually written and quoted in pairs. They consist simply of 10 numbers and there is no area code within France. Cheap rates apply 10:30pm–8am weekdays, or after 2pm on Saturday at weekends.

Dialling abroad You can make international calls from most call boxes but it may be more convenient to use a booth in a post office. To make an international call, lift the receiver, insert the money or card, dial 00, wait for the tone to change, then dial the country code followed by the STD number (omitting the initial 0).

The international dialling codes are:

- **Australia** 61
- **Canada** 1
- **Ireland** 353
- **New Zealand** 64
- **UK** 44
- **US** 1.

Dial 13 for the operator, 12 for directory enquiries. For reverse-charge calls (collect) ask the operator for a PCV (*pay-say-vay*) call (available only to destinations outside France).

Language guide

Despite nationalist dreams and ambitions, the language of Brittany is French. English is spoken widely in Channel port towns (St-Malo and Roscoff) or resorts popular with the English such as Dinard or Bénodet. You don't need to speak a word of Breton to get by in Brittany, but a few words may add to your enjoyment of a visit.

Everyday Breton expressions

good day	*demat*
goodbye	*kenavo*
thank you	*trugarez*
festival	*fest-noz*
Brittany	*Breizh (BZH)*
good health	*yermat*

Breton place-names

aber	estuary
aven	river
beg	peak
dol	table
enez	island
iliz	church
kastell	castle
ker	village, house
lann	hermitage
lech	flat stone
menez	mountain
meur	important, big
mor	sea
penn	head, summit
plou	parish
pors	port
roc'h	rock
ti	house

Basic phrases in French

yes	*oui*
no	*non*
thank you	*merci*
please	*s'il vous plaît*
hello	*bonjour*
good evening	*bon soir*
good night	*bonne nuit*
goodbye	*au revoir*
can you show me...?	*pouvez-vous m'indiquer...?*
the way to...?	*la direction de...?*
where is...?	*où se trouve...?*
I would like	*je voudrais*
we would like	*on voudrait*
how many/much?	*combien?*
this one	*ceci*
that one	*cela*
that's enough	*ça suffit*
left	*à gauche*
right	*à droite*
near	*près*
straight on	*tout droit*
opposite	*en face de*
what time?	*à quelle heure?*

Painted wood carvings, Locronan

Emergencies

Crime and police

Brittany is generally safe and peaceful but, as in all holiday areas, opportunist theft is a problem. Take out good insurance before you go and don't tempt crime by leaving valuables on view in your car or unsupervised on beaches. Be wary of pickpockets on public transport and in other busy places. If anything is stolen from you, report it immediately to the police. They will ask

Policing the pardon

you to sign a statement. Police stations are called *commissariats de police* in towns and *gendarmeries* in rural areas (in emergencies, tel: 17).

Embassies and consulates

All the main national embassies are in Paris. You should contact them only in dire emergencies, such as the theft of your passport. Dial the appropriate 10-digit number beginning with 01.

- **Australia** 4 rue Jean-Rey, 75015 Paris (tel: 01 40 59 33 00).
- **Canada** 35 avenue Montaigne, 75008 Paris (tel: 01 44 43 29 00).
- **Ireland** 4 rue Rude 75016 Paris (tel: 01 44 17 67 00).
- **New Zealand** 7 ter rue Léonard-de-Vinci, 75016 Paris (tel: 01 45 00 24 11).
- **South Africa** 59 quai d'Orsay, 75007 Paris (tel: 01 53 59 23 23).
- **UK** 35 rue du Faubourg-St-Honoré, 75008 Paris (tel: 01 44 51 31 00). Consulate: 16 rue d'Anjou, 75008 (tel: 01 44 51 31 02).
- **US** 2 avenue Gabriel, 75008 Paris (tel: 01 43 12 22 22). Consulate: 2 rue St-Florentin, 75001 (tel: 08 36 70 14 88).

A consul (or honorary consul) can issue passports, contact relatives and advise on transferring funds. The only one in Brittany is British and is at 8 boulevard des Maréchaux, 35800 Dinard (tel: 02 99 46 26 64).

Emergency telephone numbers

For police or ambulance call 17, for the fire brigade (*pompiers*) 18. In cities you can also call for the 15 SAMU (Service d'Aide Medicale d'Urgence) ambulance service.

Lost property

If you are unlucky enough to lose something, contact the nearest police station (*gendarmerie* or *commissariat de police*) within 24 hours of discovering the loss. Take your passport (if you still have it!). Obtain a copy of the police report if you intend claiming on your insurance. If you lose your credit cards, contact the nearest bank displaying the appropriate sign (Carte Bleue/Visa or Eurocard/Access).

Lost card hotlines If you lose your credit card, call:

- **Carte Bleue/Visa**, tel: 08 03 00 59 59.
- **American Express**, tel: 01 47 77 72 00.

Health, vaccinations and pharmacies

No vaccinations are specifically required or recommended for travellers to France. Rabies is still technically endemic in France but it is very rare in Brittany. To be absolutely safe, however, don't touch any local animals, and if you are bitten seek medical attention however minor the wound. Aside from this, the worst ailment you are likely to suffer in Brittany is an occasional mosquito bite, or (if you are unlucky) a bout of 'holiday tummy', particularly if you enjoy shellfish. Tap water is safe to drink, but bottled water generally tastes better.

Accidents and illnesses can strike anywhere, however, so you need to be prepared. EU residents are entitled to reciprocal health treatment in France (take the correct form – E11 – with you), but only part of the expenses incurred are reimbursed (repatriation is excluded), and this is no substitute for adequate medical insurance. Non-EU residents should check the validity of their personal health insurance carefully before travelling.

Chemists (*pharmacies*) are recognisable by a green cross and are usually open six days a week. Pharmacists in France are trained to diagnose and treat minor complaints and can give first aid on request (they may charge a fee). They can also provide the name of a doctor or dentist. They are not allowed to dispense prescriptions from foreign doctors, so take a good supply of any medicines you need regularly. A rota of local pharmacies on duty (*pharmacie de garde*) outside normal hours should be posted on the doors of chemists and in local newspapers, or ask at the police station.

A picturesque pharmacie *at Landerneau*

Other information

Camping and self-catering

Brittany has numerous campsites and a huge number of *gîtes*. The *Gîte de France Handbook* lists over 2,500 self-catering holiday homes in France (see also page 266).

Camping organisations

- **Camping Plus** 69 Westbourne Grove, London W2 4UJ (tel: 0171 792 1944); or PIBS-CP26 – 56008 Vannes Cedex (tel: 02 97 42 55 83).
- **Eurocamp** 28 Princess Street, Knutsford, Cheshire WA16 6BN (tel: 01565 633844).
- **Keycamp Holidays** Ellerman House, 92–6 Lind Road, Sutton, Surrey SM1 4PL (tel: 0181 395 8565).

Self-catering organisations

- **Maison des Gîtes de France** 59 rue St-Lazare, 75009 Paris (tel: 01 49 70 75 75).

Camping at Rothéneuf

- **Gîtes de France** 178 Piccadilly, London W1V 0AL (tel: 0891 24 41 23).
- **Maison de la Bretagne – Paris** 203 boulevard St-Germain, 75007 Paris (tel: 01 53 63 11 50).
- **Brittany Ferries** The Brittany Centre, Wharf Road, Portsmouth PO2 8RU (tel: 01705 827701).
- **Service de Réservation du Relais des Gîtes Ruraux** Côtes-d'Armor: Maison du Tourisme, 21 rue des Promenades, BP4536, 22045 St-Brieuc, Cedex 2 (tel: 02 96 62 21 73); Finistère: 5 allée Sully, 29322 Quimper, Cedex (tel: 02 98 52 48 00); Ille-et-Vilaine: 8 rue de Coëtquen BP5093, 35061 Rennes, Cedex 3 (tel: 02 99 78 47 57); Loire-Atlantique: Gîtes de France, 1 allée Baco BP3215, 44032 Nantes, Cedex 1 (tel: 02 51 72 95 65); Morbihan: 2 rue du Château, BP328, 56403 Auray, Cedex (tel: 02 97 56 48 12).
- **Relais des Gîtes** 8 rue de Coëtquen BP5093, 35061 Rennes, Cedex 3 (tel: 02 99 78 47 57).

Visitors with disabilities
Facilities for the disabled have improved greatly in France. A useful publication is *Guide Rousseau H…comme Handicaps.* There are five guides, one for each main area of France according to the first two digits of its telephone number (Brittany is 02). Order a copy in the UK from the **European Bookshop**, 5 Warwick Street, London W1R 1RA (tel: 0171 734 5259), or from the publishers, **Association France Handicaps**,

Local produce on sale at Pleyben, Armorique

9 rue Luce-de-Lancival, 77340 Pontault-Combault (tel: 01 60 28 50 12). Alternatively, contact **Le Comité National Français de Liaison pour la Réadaptation des Handicapés**, 236 bis rue de Tolbiac, 75013 Paris (tel: 01 53 80 66 66).

Opening times
Shops Food shops generally open Monday to Saturday 8am–8.30pm,

CONVERSION CHARTS

FROM	TO	MULTIPLY BY
Inches	Centimetres	2.54
Centimetres	Inches	0.3937
Feet	Metres	0.3048
Metres	Feet	3.2810
Yards	Metres	0.9144
Metres	Yards	1.0940
Miles	Kilometres	1.6090
Kilometres	Miles	0.6214
Acres	Hectares	0.4047
Hectares	Acres	2.4710
Gallons	Litres	4.5460
Litres	Gallons	0.2200
Ounces	Grams	28.35
Grams	Ounces	0.0353
Pounds	Grams	453.6
Grams	Pounds	0.0022
Pounds	Kilograms	0.4536
Kilograms	Pounds	2.205
Tons	Tonnes	1.0160
Tonnes	Tons	0.9842

MEN'S SUITS

UK	36	38	40	42	44	46	48
Rest of Europe	46	48	50	52	54	56	58
US	36	38	40	42	44	46	48

DRESS SIZES

UK	8	10	12	14	16	18
France	36	38	40	42	44	46
Italy	38	40	42	44	46	48
Rest of Europe	34	36	38	40	42	44
US	6	8	10	12	14	16

MEN'S SHIRTS

UK	14	14.5	15	15.5	16	16.5	17
Rest of Europe	36	37	38	39/40	41	42	43
US	14	14.5	15	15.5	16	16.5	17

MEN'S SHOES

UK	7	7.5	8.5	9.5	10.5	11
Rest of Europe	41	42	43	44	45	46
US	8	8.5	9.5	10.5	11.5	12

WOMEN'S SHOES

UK	4.5	5	5.5	6	6.5	7
Rest of Europe	38	38	39	39	40	41
US	6	6.5	7	7.5	8	8.5

Restaurants by St-Malo's ramparts

while other shops open later (at 9 or 9.30). *Boulangeries* (bakeries) open on Sunday too. Half-day closing varies but is often Monday. Lunchtime closing is usually 12–2 but supermarkets stay open all day and may be open later too. Nearly every town in Brittany holds a weekly market.

Banks You can assume all banks open at least 9–noon and 2–4. Some open Saturday mornings but may close on Monday (beware of national holidays – banks close early the day before). *Bureaux de change* at international airports operate daily 6am–11pm.

Museums and other sights National museums close on Tuesdays, others often on Mondays. Most close on major public holidays. In Brittany, opening hours for tourist sights are seasonal, with much longer summer hours. Many sights close completely

Souvenirs for sale in Dinan

during the winter (October to Easter). Check opening hours at the local tourist office if you wish to visit something in particular. (Ask about entry fees as well, since these vary greatly.)

Post offices These are generally open 8–5, 6 or 7 on weekdays, and 8–noon on Saturday. Smaller offices close at lunchtimes.

Places of worship
Brittany is a strongly Catholic region and every town or village has a thriving church community. Check noticeboards to see what time masses start. Protestant churches can be found in large towns. Other denominations and faiths may be less well represented – ask at the tourist office or town hall.

Toilets
Public toilets can be found in shopping centres, petrol stations, hypermarkets and so on. Men are *Messieurs*; women are *Dames*. Standards are variable, so take advantage of facilities when you are in cafés, restaurants, hotels or museums, as these are often better kept than average.

Electricity
Nearly everywhere in Brittany operates at 220 volts, 50Hz. Electric sockets take plugs with two round pins. Take an adapter for non-continental appliances. US and Canadian visitors may require a transformer too.

The cider museum at Argol

The Maison de la Reine Anne is one of Morlaix's most attractive buildings

Tourist offices

The French Government Tourist Office (FGTO) publishes a great deal of literature about France, available from the following addresses:

- **Australia** French Tourist Bureau, BNP Building, 12th Floor, 12 Castlereagh Street, Sydney NSW 2000 (tel: 2 231 5244).
- **Canada** Représentation Française du Tourisme, 1981 Avenue McGill College, Suite 490, Montreal, PQ H3A 2W9 (tel: 514 288 4264).
- **Ireland** FGTO, 35 Lower Abbey Street, Dublin 1 (tel: 1 70 34046).
- **UK** FGTO, 178 Piccadilly, London W1V 0AL (tel: 0891 244123).
- **US** FGTO, 444 Madison Ave, 16th Floor, New York, NY 10020 (tel: 212/838-7800).

Tourist offices in Brittany

Nearly every small town or resort has its own *Office du Tourisme* or *Syndicat d'Initiative* (recognisable by a large letter **i**). Many of these are seasonal.

- **Regional tourist office** (Comité Régional de Tourisme) 1 rue Raoul Ponchon, 35069 Rennes, Cedex (tel: 02 99 36 15 15).
- **Côtes-d'Armor** Maison du Tourisme, 29 rue des Promenades, BP 4620, 22046 St-Brieuc (tel: 02 96 62 72 15).
- **Finistère** 11 rue Théodore le Hars, BP1419, 29104 Quimper, Cedex (tel: 02 98 76 20 70).
- **Ille-et-Vilaine** 4 rue Jean-Jaurès, BP6046, 35060 Rennes, Cedex 3 (tel 02 99 78 47 47).
- **Morbihan** Hôtel du Département, rue St-Tropez, BP400, 56009 Vannes, Cedex (tel: 02 97 54 06 56).
- **Loire-Atlantique** Comité Départmental du Tourisme, 2 allée Baco, 44000 Nantes (tel: 02 51 72 95 30).

Hotels & Restaurants

Accommodation

Brittany offers a vast range of accommodation to suit all tastes and pockets. Much of it is self-catering in campsites and *gîtes* (see page 260). Besides conventional hotels you have a choice of staying in luxurious châteaux, practical hostels or cosily *en famille* in France's expanding network of working farms or *chambres d'hôtes* (bed and breakfasts).

Generally speaking, accommodation in Brittany caters for families. It is unlikely to be dauntingly exclusive or snooty, or bursting with priceless antiques and designer furnishings. Many establishments are fairly simple and family run. Summer bookings are heavy, especially during the peak French holiday season (July and August), so it's best to book in advance to make sure of a place. It is usually easier to find a bed inland than on the coast. If you reserve in advance, you will usually be asked for a deposit (*arrhes*) – send a Eurocheque or international money order to avoid bank charges. Several agencies will organise bookings in registered chains for you. For a small fee, tourist offices will make reservations for up to a week ahead if you visit them in person.

Hotels Brittany has about 1,000 registered hotels. French hotels are officially graded from one to four stars, with an additional 'luxury' category, depending on the level of facilities offered. A full list of registered hotels is available from the tourist office. Other groups of hotels produce separate brochures (often available free in tourist offices). One of the best known and most popular is the *Fédération des Logis de France*, consisting of small, inexpensive, family-run hotels, often of considerable character. There are over 300 *logis* throughout Brittany, many with good home cooking. The *logis* guide is available in bookshops.

By law, hotel tariffs must be clearly visible in the reception area and in each bedroom. Prices are usually quoted per room (top-range hotels sometimes whack on an obligatory 15 per cent service charge when you settle the bill) and do not include breakfast. Hotel breakfasts are in any case generally poor value. You are much better finding a local café or *pâtisserie* to satisfy early-morning hunger pangs. In high season many hotels have an awkward habit of insisting guests pay half-board (*demi-pension*). This may be good value, and no hardship if there's a decent cook, but you may prefer to eat out sometimes. On the other hand, if you particularly wish to try a hotel restaurant it can be annoying to find it closed (often the case on Sunday or Monday evenings).

If you are travelling solo you may still have to pay the double-room rate; singles are rare, and often unpleasantly poky or ill-equipped. Negotiate for a discount if you can. Rooms with only a shower are cheaper than those with a bath; if you can make do with a public bathroom you should pay much less.

Gîtes A French *gîte* is a self-catering country holiday home, often a converted farmhouse or cottage. Many belong to a national government-run scheme called Gîtes de France. These are classified by ears of corn, from one to four depending on the level of sophistication; others are graded by 'nests' (Nids Vacances), from one to three.

To find a good *gîte* you should book well in advance (the previous autumn if possible) – by either contacting the owner direct (the FGTO has a list of addresses and phone numbers of local *gîtes*) or organising your booking through Gîtes de France (a commission is charged). Many holiday companies, including Brittany Ferries (one of the largest operators) have selections of *gîtes* in their brochures.

Before setting off on a *gîte* holiday, take careful note of what you may need to take with you. Bed linen, towels, teapots, kettles and so on may not be supplied. You may even like to take your own pillows to avoid the dreaded French bolsters.

Gîtes d'étape These are large, communal hostels, often in farmhouses, which offer simple, dormitory-style accommodation for walkers, riders and lovers of the outdoors. There are comparatively few in Brittany.

Chambres d'hôtes The term 'bed and breakfast' as understood in Britain or some other countries doesn't quite describe the French experience, which is catching on fast as this is a sociable and interesting way to explore France. Establishments vary from grand châteaux to simple rural homes. You are generally provided with an evening meal and are expected to join in family life, so it helps if you can speak a little French.

Local tourist offices provide lists of *chambres d'hôtes*, or you can obtain the FGTO booklet in advance. The associations Château Acceuil or Châteaux et Manoirs de Bretagne cater for the top end of the market. The Maison des Gîtes de France (see page 260) publishes a yearly directory of all the *chambres d'hôtes* in France, classified in the same way as the *gîtes*; there are also smaller regional booklets available. Bed and Breakfast (France), International Reservations Centre, PO Box 66, Henley-on-Thames, Oxfordshire RG9 1XS; tel: 01491 578803) will also handle reservations from the US, Canada, Australia and so on.

Camping Some of France's best campsites can be found in Brittany, especially along the popular holiday coasts of Cornouaille and Trégor. You can find them on lovely beaches, in woods or even in the grounds of châteaux. Officially they are graded from one to four stars and all are required to have a source of clean running water, daily refuse collection and a telephone. After that you progress through any number of layers to on-site swimming pools, restaurants, supermarkets and entertainment. Most sites have a mixture of free pitches for your own tent, caravan or campervan, and fixed tents, static caravans or chalet-style huts.

If you book a package camping holiday you will probably get a fully equipped tent on one of the better sites and a courier to look after you. Don't expect virgin wilderness or much experience of the great outdoors on such a holiday (these sites are generally both organised and crowded), but it saves you investing in your own equipment and is a good idea for novice or gregarious campers.

Alternatively, you can use a reservation agency – you take your own equipment but bookings are organised for you (see page 260). Independent camping obviously gives you the choice of more peaceful locations and flexibility. If you prefer less organised camping, look for signs saying *Camping à la ferme* or *Aire naturelle de camping*. You don't have to use an official site, but *camping sauvage* is strictly prohibited in nature reserves or regional parks. Some sites require you to present a camping *carnet* (permit), available to members of the Automobile Association or from various camping organisations.

In July and August many campsites are fully booked, while out of high season facilities may be shut. Useful guides for independent campers include the Michelin *Camping Caravanning France* and *Camping à la ferme*.

The list of accommodation that follows has been divided into three price categories, based on prices for a double room in high season:

- **budget (£)**–below 300FF
- **moderate (££)**–300–500FF
- **expensive (£££)**–above 500FF

Note, these categories serve as a general guide only: hotels often have a very wide range of prices, depending on the season and the facilities in each room. If possible, inspect a bedroom before accepting it, or make it clear when booking what facilities you require.

Hotels and restaurants are listed under the nearest main-entry place-name in the gazetteer; this may be some distance from the establishment itself.

THE EMERALD COAST

Cancale

Continental (££) quai Thomas (tel: 02 99 89 60 16). Cheerful terraced building with bright awnings amid a bustling line of seafood restaurants. Excellently placed overlooking the harbour, with the oysterbeds almost at arm's length. Choose a room with a sea view if you can. Oysters are served (see restaurant section).

Maisons de Bricourt (£££) rue Du Guesclin (tel: 02 99 89 64 76). Accommodation in this celebrated restaurant-with-rooms is in two locations. Some rooms are in an elegantly furnished old stone manor house on clifftops overlooking the bay of Mont-St-Michel. Antiques, chandeliers and lovely china grace just six bedrooms. A new annexe has just been opened about 3km away, again with bay views. The memorable food earns two Michelin rosettes (see restaurant section).

Pointe du Grouin (££) Pointe du Grouin (tel: 02 99 89 60 55). Popular pitstop for walkers and bird-watchers on a scenic headland overlooking Ile des Landes. Overrun with passing trade at summer lunchtimes, but its location is hard to beat when the crowds depart. Smart and comfortable with an unpretentious brasserie adjacent.

Tirel-Guérin (££) gare de la Gouesnière, St-Méloir-des-Ondes (tel: 02 99 89 10 46). Modern hotel about 4km inland amid cabbage fields. Charming owners, large bedrooms and excellent food (see restaurant section). Indoor swimming pool.

Dinan

Arvor (££) 5 rue Pavie (tel: 02 96 39 21 22). Very central, pleasantly furnished in a former convent building near the tourist office. Parking tricky.

D'Avaugour (££) 1 place du Champ (tel: 02 96 39 07 49). Thoroughly well-established, reliable hotel overlooking place Du Guesclin in the heart of historic Dinan. Has been smartly refurbished, but retains some old-world charm. Very convenient for sightseeing. Good food in garden restaurant in rampart walls.

Le Challonge (£) 29 place Du Guesclin (tel: 02 96 87 16 30). Very close to D'Avaugour (see above), but a cheaper option – a neat, cheerful hotel with attractive, modern rooms. Road noise may be a problem in some of the rooms. Good brasserie-restaurant.

Moulin de la Fontaine (££) Vallée de la Fontaine des Eaux (tel: 02 96 87 92 09). An 18th-century watermill in magnificent countryside, with its own gardens and lake. Convenient for the St-Malo ferry and within easy walking distance of Dinan. Dinner available on request. British hosts can offer advise on local history.

La Porte St-Malo (£) 35 rue St-Malo (tel: 02 96 39 19 76). A stone's throw beyond the city gates, easily accessible by car yet lies a mere stroll from the old town. Simple rooms with touches of character. Has a popular local bar and some patio gardens but no restaurant.

La Renardais (£) Le Repos (tel: 02 96 86 89 81). This stone-built country house on the outskirts of the village of Ploüer-sur-Rance preserves its original charm, though restoration has added modern comforts. In summer meals are served in the terraced floral gardens. The beach is just 15 minutes away.

Dinard

Altaïr (££) 18 boulevard Féart (tel: 02 99 46 13 58). Tall, dignified town house set back from the sea. The public areas are furnished with lots of polished wood and antique mirrors; the bedrooms are variable – some are fairly plain, others are modern. Has one of the town's most renowned restaurants (see restaurant section).
Hotel Amethyste (£) pl du Calvaire (tel: 02 99 46 61 81). A friendly place in the town centre, just 100m from the beach, suitable for families. The comfortable bedrooms all have modern facilities. A bar and ice-cream parlour with chairs set outside add to the enjoyment of summer days.
Inter Hotel Balmorel (££) 26 rue du Ml-Leclerc (tel: 02 99 46 16 97). In the town centre, close to the beach, casino and seaside promenade. Interior and guest rooms decorated with traditional furnishings. Pleasant bar where guests can enjoy an aperitif before an evening meal in one of Dinard's retaurants.
Manoir de la Rance (£££) Pleurtuit, la Jouvente (tel: 02 99 88 53 76). Converted manor overlooking the Rance estuary in marvellously peaceful countryside. Garden where breakfasts, teas and drinks are served. Friendly owners. Relaxing, eclectic furnishings. No restaurant.
La Plage (££) 3 boulevard Féart (tel: 02 99 46 14 87). Attractive, well-located hotel near the casino and Plage de l'Ecluse, with partial sea views. Comfortable, well-equipped rooms. Excellent, friendly restaurant (see restaurant section) – half-board is good value.
La Valée (££) 6 av George V (tel: 02 99 46 94 00). Peacefully situated by the sea, yet only a short walk from the town centre, this hotel makes an excellent base for a holiday. The menu in the hotel restaurant offers lobster and other seafood specialities.

Erquy

Hôtel Beauséjour (£) 21 rue de la Corniche (tel: 02 96 72 30 39). Very good small *Logis de France*, overlooking the sea. Garden, parking facilities and a choice of reasonable menus including a children's menu.

Rance Valley

L'Abri des Flots (£) Bord de Rance, Mordreuc (tel: 02 96 83 20 43). Very simple stone-built bar-hotel on the Rance river and overlooking a ruined islet fortress. Cheap and cheerful, with good food.

Sables d'Or-les Pins

Le Manoir St-Michel (££) la Carquois (tel: 02 96 41 48 87). Fifteenth-century stone manor house surrounded by velvety lawns overlooking a scenic slab of coastline. Comfortably furnished in local style, with log fires. No restaurant.

St-Cast-le-Guildo

Des Dunes (££) rue Primauguet (tel: 02 96 41 80 31). Modern, comfortable hotel a block from the beach. Feels reassuring and solid, if not especially imaginative. Good food and facilities.

St-Malo

Ajoncs d'Or (£££) 10 rue des Forgeurs (tel: 02 99 40 85 03). Comfortable, reliable *intra-muros* hotel, old-fashioned but smartly Gallic inside. Fairly peaceful corner site, but in the heart of the old town. Garage parking. No restaurant.
L'Ascott (£££) 35 Rue Chapitre (tel: 02 99 81 89 93). This 19th-century manor house has been elegantly renovated. Set on the River Rance estuary, it has picturesque gardens, is close to the beach and forest areas and easily accessible from the motorway.
Hôtel Brocéliande (££) 43 chaussée du Sillon (tel: 02 99 20 62 62). Small, stylish hotel facing the long beaches near Paramé, set back from the seafront road. No restaurant.
Les Charmettes (£) 64 boulevard Hébert (tel: 02 99 56 07 31). Inexpensive little *pension* consisting of two tranquil houses (one being simpler and cheaper than the other) overlooking the sea near Paramé.
Hotel France & Chateaubriand (££) (tel: 02 99 56 66 52). Seconds from the beach, in the historic part of the city. The rooms are comfortable with either views of the sea or yachting harbour. The restaurant serves a choice of fresh fish and seafood.
La Goelettrie (£) (tel: 02 99 81 92 64). A stone-built residence, close to the sea. Some rooms have sea views. On Monday, Wednesday and Friday nights Breton specialities are served in the restaurant. Regional breakfasts served and children under two can stay free of charge.
La Korrigane (£££) 39 rue le Pomellec, St-Servan (tel: 02 99 81 65 85). Graceful 19th-century mansion in quietish suburb, 5 minutes from the sea. Many antiques and *objets d'art*, slightly daunting atmosphere but friendly owners. Garden. No restaurant.
La Rance (££) 15 quai Sébastopol, St-Servan (tel: 02 99 81 78 63). Civilised small hotel near quiet Port Solidor. Clean, well-equipped rooms, some with excellent views. Satellite TV accompanies traditional furnishings and some antiques. Good breakfast; courteous owners. No restaurant (try L'Atre just down the road).
Le Valmarin (£££) 7 rue Jean XXIII, St-Servan (tel: 02 99 81 94 76). If you would like to see what a *malouinière* looks like, stay here. This former corsair's home has palatially sized rooms in peaceful grounds, and is elegant and restful. No restaurant.

La Villefromoy (£££) 7 boulevard Hébert (tel: 02 99 40 92 20). Out on the Paramé side of town, a beautiful old mansion (actually two houses cleverly joined together) of great distinction inside and out. Furnishings are luxurious, rooms bright and tasteful, some with sea views. Garden for drinks and breakfasts.

Le Val André

De la Mer (£) 63 rue Amiral Charner (tel: 02 96 72 20 44). Simple and unpretentious; on the road behind the beach. Friendly staff and excellent seafood (see restaurant section). A functional motel annexe called Nuit et Jour offers overnighting for families, though you probably wouldn't want to spend your whole holiday here.

THE PINK GRANITE COAST

Armorique Corniche

Le Ty-Pont (£) St-Jean-du-Doigt (tel: 02 98 67 85 94). One of those delectable French finds that are all too rare: a simple, friendly and very inexpensive family-run seaside hotel with generous home cooking.

Guingamp

Château de Brélidy (£££) Brélidy (tel: 02 96 95 69 38). Tastefully furnished *chambres d'hôtes* (including 10 rooms in period style) in this carefully restored 16th-century castle promise an interesting sojourn. Dinner by arrangement. Extensive parkland.
Relais du Roy (££) 42 place du Centre (tel: 02 96 43 76 62). Well-run stone hotel on the market square, with features of historic interest and well-modernised bathrooms. A useful touring base inland.

Lannion

La Porte de France (£) 5 rue Savidan (tel: 02 96 46 54 81). Attractive stone coaching inn on the edge of the old town; old-fashioned and somewhat eccentric inside. The firelit bar is popular with locals. No restaurant.

Paimpol

Le Barbu (£££) pointe de l'Arcouest (tel: 02 96 55 86 98). Right by the Bréhat ferry terminal, overlooking a marvellous stretch of coast. Comfortable modern furnishings and picture windows. Has a swimming pool and a seafood restaurant.
Le Repaire de Kerroc'h (££) 29 quai Morand (tel: 02 96 20 50 13). Imposing former corsair's house on the harbour, refurbished in smart traditional style. Very comfortable spacious bedrooms and courteous, affable service. See also restaurant section.

Perros-Guirec

Les Feux des Iles (£££) 53 boulevard Clemenceau (tel: 02 96 23 22 94). Tall stone house in gardens overlooking the bay. Rooms vary in style and size but in general are well furnished. Panoramic sea views and a tennis court. The emphasis is on the food (see restaurant section).
Hermitage Hotel (££) 20 rue la Montreer (tel: 02 96 23 21 22). A friendly, relaxed town-centre hotel surrounded by a large garden. Rooms are well-equipped and comfortable. Close to sea and forest areas.
Le Sphinx (£££) chemin de la Messe (tel: 02 96 23 25 42). Belle Epoque stone house perched on clifftops in a residential area. Good sea views from terraced bedrooms and open-plan bar-restaurant. Light, modern furnishings.

Plougrescant

Manoir de Kergrec'h (£££) (tel: 02 96 92 56 06). One of the most successful and delightful of all Breton hotel-châteaux – a tasteful period interior without a wrong note anywhere. Extremely peaceful setting in extensive grounds by the sea. Charming and unassuming owners (a viscount and his wife). Dinner by prior arrangement only.

St-Quay-Portrieux

Le Gerbot d'Avoine (£) 2 boulevard du Littoral (tel: 02 96 70 40 09). Though shabby and dated in some public areas, this modest establishment has exceedingly high standards of hospitality. Staff take duties seriously and bedrooms are spacious and comfortable. Food, alas, isn't up to much.

Trébeurden

Auberge de Jeunesse (£) (tel: 02 96 23 52 22). Quietly positioned just outside the resort, near the Marais du Quellen nature reserve, this modern youth hostel is pleasantly equipped and overlooks a splendid section of the coastline. Good local birdwatching and megaliths.
Manoir de Lan Kerellec (£££) (tel: 02 96 15 47 47). Peaceful manor located in the resort overlooking marvellous coastal scenery. Expensive, exclusive catering for hedonists. Nautically themed dining room takes advantage of the excellent views.
Ti al Lannec (£££) allée de Mézo-Guen (tel: 02 96 15 01 01). One of Brittany's most appealing hotels; a stay here is a real treat. Wonderful views from all bedrooms, which are individually decorated and luxurious. New health club. Children welcome.

Trégastel

Bellevue (££) 20 rue des Calculots (tel: 02 96 23 88 18). Though this grand manor lacks the distinction of the Trébeurden hotels (see above) it is none the less comfortable and quiet, with gardens running down to the sea.

Tréguier

Kastell Dinec'h (££) route de Lannion (tel: 02 96 92 49 39). Handsomely converted farmhouse in a rural setting about 2km from the town centre. Stylish bedrooms with a mix of period and modern furniture. Relaxing and family-oriented. Swimming pool. See also restaurant section.

NORTH FINISTÈRE

Brignogan-Plages

Castel Régis (££) plage du Garo (tel: 02 98 83 40 22). Superbly located by lovely rock and sand beaches. Furnishings are fairly plain but the bedrooms (mostly in rustic bungalows) are spacious and peaceful. Swimming pool, tennis and mini-golf. Good, if pricey, restaurant.

Carantec

Pors-Pol (£) 7 rue Surcouf (tel: 02 98 67 00 52). Appealing family hotel in a large garden overlooking a small beach. Relaxing, home-like atmosphere, but bedrooms are on the small side. Good home cooking.

Le Conquet

La Pointe Sainte-Barbe (££) (tel: 02 98 89 00 26). An ugly, dated building in this otherwise attractive grey fishing town, but friendly staff and panoramic views compensate. Practical, simple bedrooms, some very cheap. From the breakfast room you can decide how sick you're going to feel on the crossing to Ouessant.

Le Relais du Vieux Port (£) 1 quai Drellach (tel: 02 98 89 15 91). Simple restaurant-with-rooms by the harbour (see restaurant section). Spacious, stylish bedrooms, all with views.

Morlaix

L'Europe (££) 1 rue Aiguillon (tel: 02 98 62 11 99). Well-run if slightly old-fashioned central hotel. Conventional furnishings enlivened by a few historic touches (17th-century panelling, baroque plasterwork). Well placed for exploring the old town.

Du Port (£) 3 quai de Léon (tel: 02 98 88 07 54). Inexpensive bar-hotel in a pretty, pinkwashed building by the port and viaduct. Modern, austere interior.

Ouessant, Ile d'

Duchesse Anne (£) Lampaul (tel: 02 98 48 80 25). Just outside the village on a quiet breezy hill above the port. Simple, traditional and popular dining room.

Roc'h-ar-Mor (£) Lampaul (tel: 02 98 48 80 19). Of the three more-or-less basic hotels in the village, the Roc'h-ar-Mor has the attraction of a grassy walled garden overlooking the sea, where bar lunches can be enjoyed.

Plouescat

L'Azou (£) rue Général Leclerc (tel: 02 98 69 60 16). Simple little hotel in the village centre, set back from the street around a courtyard. Rooms are nothing special; the emphasis here is on the food (mostly fish). When dinner is served, nothing else matters.

La Caravelle (£) 20 rue de Calvaire (tel: 02 98 69 61 75). Just 15 minutes from Roscoff ferry terminal, this comfortable, simply furnished establishment is ideal for an overnight stop. The restaurant has a high standard of home cooked dishes with seafood specialities.

Roscoff

Les Alizés (£) quai d'Auxerre (tel: 02 98 69 72 22). Pretty, shuttered stone house with a terrace overlooking the old port. Well-furnished bedrooms and friendly staff. Excellent value.

Bellevue (££) rue Jeanne d'Arc (tel: 02 98 61 23 38). Attractive modern hotel with superb sea views at the east end of the bay. Spruce but unpretentious, with easy parking opposite. Good seafood restaurant.

Le Brittany (£££) boulevard Ste-Barbe (tel: 02 98 69 70 78). An 18th-century manor house at the east end of the bay near the ferry terminal. Tastefully furnished with antiques, it has a sophisticated but unpompous air – transient ferry clients keep it bustling. Swimming pool. Notable food (see restaurant section).

Du Centre (£) 5 rue Gambetta (tel: 02 98 61 24 25). Popular bar-restaurant with simple rooms, close to the old harbour and boats to Ile de Batz. The bar, Chez Janie, is a well-known local haunt decorated with photos of old Roscoff and 'Onion Johnnies'. Cheerful, informal; can get a little noisy. Very popular with ferry travellers.

Gulf Stream (££) rue Marquise-de-Kergariou (tel: 02 98 69 73 19). Smart modern resort hotel at the quiet west end of town.
Large gardens, sea views and a swimming pool.

Talabardon (££) place de l'Eglise (tel: 02 98 61 24 95). Gracious stone building amid the corsairs' houses around the church. Smartly furnished interior; some sea views. Restaurant.

St-Mathieu, Pointe de

Corrotel-Pointe St-Mathieu (££) (tel: 02 98 89 00 19). Bits of stone cladding and crypt-like vaulting take the modern edge off this somewhat bleak hotel-restaurant by the ruins of the old abbey. Smartly refurbished, the hotel has a brasserie for light snacks.

ARMORIQUE

Arrée, Monts d'

Les Voyageurs (£) Sizun (tel: 02 98 68 80 35). The location, right beside Sizun's church, makes this simple place worth a mention; otherwise, it is a practical but unremarkable choice.

Châteaulin

Au Bon Acceuil (££) Port-Launay (tel: 02 98 86 15 77). Riverside building with stripy awnings and shutters. Rooms are simple but clean and neat. Busy road may cause some traffic noise during the day. Beyond are the clear salmon waters of the Aulne.

Crozon, Presqu'île de

La Mer (£) le Fret (tel: 02 98 27 61 90). Pleasing stone *logis* overlooking the harbour where boats arrive from Brest. Simple, old-fashioned bedrooms. See also restaurant section.

Relais-Motel de Pors-Morvan (££) Pors-Morvan, Plomodiern (tel: 02 98 81 53 23). Nineteenth-century stone farm buildings cleverly converted into stylish motel accommodation. *Crêpes* and snacks served. Tennis. About 6km from the sea.

Le Faou

Le Relais de la Place (£) (tel: 02 98 81 91 19). The plain exterior belies a good-value, well-run hotel-restaurant on the town square (see also restaurant section).

La Vieille Renommée (££) (tel: 02 98 81 90 31). More imposing architecture initially gives this establishment the edge over its nearby rival (see above), but inside it is equally simple though a little pricier. Its corner site may make it a little noisy.

Huelgoat

Hôtel du Lac (£) 9 rue du Général de Gaulle, (tel: 02 98 99 71 14). Huelgoat has little to offer its visitors in the way of accommodation, except this small *Logis de France* overlooking the picturesque lake. Good restaurant serving traditional Breton cuisine. See also restaurant section.

Lampaul-Guimiliau

De l'Enclos (£) (tel: 02 98 68 77 08). Modern, motel-style *logis* beside one of the region's most famous churches. Guests are given a friendly welcome.

Landerneau

Le Clos du Pontic (££) rue du Pontic (tel: 02 98 21 50 91). Unusual turreted house in peaceful shady gardens some way from the town centre, providing an impersonal but agreeable stay. Most of the well-equipped bedrooms are in a pleasant modern wing with good facilities (such as a coffee bar). Come and go as you please. Attractive restaurant.

Morgat

Julia (£) 43 rue du Tréflez (tel: 02 98 27 05 89). A good traditional hotel-restaurant with sea views. Interior furnishings are attractive and modern.

St-Thégonnec

Auberge St-Thégonnec (££) place de la Mairie (tel: 02 98 79 61 18). The modern, slightly bleak air of contract furnishings dissipates once you settle down to a meal here (see restaurant section). Spacious, well-equipped bedrooms, some overlooking quiet gardens. Innovative telephones enable you to receive outside calls directly to your room. The famous parish close is opposite.

CORNOUAILLE

Audierne

Le Goyen (£££) le port (tel: 02 98 70 08 88). Imposing and grandly furnished, overlooking harbour and estuary. Furnishings are stylishly traditional; the atmosphere refined but relaxed. Celebrated for its food (see restaurant section).

Beg-Meil

Belle Vue (£) Cap-Coz (tel: 02 98 56 00 33). Pleasant, well-kept, family-oriented *logis* close to the beaches of Cap-Coz. Simple rustic furnishings. Garden, terrace and restaurant. Cliff walks.

La Pointe (£) Cap-Coz (tel: 02 98 56 01 63). Nestling on a narrow spit of sand just 20m from the sea on either side, this is a simple, family hotel with some fairly rudimentary bedrooms; those in the newer wing are more comfortable.

Thalamot (££) le Chemin-Creux (tel: 02 98 94 97 38). Idiosyncratic and relaxing hotel near the beach in a shady garden. Simple bedrooms in a newer wing. Restaurant.

Bélon

Manoir de Kertalg (£££) route de Riec-sur-Bélon, Moëlan-sur-Mer (tel: 02 98 39 77 77). Delightful granite manor house, hidden in a vast forested park along the Bélon estuary, close to Pont-Aven and fine,sandy beaches. River fishing, forest walks. Restaurants near by. Seafood in the evening on request.

Les Moulins du Duc (£££) Moëlan-sur-Mer (tel: 02 98 39 60 73). Luxury hotel converted from a 16th-century mill in deep countryside. Ponds and streams cover much of the extensive grounds. The bedrooms are in stone cottages picturesquely modernised but retaining bits of mill machinery and antique furnishings. Excellent food (see restaurant section).

Bénodet

Amoric Hotel (££-£££) 3 rue de Penfoul (tel: 02 98 57 04 03). This hotel is surrounded by peaceful flower-filled gardens and has a pleasant bar and terrace where visitors can relax. The rooms are smartly furnished and have en-suite facilities. Close to beach and harbour.

Domaine de Kereven (££) route de Quimper (tel: 02 98 57 02 46). If Bénodet were not so poorly stocked with pleasant accommodation, this plain, inoffensive hotel some way out of the resort might not get a mention. As it is, it is worth considering: well kept, peaceful and welcoming.

Kastel-Moor and Ker-Moor (££) avenue de la Plage (tel: 02 98 57 05 01). Twin hotels

sharing a large garden, with swimming pool and tennis courts, across the road from the beach resort.
Ker Vennaik (£-££) 45 av de la Plage (tel: 02 98 57 15 40). Peaceful accommodation in congenial bedrooms, with views of the hotel's colourful gardens. Bar and brasserie available.
Menez-Frost (££) 4 rue J Chacot (tel: 02 98 57 03 09). Large and rambling in extensive grounds with a pool. Somewhat dreary but the welcome is quite civilised. Some self-catering. No restaurant.
Le Minaret (££) corniche de l'Estuaire (tel: 02 98 57 03 13). Curious Moorish architecture dating from the 1920s gives some distinction. The bedrooms disappoint but the location and views are superb. None too friendly in high season. Lovely gardens with a terraced bar lead towards the beach.
Ste-Marine (£) 19 rue du Bac, Ste-Marine (tel: 02 98 56 34 79). Simple, pretty old house in a lovely position overlooking the picturesque harbour. Tables set outside.

Concarneau
Auberge de Jeunesse (£) quai de la Croix (tel: 02 98 97 03 47). Beautifully located youth hostel by the water's edge. The marine biology institute is next door. A short stroll to the Ville Close.
La Bonne Auberge (£) le Cabellou (tel: 02 98 97 04 30). Attractive gabled white house on the southern side of town in a peaceful resort area. Fairly spartan inside but it has some character, and a pleasant garden.
Le Galion (££) 15 rue St-Guénolé, Ville Close (tel: 02 98 97 30 16). Since this is the only accommodation within the old walled citadel, its limited rooms are always in demand. As it need curry no favours, service is peremptory and haughty. None the less, the tastefully furnished rooms have charm and sophistication. See also restaurant section.
De l'Océan (£££) plage des Sables Blancs (tel: 02 98 50 53 50). Large, modern resort hotel with lots of somewhat impersonal facilities. Sea views, although the hotel stands behind a busy road.
Plage des Sables Blancs (££) plage des Sables Blancs (tel: 02 98 97 01 39). Right on the sea front, close to the town. A good place for a relaxing holiday on the coast. Some rooms have excellent views of the fine, sandy beaches.

Douarnenez
Ty Mad (££) plage St-Jean (tel: 02 98 74 00 53). Tall, shuttered, well-kept hotel in a quiet corner at the top of the town, with a garden and views of the church and sea. Though accessible only via tortuous back-streets, signposting is obliging from the port.
Kerléguer (££) (tel: 02 98 92 34 64). Guests can choose to stay in the family home on this old farm or in a separate ivy-clad stone cottage. It is close to the village and within easy distance from the sea.
Manoir de Kervent (££) Pouldavid (tel: 02 98 92 04 90). You are assured of a warm welcome at this residence where discounts for children under 5 years are available. Both the beach and forest area are close at hand.

La Forêt-Fouesnant
De l'Espérance (£) place de l'Eglise (tel: 02 98 56 96 58). A modest stone-built house by the church in the village centre. Lush gardens behind. The rooms are of variable quality and price; the quieter ones are at the rear.
Manoir du Stang (£££) (tel: 02 98 56 97 37). Ornate 16th-century château, regally furnished in period style. Frosty reception may take the edge off first impressions but the rooms are very comfortable. Extensive parkland.

Fouesnant
Armorique (£) 33 rue de Cornouaille (tel: 02 98 56 00 19). Good-value, friendly, family-run place in the main street. The bar and dining room give on to a courtyard full of hydrangeas.
De la Pointe de Mousterlin (£–££) Mousterlin Plages (tel: 02 98 56 04 12). A stone's throw from the splendid beaches at Mousterlin point, this is an ideal choice for a relaxing family holiday. Some of the larger rooms have balconies. Fresh local fish is served in the restaurant.

Locronan
Manoir de Moëllien (££) Plonévez-Porzay (tel: 02 98 92 50 40). The name recalls Chateaubriand's lover, Thérèse de Moëllien, whose home this lovely 17th-century manor once was. Now carefully restored, thriving and peaceful, it has attractive rooms. These are in a stable annexe, though, and can seem a little damp and chilly in bad weather. Excellent breakfast. Book ahead to avoid disappointment.
Du Prieuré (££) (tel: 02 98 91 70 89). This attractive granite *logis* on the edge of the lovely old town makes an excellent base, though it lacks interesting views. Some refurbished bedrooms and an imposing arched and beamed dining room. Expect the crowds in season.

Montagnes Noires
Le Relais de Cornouaille (£) 9 rue Paul Sérusier, Châteauneuf-du-Faou (tel: 02 98 81 75 36). Down-to-earth central hotel-restaurant adorned with flower-filled window-boxes. A good place to have lunch or to use as a base for exploring the Montagnes Noires.

Pont-Aven
Ajoncs d'Or (££) place Hôtel de Ville (tel: 02 98 06 02 06). Very central and friendly: the best value in this overrun tourist town. Old-fashioned, sensible furnishings and plenty of appropriate artworks.

Kermentec (£) (tel: 02 98 06 07 60). Bed-and-breakfast accommodation in a stone house in the hills of Pont-Aven. Visitors may breakfast outside in the sunshine or by the fire on winter mornings. Swimming, beaches, river sports and golf facilities are all within easy reach.
Moulin de Rosmadec (£££) (tel: 02 98 06 00 22). Easy to find by the bridge in the village centre, this appealing restaurant-with-rooms has been converted from one of the original windmills for which the town is famous. Water rushing by may make it hard to sleep. Furnishings are very pretty, and rooms need booking ahead. These are a sideline to the food, however (see restaurant section).
Roz-Aven (£££) 11 quai Théodore Botrel (tel: 02 98 06 13 06). Pretty waterfront inn with comfortable if somewhat overpriced Louis XIV rooms. No restaurant, though there is a local bar.

Pont-l'Abbé

Chateau Hotel de Kernuz (££) rte de Penmarc'h (tel: 02 98 87 01 59). A 16th-century residence in secluded grounds with ancient oak trees and wide lawns. The interior is equisitely decorated and the bedrooms provide a high level of comfort.
De Bretagne (££) 24 place de la République (tel: 02 98 87 17 22). Central hotel on the main square (plenty of parking). Smart, civilised rooms – the most peaceful ones are at the rear – and excellent food (see restaurant section). Friendly owners.

Port-Manec'h

Chez Pierre (££) Raguenez-Plage (tel: 02 98 06 81 06). Stone house in the village centre with attractive gardens and a popular restaurant (good food but very slow service). Comfortably furnished bedrooms and lounge areas.
Le Men-Du (££) Raguenez-Plage (tel: 02 98 06 84 22). White-painted building in splendid isolation overlooking the beach and a tidal island. Friendly, inexpensive and comfortable. No restaurant.
Du Port (£) 30 rue de l'Aven (tel: 02 98 06 82 17). Agreeable family *logis* with partial sea views over scenic coastline. Simple furnishings. Garden.

Quimper

Château de Guilguiffin (£££) Landulec 29710 (tel: 02 98 91 52 11). On the D874 south of Quimper, this large château is set amid magnificent parkland. No restaurant but arrangements can be made for brunch or buffet supper. Price includes breakfast.
Gradlon (££) 30 rue de Brest (tel: 02 98 95 04 39). Solid, comfortably furnished town hotel a short walk from the cathedral. Garden in summer, log fires in winter.
Hotel Mascotte (££) 6 rue Theodore le Hars (tel: 02 98 53 37 37). A town-centre hotel surrounded by lively streets. The modern bedrooms have good amenities. Comfortable lounge, bar and restaurant. Good access to the motorway.

Quimperlé

Auberge de Toulfoën (£) route du Pouldu (tel: 02 98 96 00 29). Country coaching inn serving good lunches near the Forêt de Carnoët. Simple rooms available.

Ste-Anne-la-Palud

La Plage (£££) (tel: 02 98 92 50 12). Isolated, luxurious beach hotel at high-water mark. Impressively furnished and equipped, it attracts a notably well-heeled (and generally older) clientele. Excellent food (see restaurant section).

Sizun, Cap

Baie des Trépassés (££) Plogoff (tel: 02 98 70 61 34) and Pointe du Van (££) Plogoff (tel: 02 98 70 62 79). Twin hotels on a scenic bay near **Pointe du Raz**. Rather spartan inside, but excellent coastal scenery and sandy beaches.
Le Clos de 4 Saisons (£) 2 rue de la Paix (tel: 02 98 68 80 19). Peaceful accommodation in a building with plenty of character, surrounded by a pretty park. The restaurant, housed in the oldest part of the building, offers inventive cuisine using local produce.
Kermoor (£) Plage du Loch, Plogoff (tel: 02 98 70 62 06). Simple hotel overlooking a lovely stretch of sand. Renovated in 1998. Cheerful seafood restaurant.

MORBIHAN

Auray

L'Auberge (££) 56 route de Vannes, Ste-Anne-d'Auray (tel: 02 97 57 61 55). Attractive, old-world inn, traditionally furnished with dark wood and candelabra. Light, fresh fabrics in the bedrooms. Garden. See also restaurant section.
La Croix Blanche (£) 25 rue de Vannes, Ste-Anne-d'Auray (tel: 02 97 57 64 44). Pleasing older-style building on the edge of town, decently furnished. Popular haunt with pilgrims.

Belle-Ile

Atlantique (££) quai de l'Acadie (tel: 02 97 31 80 11). Perhaps the most appealing of the three attractive and well-kept hotels just below the citadel by the landing stage in le Palais. An elegant yellow-washed building with dormers, comfortably furnished rooms and an animated bar-restaurant, Le Grand Café, downstairs.
Castel Clara (£££) Anse de Goulphar (tel: 02 97 31 84 21). Luxury hotel-restaurant overlooking one of Belle-Ile's most picturesque sections of coastline. A substantial modern white and grey block with balconied rooms. Many facilities, including tennis, swimming

pool and thalassotherapy. A constant stream of coach parties heads for lunch at the adjacent establishment.
Phare (£) Sauzon (tel: 02 97 31 60 36). Right by the lighthouse in this charming fishing port. A simple, pretty building of great appeal.
Hotel-Village la Desirade (££) Le petit Cosquet (tel: 02 97 31 70 70). A visit to La Desirade will be a memorable experience. Décor in the rooms is themed, ranging from Tuscan style to oriental elegance. A colourful garden creates a charming setting for a peaceful and relaxing stay. Heated outdoor swimming pool.

Carnac

L'Alcyone (££) Impasse de Beaumer, Carnac Plage (tel: 02 97 52 78 11). Guests at this Breton house are welcomed by the friendly owners, and can enjoy home cooking in a calm and peaceful environment. Salt-water swimming pool, tennis, horse-riding and golf are all available near by. Also, beach clubs for children.

Hotel Celtique (££) 17 av de Kermario, Carnac Plage (tel: 02 97 52 11 49). Quietly positioned among pine trees at Carnac Plage. Close to the beach and with a heated outdoor swimming pool, sauna and jacuzzi. Bicycle rental available.
La Marine (££) 4 place de la Chapelle (tel: 02 97 52 07 33). A good base in the town centre, useful for exploring the megaliths and the Musée de Préhistoire, which is close by. A well-kept building with modern blue and white furnishings, respectable light, clean rooms and a terraced seafood restaurant (see restaurant section).
Les Rochers (££) 6 boulevard de la Base Nautique (tel: 02 97 52 10 09). One of the more agreeable options in Carnac's beach resort. Notably welcoming (unlike some of its competitors), and attractively furnished with cane rattan chairs and plants, in a prime sea-facing position near the yacht club.

Le Faouët

La Croix d'Or (£) 9 place Bellanger (tel: 02 97 23 07 33). A handsome building on the main square, overlooking the splendid covered wooden marketplace. A reliable base for exploring local chapels and places of interest in this attractive town.

Josselin

Château (££) (tel: 02 97 22 20 11). Imposing dormered building occupying a prime site on the opposite bank from the castle. The interior is dowdily respectable and fairly quiet.
Hôtel du Roi Arthur (£££) Le Lac au Duc, Ploërmel (tel: 02 97 73 64 64). Extremely comfortable hotel next to a lake and a nine-hole golf course. Facilities include an indoor swimming pool, fitness club and air-conditioned restaurant.

Locmariaquer

L'Escale (££) Place Dariorigum (tel: 02 97 57 32 51). Well positioned by the waterfront, a modern white building, plainly furnished but comfortable, with good views from many rooms. Rustic, sea-facing restaurant.
Lautram (£) place de l'Eglise (tel: 02 97 57 31 32). Well-kept small hotel opposite the church, close to the harbour. Some garden rooms in the rear annexe. Seafood restaurant.

Ploërmel

Le Cobh (££) 10 rue des Forges (tel: 02 97 74 00 49). Well-run town-centre hotel of unusual character. Attractively furnished public areas and well-equipped bedrooms. Garage parking. Restaurant.
Golf Hotel du Roi Arther (££–£££) Le Lac au Duc (tel: 02 97 73 64 64). Set beside the legendary forest of Broceliand and overlooking the Lac au Duc, the largest natural lake in Brittany. Facilities include a 9-hole golf course, indoor swimming pool and gym. Apartments in the grounds are also available.

Pontivy

Le Rohan Wesseling (££) 90 rue Nationale (tel: 02 97 25 02 01). This comfortable business hotel in a typical period building in the Napoleonic quarter has no particular charm, but is well managed and fairly quiet, with good facilities and a small garden set with tables. Park and old town near by.
Le Vieux Moulin (£) St-Nicolas-des-Eaux (tel: 02 97 51 81 09). Attractive, simple village inn overlooking the River Blavet. Comfortable, well-equipped rooms and a restaurant. A good touring base.

Port-Louis

Commerce (£) 1 place du Marché (tel: 02 97 82 46 05). A no-nonsense commercial *logis* in the heart of this peaceful town, a more-than-adequate base for a night or two, with 1960s time-warp furnishings, a pleasant garden and plenty of local atmosphere. The restaurant is worth considering – you may not find anywhere else to eat!

Quiberon, Presqu'île de

L'Océan (£) 7 quai de l'Océan, Port-Maria (tel: 02 97 50 07 58). Useful base for visiting Belle-Ile, convenient for the *gare maritime*. Modern furnishings but bedrooms are very small.
La Petite Sirène (££) 15 boulevard René Cassin, Quiberon (tel: 02 97 50 17 34). Well-appointed hotel at the southern tip of the Quiberon peninsula, overlooking the sea and close to the thalassotherapy centre. The restaurant serves good meals at moderate prices. Short walk to the beach and casino.

Rhuys, Presqu'île de

Le Mûr du Roy (£) Penvins (tel: 02 97 67 34 08). Low, slate-roofed cottage in a peaceful coastal location, simply but attractively furnished. Friendly atmosphere. There is a restaurant, or try the excellent Espadon, also in the village.

La Roche-Bernard

Auberge Bretonne (£££) 2 place Duguesclin (tel: 02 99 90 60 28). Celebrated restaurant-with-rooms (see restaurant section) in the town centre. Well-kept exterior with blue shutters and window-boxes. Very smartly furnished.

Auberge des Deux Magots (££) 1 place du Bouffay (tel: 02 99 90 60 75). Pretty stone and white-painted building in a quiet enclave near the town hall, with cheerful red awnings. Bedrooms more urbanely grand. See also restaurant section.

De Bretagne (£) 15 rue Crespel de la Touche (tel: 02 99 90 60 65). This pleasant roadside hotel near the new road bridge has much local competition, but you could do worse if everywhere else is full. Clean and well equipped. No restaurant.

Le Colibri (£) 1 rue du Four (tel: 02 99 90 66 01). A pleasant, friendly, central hotel in a quiet part of the old town. Private parking. No restaurant, but a light, attractive breakfast room.

Domaine de Bodeuc (£££) (tel: 02 99 90 89 63). An elegant, creeper-covered small manor house about 5km from town, signposted off the Redon road. Peaceful setting in 15ha of parkland. The interior is furnished with great flair and taste and there is an intimate, country-house atmosphere. Breakfast only as yet (but what a breakfast!). Restaurant for residents only.

Domaine de Rochevilaine (£££) pointe de Pen Lan, Billiers (tel: 02 97 41 61 61). Unusual, rambling, village-like complex right by the sea, originally converted from old watch-post buildings. Inside it is luxurious and relaxing, with magnificent views. Expensive restaurant. See also restaurant section.

Glycines (£) place de l'Eglise, Billiers (tel: 02 97 41 64 63). A much cheaper and simpler *logis* alternative, with sea and salt-marsh views and good fish suppers.

Le Manoir du Rodoir (£££) route de Nantes (tel: 02 99 90 82 68). A fine stone house (once an old forge) set well off the road in its own grounds. Beautifully furnished like an English country-house inside (the owners are British), it is tasteful and comfortable throughout. See also restaurant section.

Rochefort-en-Terre

De Bretagne (£££) Questembert (tel: 02 97 26 11 12). In the village centre, a renowned restaurant-with-rooms (see restaurant section), grandly furnished but quite intimate in scale. Very comfortable, serene bedrooms. Garden.

Château de Talhouët (£££) off Molac road, NW (tel: 02 97 43 34 72). Classy *chambres d'hôtes* in a lovely stone château with fine gardens. Inside all is peace, good taste and understated luxury. Rooms vary greatly in style and price, but all are immensely comfortable. The quiet professionalism behind this operation leaves you completely relaxed.

Vannes

Hotel Mascotte (££) av Jean Monet (tel: 02 97 47 59 60). A splendid situation, close to the bay of Morbihan and near the historic centre, makes this an excellent base for exploring the town. Sound-proofed bedrooms ensure a peaceful night. Light, simple cuisine is served in the restaurant.

Manche Océan (££) 31 rue du Lieut Col Maury (tel: 02 97 47 26 46). Peaceful, comfortable accommodation in a friendly, family-run establishment in the historic centre of the town. Convenient for shops, restaurants and major sights.

L'Oasis (£) route de Conleau (tel: 02 97 40 82 05). On the face of it there is not much to distinguish this functional roadside business hotel in dull suburban surroundings. But Vannes has little to offer in the way of attractive hotels and you could do worse than this friendly, well-equipped place. Good value, easy parking, and a short drive to the ferry terminals for the Golfe du Morbihan.

Le Roof (££) presqu'île de Conleau (tel: 02 97 63 47 47). A modern building occupying an enviable waterfront site some way from the old town. Family-run, though its bland furnishings lack character. Much praised for its friendly staff and cheerful atmosphere. Good facilities and spacious, comfortable rooms. The terraced restaurant overlooks the bay and a constant flurry of boats.

Les Vénètes (££) la pointe d'Arradon, Arradon (tel: 02 97 44 03 11). Peacefully located west of Vannes on the Golfe du Morbihan, understandably popular in summer. The restaurant and most bedrooms have tranquil views of boats and islands. Simply but pleasantly furnished.

INLAND BRITTANY

Combourg

Du Château (££) 1 place Chateaubriand (tel: 02 99 73 00 38). Well-established hotel near the castle and lake, comfortably furnished throughout. Annexe bedrooms are modern and very well equipped.

Château de la Bourbansais (£££) Pleugueneuc (tel: 02 99 69 40 07). The area around Combourg is dotted with castles; this one was built in 1583 on an ancient Gallo-Roman site. French-style gardens, woods, zoo and children's play area; fishing and hunting in season; nature trail.

Château de la Motte Beaumanoir (£££) Pleugueneuc (tel: 02 99 69 46 01). Opulent, refurbished château set in extensive grounds. Buildings date from the 15th and 18th centuries and are furnished in *Directoire* style. Swimming pool, tennis and many other leisure facilities ensure a pampered stay.

Du Lac (£) 2 place Chateaubriand (tel: 02 99 73 05 65). Cheaper and simpler than its neighbour across the road, this enjoys good lake views. Good restaurant; bedrooms rather dated.
Aux Voyageurs (£) Tinténiac (tel: 02 99 68 02 21). Simple village *logis* – bustling and popular. Restaurant (live lobsters on display) and private garden.

Fougères
Balzac (£) 15 rue Nationale et rue Chateaubriand (tel: 02 99 99 42 46). Useful central base in the upper town. Pleasant welcome; old-fashioned furnishings. No restaurant.

Hédé
Vieux Moulin (£) (tel: 02 99 45 45 70). Pretty old inn in a lovely setting. Simply furnished inside, with good dining room.

Mûr-de-Bretagne
L'Abbaye Bon-Repos (£) Bon-Repos, St-Gelven, Gouarec (tel: 02 96 24 98 38). Unusual guesthouse converted from 12th-century abbey ruins in an idyllic spot. Be warned, there are *son et lumière* shows occasionally in summer. Banqueting hall restaurant.

Auberge Grand' Maison (££) 1 rue Léon le Cerf (tel: 02 96 28 51 10). Stylish if slightly cramped inn in the village centre. Ambitious food (see restaurant section). Bedrooms vary greatly in standard and price and some are quite small.
Auberge Kreisker (£) 11 place Kreisker, St-Nicolas-du-Pélem (tel: 02 96 29 51 20). Distinctive small hotel in the village centre with creaking floors and quasi box beds in some rooms. A useful touring base.
Beau-Rivage (£) Caurel, Lac de Guérledan (tel: 02 96 28 52 15). Modern building overlooking the lake. Take a room with a view. Terrace restaurant. Many watersports facilities near by.
Du Blavet (£) Gouarec (tel: 02 96 24 90 03). Tall and interesting – overlooking the point where the Nantes–Brest canal meets the River Blavet. A busy road runs close by; otherwise the surrounding countryside is very peaceful. Period Breton furniture; some rooms a little musty. Good food.

Paimpont, Forêt de
Relais de Brocéliande (££) Paimpont (tel: 02 99 07 81 07). Old inn, quirkily old-fashioned, and with charming secluded gardens. Lively local bar-restaurant adorned with hunting trophies.

Rennes
Ar Milin (££) 30 rue de Paris, Châteaubourg (tel: 02 99 00 30 91). Large, comfortable roadside hotel (a converted flour mill) between Rennes and Vitré. Many facilities and extensive gardens landscaped around the river bank.
Hotel Lecoq-Gadby (£££) 156 rue d'Antrain (tel: 02 99 38 05 55). Quite an institution. This elegantly furnished establishment, which provides a comfortably relaxing stay, is patronised by many famous personalities. Enjoy the open terrace and solarium. *A la carte* and fixed-price menus in the restaurant. Easy access to the motorway.
Hôtel des Lices (££) 7 place des Lices (tel: 02 99 79 14 81). Modern, thoroughly civilised and small; on the edge of the old town. Parking available near by. Excellent, neat little bedrooms, friendly welcome and good breakfast.
Pen'Roc (££) le Peinière-en-St-Didier (tel: 02 99 00 33 02). Excellent modern hotel by a small pilgrimage chapel. Smart, stylish furnishings, unfailingly courteous staff and ambitious food (see restaurant section). Many facilities (including satellite TV) and a substantial proportion of conference trade. Note – not to be confused with the adjacent hotel on the same site.

LOIRE-ATLANTIQUE

Batz-sur-Mer
Le Lichen de la Mer (££) Baie du Manérick (tel: 02 40 23 91 92). Pleasant, well-cared-for detached house along the seafront road. Solid, traditional furnishings and good views. Separate restaurant l'Atlantide (see restaurant section).

La Baule
Le Castel Marie-Louise (£££) 1 rue Andrieu (tel: 02 40 11 48 38). One of la Baule's most exclusive hotels, in an imposingly turreted Belle Epoque mansion. Immaculate gardens, sea-water pool (at Hôtel Hermitage). Celebrated food (see restaurant section).
La Lutetia (££) 13 av des Evens (tel: 02 40 60 25 81). The Lutetia is just a stone's throw from what is reputed to be Europe's finest beach. Though the building retains its original façade, the interior has been completely renovated, with comfortable rooms. An elegant restaurant creates regional cuisine using local produce.
La Palmeraie (££) 7 allée des Cormorans (tel: 02 40 60 24 41). One of la Baule's best-loved hotels, a *logis* set in a quiet corner of the residential belt between beach and high street. Not particularly stylish, but reassuringly reliable. Palm-shaded terraces.
Ty-Gwenn (£) 25 avenue de la Grande Dune (tel: 02 40 60 37 07). Simple, pretty family-run guest-house. Quiet surroundings, short walk to the beach.

Brière
Auberge de Kerhinet (££) Kerhinet (tel: 02 40 61 91 46). Typical thatched cottage converted into an attractive (if somewhat *touristique*) *logis*. Dining room (see restaurant section).

Le Croisic

L'Estacade (££) 4–5 quai du Lénigo (tel: 02 40 23 03 77). Bustling bar-hotel on the waterfront by the *criée* and busy harbour. The bar area is traditional; the best bedrooms are modern and stylish. See also restaurant section.
Grand Hotel de l'Océan (££) plage de Port-Lin (tel: 02 40 62 90 03). Port-Lin's smartest hotel, a boxy, low-rise white block occupying a prime site by the Atlantic. Spacious, traditionally furnished public areas with big picture-windows. See restaurant section.
Les Nids (£) plage de Port-Lin (tel: 02 40 23 00 63). Civilised *logis* peacefully set a block back from Atlantic seafront; partial sea views. Separate restaurant near by (see restaurant section). Fairly basic, old-fashioned rooms.

Guérande

Loscolo (££) Pointe de Loscolo, Pénestin (tel: 02 99 90 31 90). Beautifully situated on one of Loire-Atlantique's prettiest stretches of coast, overlooking the Plage de la Mine d'Or. Quiet, friendly, well-run and attractively furnished – in short, a charmer.
De la Pointe (£) Piriac-sur-Mer (tel: 02 40 23 50 04). Daudet stayed here, says a plaque outside. A useful, modest base in a pretty fishing town of old half-timbered houses. Good beaches near by.
Roc Maria (££) 1 rue des Halles (tel: 02 40 24 90 51). A 15th-century gem tucked in the heart of the old walled town. Attractively furnished, with a lovely *crêperie*.

Nantes

Amiral (££) 26 bis rue Scribe (tel: 02 40 69 20 21). A neat, practical, modern hotel near Place Graslin, with attractive furnishings and welcoming staff. Plenty of restaurants, shops and nightlife all around, and a car park near by (though tricky to find by car).
Du Château (£) 5 place de la Duchesse-Anne (tel: 02 40 74 17 16). The accommodation section is run separately from the excellent Auberge du Château (see restaurant section), but provides basic, convenient lodgings should you want to spend more on food than sleeping. Views of the castle from front rooms, and some traffic noise.
Duchesse Anne (££) 3–4 place de la Duchesse Anne (tel: 02 51 86 78 78). Grandiose old-fashioned hotel overlooking the castle. No-frills, shabby in parts, but spacious, comfortable rooms, helpful staff, and – not least of Nantes' wonders – garage parking. Good value.
L'Hôtel (££) 6 rue Henri IV (tel: 02 40 29 30 31). This is *the* place for a sophisticated stay in Nantes. A chic interior of cane and cashmere, *objets d'art* and beautifully co-ordinated colour schemes. Prices are geared towards business travellers (cheaper at weekends) and quoted in *euros*, but are surprisingly reasonable. No restaurant.
Le Jules Verne (££) 3 rue du Couëdic (tel: 02 40 35 74 50). All is sleek, black and minimalist in this hotel in the heart of the old town near Place Royale. Plants take the edge off the starkness and bedrooms are well equipped.
Novotel Nantes (££) 3 rue de Valmy (tel: 02 51 82 00 00). A modern, town-centre establishment with well-equipped rooms. An excellent choice for travellers anticipating a late arrival as food can be ordered at any time. Guests with disabilities are well catered for.

Redon

La Belle Anguille (£) route de Ste-Marie (tel: 02 99 72 31 02). Three kilometres outside town, in tranquil countryside overlooking a lovely stretch of river. Simple and family-run: makes no extravagant claims, and concentrates on what it does best – its food (see restaurant section). Bedrooms are clean and bright.
Chandouineau (££) 10 avenue de la Gare (tel: 02 99 71 02 04). A fairly charmless location by the railway station but conveniently near to the old town. Inside it has character, quite grand furnishings and large, old-fashioned rooms. Its restaurant is a high spot (see restaurant section).

RESTAURANTS

The following restaurants are divided into three price categories, based on the cost of a meal excluding drinks:

- **budget (£)** – below 120FF
- **moderate (££)** – 120F–300FF
- **expensive (£££)** – above 300FF

These should be viewed as a rough guideline only; many restaurants have an enormous range of menus and individual dishes. Even famous and august places may have a set-lunch menu well within your budget, and it would be a shame to leave Brittany without tasting some really first-class seafood.

THE EMERALD COAST

Cancale

Continental (££) quai Thomas (tel: 02 99 89 60 16). An excellent place to sample Cancale's oysters, preferably on the terrace towards sunset. See also hotel section.
Maisons de Bricourt (£££) rue Du Guesclin (tel: 02 99 89 64 76). The memorable food in this smart establishment earns two Michelin rosettes and four red Gault Millau *toques*, and some consider it Brittany's top restaurant. See also hotel section.
Le Narval (££) 20 quai Gambetta (tel: 02 99 89 63 12). Good seafood, appetisingly displayed by the door. The upstairs dining room

has a view over the harbour if the tables outside are occupied.
Tirel-Guérin (££) gare de la Gouesnière, St-Méloir-des-Ondes (tel: 02 99 89 10 46). A Michelin star has been awarded for the food here, though residents may find the set menus change too infrequently. Plush dining room of drapes and tassels. Famous for lobster. See also hotel section.

Dinan
D'Avaugour (££) 1 place du Champ Clos (tel: 02 96 39 07 49). An airy restaurant overlooking place Du Guesclin in the historic heart of town.
La Caravelle (££) 14 place Duclos (tel: 02 96 39 00 11). Rustic setting for straightforward, high-quality dishes such as oysters and fillet of beef.
Mère Pourcel (££) 3 place des Merciers (tel: 02 96 39 03 80). Lovely old 15th-century house with a magnificent oak staircase. Copious helpings. Tables outside.
Les Terrasses (££) (tel: 02 96 39 09 60). Delightful waterfront setting at the port by the bridge.

Dinard
Altaïr (££) 18 boulevard Féart (tel: 02 99 46 13 58). Perhaps Dinard's best restaurant, simple but imaginative, in a highly traditional dining room of polished Breton furniture. See also hotel section.
La Plage (££) 3 boulevard Féart (tel: 02 99 46 14 87). The restaurant at this hotel is **Le Trézen**, with attractive menus served in an intimate, informal dining room. See also hotel section.

Erquy
L'Escurial (££) boulevard de la Mer (tel: 02 96 72 31 56). Local scallops (*coquilles*) are the speciality in this deceptively ordinary-looking place by the workmanlike harbour.

Fréhel, Cap
La Fauconnière (£) (tel: 02 96 41 54 20). Cliff-edge restaurant in a spectacular location, popular with walkers and bird-watchers. Simple fare such as omelettes, fresh fish and the like.

St-Cast-le-Guildo
Le Biniou (££) Pen Guen (tel: 02 96 41 94 53). Attractive fish restaurant set above the beach. Rustic but up-market.

St-Malo
L'Atre (££) 7 esplanade St-Menguy, Port Solidor, St-Servan (tel: 02 99 81 68 39). Views over the Solidor beach and Rance estuary from this appealing small restaurant. It has more than seafood, though fish is what it does best, with good Muscadet.
Café de l'Univers (££) place Chateaubriand (tel: 02 99 40 89 52). A popular place within the walls of the old town specialising in seafood. Late dinners served.
Crêperie Chez Chantal (£) 2 place aux Herbes (tel: 02 99 40 93 97). Offering a grand choice of *crêpe* fillings, especially seafood, at reasonable prices. Pleasant dining room.
A la Duchesse Anne (££) 5 place Guy La Chambre (tel: 02 99 40 85 33). One of St-Malo's most celebrated eating places, always bustling, by the rampart walls. It specialises in grilled lobster and *tarte tatin*. No set menus but not outrageously expensive. Book well ahead.
Tea-Time (£) 4 Grande-Rue (tel: 02 99 40 89 12). A tea shop near the walls. Heartily French despite the English connotations, but you can have an English breakfast here. Coffee is served in thin porcelain and there are marvellous cakes.

Le Val André
La Cotriade (££) port de Piégu (tel: 02 96 63 06 90). This small harbourside restaurant has a big reputation for excellent seafood with exquisite sauces. Book ahead to avoid disappointment.
De la Mer (£) 63 rue Amiral Charner (tel: 02 96 72 20 44). Wonderful *moules* here, hence its popularity with locals, but all is simple, friendly and cheerful. See also hotel section.

THE PINK GRANITE COAST

Belle-Isle-en-Terre
Le Relais de l'Argoat (£) (tel: 02 96 43 00 34). Inexpensive *logis* with good regional menus and honest country cooking.

Bréhat, Ile de
Bellevue (££) Port Clos (tel: 02 96 20 00 05). Small informal hotel-restaurant near the landing stage, offering a quayside terrace and fresh seafood.

Lannion
Le Serpolet (££) 1 rue Félix le Dantec (tel: 02 96 46 50 23). Attractive stone restaurant in a quiet side-street. Excellent fish and desserts.

Paimpol
Aux Pesked (££) 59 rue du Légué, Saint-Brieuc (tel: 02 96 33 34 65). Classy, with a moderately priced weekday menu; fish specialities.
Café du Port (££) Porz-Even. Excellent seafood in a terraced restaurant by the quayside.
Le Repair de Kerroc'h (££) 29 quai Morand (tel: 02 96 20 50 13). Local ingredients figure in the mostly fishy dishes, and the upgraded terrace restaurant now hums with activity. See also hotel section.
Vieille Tour (££) 13 rue Eglise (tel: 02 96 20 83 18). Set in a small stone house. Praised by Michelin for its good set meals (*à la carte* can be pricey).

Perros-Guirec
Les Feux des Iles (££) 53 boulevard Clemenceau (tel: 02 96 23 22 94). The dining room takes full advantage of the views but don't be distracted too much: the food is excellent. See also hotel section.

Ploumanac'h
Rochers (£££) (tel: 02 96 91 44 49). Wonderful views of the pink granite complement elaborate lobster dishes and Calvados pancakes. Advance booking essential.

St-Quay-Portrieux
Ker–Moor (££) 13 rue du Président le Sénécal (tel: 02 96 70 52 22). With a garden and panoramic view of the Bay of Saint-Brieuc; close to the beach. The house speciality is scallops.

Trébeurden
Ti Al-Lannec (££) 14 allée de Mézo-Guen (tel: 02 96 15 00 01). With a panoramic sea view and terrace. Meals are served outside in the summer. Speciality: salad of scallops fried with truffles. Moderately priced lunchtime menu.

Tréguier
Auberge du Trégor (£) (tel: 02 96 92 32 34). If you prefer to stay in town during the evening, this little place is moderately priced.
Kastell Dinec'h route de Lannion (tel: 02 96 92 49 39). Good home cooking wins a Michelin accolade, so the obligatory half-board at this hotel is no hardship. See also hotel section.

NORTH FINISTÈRE

Plouguerneau
Castel Ac'h (£) Plage de Lilia, 5km north-west of Plouguerneau (tel: 02 98 04 70 11). Lovely view of the rugged west coast. Lunchtime menu good value. Children's menu. Rooms available.

Le Conquet
Le Relais du Vieux Port (£) 1 quai Drellach (tel: 02 98 89 15 91). A variety of snacks, *crêpes* and salads is served to the accompaniment of gentle piano music. See also hotel section.

Kerjean
Crêperie le Pressoir (£) 9 place de l'Europe, Plouescat (tel: 02 98 69 60 46). This *crêperie*, open daily in July and August, specialises in seafood *crêpes* and mussels in cream. Children's menu available.

Morlaix
La Marée Bleue (££) 3 rampe St-Mélaine (tel: 02 98 63 24 21). Close to the tourist office in one of Morlaix's picturesque *venelles* (alleys). Traditional cooking, good set menus and interesting wines.

Roscoff
Le Brittany (££) boulevard Ste-Barbe (tel: 02 98 69 70 78). Fish menus *par excellence* are served in Le Yachtman, the renowned restaurant at the Brittany hotel. A series of stone arches allows sea views through the granite walls. See also hotel section.
Chardons Bleus (££) 4 rue Amiral Réveillère (tel: 02 98 69 72 03). Friendly hotel-restaurant a block behind the port. Children's menus available.
Crêperie de la Poste (£) rue Gambetta (tel: 02 98 69 72 81). Serves a wide range of pancakes in a plain, workaday dining room popular with ferry travellers.
Le Temps de Vivre (££) place de l'Eglise (tel: 02 98 61 27 28). Possibly the best place in town, with excellent views of the Ile de Batz. Seafood and local vegetables are served in an attractive dining room.

ARMORIQUE

Arrée, Monts d'
Milin Kerroch (£) Sizun (tel: 02 98 68 81 56). At the entrance to the village, in the Centre de Loisirs, a converted watermill serving a wide variety of *crêpes*.

Camaret-sur-Mer
Hotel de France (££) quai G Toudouze (tel: 02 98 27 93 06). One of the best choices for local seafood in a port area crammed with fish restaurants. Good views from first-floor windows.

Carhaix-Plouguer
Auberge du Poher (££) route de Lorient (tel: 02 98 99 51 18). Pretty, rustic restaurant serving regional Breton food with earthy dishes such as *tripes* and *andouilles*.

Crozon, Presqu'île de
La Mer (£) le Fret (tel: 02 98 27 61 90). Terraces and picture windows make the most of the views, though the food is worth concentrating on too. See also hotel section.
La Salicorne (£) 42 boulevard de la Plage, Morgat (tel: 02 98 27 05 68). Open during the summer months; traditional cuisine including roasted monkfish on a layer of leeks and a delicious *crêpe* filled with crispy apple in caramelised sugar flavoured with *chouchenn* (honey brandy).

Le Faou
Le Relais de la Place (£) (tel: 02 98 81 91 19). The outside is plain, but the cooking is honest and very good value. See also hotel section.

Guimiliau
Ar Chupen (£) (tel: 02 98 68 73 63). This *crêperie* near the church deals with any sudden appetite worked up in the parish close. A *crêpe du pagan* sounds quite an antidote to spiritual thoughts.

Huelgoat

Restaurant du Lac (£) 9 rue du Général de Gaulle (tel: 02 98 99 71 14). The best restaurant in this beautiful tourist spot, with a good lunch menu and special children's menu. Serving typical Breton dishes, including pork grilled over a wood fire, chicken cooked in cider, and Breton *far*. See also hotel section.
La Chouette Bleue (£) rue du Lac (tel: 02 98 99 78 19). Ice-cream and *crêperie* bar at the end of the main street. Swift service in a spacious, rustic dining room.

Landerneau

L'Amandier (££) 55 route de Brest (tel: 02 98 85 10 89). Traditional hotel with an excellent restaurant and brasserie.
La Mairie (££) 9 rue de la Tour d'Auvergne (tel: 02 98 85 01 83). Attractive establishment overlooking the scenic Pont de Rohan.

Landivisiau

L'Avenue (£) 16 avenue Coat Meur (tel: 02 98 68 11 67).Cheap restaurant specialising in traditional Breton dishes: scallops, *kig ha farz* (a kind of stew), *tripes à la bretonne.*
L'Enclos (££) rue de Saint-Jaques, Lampaul-Guimiliau (tel: 02 98 68 77 08). Specialities such as monkfish cooked in cider and *gambas à la bretonne.*
Milin an Elorn (£) ancienne route de Landivisiau, la Roche-Maurice (tel: 02 98 20 41 46). *Crêperie* and grill restaurant in a converted watermill.

St-Thégonnec

Auberge St-Thégonnec (££) place de la Mairie (tel: 02 98 79 61 18). Some of the region's most accomplished cooking is served here, at surprisingly unfrightening prices. Regional Breton menus are served in the gardens in summer. See also hotel section.

CORNOUAILLE

Audierne

Le Goyen (£££) le port (tel: 02 98 70 08 88). The lovely restaurant at this hotel overlooks a splendid sweep of estuary and serves a mix of traditional and *nouvelle* cuisine. Stick to set menus or you may be in for a shock when the bill arrives. See also hotel section.

Bélon

Chez Jacky (££) Riec-sur-Bélon (tel: 02 98 06 90 32). Oyster farm-cum-restaurant overlooking the River Bélon.
Le Kerfany (££) Blorimond, route du Port de Bélon, Moëlan-sur-Mer (tel: 02 98 71 00 46). Serving several menus over a wide price range. Specialities include seafood and Breton *far.*
Les Moulins du Duc (£££) Moëlan-sur-Mer (tel: 02 98 39 60 73). Top-quality food is served in two candlelit dining rooms, one of which is non-smoking. See also hotel section.
Le Puits Gourmand (£) 13 rue Pont Ar Laer, Moëlan-sur-Mer (tel: 02 98 39 65 70). Speciality: fillet of duck cooked in *pommeau de Bretagne*, a kind of apple wine.

Bénodet

L'Agape (£££) la Plage, Ste-Marine (tel: 02 98 56 32 70). Close to the beach in a small resort: elegant, with expensive menus carefully presented.
La Ferme du Letty (££) le Letty Izella (tel: 02 98 57 01 27). This old stone farmhouse by the lagoon produces some of the most enjoyable food in the resort. Though it retains some of its rustic simplicity, it now has an air of quiet sophistication, with summer terraces, winter fires and obliging waiters.

Concarneau

Chez Armande (£) 15 bis avenue Dr Nicolas (tel: 02 98 97 00 76). Old-fashioned family-run place serving simple, unpretentious fish dishes.
La Coquille (££) quai Moros (tel: 02 98 97 08 52). Classy but down-to-earth fish restaurant by the new port.
Crêperie des Remparts (££) 31 rue Théophile-Louàrn, Ville Close (tel: 02 98 50 65 66). This *crêperie* in the old walled town is an excellent place to sample *crêpes* and *galettes.*
Le Galion (£££) 15 rue St-Guénolé, Ville Close (tel: 02 98 97 30 16). All beams, stone and flower tubs; retains its Michelin accolades although some critics have found the *nouvelle* portions too meagre. See also hotel section.
La Porte au Vin (££) 9 place St-Guénolé, Ville Close (tel: 02 98 97 38 11). This restaurant-cum-*crêperie* offers inexpensive imaginative menus, combining fish stews and seaweed *crêpes.*

Douarnenez

Restaurant de la Criée (££) terre-plein du Port (tel: 02 98 92 13 55). This plain restaurant in the port authority building produces brilliantly fresh seafood in enormous quantities.

Locronan

Au Fer à Cheval (££) (tel: 02 98 91 70 74). Busy town-centre restaurant with excellent views of the fine main square. Noisy bar downstairs.

Pont-Aven

Auberge La Taupinière (£££) route de Concarneau (tel: 02 98 06 03 12). Locals consider the trek out of town worth it for prime regional cooking. Elegant dining room and good service.

Moulin de Rosmadec (£££) (tel: 02 98 06 00 22). In an old mill house near the town centre, producing justifiably famous food, this is by no means cheap. Interior combines elegance with old-world Breton charm. See also hotel section.

Pont-l'Abbé

De Bretagne (£) 24 place de la République (tel: 02 98 87 17 22). The owner, an ex-fisherman, naturally specialises in fish, producing delectable dishes at reasonable prices. See also hotel section.

Quimper

L'Ambroisie (££–£££) 49 rue Elle-Fréron (tel: 02 98 95 00 02). Close to the cathedral, serving excellent fish dishes. Also noted for its delicious desserts.
Au Vieux Quimper (£) 20 rue Verdelet (tel: 02 98 95 31 34). Popular *crêperie* in the old town serving food all day.
Le Capucin Gourmand (£££) 29 rue Réguaires (tel: 02 98 95 43 12). For serious eating in Quimper this wins the accolades, mostly for elaborate fish dishes.
Grand Café de Bretagne (£) 18 rue du Parc (tel: 02 98 95 00 13). Lively brasserie by the river, with a wide range of snacks and more substantial meals at all prices.
Taverne des Cariatides (£) 4 rue Guéodet (tel: 02 98 95 15 14). Another well-frequented *crêperie*, as much for its curious architecture as its huge range of pancakes.

Quimperlé

Ty-Gwechall (£) 4 rue Mellac, Haute Ville (tel: 02 98 96 30 63). *Crêperie* at the top of the town. Unconventional fillings such as carrots, chutney, and lots of other things too.

Ste-Anne-la-Palud

La Plage (£££) (tel: 02 98 92 50 12). Inventive cuisine in luxurious and elegant surroundings. See also hotel section.

MORBIHAN

Auray

L'Armoric (£) place St-Sauveur, St-Goustan (tel: 02 97 24 10 36). Bustling bar-restaurant occupying the best position on the main square of the old town.
L'Auberge (££) 56 route de Vannes, Ste-Anne-d'Auray (tel: 02 97 57 61 55). Candlelit restaurant using local produce to serve up highly imaginative and affordable food. See also hotel section.
La Closerie de Kerdrain (£££) 20 rue Louis-Billet (tel: 02 97 56 61 27). Accomplished traditional fare in an attractive Renaissance mansion just outside the town centre. Book ahead.

Belle-Ile

Contre Quai (££) rue St-Nicolas, Sauzon (tel: 02 97 31 60 60). Reputable fish restaurant in one of Belle-Ile's prettiest coastal villages.
Roz Avel (££) behind the church, Sauzon (tel: 02 97 31 61 48). Meals served outside in summer; book in advance.

Carnac

Auberge de Kérank (££) route Quiberon, Plouharnel (tel: 02 97 52 35 36). A rustic-style establishment near the Quiberon peninsula.
La Marine (££) 4 place de la Chapelle (tel: 02 97 52 07 33). The Bistrot du Pêcheur here is one of the most cheerful and convenient places to eat in the upper town. Fortify yourself with a delicious fishy lunch before megalith-hunting. See also hotel section.
Le Ratelier (£) 4 chemin du Douët (tel: 02 97 52 05 04). Country house hotel with good food, a little way out of the centre.

Hennebont

Château de Locguénolé (£££) route de Port-Louis, Kervignac (tel: 02 97 76 29 04). Some find the awesome reputation of this elegant riverside hotel overblown, but its restaurant is highly acclaimed. Eating here in the evening can be expensive; weekday lunches are just about affordable.

Lorient

L'Amphitryon (£££) 127 rue Col Müller (tel: 02 97 83 34 04). Serving elaborate, reverential cuisine (with prices to match) this choice is for serious foodies. Has earned a Michelin rosette.
Café Leffe 'Le Skipper' (£) maison de la Mer, quai de Rohan (tel: 02 97 21 21 30). Handily placed brasserie providing sustenance for visitors to Lorient's tourist attractions, or ferry travellers bound for the islands. With a covered terrace downstairs and a conservatory seafood restaurant upstairs.
Le Victor Hugo (££) 36 rue Lazare-Carnot (tel: 02 97 64 26 54). Easy to miss on a dull busy street, but not far from the marina. Family-run, with good set menus served in a spacious, leafy dining room. Accommodation also available.

Morbihan, Golfe du

L'Escale (££) Ile d'Arz (tel: 02 97 44 32 15) Modern hotel-restaurant on the seafront, a popular lunch stopover on gulf cruises. Seafood specialities.
Er Lannic (£) Baden Port Blanc (tel: 02 97 57 07 07). Charming granite house with tables outside. This *crêperie* offers travellers a pleasant way to wait for the Ile aux Moines boat.
Le San Francisco (££) Ile aux Moines (tel: 02 97 26 31 52). This seafood restaurant overlooks the harbour and has splendid views of the Golfe du Morbihan. Speciality dishes include fried *gambas* with aniseed sauce.

Pontivy

La Pommeraie (£) 17 quai du Couvent (tel: 02 97 25 60 09). In the medieval part of the town, close to the castle. Good lunchtime menu.

Quiberon, Presqu'île de

Ancienne Forge (££) 20 rue de Verdun, Port-Maria (tel: 02 97 50 18 64). Quiet and pretty, tucked away from the seafront in a cul-de-sac.
La Criée (£) quai de l'Océan, Port-Maria (tel: 02 97 30 53 09). Informal, inexpensive quayside fish restaurant, popular with families. What they serve is either scribbled on the blackboard or awaiting inspection on fishmonger's trays.

Rhuys, Presqu'île de

Le Grand Large (££) rue du Phare, Port-Navalo (tel: 02 97 53 71 58). Smart restaurant in the ritzy marina development overlooking the waterfront, serving seafood specialities full of eastern promise.

La Roche-Bernard

Auberge Bretonne (£££) 2 place Duguesclin (tel: 02 99 90 60 28). A celebrated restaurant, where ambitious food is served up in sophisticated surroundings that are arranged around a garden courtyard. See also hotel section.
Auberge des Deux Magots (££) 1 place du Bouffay (tel: 02 99 90 60 75). Stylish, country-style décor with lively frescoes. Cheerful, unpretentious menus. See also hotel section.
Domaine de Rochevilaine (£££) Pointe de Pen Lan, Billiers (tel: 02 97 41 61 61). At the entrance of the Rhuys peninsula. The dining-room overlooks the sea. Superb seafood platter. See also hotel section.
La Douanerie (£) quai de la Douane (tel: 02 99 90 62 57). Pleasant quayside restaurant serving fresh seafood. Simpler fare such as pizza, pasta and ice-cream is also on offer.
Le Manoir du Rodoir (£££) route de Nantes (tel: 02 99 90 82 68). Celebrated restaurant run with flair, enthusiasm and great sureness of touch. See also hotel section.

Rochefort-en-Terre

Le Bretagne (£££) Questembert (tel: 02 97 26 11 12). This famous *Relais de Campagne restaurant* has ambitious *nouvelle cuisine* in gracious panelled surroundings. See also hotel section.
Lion d'Or (££) (tel: 02 97 43 32 80). This is the best restaurant in town and is housed in one of its prettiest buildings, dating from the 16th century.

Vannes

La Huche à Pain (£) 23 place des Lices (tel: 02 97 47 23 76). Popular *pâtisserie* where you can buy delicious Breton cakes such as *kouignamann.*
Les Logoden (£) Arradon (tel: 02 97 44 03 35). Good-value restaurant opposite the post office in the town centre.
Le Pressoir (£££) 7 rue Hôpital, St-Avé (tel: 02 97 60 87 63). Renowned restaurant in rustic-style Louis XIII setting just north of the town. Menu includes a good range of meat and fish dishes.
Crêperie des Ramparts (£) 18 rue des Vierges (tel: 02 97 54 26 09). Charming place situated on pedestrian street. Specialities include *crêpe* with mussels and garlic butter or spinach, bacon and fresh cream.
Le Richemont (££) place de la Gare (tel: 02 97 47 12 95). Some way from the old town, but worth the trek for such accomplished and reasonably priced food.

INLAND BRITTANY

Fougères

Les Voyageurs (£) 10 place Gambetta (tel: 02 99 99 14 17). The restaurant in this traditional commercial hotel (under separate management) produces good food, albeit in a fairly charmless and noisy setting. Book ahead.

Hédé

La Vieille Auberge (££) route de St-Malo (tel: 02 99 45 46 25). Pretty terraced restaurant in a granite house by a pond. Fish specialities.

Mûr-de-Bretagne

Auberge Grand' Maison (££) 1 rue Léon le Cerf (tel: 02 96 28 51 10). Ambitious modern cooking in smart surroundings. Elaborate dishes, but set menus can be good value. Delicious desserts. See also hotel section.
Les Blés d'Or (£) 17 place de l'Eglise (tel: 02 96 26 04 89). Popular *crêperie* on the main square.

Paimpont, Forêt de

Manoir du Tertre (££) Paimpont, off D71 Beignon road (tel: 02 99 07 81 02). Dinner in this eccentric rural setting can prove startlingly interesting and good value, though the accommodation is a little on the frowsty side.

Rennes

Auberge St-Saveur (££) 6 rue St-Saveur (tel: 02 99 79 32 56). Breton lobster and other shellfish and fish dishes served in a traditional atmosphere in an historic 18th-century building.
Chouin (££) 12 rue d'Isly (tel: 02 99 30 87 86). This smart restaurant is attached to a fish shop. The lunchtime menu is particularly good value.
Le Corsaire (££) 52 rue Antrain (tel: 02 99 36 33 69). Accomplished classic food in a chic setting. Good wine list.

Le Four à Ban (££) 4 rue St Mélanie (tel: 02 99 38 72 85). Very good-value lunch menu in 18th-century surroundings. The chef only uses fresh produce in season. Parking near by.
Le Khalifa (£) 20 haut de la place des Lices (tel: 02 99 30 87 30). Serving interesting Moroccan food in the lively student quarter of the old town.
Maison de la Galette (£) 6 place Ste-Anne (tel: 02 99 79 01 43). Lively *crêperie* in the heart of the old town. Prompt, friendly service. Always bustling; views of medieval Rennes all round.
Pen'Roc (££) la Peinière-en-St-Didier (tel: 02 99 00 33 02). Much home-grown produce appears on the menu in this attractive, sophisticated *logis*. See also hotel section.
Le Robien (£) 18 rue de Robien (tel: 02 99 36 13 26). Traditional cuisine served on a sunny terrace decorated with flowers in summer.
Saint-Germain-des-Champs (£) 12 rue Vau St-Germain (tel: 02 99 79 25 52). Health-food and vegetarian meals using organically grown produce. Meals outside in summer.

Vitré

Petit-Billot (££) 5 place Maréchal Leclerc (tel: 02 99 74 68 88). Hotel-restaurant close to the old walled town. Good, moderately priced set menus.
Taverne de l'Ecu (££) 12 rue Beaudrairie (tel: 02 99 75 11 09). A taste of the old town in a pretty 17th-century building a stone's throw from the castle.

LOIRE-ATLANTIQUE

Batz-sur-Mer

L'Atlantide (££) 59 boulevard de la Mer (tel: 02 40 23 92 20). Attractive seafood restaurant along the main coast road, under the same management as Le Lichen (see hotel section).

La Baule

Le Castel Marie-Louise (£££) 1 rue Audrieu (tel: 02 40 11 48 38). Top-range cuisine is served in this exclusive *Relais et Châteaux* establishment. The surroundings are elegant and formal but also quite intimate. See also hotel section.

Brière

Auberge de Kerhinet (££) Kerhinet (tel: 02 40 61 91 46). A wide range of dishes are served in the attractive beamed dining room of this small hotel. See also hotel section.
Auberge du Parc (££) Ile de Fédrun (tel: 02 40 88 53 01). Typical thatched cottage where you can sample popular local dishes including pike, eel, tench and duck. Children's menus available.

Le Croisic

L'Estacade (££) 4–5 quai du Lénigo (tel: 02 40 23 03 77). Old-fashioned family-run brasserie near the harbour, popular with locals. Copious helpings of seafood. See also hotel section.
Grand Hotel de l'Océan (£££) plage de Port-Lin (tel: 02 40 62 90 03). Prime seafood served in a comfortable dining room with magnificent Atlantic views. See also hotel section.
Les Nids (£) plage de Port-Lin (tel: 02 40 23 00 63). The separate restaurant of this *logis* on the Atlantic side of town makes a more than useful place to eat. The menus are elaborate and generous. See also hotel section.
Océarium (£) avenue de St-Goustan (tel: 02 40 23 02 44). Le Croisic's splendid aquarium is a useful place to pick up an ice-cream or quick snack (parade of cafés and shops directly outside).

Guérande

Les Remparts (££) boulevard du Nord (tel: 02 40 24 90 69). Good set menus available in this traditional hotel by the walls.

Nantes

Auberge du Château (££) 5 place de la Duchesse-Anne (tel: 02 40 74 31 85). Excellent, imaginative food, just opposite the castle. A good choice if you are staying near by (see hotel section).
La Cigale (££) 4 place Graslin (tel: 02 51 84 94 94). A must at least for coffee if you are exploring the old town. Gorgeous *fin-de-siècle* brasserie with intact interior. Good seafood lunches and cakes.
L'Esquinade (££) 7 rue St-Denis (tel: 02 40 48 17 22). Elegant little place near the cathedral with a cosy dining room and plenty of choice.
La Grill'homière (£) 6 rue Albert Londres (tel: 02 40 50 78 72). Reasonably priced menus and children's menu. Specialities: grilled meat and fish.
La Mangeoire (£) 10 rue des Petites-Ecuries (tel: 02 40 48 70 83). Excellent country cooking using game, meat and fish. Unpretentious good-value.

Redon

La Belle Anguille (£) route de Ste-Marie (tel: 02 99 72 31 02). On a lovely stretch of riverside scenery, the best kind of simple, rustic restaurant-with-rooms using local produce to good effect. See also hotel section.
La Bogue (££) 3 rue des Etats (tel: 02 99 71 12 95). Enterprising regional cooking in an appealingly traditional setting near the town centre. Chestnuts feature on the menu in season.
Jean-Marc Chandouineau (££) 10 avenue de la Gare (tel: 02 99 71 02 04). Accomplished cooking by one of Redon's best chefs, in surprisingly grand surroundings near the railway station. See also hotel section.

Index

M

N

O

Picture Credits

J ALLAN CASH PHOTOLIBRARY 77 Ile de Bréhat, 98 Brest docks, 99 Brest Castle, 112a Roscoff, crabs, 196 Quiberon rocks. **BRITTANY FERRIES PHOTO LIBRARY** 113b teashop, 113c Brittany ferry. **CDT FINISTÈRE** 111b aber. **JOHN FISHER** 97b le Folgoët, 109 Ile d'Ouessant, 180 Belle-Isle-en-Terre ferry, 181 Sauzon lighthouse, 185a Carnac, 254 trams at Nantes, 255 ferry queue, 258 le Folgoët, policeman. **MARY EVANS PICTURE LIBRARY** 18a Tristan and Isolde, 18b Tristan and Isolde, 20b Yves, 32a Roman galley, 33b Julius Caesar, 40b Louis XIV, 41a Colbert, 41b Jules Verne. **FRENCH RAILWAYS LTD** 44a TGV trains. **HULTON DEUTSCH COLLECTION** 42a General de Gaulle and Eisenhower, 43a Rennes, French women watch Americans. **IMAGE BANK** front cover (b). **THE MANSELL COLLECTION LTD** 34a Battle of Auray, 34b Jean de Montfort, 35a Du Guesclin, 36b Charles VIII, 37 Anne of Brittany, 38b Jacques Cartier, 39 Cardinal de Richelieu, 179a The Arrest of Georges Cadoudal, 179b Georges Cadoudal. **POWERSTOCK/ZEFA** front cover (a). **SPECTRUM COLOUR LIBRARY** 186 Hennebont, 187 Iron Well, 191 Lorient market, 192a Pointe du Percho, 249 P & O Ferry at Calais. **TONY STONE** front cover (c). **WERNER FORMAN ARCHIVE LTD** 32b Camp d'Artus, 33a Kermaria Stone (Musée des Antiquités Nationales, Saint-Germain-en-Laye).

The remaining photographs are held in the AA PHOTO LIBRARY and were taken by: A Baker 11a, 13b, 28, 56a, 59b, 82, 143a, 160a, 168, 169, 171, 177, 203, 215, 243b, 259; S Day back cover, 3, 5a, 6/7, 7, 9, 10b, 13a, 14b, 16b, 16c, 17, 24b, 25, 29, 35b, 36a, 38a, 40a, 45, 46, 48, 49, 50, 51a, 51b, 52, 53, 54a, 54b, 55, 56b, 57a, 57b, 58, 59a, 62, 63, 64a, 64b, 65a, 65b, 67a, 67b, 68a, 68b, 69a, 69b, 113a, 126a, 151b, 155b, 176a, 184b, 194b, 195, 204, 206b, 207a, 207b, 208, 209a, 209b, 210a, 210b, 211a, 211b, 214a, 214b, 217a, 217b, 218, 219a, 220a, 220b, 221a, 221b, 222a, 222b, 223, 224, 225a, 225b, 247, 248, 262a, 262b, 265; J Edmanson 150b, 231, 235; P Kenward 44c, 253; R Moore 61b; T Oliver 16a; K Paterson 256; C Sawyer 60, 61a; B Smith spine, 116, 127b, 139a; A Souter 128b; R Strange 2, 4, 5b, 5c, 8, 10a, 11b, 12a, 14a, 15, 19b, 21, 22a, 22b, 22c, 23, 24/5, 26a, 27a, 27b, 30a, 30b, 31a, 31b, 42b, 43b, 44b, 72a, 73, 74, 75b, 78a, 78b, 80, 84, 85a, 85b, 86, 87a, 87b, 88a, 88b, 89a, 89b, 89c, 90a, 96, 97a, 100, 101a, 101b, 104, 106, 107, 111a, 114, 115a, 115b, 117, 118, 119a, 120a, 121, 122, 123, 124a, 124b, 125, 126b, 127a, 129a, 129b, 130a, 131, 132a, 132b, 133, 134, 135a, 135b, 136a, 136b, 137a, 137b, 140, 142, 143b, 144, 145a, 145b, 146a, 146b, 147, 148, 149a, 149b, 149c, 150a, 151a, 152, 153a, 153b, 154, 155a, 155c, 156, 157, 158a, 158b, 159a, 159b, 160b, 161a, 161b, 162, 163a, 164a, 164b, 165a, 166a, 166b, 167, 170, 172a, 172b, 173, 174, 175, 176b, 178a, 178b, 182, 184a, 185b, 188, 189, 190, 192b, 193, 194a, 197, 198a, 198b, 199, 200a, 200b, 201a, 201b, 226, 228a, 228b, 230a, 230b, 233a, 233b, 236, 237, 238, 239, 241, 242a, 242b, 244, 245a, 245b, 246, 251, 257, 263, 264; R Victor spine, 4, 12b, 19a, 20a, 66, 70, 72b, 75a, 79, 81, 83, 90b, 91, 92, 93, 94, 102a, 102b, 103a, 103b, 103c, 105, 110, 112b, 119b, 120b, 128, 130b, 163b, 165b, 183a, 183b, 206a, 212, 213, 216, 229, 234, 243a, 250, 252, 260, 261

Contributors

Revision copy editor: Nia Williams **Original copy editor:** Jane Middleton
Revision verifier: Elisabeth Morris **Cover design:** Carroll Associates